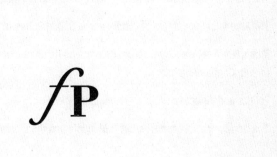

Also by Steve Gillon:

The American Paradox: A History of the United States Since 1945

The American Experiment: A History of the United States (Vol. II)

That's Not What We Meant To Do: Reform and Its Unintended Consequences in 20th Century America

Politics and Vision: The ADA and American Liberalism

The Democrats' Dilemma: Walter F. Mondale and the Liberal Legacy

BOOMER NATION

THE LARGEST AND RICHEST GENERATION EVER AND HOW IT CHANGED AMERICA

STEVE GILLON

Free Press
New York London Toronto Sydney

FREE PRESS
A Division of Simon & Schuster, Inc.
1230 Avenue of the Americas
New York, NY 10020

FREE PRESS and colophon are trademarks of Simon & Schuster, Inc.

For information about special discounts for bulk purchases, please contact Simon & Schuster Special Sales: 1-800-456-6798 or business@simonandschuster.com

Designed by Nancy Singer Olaguera

Manufactured in the United States of America
10   9   8   7   6   5   4   3   2   1

The IKEA commercial reproduced on page 133 of this book is used with the permission of Inter IKEA Systems B.V.

Library of Congress Cataloging-in-Publication Data

Gillon, Steve
     Boomer nation: the largest and richest generation ever and how it changed America / Steve Gillon.
          p. cm.
     Includes bibliographical references and index.
     1. Baby boom generation—United States. 2. Baby boom generation—United States—Biography. 3. United States—Social Conditions—1945– I. Title.

HN59.G55 2004
305.24'0973—dc22

2004040350

ISBN 0-7432-2947-9

This book is dedicated to the memory of
"Uncle Bill"—William G. Parker
(1930–2003)

CONTENTS

ACKNOWLEDGMENTS

I could not have written this book without the support of the University of Oklahoma, the insight of many colleagues and scholars, and the encouragement of friends. I am indebted to David Boren, president of the University of Oklahoma, for having the faith to make me the first dean of the Honors College, and to Provost Nancy Mergler for giving me the freedom to work on this project. Associate Dean Carolyn Morgan handled many of my day-to-day responsibilities with typical grace and consummate skill. Executive assistant Mindy Jones protected me from interruptions, helped organize my hectic schedule, and provided a daily ration of chocolate. Research assistants George Milne, Heather Clemmer, and Kellie Moss at OU, and Andrew Kinney at Harvard, provided a steady stream of useful material and valuable insight. Gary Ginsberg and Ken Orkin, close friends and tough critics, offered many helpful suggestions, as did Susan Werbe. My agent, Esther Newberg, provided advice, support, and encouragement when it was most needed.

At the Free Press, Bruce Nichols guided the project from beginning to end, making numerous helpful comments and suggestions along the way. His strong editorial hand helped mold this book in countless ways. Celia Knight's careful copyediting saved me from many embarrassing mistakes.

Of course, it would have been impossible to write this book without the support of the six people whose lives provide the narrative thread. Fran Visco, Marshall Herskovitz, Alberta Wilson, Bobby Muller, Donny Deutsch, and Elizabeth Platter-Zyberk took time from their busy schedules to talk with me about their lives. They encouraged friends and colleagues to do the same. Special thanks to the assistants who helped schedule the time: Erin Meyers, Vonda LePage, Shannon Tracy, Cyndi Song, and Josh Gummersall.

Most of all, I would like to thank Abbe Raven, the general manager of the Arts and Education (A&E) television network. It was nearly a decade ago, when she was the head of programming at the History Channel, that Abbe gave me my first opportunity on television. Over the years, as she has risen through the ranks, Abbe has carried me along with her, offering more opportunities than I could ever have imagined, and certainly more than I deserve. But she has not been alone. I am also indebted to the many other friends and colleagues at A&E and the History Channel: Nick Davatzes, Dan Davids, Charlie Maday, Susan Werbe, Artie Scheff, Libby O'Connell, Nancy Dubuc, Steven Jack, Anthony Giacchino, and John Verhoff.

BOOMER
NATION

(Please note: I have used endnotes for all references to primary and secondary materials. All other quotes are taken from author interviews.)

THE LONG BOOM

It seems to me," observed a British visitor to America in 1958, "that every other young housewife I see is pregnant." The Baby Boom may have been obvious to everyone by 1958, but it caught most Americans by surprise when it started at the end of World War II. In 1946 the census's experts viewed the upsurge in births as temporary and predicted an increase of only 5 million for the rest of the decade. How wrong they were! In 1948 the nation's mothers gave birth to 4 million babies—a child was born every eight seconds. By the end of the decade nearly 9 million babies had been born. The census planners had miscalculated by over 50 percent. (By comparison, the pollsters who predicted Tom Dewey's victory over President Harry Truman in 1948 missed by only 5 percent.)

And the babies kept coming. In January 1953 General Electric announced that it would award five shares of stock to any employee who had a baby on October 15, the company's seventy-fifth anniversary. The company said it expected about 13 winners. Instead, 189 children were born on that day. By 1959 there were over 50 million children under the age of 14 living in the United States. Together they made up over 30 percent of the population. There were as many children in 1959 as there were people living in the United States in 1881. To keep track of the boom, the Commerce Department established a "census clock" in the lobby of its Washington, D.C., headquarters. Multicolored flashing lights on the clock signaled a birth every 7½ seconds, a death every 20 seconds, the arrival of a new immigrant every 1½ minutes, and the departure of an emigrant every 20 minutes. The result was an increase in population of one person every 11 seconds.

The Baby Boom would prove to be the single greatest demographic event in American history—more significant, even, than the staggering loss of life during the Civil War. Boomers were so disproportionately numerous, so affluent, so blessed by the cold peace of the Cold War (Vietnam notwithstanding) that they would have the motive, means, and opportunity to reshape the nation. How they did so, and what it means for America today, have been grossly misunderstood. The Boomers have been dismissed by many commentators as selfish or self-indulgent, a generation that never had to make the sacrifices of its predecessors in fighting a major war or battling a great depression; a generation that had too much sexual freedom, that invented the "me decade" of the 1970s, and that spent a small fortune on therapy and "self-actualization." But this stereotype is short-sighted and misses other very different trends that have also been Boomer driven—the explosion of new religious denominations and steady rise in churchgoing; the explosion of charitable giving; the explosion of entrepreneurship—all of which became most evident in the 1970s and 1980s as the Boomers rose to adulthood. Though they pushed the country toward liberalism when they were young, they pushed it right back to conservatism when they grew older. Beneath all the contradictions, there is a strong signal: they have reshaped an entire culture around their own single cohort.

Some saw it coming. Expectations of peace and prosperity were directly tied to the proliferation of future consumers. "Just imagine how much these extra people, these new markets, will absorb—in food, in clothing, in gadgets, in housing, in services," gushed Sylvia Porter. "Our factories must expand just to keep pace." In 1958 *Life* magazine called children the "Built-in Recession Cure," concluding that all babies were potential consumers who spearheaded "a brand-new market for food, clothing, and shelter." Signs in the New York City subway read: "Your future is great in a growing America. Every day 11,000 babies are born in America. This means new business, new jobs, new opportunities."

There has never been a simple or wholly satisfactory explanation of why the Boom occurred in the first place. One obvious reason was that young couples who had delayed getting married during World War II decided to make up for lost time. Yet as the decade progressed, the median age of those getting married hit historic lows—20.1 years for women and 22.5 for men. Young couples were starting families earlier and continuing to have children over a longer period of time. At the same time changing cultural attitudes toward sexuality and pregnancy created a "procreation ethic" that encouraged young couples to have children. Popular television shows and magazine stories celebrated the joys of pregnancy and motherhood, as did advertisers. "I'm Alice Cook," declared a suburban housewife in one aspirin commercial. "I have six children, and they come in all shapes and sizes. So do their colds." Perhaps people felt comfortable having more children while a growing economy buoyed their hopes for the future. The Serviceman's Readjustment Act, popularly known as the GI bill, which Congress passed in 1944, pumped millions of dollars into the economy by providing veterans with unemployment compensation, medical benefits, loans to start new business, and tuition benefits for continuing education. Certainly modern science contributed to the fertility euphoria by conquering diseases that had plagued people for centuries. Antibiotics and other new drugs subdued diseases such as tuberculosis, diphtheria, whooping cough, and measles. The most significant achievement was the victory over poliomyelitis (polio), most of whose victims were children. Between 1947 and 1951 this crippling disease struck an annual average of 39,000 Americans. In 1955 Dr. Jonas Salk of the Pittsburgh Medical School developed the first effective vaccine against polio, and by 1960 vaccines had practically eliminated the disease in the United States.

Yet if peace, prosperity, and health explained the Boom, it would have continued in spite of Vietnam (after all, Korea didn't even slow it down) and in spite of the Pill. It came to an end before feminism gave women an economic alternative to marriage and family. Perhaps, then, it was a cultural tipping point at which the causes coalesced just enough, and networks of individuals jumped on the bandwagon just enough, to launch a procreation fad that tipped back toward "normal" birthrates (and continued tipping lower than ever) only by 1964. It isn't a satisfying explanation, but some social phenomena are remarkably resistant to simple explanations.

American historians have neglected the importance of generations in history. "Among democratic nations," Alexis de Tocqueville wrote in the 1830s, "each new generation is a new people." In the 1930s the social scientist Karl Mannheim argued that decisive events in their early adult years could shape the consciousness of an entire generation. "Early impressions," Mannheim wrote, "tend to coalesce into a natural view of the world." More recently, in their book *Generations,* journalists William Strauss and Neil Howe attempted to divide four centuries of American history into eighteen generations. They even claim that conflict between these recurring generations offers "an important explanation for why the story of America unfolds as it does" and a model for predicting the future. Of course it is not so simple—most generations do not have obvious beginnings and endings, nor do their members tend to view one another as fellow travelers.

Demographers themselves do not always agree on the exact dates or titles for each age group. In general most Americans living today fall into one of a handful of broad generational categories. The Depression and World War II were the defining experiences of the now famous "GI Generation," or "Greatest Generation," as the TV anchorman Tom Brokaw called them. Born before 1930, they represented about 16 percent of the adult population in 1998. Those born between 1930 and 1945 are often lumped together as the "Swing Generation" or occasionally split into a separate "War Babies" group born after 1941. Together they represent approximately 15 percent of adults. Boomers, usually dated between 1946 and 1964, account for about 39 percent of Americans over the age of 18 and 29 percent of the total population. They were followed by "Generation X," or the "Baby Busters" (1965–1976), who represent 22 percent of adults, and the Baby Boomlet, the children of the Boomers, born between 1977 and 1995.

Yet of all these groups, only the Boomers have the coherence and importance of a cohort defined by its age. The Depression and the war profoundly affected all Americans alive at the time. The incoherence of the Gen Xers, and the silly debates about what to call their successors, suggest that the birthdates of everyone under age 40 are not that useful in predicting their behavior or interests. But the Boom is an exception, thanks to its enormous size. It wrapped our culture around itself like no other generation before or since. While past generations have shared common experiences, they developed only a loose sense of generational identity. Largely because of their size and the emergence of mass media, especially television, Boomers are the first generation to have a defined sense of themselves as a single entity.

The Baby Boom's special status is derived first and foremost from its enormous size, especially in comparison to the smaller generations that came immediately before and after. Nearly 80 million American children were born between 1945 and 1964. The Swing generation that preceded the Boomers produced only 30 million. The widespread use of the Pill that began in 1964 reduced births for Generation X (1965–1977) to fewer than 45 million The result was a demographic spike in births that starts at the end of World War II and ends at the beginning of the Vietnam War.

It is not just their size that has made Boomers unique. Almost from the time they were conceived, Boomers were dissected, analyzed, and pitched to by modern marketers, who reinforced a sense of generational distinctiveness. "By pitching so many things to us all the time that were only and specifically for us, the mass media insisted that *we* mattered," Susan Douglas wrote about the experience of young girls growing up in the 1950s. "Once you're a market—especially a really big market—you can change history." The amount of money spent to advertise products doubled during the decade from $6 billion to over $12 billion. Toy companies led the way. In 1958, 64 toy manufacturers spent $3.5 million on television ads. The following year, 121 companies spent $6.5 million. By the end of the century, marketing budgets would be many times that amount. The Boomer era has witnessed and encouraged a marketing explosion far greater than the much-hyped birth of mass advertising in the early 20th century. By some estimates, children raised on shows like *The Mickey Mouse Club* and *Howdy Doody* saw more than 500 hours of ads by the age of 6. By the time they were age 21, most Boomers had seen more than 300,000 commercials.

Eugene Gilbert, who referred to himself as the Pied Piper of the Youth Market, did more than anyone else to target the Boomers even while they were young. "Our salient discovery is that within the past decade [1950s] the teen-agers have become a separate and distinct group in our society," he observed. His syndicated column, "What Young People Are Thinking," ran in more than 300 newspapers in the late 1950s. He collected and then sold to marketers information about the evolving teen consumers. Gilbert estimated that the average teenager had $10 a week to spend in 1958 compared with $2.50 in 1944 and that teens spent more than $10 billion a year on products. He discovered that teenage girls annually spent $20 million on lipstick, $25 million on deodorant, and $9 million on permanents. Male teenagers owned 2 million electric razors. Together they spent about $75 million on pop records. Perhaps Gilbert's greatest insight was that teenagers could convince their parents to purchase a new car or stylish clothing. Gilbert found that half of the 4 million kids who watched *Captain Kangaroo* went shopping with their mothers three times a week, and 80 percent of them pleaded with their mothers to buy products they had seen plugged on the show.

He was right, at least in general. Boomers would change America by serving as a target, a magnet, and an immovable object just as much as by their own actions. Their impact can be seen in something as simple as changing car fashions. In the 1950s Boomer parents purchased large cars, ideal for transporting small children. In the 1960s Boomers fresh out of high school wanted sporty Mustangs, which rolled off the production line for the first time in 1964, or unconventional Volkswagen Beetles. In the 1970s and 1980s struggling Boomers moved into their first jobs, and as they started families of their own, they looked to economical imports like the Toyota Corolla or the Honda Accord. In the 1990s manufacturers tried appealing directly to Boomer women with children by developing the minivan. (Boomers made up 61 percent of Chrysler minivan owners compared to 42 percent of passenger cars.) As their children grew up and left home, many Boomer men tried to reclaim their youth by purchasing more sporty cars, like the popular BMW Z3, marketed to 40- and 55-year-olds as a "weekend reward."

Boomers were raised in a period of unprecedented prosperity and unparalleled expectations about the future. America emerged from World War II with new military might and a desire to shape the world. Keynesian economics gave people the belief they had conquered the boom-and-bust cycle that had plagued societies in the past. Between 1940 and 1960 the gross national product (GNP) more than doubled, from $227 billion to $488 billion. The median family income rose from $3,083 to $5,657, and real wages climbed by almost 30 percent. By 1960 a record 66.5 million Americans held jobs. Unlike in earlier boom times, runaway prices did not eat up rising income: inflation averaged only 1.5 percent annually in the 1950s. "Never had so many people, anywhere, been so well off," the editors of *U.S. News & World Report* concluded in 1957.

Education played a central role in the development of a distinct Baby Boom culture. Many states passed mandatory school attendance laws after World War II in an effort to expose America's youth to middle-class values of respectability and hard work. In 1930 only 50 percent of children aged 14 to 17 were students. By 1950 the ratio increased to 73 percent. In response to the enormous demand for space, school districts rushed to open new schools and add on new classrooms. During the 1950s California opened one school every week. In 1954 alone more than 60,000 new classrooms were built. Instead of becoming "vast instruments of American democracy," as Harvard president James Bryant Conant said they would, American high schools provided a perfect breeding ground for a subversive "youth culture." Large new schools swelling with thousands of teenagers encouraged young people to look to their peers, and not their parents, for direction and approval. "Adolescents today are cut off, probably more than ever before, from the adult society," observed James Coleman in *The Adolescent Society.* "They are dumped into a society of their peers, whose habitats are the halls and classrooms of their schools, the teen-age canteens, the corner drugstore, the automobile." After swelling primary school playgrounds in the 1950s, Boomers overran college campuses in the 1960s, changing higher education along the way.

That youth culture found its most powerful expression in popular music. "Rock was a language that taught the baby boomers about themselves," observed Landon Jones, author of *Great Expectations.* The transistor radio allowed the new music to penetrate deep into teen culture. In 1954 "Rock Around the Clock," became, according to music critic Lillian Roxon, "the first assault to have a special secret defiant meaning for teenagers only. It was the first inkling teenagers had that they might be a force to be reckoned with in numbers alone. If there could be one song, there could be others; there would be a whole world of songs, and then a whole world." While Boomers were twisting their hips to the beat of "Jailhouse Rock," their older brothers and sisters were still swooning over Doris Day. Because it was so closely identified with teen culture, rock appeared more rebellious than it was during the 1950s, when most of the music still dealt with the familiar themes of romance and dance. It was during the 1960s that rock became the emblem of rebellion of the younger generation against the world their parents had created. "Hope I die before I get old," a lyric from The Who's "My Generation," was an apt rallying cry for a newly self-aware cohort.

The institution that solidified the sense of generational identity more than any other was television. "Television itself is a baby boomer, it's a baby-boom instrument," said former NBC head Brandon Tartikoff. "The baby-boom generation has never known a living environment in which there wasn't a television." Television—along with the marketers who used it—and music gave Boomers a common language and created the first integrated national culture. That is not to say that America's national culture was created in postwar America. Our political system was built on a foundation of shared beliefs; the growth of big business, along with mass circulation magazines, Hollywood movies, professional sports teams, and radio in the early 20th century had created the fragile scaffolding of a shared culture. In the 1920s the grandparents of Boomers in small towns and big cities flocked to new movie houses to see stars such as Douglas Fairbanks, Charlie Chaplin, Clara Bow, and Joan Crawford. In 1927, 150,000 people paid to see Gene Tunney defeat Jack Dempsey in Chicago, but more than 50 million listened to the bout on radio. The radio allowed Boomer parents to listen collectively to the soothing voice of Franklin Roosevelt as he reassured them through the trauma of depression and war.

Movies and radio, however, could not match television's power to mold a common culture. Television separated the Boomers from every previous generation. Mass production and technological advances in the 1950s allowed most American families to own a set. The size of the screen expanded from 12 inches to 19 and 21 inches; even as color was introduced in 1953, the cost of the sets declined from $700 in the late 1940s to as little as $200 by 1955. In 1948 there were fewer than 400,000 TV sets in the country. Four years later there were nearly 19 million. By 1960 nine out of every ten American homes had a TV, and the average set was turned on for at least six hours every day. The following year for the first time, television surpassed radio and print as the primary source of news for most Americans. According to the political scientist Paul Light, the average Baby Boomer had viewed between 12,000 and 15,000 hours of television by age 16.

Starting in the 1950s Americans across the country watched the same shows, laughed at the same jokes, and watched the same news stories unfold. Most shows avoided controversy and celebrated rugged individualism and family togetherness. Families were intact, men worked during the day, and women stayed at home. No one was ever sick. No one was poor. *Father Knows Best* presented the ideal American family. Jim Anderson, an insurance agent in the prosperous midwestern town of Springfield, provided for the family and solved the crisis of the day. His supportive wife, Margaret, tended to housekeeping and watched over their three wholesome kids: Bud, Betty, and Kathy. Many other shows—*Leave It to Beaver, The Adventures of Ozzie and Harriet*—presented similar rosy portraits of the American family. "Ward," a caring and always well-dressed June Cleaver repeated many times, "I'm worried about the Beaver."

Television transformed American social habits. Studies showed that the average household watched five hours of television a day. Most viewers confessed to reading fewer books and magazines after purchasing a TV set. When a popular show was on, all the toilets in the nation flushed at the same time, during commercial breaks and when the program ended. Saturated by commercials, children could recite the Pepsi-Cola theme song—"Pepsi-Cola hits the spot / twelve full ounces, that's a lot"—before they learned the national anthem. They may not have been able to read, but children had no trouble recognizing the word *detergent*. As the poet T. S. Eliot observed, television provided a valuable shared experience, but it was "a medium of entertainment which permits millions of people to listen to the same joke at the same time, and yet remain lonesome."

As young children, Boomers grew up watching wholesome family shows, but they came of age in the 1960s seeing police dogs and fire hoses turned against innocent protesters on the news. Americans sat in their living rooms viewing images of bombs exploding on Vietnamese villages the same way that had once seen Beaver fret over his school science project. "Vietnam made us a television nation," observed media critic Tom Shales. "We lived through years of darkness and emerged from them media-wise. Even media-obsessed." Television served as a national mirror for the Boomer generation. They thought about the world in television images and used its lexicon to communicate with each other.

If television ads bombarded Boomers with images of the good life filled with a cornucopia of new consumer products, a late-blooming fad for Sigmund Freud gave permission to use them. By the time the Viennese psychoanalyst traveled to the United States in 1909, his theories that early childhood development shaped adult behavior had already been widely disseminated and nearly universally dismissed in Europe. In the United States, however, left-leaning intellectuals and social reformers latched on to his critique of sexual repression and emphasis on the importance of the environment in shaping behavior as a useful antidote to staid Victorian culture. After World War II Freud's ideas gained wide currency in the United States. In 1947 *Life* magazine featured an article titled "Psychoanalysis" that emphasized that "repressed sexual desires" and "infantile experiences" were the cause of adult unhappiness. Articles about Freud became a regular feature in other popular magazines—*Time, Atlantic Monthly, Look,* and *Life*—as well as mainstream newspapers. References to Freudian slips became a part of everyday vocabulary, and Freud's emphasis on the unconscious, guilt, sublimation, and repression changed the way people thought of themselves and the way they related to each other.

Thanks to Dr. Benjamin Spock, Boomers—often called "Spock babies"—had Freud mixed with their baby formula. "Benjamin Spock probably did more than any single individual to disseminate the theory of Sigmund Freud in America," observed the psychiatrist and Freudian critic E. Fuller Torrey. Spock, whose *The Common Sense Book of Baby and Child* (1946) served as the bible for Boomer parents, had attended the New York Psychoanalytic Institute in the 1930s and was determined to bring Freud and his ideas to a mass audience. Spock rejected his own upbringing, which emphasized strict feeding schedules and unchanging routines, and insisted that parents respond to the needs and schedules of their children. "Trust yourself, you know more than you think you do," he reassured worried new parents. His ideas reflected the optimism of the age, reinforcing that personality was malleable if only parents developed the right skills. Along with practical advice about colic, toilet training, and temper tantrums, Spock offered parents sugar-coated doses of Freudian psychology. Since he believed that most adult problems began in childhood, Spock instructed parents about concepts of "sibling rivalry" and used Freud's Oedipus complex to explain the behavior of 6-year-olds. "The noblest things that man has thought and made are partly the product of his longing for and renunciation of his beloved parent," he wrote. Whether they purchased the book, as one of five mothers did, borrowed it from their local library, read the excerpts in magazines and newspapers, or listened to him on television, Boomer mothers found it impossible to escape Spock's influence. In a December 1955 episode of *I Love Lucy,* the husband-wife team of Lucille Ball and Desi Arnaz flipped through a dog-eared copy of Spock's book to decide whether to send "little Ricky" to nursery school. (The answer was yes.)

Later, when many Spock babies grew up to be campus protesters and feminists, conservatives traced these trends back to their permissive upbringing. The problem, however, is that most of the conservative critics, and many future New Right disciples, were also Spock babies. Although Spock emerged as an outspoken liberal activist during the 1960s, the Freudian ideals he espoused had more of a cultural than a political impact on the Baby Boom generation. The emphasis on individual psychology and the discovery of "inner" happiness produced a generation consumed with finding self-fulfillment. "The overwhelming success of Freudianism in America lies in the general insistence on individual fulfillment, satisfaction and happiness," social critic Alfred Kazin observed in 1956. "The insistence on personal happiness represents the most revolutionary force in modern times."

It has become a cliché, though true, to say that Boomers replaced the ethic of sacrifice and self-denial of the Greatest Generation with the ethic of self-fulfillment of the '60s generation. As Kenneth Keniston wrote in *Young Radicals: Notes on Committed Youth,* the parents of Baby Boomers were raised on rules that "emphasized respect, the control of impulse, obedience to authority, and the traditional . . . values of hard work, deferred gratification, and self-restraint." According to the pollster Daniel Yankelovich, instead of asking, "Will I be able to make a living?" Boomers, in contrast to their parents, wanted to know, "How can I find self-fulfillment?" Their search for self-fulfillment often found expression in language borrowed from pop psychology. Not surprisingly, the word *lifestyle,* which, in the words of one cultural historian, "suggested free choice, the uninhibited search for what looked and felt right," made its first appearance in Webster's dictionary in 1961. By the 1970s everybody was talking about "reaching their potential," working "to keep in touch with their feelings," to be "true to one's self." Implicit in the Boomer faith in self-fulfillment was a powerful streak of individualism, a willingness to question authority and established rules, and a disdain for bureaucracy. In 1940 only 11 percent of women and 20 percent of men agreed with the statement, "I am an important person." By 1990 over 60 percent of both sexes agreed with the statement.

When future historians look back at the contribution made by the Boomer generation, they will no doubt place the expansion of individual freedom at the top of the list of achievements. Boomers not only cheered on the civil rights movement, they spearheaded the feminist cause in the 1970s, and fought for a host of new rights and responsibilities—not just gay rights, handicapped rights, the right to privacy, but the responsibility of everyone to participate in the economy, or more generally just to become engaged in the culture—that changed the tone and character of modern life. Their emphasis on individual rights and the underlying challenge to authority led to a dramatic democratization of American culture. The Founding Generation (the real "greatest generation") forged the American experiment based on the "inalienable rights" of "life, liberty, and the pursuit of happiness," even if only property-owning white men were able to enjoy those rights. The World War II generation saved that experiment from the imminent threat of Nazi tyranny at the same time that it enforced segregation at home. The Boomer generation was the first to realize the American dream of equal opportunity for all its citizens. Boomers have not solved all of America's problems, and they have created new ones of their own. But it cannot be denied that this generation has strengthened the foundation of American freedom. The Boomers inherited a thriving republic from their parents, and they are passing on to their children a society that is even more open, dynamic, energetic, and innovative.

It has become fashionable to bash Boomers—to dismiss the entire generation as self-centered and narcissistic. But this criticism sells the Boomer generation short. Much of the debate over the Boomer legacy has its roots in the 1960s when the generation emerged on the national scene. The civil wars of the 1960s were less bloody than the battle between North and South a century earlier, but their impact on American society and politics was no less profound. Grumpy conservatives blame Boomers for their reckless assault on authority, for precipitating a decline of traditional standards, and for creating a culture of dissent. Utopian-minded liberals feel betrayed by Boomers who, after a promising start, became more interested in acquiring status and wealth than in changing the world. Although they have clearly disappointed partisans on both the right and the left, Boomers have achieved something that eluded both the Roosevelt and Reagan revolutions: a general sense of happiness. In 2000, surveys by *USA Today*, CNN, and the Gallup Organization showed an unprecedented 83 percent of Americans expressed satisfaction with the economy, 73 percent believed they were better off personally than they were in 1992, and 69 percent were satisfied with the state of affairs in the country. And they were optimistic about the future: Two-thirds believed the next generation would have a better life than their parents had had.

In the end Boomers have transformed American society and institutions, but not always in ways they had anticipated or like to remember. The Boomer generation replaced the political struggles of the 1960s with the culture wars of the 1980s. In the 1960s Americans clashed over fundamental questions of power in society: redistributing wealth, empowering African Americans, debating America's place in the world. After the 1970s debate in America often centered around culture and the proper limits of individual expression. Political debates in America are no longer about power but about "values." But the culture war, and the heated debate between left and right often dramatized on television talk shows, disguise a fundamental reality. Not only do Boomers control most major institutions in America, but the ethic of self-fulfillment and the broader definition of individualism have seeped into every corner of American society and culture. Today, Boomer culture is American culture.

■

There is no agreement about the dates that make up the Baby Boom, although most observers define it as those born between 1946, when births started their dramatic climb, and 1964, when widespread use of the Pill contributed to a decline in birthrates. During that period roughly 76 million babies were born, making the postwar Baby Boom the largest generation in history. Yet an eighteen-year span is a very long time, and as I looked at the history of the nation through the lens of that generation, I found it useful to divide the giant generation into two groups. What I call Boomers are those born between 1945 and 1957, when the birthrate leveled off—this leading edge of the generation was the group that changed the country. "Shadow Boomers" are those born between 1958 and 1964, maintaining the momentum of the Boomers but not changing its impact. Certainly the life experiences of a child born in 1946 were very different from one born in 1964. The early generation of Baby Boomers grew up with rock and roll, the *Mickey Mouse Club,* prosperity, crewcuts, the idealism of John F. Kennedy, and the social struggles of the 1960s. A child born in 1964 confronted a world of oil embargos, stagflation, Watergate, sideburns, and disco balls. Older Baby Boomers spent much of their lives trying to reconcile their youthful idealism with social reality. Younger Boomers, raised in an age of cynicism, had less idealism to compromise.

According to the economist Mark Berger, college-educated Baby Boomers born after 1957 earned 10 percent less over their lifetimes than those born just the year earlier. "If you were born in 1957," Berger said, "you may be in this same size group as those born in 1953, but you've got all those people in front of you who already entered the workforce, so things looked a little worse." Polls showed that Boomers born after 1957 were more likely to question their ability to influence government policy and less likely to support the 1960s Great Society legislation. There is also the issue of family birth order: Those born in the early stage of the Baby Boom were most likely to be the firstborn, and some studies suggest that birth order can shape personality.

There is also evidence to suggest that older Boomers were more likely to be raised by lenient parents. In 1946 Dr. Benjamin Spock debuted his *Common Sense Book of Baby and Child Care.* By the late 1950s, however, growing concern about juvenile delinquency led Spock to reconsider his approach. In 1957 he revised his book, admitted that he had erred on the side of permissiveness, and counseled parents to provide more structure and discipline for their children. Mothers took the new message to heart. A major study of child-rearing practices concluded, "By 1960, the mothers studied were more similar to the 1940 sample and displayed less babying, protectiveness, affection, and approval than 1950 mothers."

This book varies from standard discussions of the Boomers in one other way. The problem with most of the literature examining the Baby Boom is that it takes a static view of the life cycle. Generations, like individuals, change and evolve as they move from childhood, to teenagers, to adults. Until recently social psychologists paid little attention to development beyond adolescence. Not only does the Freudian notion that most personality traits are formed in childhood and early adolescence still hold considerable influence, but until recently, most people did not have to worry about midlife development because they did not live long enough to experience it. Before 1900 the average life expectancy of Americans was less than 50 years; a 40-year-old man was considered old. "People thought of being little and then of being old," observed Yale historian John Demos. "But the middle part was not articulated as a distinct stage."

As life expectancy expanded in the 20th century, some observers speculated about the possibility of a generational life cycle. From Spanish philosopher José Ortega y Gasset, to psychologists Erik Erikson and Daniel Levinson, to popular writer Gail Sheehy, the life cycle has been divided into variously defined segments. The underlying premise of this book is that it is possible to understand American history since 1945 by charting the life cycle of the Baby Boom. I have broken down modern America into three eras. The first era, which I have called the Cult of Youth, corresponds with the childhood and early adulthood of the generation. It extends from the 1950s through the late 1970s when the youngest of the Baby Boomers (those born in 1957) would either be entering the workforce in large numbers or preparing to graduate from college. The second era, called the Great Shift, covers the years of middle adulthood, from roughly the late 1970s to the early 1990s. It was when the Boomers became breadwinners and parents that American politics lurched to the right; as Churchill said, "Any young man who isn't a socialist hasn't got a heart, but any old man who is a socialist hasn't got a head." The third era, Boomer Nation, describes Boomers at their peak of power during the 1990s, perhaps best symbolized by Bill Clinton's election as president in 1992.

It is not my intention to suggest that the handful of people chosen for this study are representative of a generation as large and diverse as the Baby Boomers. They are not. Their lives do, however, illuminate some of the broad themes of the age. The characters are not household names, but they have all been influential in their respective professions, and they have, in ways large and small, helped to define what it means to be a Boomer. Each character touches on the story of an important dimension of postwar life—television, advertising, religion, architecture, feminism, and the Vietnam War. Other important aspects of Boomer culture—music and technology, for example—arise only indirectly. Of course not all Boomers believe the same things or act the same way. They find themselves on all sides of contentious social and political issues. They are Democrats, Republicans, independents, and "none of the above." Some go to church, some do not. Nevertheless, collectively, there is a signal beneath the noise, driven by their age and common interests. Boomers have remade America in ways large and small, with all the drama of history. This is their story.

CAST OF CHARACTERS

Bobby Muller (1945) joined the marines after college and went to Vietnam to fight communism. In 1969 a Vietcong bullet ripped through his body, puncturing his lungs and severing his spinal cord, leaving him paralyzed from the waist down. His story, and the story of the Vietnam Veterans of America, which he helped found, sheds light on how the most controversial event of the Baby Boom generation continues to haunt the nation.

Fran Visco (1948), a respected Philadelphia lawyer, was diagnosed with breast cancer in 1987. In 1991 she was elected president of the National Breast Cancer Coalition. Visco's life sheds light on the evolution of the women's movement, the rise of powerful grassroots lobbying groups, and the growing concern among aging Boomers about health issues.

Elizabeth Platter-Zyberk (1950) is a Miami-based architect who, with her husband, Andres Duaney, designed Seaside, Florida, in the 1980s. The new urbanism articulated their generation's nostalgia for a lost sense of community. In the 1990s Platter-Zyberk was on the cutting edge of a movement among Boomers to find a new balance between tradition and change, individualism and community.

Marshall Herskovitz (1952), writer-producer, is, along with his creative partner, Ed Zwick, perhaps the most thoughtful, and certainly the most introspective, chronicler of Baby Boomers. His *thirtysomething,* which premiered on ABC in 1987, captured the anxiety of a handful of young adults trying to reconcile their grand expectations of life with the cold, hard realities of making a living and sustaining relationships.

Alberta Haile (Wilson) (1954) is an education reformer and school choice advocate who once dropped out of high school. Her life revolved around drugs and sex until she discovered religion in the 1970s. Her life journey has been more dramatic, and more tragic, than most others, but her story sheds light on two interrelated themes of the Baby Boom generation: the rise of religious fundamentalism and the powerful conservative backlash against liberalism.

Donny Deutsch (1957) transformed his father's small boutique advertising firm into one of the most influential and creative agencies in the country. He also experienced something unique to a large number of Boomers: an extended adolescence. Father and son are symbolic of the two generations. Together their story underscores the bonds of mutual affection and skill that tie together the "Greatest Generation" and the "Boomer generation."

PART I

THE CULT OF YOUTH:
1945–1978

The Boomers came from different backgrounds, were raised in varied circumstances, and endured unique personal crises. But they were all children at some point in the 1950s, teenagers at some point in the 1960s, and young adults by the end of the 1970s. That simple demographic observation goes a long way to explaining American politics and culture in the first few decades after World War II. The flood of babies made America of the 1950s a child-centered nation, where parents, teachers, and marketers labored to satisfy their every need and desire. "The twentieth century is not likely to be the Century of the Common Man," groused the sociologist David Reisman, "but the Century of the Child." In the typical American home of the 1950s, he noted, "It is the parents, and especially the fathers, who are marginal, who are in a precarious position, who are frightened conformists, while the children hold the strategic initiative."

As questioning, skeptical, and self-aware teenagers, Boomers would transform the 1960s into a decade of social experimentation and cultural liberalism. In 1965, 41 percent of all Americans were under the age of 20. Unlike their parents, who often started working in their late teens and early twenties, many Boomers had the advantage of extending their adolescence by going to college. College enrollments soared from 3.6 million in 1960 to almost 8 million in 1970. Before World War II there were no colleges or universities with more than 15,000 students. By 1970 more than fifty schools had 30,000 students stuffed on their campuses. Between 1958 and 1970 the University of Wisconsin saw its enrollment swell from 14,000 to 35,000; the University of Minnesota doubled to over 40,000, and other large state universities witnessed similar increases.

With so many young people concentrated in one place, it is little wonder that college campuses became the seedbed of youth protest. "We are people of this generation, bred in at least modest comfort, housed now in universities, looking uncomfortably to the world we inherit," declared the Port Huron Statement, the founding document of the New Left. "Probably never before in human history," wrote Richard Flacks, "has a society brought together such a large number of potential dissidents . . . under conditions that so greatly facilitated their mutual influence." Lyndon Johnson's decision to escalate the Vietnam War in 1965 provided the spark that ignited the generation.

Boomers were not the driving force of the social clash of the 1960s, but they absorbed and institutionalized its lessons. It was the ripple effect of the decade—the loosening of social mores about sex and drugs, along with the challenge to all forms of authority—that produced a revolution in social values. Boomers insisted on a new informality that is hard to overstate. "In the '70s, hardly anybody was a hippie, because everybody was," declared one observer. Emblems of '60s protest, like long hair and casual dress, would gain mainstream appeal during the 1970s. Even notable fashion failures—blue polyester leisure suits, and wide, pointy collars—reflected a rebellion against the formality of an older generation.

The story of the first thirty years of the Boom is a story of baby culture turning into youthful celebration, with all the self-absorption inherent in young people (which unfortunately and unfairly tainted the Boomers as self-absorbed for life). The best selling self-help book of the 1970s would be *Looking Out for #1*. "If we can learn to love and nurture ourselves," said the authors of *How to Be Your Own Best Friend*, "we will find ourselves richer than we ever imagined." For many Boomers, the search included discovering repressed sexual feelings. Culturally, at least, the 1970s were the "Me Decade," as Tom

Wolfe described it in his famous 1976 *New York* magazine article. "The old alchemical dream was changing base metals into gold," he wrote. "The new alchemical dream is: changing one's personality—remaking, remodeling, elevating and polishing one's very self . . . and observing, studying and doting on it."

While Boomers redefined the political and social landscape, they continued to exercise their greatest influence on the economy. At heart the Boomers were consumers, not revolutionaries. As they moved through the life cycle, marketers and manufacturers moved with them. "The high-school set has graduated from the ice-cream, soda-fountain and bicycle circuit into the big leagues of U.S. consumption," *Newsweek* noted in 1966. That year high school students—a small subset of Boomers—were responsible for buying 16 percent of cosmetics, 45 percent of soft drinks, 24 percent of wristwatches, 81 percent of single records, and 30 percent of all cameras sold in the United States. Companies recognized the potential of the lucrative young adult market. "The sheer weight of numbers makes the youth of this country a factor that just cannot be ignored," a Ford executive declared in 1966, two years after producing the first Mustang. "Frankly, we are going all out." American Airlines tried to capture teen loyalty by offering them half-priced flights. Retailer Montgomery Ward began its annual catalogue with a seventy-seven-page supplement on girls' fashions entitled "Young America in Action." Even companies not selling directly to Boomers tried looking young. "The baby boom was so overwhelming that it made everybody think young," said advertising pioneer Mary Wells Lawrence, who gave fledgling Braniff Airlines a youthful facelift.

The end of the first period of Boomer history would be fraught with economic challenge, however. During the 1950s and 1960s the number of people joining the workforce increased at a steady pace of roughly 1 million a year. As Boomers graduated from college and started looking for jobs in the 1970s, the economy had to absorb more than 2 million new workers every year. Their numbers may have promised an age of expanded consumer choices and greater cultural freedom, but the unprecedented size of the generation also meant increased competition for jobs, helping to produce both high unemployment and soaring inflation in the 1970s. "It's just as if you had a big crop of wheat," said economist Richard Freeman. "Wheat prices fall." A generation raised on expectations of the good life would confront the cold, hard reality that their quality of life could actually decline.

ONE

THE BOOMER GENERATION

Fran, age 4;

Marshall and family, 1950s;

Alberta, age 2.

A history of the Baby Boom generation could start in any town or city in the country. This one starts in Philadelphia. Filled with two-story brick row houses on narrow streets that radiated out from the city center to the nearby streetcar suburbs of Germantown, Overbrook, and Wynnefield, Philadelphia is neither more nor less typical a Boomer locale than Topeka, Los Angeles, or Peoria. Like most other American cities, Philadelphia gained new industry, new jobs, and new workers during World War II. Memories of the Depression faded as the demands for war materiel boosted the local economy, providing jobs for one of every four workers. Women made up nearly 40 percent of the industrial workforce, and the city saw its black workforce double. With the exception of a few labor disputes, Philadelphians united in the effort to defeat the Nazis. In every neighborhood of this deeply divided city—Italian, Jewish, black, Polish, and Irish—blue star banners (indicating that a child was in the service) hung proudly in the windows, providing a poignant reminder of the common sense of sacrifice that gripped the city.

Residents released their pent-up demand at the end of the war by getting married, having babies, and moving to the suburbs. The number of marriage licenses in Philadelphia doubled between 1945 and 1946. During the 1950s the suburban population swelled from 700,000 to 2.3 million. The local Yellow Cab company discussed plans for helicopter service between the city and suburbs. With wartime rationing lifted, many residents went on a shopping spree, buying new cars and filling their houses with all the latest gadgets: refrigerators, washing machines, and dishwashers. None, however, proved as popular as the television. In 1946 there were fourteen companies producing 6,476 television sets. In 1948 there were seventy-five companies churning out nearly 1 million receivers. That year the general manager of local WFIL-TV lured all three national political conventions (Democratic, Republican, and Progressives) to Philadelphia by pointing out that the city was hooked up to a cable that linked nine cities on the East Coast. These nine cities had seventeen television stations that could potentially reach one-third of the electoral votes, while other stations would be shipped kinescopes to be broadcast the following day. The television age had begun.

Television and the Boomers grew up together, but it was an uneasy relationship. During the 1950s, despite television images of caring mothers and attentive fathers, in the lives of many Boomers, fathers did not always know best (or even come home), sometimes mothers stayed home and drank, and many kids could not afford a Davy Crockett coonskin cap. Boomers grew up amid rising expectations about the future—expectations whetted by marketers hawking new products. But their lives often fell short of those expectations. Boosters claimed that television would not only bring families together, it would instill faith in government. "A people able to keep that well informed about the working of its government is unlikely ever to question the power of democracy," opined an RCA executive after watching the Truman inaugural on the screen. The irony of growing up in the 1950s was that consumption and television, two ingredients in a recipe for conformity and contentment, instead produced an explosive mix of power and skepticism that would find full expression in the 1960s.

The birth of the Boomers can be chronicled in ways big and small. In 1939 Thayer, Inc., the largest manufacturer of baby strollers, had stroller sales of $200,000. In 1953 it would sell $7 million worth of them. Sales of baby food rose from 2.7 million cases in 1941 to 15 million in 1947. As children, Boomers transformed America into a nation of schools, suburbs, and station wagons. Elementary school enrollment increased from 21 million in 1950 to 30 million by the end of the decade. As *Business Week* noted, children have two characteristics that make them good targets for advertisers: They "fall for fads and new products at the drop of a hat," and they "have a very big vote in family buying decisions." In 1947 more than sixty-four Sunday newspapers established "the baby corner," a feature design for advertisers trying to reach the baby market. In 1956 Kellogg responded to the young Boomers' penchant for choice by introducing its new variety-pack cereals. The number of toy companies doubled between 1942 and 1947.

For Marshall Herskovitz, the third of three sons, born in 1952 into an educated, Jewish family in a suburb of Philadelphia, the television sets that everyone bought would be a blessing and a curse. He was a remarkably precocious, sensitive, and introspective child. "I have a lot of happy memories from my childhood," he recalls, "but I also know that I was very anxious and alienated." Tall and thin, he lacked the athletic ability of his peers. Marshall had a hard time fitting into a world where boys were supposed to be stoic and tough, and women were gentle and emotional. He watched westerns on television every week, but he never identified with the cowboys. "I was very aware as a boy that I was not living up to the male sort of ideal of our culture as I was seeing it on the cowboy shows and the war movies," he reflects. "I was ashamed of that." He wanted to read books and magazines, talk about ideas, and share his feelings.

Television presented a sterile image of family life with clearly defined gender roles, where fathers made all the decisions and mothers made dinner. But gender roles were reversed in his family. His father, a successful cabinetmaker, was warm and soft. He was well read and often talked about poetry and literature. "He was an immensely kind man who was empathetic to the concerns of growing young males," recalls childhood friend John Morse. "He was very supportive of whatever psychological or social crisis we were going through. You could always count on a sympathetic hearing from Marshall's father." "My dad was a very caring and sensitive guy," recalls Marshall's older brother, Bart. "He was a sensitive soul who was never comfortable with conflict." His mother, who went on to earn a doctorate in education and work as a college therapist, was strong, assertive, and demanding. "You had to always be reaching for more" in dealing with her, Marshall says.

Marshall might have had anxieties in any era, of course, but the Boomer era channeled them through the peak years of psychoanalysis. "I felt like a freak essentially," he reflects. "I felt there was something wrong with me. I grew up with this internal split, of feeling a certain way and looking around me and not seeing other men who felt that way and not really knowing what to do about that." For most of his life he suffered from chronic stomach problems, which he believed was associated with anxiety. Marshall spent hours trying to figure out why he was different, why the world made such little sense to him. He often used his imagination to escape. As a child he was constantly playing war games, dressing up as an American commando, sabotaging German plants, assassinating Nazi officers. He lived near a school, which in his and his friends' imaginations was transformed into a German heavy water plant, which could be used by the Germans to produce a nuclear weapon. They would scale the fence, pretending to plant explosives. He even created imaginary friends. He would often regale his brothers about the exploits of two imaginary firemen, Giga and Jerry, who fought fires and saved lives. There seemed to be a new adventure every day.

His parents encouraged his introspection. His father had dabbled in psychoanalysis during World War II, and his mom worked as a therapist. While they encouraged their children to explore their feelings, they were less successful at creating an environment for sharing and communicating them. "He was exposed at a very young age to the fact that humans had drives and urges within them, which they are not fully aware of or comfortable with," recalls Morse. "He was very aware of how someone had to manage their own ambivalence in life. The more you come to understand your own inner drives and needs, the better able you are to manage them." Not only the later memories but even his parents' initial reactions were offered in the language of therapy.

America in the 1950s placed great emphasis on conformity, on blending in and not standing out. Like the social scientist David Riesman, who documented America's changing social psychology in *The Lonely Crowd* (1950), Marshall distinguished between "inner feelings"—genuine and real—and socially imposed values, which were contrived and artificial. The new mass culture was prescriptive and ubiquitous. Popular television shows and advertisements depicted men as tough-minded and decisive; women were soft and always deferential. But the same consumer culture that imposed standard rules of behavior also encouraged people to satisfy their private desires. An introspective and sensitive child, Marshall was very aware that the images he saw about the way people were supposed to behave contradicted his family life and his inner emotions and feelings. It was this exploration of his own inner feelings, and his attempt to come to terms with the conflict between his inner turmoil and the expectations imposed by the outside world, that formed the foundation of the characters he would create later in life.

Marshall would eventually set out to remake television programming. He never stopped criticizing his childhood shows. The sitcoms were superficial, focusing on surface reactions without any exploration of the underlying emotion or sentiment that really shaped how people behaved. Television was an escape, a fantasy. "Why didn't people say goodbye when they finished a telephone call?" he used to ask. "Why did they never go to the bathroom?" On shows like *Leave It to Beaver* and *My Three Sons,* people never showed real emotion. They never got angry. No one suffered from anxiety attacks. The sitcoms focused each week around some dramatic event that was blown out of proportion, but they failed to show how people actually lived their lives.

For Marshall, the 1960s, from secondary school through high school, would be a breath of fresh air. Part of the change was the contrast between the staid, stodgy style of Dwight Eisenhower and the youthful energy of John F. Kennedy, elected when Marshall was 8 years old. "The nation is getting accustomed to an intense young face at the White House instead of the benign and fatherly image of an elder statesman," the *New York Times* editorialized a few days after

JFK took office. "The toys at the foot of the stairs belong to children, not to grandchildren."

At the beginning of the 1960s people seemed more willing to express their feelings. Even while Boomers were in junior high and elementary school, young people, in particular, began to challenge convention and authority. In the 1950s African Americans led a handful of dramatic protests against segregation at places like Montgomery, Alabama, and Little Rock, Arkansas, but the movement was relatively small. On February 1, 1960, four freshmen at North Carolina Agricultural and Technical College in Greensboro, North Carolina, christened the new decade when they refused to give up their seats at the local Woolworth's lunch counter. That protest galvanized an expansion of the movement that would eventually turn to militancy and make protest and demonstrations part of the daily, and sometimes deadly, news stories of the decade.

At the same time a small group of artists and writers planted the seeds for rejecting the tenets of modern industrial society: materialism, self-denial, sexual repression, and the work ethic. Writer Jack Kerouac, whose best-selling *On the Road* appeared in 1957, coined the term *beat* to express the "weariness with all the forms of the modern industrial state." In 1955 poet Allen Ginsberg, a Jew and homosexual, who was deeply versed in Zen Buddhism, emerged as one of the leaders of the movement when he recited his poem "Howl" to a small audience in San Francisco. "Howl" railed against "Robot apartments! invincible suburbs! skeleton treasuries! blind capitalists! demonic industries!" The Beats embraced open sexuality and free drug use as keys to spiritual liberation. By the early 1960s the Beat message, popularized in inexpensive paperback novels, television, and movies, had gained wide acceptance among young people and formed the backbone of the counterculture movement. The Beats themselves were not Boomers, but the counterculture they helped define would be embraced by the generation.

In 1962 Marshall transferred from public school to Miquon, a progressive private school outside Philadelphia. The school had been around since the Depression, and its faculty was decidedly unconventional. Many of Marshall's teachers had been members of the Communist Party expelled from the Philadelphia public school system during the 1950s. Rooted in the progressive tradition of John Dewey, the school nurtured creative thinking and encouraged an informal democratic style in the classroom where teachers and students were equals. Students called the teachers by their first names, and they were allowed to wear jeans to class. Marshall spent less than two years at the school, but it had a profound impact on him. It exposed him not only to new, radical ideas about politics, but also to the child-centered approach to education, an invention of the 1930s that flourished as the Boomers made America itself utterly child centered. It would also encourage his creativity. "It propelled him into believing in his intellect even more, and in his curiosity and creativity," recalls his brother Bart. Marshall's "search for authenticity" had begun.

If Marshall was a suburban child with urbane new anxieties, Frances Mary Visco was born into a traditionally Catholic family in the heart of the city. She arrived on January 8, 1948, at Temple University Hospital. Yet Fran too had a home life that was far removed from her favorite TV shows. "Television was fantasyland," she recalls. "Everything was nice and pleasant." She grew up living in her grandparents' house in an Italian working-class community in West Philadelphia. Fran's mom and three siblings—Louis, Monica, and Christina—shared the three-bedroom row home with their grandparents and their occasionally present father. On television Ward Cleaver was always around, well dressed, prepared to offer sound fatherly advice for life's little troubles. "My father was a problem," Fran reflects with somber understatement.

Louis Visco had big dreams, which he thought he could realize by gambling, primarily on horses. He made a decent living operating a small printing press in the city, but in his desire to make it big, he managed to gamble away most of his money, and some that did not belong to him. Fran grew up hiding from bill collectors pounding on the front door. Or they would call on the phone. When she told them, often truthfully, that her father was not home, they threatened her. "You better put him on the phone or I am going to send the sheriff to arrest you," they shouted. "I was a just a little kid," she reflects. "It was awful." At one point, Louis listed the family house, which was owned by his wife's parents, as collateral on a loan. When he defaulted, local officials posted notice that the house would be sold at a sheriff's sale. The family had to endure the humiliating and stressful ordeal of proving that the house was not his to give away.

Lucy Visco lived a quiet, pious life, stoically enduring her husband's antics. They lived with her parents, in the house she grew up in as a child, to save money. Her parents were also able to help her raise the children since she received no help from her husband. Her day started with Catholic mass at Saint Donato's every morning at 7:00 A.M. "She really didn't get to experience life very much," recalls Monica. "She had a really close family and she was very devoted to her family and she worked hard and she didn't get to have fun." When Fran was a child, Lucy went back to work as a nurse at Temple University Hospital. It was her grandmother who would greet Fran when she returned home from school. Fran's grandmother would set the table and cook dinner most nights as well.

Even in grade school, Fran assumed adult responsibilities around the house. Her mother would confide in her. Lucy knew that her husband had numerous affairs. She worried whether she possessed the emotional or financial resources to raise a family on her own. At the same time, Fran's younger siblings looked to her for guidance. "I was the oldest in the family, so I had to protect my siblings from that part of our life," she recalls. Lucy seemed content to allow things to continue: her husband gone for days, never providing them with money, the rumors of infidelity. "It was a different time then," Fran recalls. "The idea of divorce and separation were not as accepted. Here she was in an Italian Catholic family, in an Italian Catholic neighborhood surrounded by people, happy or not, who stayed together." Fran was angry with the way her father treated her mother, and she had little tolerance for Lucy's passivity. "This is not right," a sibling recalls Fran saying, "and we have to change it." She told her mother to fight back, but she rarely did. "He's okay," Lucy would say. "He'll come around. He's your father."

In 1957, when she was only 9 years old, Fran was called into the bedroom where her parents were fighting. Lucy had finally reached the breaking point. She reminded him that he had gambled away the family's money and that he was a bad influence on the children. Then she said something that stunned him: The children agreed that he should leave the house permanently. Louis faced the children and asked them one at a time whether it was true. "Do you want me to leave?" he asked. As the oldest, Fran spoke first. "We can't have this," she said. "We are a family. We're trying to make it and you are not making it easy. We've gone through this over and over and over again, and you refuse to come around." Young Louis spoke next and repeated the same list of grievances. Then they took a vote: leave or stay? They all voted him out. Fran's father packed his bags. Not a word was spoken. A few minutes later, Fran stood in the doorway watching as her father walked slowly down the street holding only a few bags of clothing.

The family situation became more desperate. "We were the family that the local parish would donate food to because my father wasn't around," reflects Monica. Lucy worried about whether she would be able to put food on the table and often borrowed money from family members to pay the bills.

Like many other young Baby Boom women, Fran received mixed messages from her mother. Lucy encouraged Fran to aim high and to believe that she could accomplish any goal she set for herself. "Remember," she repeated to her children on numerous occasions, "always hold your head up high." She was a strong role model who emerged, although reluctantly, as an independent single mother who managed to work every day while also raising a family. She sacrificed a great deal to provide a roof over their heads, food on the table, new clothes for school. More than anything else, she wanted her children to have more opportunity and more choices than she had. Yet Fran listened to her mother complain about how difficult it was to live without a husband. The message Fran heard, according to a friend, was, "Everything is wrong because my husband left me."

That mixed message was reinforced outside the home. Many Hollywood films required women to acknowledge marriage as their top priority. "Marriage is the most important thing in the world," Debbie Reynolds says in *The Tender Trap* (1955). "A woman isn't really a woman until she's been married and had children." Many leading educators discouraged women from seeking a college education. In 1950 the president of Mills College announced that education "frustrated" women. Instead of studying science and math, college women should learn the "theory and preparation of a Basque paella, of a well-marinated shish-kebab, lamb kidney sautéed in sherry, an authoritative curry." However, the decade's celebration of the American housewife failed to account for important changes in women's lives. Between 1940 and 1960 the number of women in the workforce doubled, rising from 15 percent to 30 percent. Even more striking, the proportion of married working mothers jumped 400 percent. By 1952, 2 million more women were at work than during World War II. By the early 1960s one worker in three was a woman, and three of five women workers were married.

Evidence of changing sexual behavior also challenged the celebration of traditional family life. In 1942, Alfred Kinsey, an Indiana University zoologist best known as the world's foremost authority on the North American gall wasp, decided to abandon his work on bees and turn his attention to human sexuality. Over the next few years Kinsey and his associates quizzed 5,300 men and 5,940 women about their sexual habits. He became so obsessed by the topic that his wife remarked, "I hardly see him at night since he took up sex." His *Sexual Behavior in the Human Male* (1948) and *Sexual Behavior in the Human Female* (1953) rocketed to the top of the best-seller list, where they stayed for twenty-seven weeks. The statistics shocked the nation: 86 percent of men said they had engaged in premarital sex, 50 percent said they had committed adultery before turning 40, 37 percent of men reported at least one episode of homosexual sex, and 17 percent of men who had grown up on farms claimed to have had sex with animals. Scientists pointed out serious mythological flaws in Kinsey's research, but his conclusions nevertheless received wide attention.

Those mixed messages would stick with Fran as she grew older: she wanted to be strong and independent, but she always sought the security of a relationship. It was a problem common to many older Boomers: They were old enough to absorb their parents' traditional notions of domesticity and too young to fully grasp the full flowering of feminism, which emerged only under their own leadership. They were trapped between two generations, pulled in different directions by the desires for more freedom and the security of traditional roles. Boomers were not the first generation to want to live different lives than their mothers had. "What was unique to us," noted the historian Barbara Berg, "was that we had the opportunity to act on these dreams and inspiration and to make them a reality." According to a 1993 Congressional Budget Office study Boomers born between 1945 and 1952 had a median household income of

$38,400 in 1989 compared with $25,100 for their parents. The gap narrowed for younger Boomers raised during the economic slow-down of the 1970s, but they too finished ahead of their parents: $30,000 to $22,000. Working mothers provided the economic edge for the Boomers. Only one-third of Boomer mothers worked outside the home compared to 70 percent of Boomers.

Like many other girls growing up in the 1950s, Fran felt ambiva-lent about the future. She did not want to repeat the mistakes that her mother had made, and she desired more opportunity and greater freedom, but she also felt the need to have a traditional fam-ily. Boys growing up in the 1950s could dream of having careers that surpassed their fathers' without questioning their roles as husbands and fathers. Girls did not have that luxury. They were often forced to choose between a fulfilling career and a satisfying personal life. Fran wanted both. "I always remember Fran having a boyfriend," said her close friend Felicia. "She always needed to have a man." Fran was also ambitious, resented her father's cavalier treatment of her mom, and was determined not to allow herself to be victimized.

Since life inside her home was so painful, Fran spent lots of time outside playing with friends. She possessed an outgoing, assertive personality, and, perhaps because of all the responsibility she had assumed in the house, she was more mature than many of her friends. "Fran was always the leader," says childhood friend Rose-mary Clark. "She was always the one who came up with the games. If Fran decided to go roller skating, everybody would go roller skating. She would decide if we took apart our roller skates and made scoot-ers out of them." Like many other Baby Boomers, Fran grew up on a street crowded with other children her own age. They spent a lot of time together down at the park, just around the block. In addition to games familiar to most other urban kids like stickball, they used to play mock war games. The boys would use sticks as guns and raid each others' camps, while the girls played nurse and took care of the wounded. Fran used to love reading comic books. A dime bought the latest exploits of her favorite superheroes—*Superman, Batman, Fantastic Four, The Hulk*—who always prevailed in their battle against evil. "She was always a dreamer," recalls Monica.

By all accounts Fran was an attractive, well-built young girl. "She was a real va-va-voom," says Clark. "She had breasts when no one else did." Fran was popular with the boys, and she enjoyed the attention. "Fran always got the man she wanted," recalls Felicia. There were two groups of girls in the neighborhood: the "preps" and the "nonpreps." The preps wore Oxford shoes, crewneck sweaters, and very light makeup. Fran was clearly the leader of the nonpreps. "Fran was more of the leather jacket, boots, teased hair, white lipstick and American Bandstand type," recalls Felicia. Fran would spend hours trying to make her curly hair straight. "She would put her hair on an ironing board and iron it to get it straight and then tease it," recalls a friend. "She had really big hair." On weekends they hung out at a local luncheonette in West Philadelphia to listen to the Beatles, play pinball, and meet boys.

One of the favorite places to mingle with guys was just outside *American Bandstand,* which was taped behind Fran's high school in Philadelphia. In August 1957, *Bandstand* made its debut on sixty-seven stations as a daily national afternoon dance party program. The show premiered locally on Philadelphia's WFIL in 1952 and was hosted by dj Bob Horn. In 1956, however, Horn was fired after being arrested for drunk driving. His replacement was a young, clean-cut Dick Clark, whose previous experience included reading Tootsie Roll commercials on Paul Whiteman's *TV Teen Club.* Within a month *Bandstand* was America's top-ranked daytime show and the only place where viewers could listen to popular rock and roll, week after week. "In those days, you had Ed Sullivan and Steve Allen doing variety shows, and they had no room for a Bill Haley or the Penguins singing Earth Angel," noted Clark. Before it came to an end thirty-seven years later, Clark had hosted 650,000 dancing teens and 10,000 lip-synched musical guests, and reached millions of mostly female viewers. *American Bandstand* would have more influence over rock and roll than any other source.

Many of Fran's friends would try to sneak onto the set. Since they were not allowed to wear their Catholic school uniforms on camera, they would go into the school bathroom, change their clothes, put on lipstick and makeup (forbidden in school), and tease their hair. But Fran's strict mother prevented her from joining them or from going to any dances while in high school. Fran was rebellious but respectful. She adopted the dress and the manner of a tough teen, but in four years of high school, she never received a demerit for bad behavior and she always obeyed her mother's rules.

Fran was 13 years old when John F. Kennedy took the oath of office as president in January 1961. After Kennedy announced the creation of the Peace Corps, Fran sat down and wrote a letter asking for an application to join. She had just turned 14. In the early 1960s women made up about 3 percent of law school graduates in the country. Yet at some point in the eighth or ninth grade, she knew that she wanted to join them. "I wanted to be a lawyer because I thought that I was going to represent the downtrodden." Unable to fix her mother's home, she had one professional goal: "I really wanted to fix the world."

As a child of her mother, Fran instinctively identified with people who were poor and marginalized from society. But her compassion was mixed with a strong populist streak. "I was always distrustful of people with power," she reflects. She remembers the local sheriff and the bill collectors. The family would often engage in political conversations over the dinner table. Most often, Fran lectured her brothers and sisters about contemporary political issues. According to her brother Louis, Fran had "always been an advocate." In high school she wasn't happy with the curriculum, and she fought to change it. "Because it was a Catholic high school, there were books that we were not allowed to read." She read the books anyway and could not understand why the church had banned them. "I don't think I am going to hell because I read them," she told a nun.

Prosperity is relative, and from the perspective of the 21st century, Fran's family survived on very little. Yet it came naturally to her to think of college and graduate school and a career. Boomers would be the first generation that went to college in big numbers. In 1940 less than 16 percent of high school graduates went on to college. By 1965 nearly half of all 18- to 21-year-old Boomers were in college. The best-educated generation in history, more than 84 percent of Boomers completed high school, 44.5 percent attended college, and 25.1 percent earned degrees. Along the way, they transformed higher education and learned the skills needed to eventually assume leadership roles in business, government, and entertainment. For now, however, Visco had to put her college plans on hold to support her mother and her younger siblings.

■

Fran's and Marshall's Philadelphias were very different from each other, but there was one local culture that stood even further apart than the city-suburb, Catholic-Jewish divide: urban African Americans. Between 1940 and 1950 the black population of Philadelphia swelled by 50 percent (252,757 to 378,968) while the number of whites grew by less than 1 percent (from 1,678,577 to 1,692,637). Middle-class whites fled to the surrounding suburbs, accounting for 96 percent of the population growth there and taking many jobs with them. Urban blacks were concentrated in segregated city neighborhoods with high unemployment, rising crime rates, and minimal services.

Anyone looking at census data from the 1950s, however, would have considered the Haile family, which lived on the 1600 block of Ellsworth Street in Philadelphia, a typical American family. Like 70 percent of American families, it consisted of a working father, a stay-at-home mother, and children living under the same roof. But race defined the Hailes' lives in every way. Alberta Haile was born in March 1954 and grew up in a comfortable three-story row home in a black working-class neighborhood. The family lived on the first two floors and often rented out the third floor, which was set up as a private apartment with its own kitchen. As a child Alberta was showered with toys and gifts, but her parents provided little discipline and, sadly, offered almost no affection. "Love was never mentioned in my house," she recalls. "I never have had the pleasure of hearing my dad or my mom, for that matter, tell me that they loved me."

Albert Haile was a formal man, who dressed every day with white socks, white shirt, and tie. He often wore a hat and never failed to tip it when a woman passed. He worked two jobs. Days were spent working as a liquor store clerk. After a few hours at home in the early evening, he left to work the night shift as a security guard. He always took public transportation to get around. "He knew practically all of the bus schedules and he had each one timed to within a couple of minutes," Alberta recalls. "I can see my dad now standing on the 16th Street corner of Ellsworth Street waiting for the Number 2 bus. Although he worked hard, he did not like spending money on himself. He used to stuff old newspapers into his shoes to cover the holes and protect his feet from the elements. He made enough money to provide for the family, but he was emotionally distant. On weekends he would sit and read the newspaper, rarely poking his head from beyond the pages."

Katherine Haile was an alcoholic. Many children have memories of the milkman leaving bottles on the front steps. Alberta recalls the "beer man" leaving a case of cold "Schmidts" every Friday. As Alberta grew older, her mother seemed to sink deeper and deeper into her disease. She would be absent for long periods—sometimes weeks at a time. Her father seemed helpless. "Your mother's gone again," he would say to Alberta during one of the drinking binges. There were occasions when the police would carry her home drunk, with her clothes soiled and her head bleeding from a cut caused when she hit her head after passing out. Often when she was home, she was sick and hung over. Alberta's father would help nurse her back to health. It was both painful and confusing for Alberta. "I couldn't understand all of this," she observes. "All I know is that I loved my mom and I didn't want this happening to her, but I was powerless to stop it."

There were few strong religious influences in Alberta's childhood. It seemed to her that most of the people who preached about God had more problems than she did. Both of her parents belonged to churches, but neither was very religious. Her mom was a member of the Union Baptist Church, but never attended services. She was often struck by the hypocrisy of people who misbehaved during the week, but then faithfully attended services on Sunday. She remembers her dad buying a pint of gin one Friday and getting drunk. He did not drink often, but when he did, it was sloppy. He passed out, and when he woke up the next morning, he could not find either his teeth or his glasses. But he quickly pulled himself together, went down to the bus stop, and spent most of the morning at church. Alberta attended the local Catholic church a few times with one of her girlfriends, but the rituals made little sense to her. Everything was in Latin, so she did not understand a word, and she spent most of the hour kneeling, standing, and then kneeling again.

Most days, as soon as Albert left the house in the morning, Katherine's drinking buddies would come over. She had a long-term affair with a man named Jimmy who would wait outside every morning for Mr. Haile to leave. Albert knew about the affair, but as far as Alberta could tell, he never complained about it. At one point

Jimmy was so bold as to try to rent the third-floor apartment. "I really didn't like him for a long time because he was interrupting my home and stealing my mother's affection," Alberta recalls. One day she exploded in anger, grabbed a kitchen knife, and lunged at him. Her mother intercepted the knife, and Alberta cut her hand in the scuffle. But Jimmy got the message: He never came to the house again while Alberta was home.

Since her father worked two jobs and her mother was often out drinking, Alberta spent lots of time at the houses of family friends. Alberta and the children of one of her mom's drinking buddies would spend nights together unsupervised. All were under the age of 10. They were fine by themselves except when the boyfriend, a truck driver, would decide to spend the evenings. He was a pedophile. He slept on a fold-out couch in the living room, but in order to get to the kitchen or the bathroom, he had to walk through the children's bedroom, where all the kids slept in one queen-sized bed. At night he often paced back and forth through their room, naked, making sure the children saw that he had an erection. "Then I remember on many occasions he would call those kids one by one into that room with him," says Alberta. The children, boys and girls, would lay in fearful wait. He had nicknames for each of them. "The light-skinned one he called kitten. The dark skin one he called pet. When he said kitten, kitten had to go to that room." One by one, they would return, slip silently back into bed, cover themselves with blankets, and cry. They never spoke about what took place in the other room. Alberta believes that he never called her because he knew and respected her father.

On other days, she spent nights at the house of an older friend, Carmella, who lived down the street. They would lie on the floor and watch television. Large rats used to come up through holes in the kitchen floor and try making their way to the living room. Alberta and Carmella would place a piece of plywood in the doorway connecting the kitchen and the living room to help contain them. Whenever a rat made it through the barrier, they would throw their shoes at it to scare it away.

Alberta wasn't sure what was worst: fighting off sexual predators, scaring off rats, or spending weekends with her strict grandmother who made her kneel and say prayers four times a day—in the morning, at noon, in the early evening, and again at bedtime. "As a little kid, I resented the fact that I had to go to Grandmom's every weekend, stay in a dark, dreary house, without a TV, and pray all day and night." One of Alberta's least favorite chores was emptying her grandmother's spittoon, which she kept in the bedroom and often used as a toilet at night. The only enjoyable part of the weekend came on Saturday nights when her grandmother's roommate, Mrs. Sadie, would open the door to her room and let Alberta watch her television from a chair in the hallway.

By 1963, Alberta was in the fourth grade at W. E. Childs Elementary School. She was a "good girl": obedient, respectful, and a straight A student and on the honor roll every semester. "She won all the awards," recalls a classmate. Alberta told everyone that she wanted to be a doctor when she grew up. "I think the worst thing that I did was to hide food behind the radiators in the house when I didn't like it," she recalls. But the chaos in her life was about to catch up with her.

Philadelphia's numerous Italians and sizable numbers of Jews and African Americans were a typical northern urban mix, filled out with Quakers, Poles, and Irish. The differences between each group were sharp, but the differences within them were sharper (as the particular struggles of Marshall, Fran, and Alberta attest). Philadelphia also housed first-generation immigrants, including Elizabeth Platter-Zyberk, the first American-born child of Polish immigrants who fled both German Nazis and Soviet Communists before emigrating to the United States in 1947.

Yet however unique their personal experiences, Marshall, Fran, Alberta, Elizabeth, and the millions of other Boomers shared, for the first time, a distinct sense of generational identity. Whether from Philadelphia or Oklahoma City, they watched the same television shows, badgered their parents to buy the same toys, and participated in the same fads. The theme song for *The Mickey Mouse Club*—"M-I-C-K-E-Y M-O-U-S-E!"—became the childhood anthem of the Baby Boom, while the opening credits of *Leave It to Beaver*—"starring Barbara Billingsley, Hugh Beaumont, Tony Dow—and Jerry Mathers as the Beaver"—would rattle around in their heads for decades. In 1954 the popular Disney show *Davy Crockett,* the "king of the wild frontier," made Crockett an instant hero among millions of children. Growing up in Philadelphia, Marshall Herskovitz watched the *Davy Crockett* show every week on television, listened to the theme song on the radio, and went out to play wearing his coonskin cap, shooting arrows at imaginary Indians. Kids his age across the country, in small towns and big cities, were doing the same thing. Before the fad was over, Marshall's parents and millions of others had spent more than $100 million on Crockett paraphernalia.

While Marshall got caught up in the Davy Crockett fad, Fran Visco joined hundreds of thousands of other kids and rushed out to buy a Hula Hoop in 1958. Introduced from Australia by the Wham-O Manufacturing Company in 1958 for $1.98, the thin, multicolored polyethylene tube became an instant hit with kids. Not all adults shared the enthusiasm, however. Fran's grandfather was horrified when he saw her playing with the Hula Hoop in the park. It was, he complained, "too sexually suggestive" a toy for a young girl.

Most children were only vaguely aware, or capable of understanding, the fears that may have kept their parents up at night, and preoccupied most historians: the "Red Menace," wars of national liberation, *Sputnik.* As children growing up in the 1950s, their concerns were more immediate, their worlds more limited. With the exception of the obligatory duck-and-cover air-raid drills at schools, most children filtered the dire warnings about the dangers from nuclear fallout through the prism of popular culture. *Mad,* a favorite humor magazine that reached the stands in the summer of 1952, fantasized that after a nuclear war, the *Your Hit Parade* would include songs that lovers would sing as they "walk down moonlit lanes arm in arm in arm." Hollywood monster and mutant movies, suggesting that nuclear tests had either dislodged prehistoric monsters or created new genetically altered creatures, were popular. In *The Day the Earth Stood Still* (1951), a superior race of aliens invade earth to warn humans of the dangers of nuclear weapons, threatening to destroy the planet if all nations do not abolish atomic weapons.

Even issues of war and peace were translated into debates over consumer goods. The hottest personal confrontation of the Cold War took place not on a remote battlefield but in a model American kitchen. The exchange between Vice President Richard Nixon and

Soviet Premier Nikita Khrushchev took place in July 1959, as Nixon escorted the Soviet leader through a six-room model suburban ranch house filled with shining new furniture at a Moscow exhibit that celebrated American life. Within minutes the conversation about television sets and washing machines escalated into an ideological clash between communism and capitalism. Jamming his thumb into Nixon's chest to underscore his point, Khrushchev warned, "If you want to threaten, we will answer threat with threat." Not to appear intimidated, Nixon brazenly waved his finger in Khrushchev's face, retorting that it was the Soviets, not the Americans, who threatened world peace. Later that evening at a state dinner, Nixon, still gloating over the display of American affluence, told his Soviet hosts that the United States had achieved "the ideal of prosperity for all in a classless society."

But that was the catch. For the first time in its history, a large majority of Americans really believed they had mastered the tools to guarantee prosperity at home and promote freedom abroad. Economic growth would provide the nation with the resources it needed to fund necessary social problems at home while also paying for the military needs of the Cold War. The nation, in other words, could have both guns and butter. Surveys showed that 75 percent of Americans considered themselves part of the middle class. Boomers were constantly reminded that they were growing up in an open, dynamic society where every child could grow up to realize his or her dreams. Pundits hailed the 1950s as an "age of consensus," a time when prosperity, social programs, and fear of communism rendered social protest obsolete.

Boomers were aware of the disparities between the expansive hopes of their parents' generation and the nagging social realities of postwar America. In spite of the widening prosperity, the distribution of income in America remained uneven. In 1959 a quarter of the population had no liquid assets; over half the population had no savings accounts. Although poverty had declined significantly since the Great Depression, about 40 million Americans, representing 25 percent of the population, were poor in 1960. Nowhere was the contradiction between ideals and reality more striking than in the lives of African Americans. In 1954 the Supreme Court issued a unanimous decision in *Brown v. Board of Education of Topeka, Kansas*, declaring that "in the field of public education the doctrine of 'separate but equal' has no place." But most blacks, especially in the South, still lived as second-class citizens. It was the unprecedented expectations of a better life, the hope of finally realizing the promise of America, that inspired the social and political activism of the Boomer generation.

No previous generation had been nurtured on such expansive hopes or had been so confident in their ability to change the world. In the waning days of the Eisenhower administration, the White House organized the Conference on Children and Youth. Perhaps anticipating the social turmoil that was to ensue in the coming years, the 1,400 young delegates identified racial discrimination as "the biggest moral problem of the sixties" and then backed up their words by organizing a demonstration in downtown Washington.

No one conveyed that sense of idealism better than President John F. Kennedy, who promised positive leadership, public sacrifice, and a bold effort to "get America moving again." He combined an optimistic message with a biting critique of America's problems, including an imagined "missile gap." With the help of his talented group of advisers, he carefully manufactured the image of a youthful, robust leader, hero of *PT-109* and the brilliant author of the Pulitzer Prize–winning book *Profiles in Courage* (1956). "Let the word go forth," Kennedy declared in a memorable Inaugural Address with his crisp Boston accent, that "the torch has been passed to a new generation." His call for sacrifice—"Ask not what your country can do for you, ask what you can do for your country"—was addressed to Boomer parents, but Kennedy's youthful idealism and modern style appealed to their children as well.

His assassination on November 22, 1963, was the defining moment of the Baby Boom. His death and funeral first shocked, and then mesmerized, the nation. It represented the first time a generation had experienced a historical event in a single simultaneous moment, soon after it happened. When President Kennedy was assassinated, everyone stopped to watch CBS and NBC's extraordinary, first-ever on-the-scene coverage. At 1:40 P.M. EST, CBS interrupted *As the World Turns* with a "CBS News Bulletin." Anchor Walter Cronkite announced that shots had been fired at the Kennedy motorcade. NBC was on the air sixty seconds later. At 2:38 P.M. EST, Cronkite announced in an emotion-choked voice: "From Dallas, Texas, the flash—apparently official. President Kennedy died at 1 P.M. Central Standard Time—a half hour ago." No other news story in history had been transmitted so quickly, penetrated so deeply, or grabbed the nation's attention as completely. Over 90 percent of Americans knew about Kennedy's death within two hours of the assassination. The nation ground to a standstill: Schools sent home children, businesses closed. Four out of five Americans "felt deeply the loss of someone very close and dear."

That night Fran Visco lay awake in bed, fearful that if she closed her eyes, she would never wake up. Her mother tried to comfort her. It was natural to be scared, she said, but everything would be fine. Marshall Herskovitz "spent the whole weekend feeling very frightened. Was the world coming apart?"

TWO

THE VIETNAM DIVISION

Bobby as a schoolboy;   **high school athlete;**   **Marine lieutenant;**   **on leave during Vietnam.**

Wars do more than any other event to unify and build a sense of nationhood—most of the time. And the Boomers lived in a warlike era longer than any other generation, thanks to the Cold War. But Vietnam heated into an American hot war just as the oldest boomers were reaching draft age. Whereas the Greatest Generation had the bonding experience of World War II in which nearly every eligible adult male served in the military and many others, including wives and mothers, worked in war-related industry at home, in Vietnam, only 10 percent of the 27 million draft-aged men served. For the Baby Boom generation, those who served and those who did not, Vietnam would be a source of constant division. A few young people fought; some protested against it; most managed to avoid it. Long after the last American left the rice fields of South Vietnam, Americans would continue to argue, often passionately, about the "lessons of Vietnam." The war in Southeast Asia ground to a halt in the 1970s, but the battle for the hearts and minds of the Boomers continued into the next century.

Robert Muller was born in Geneva, Switzerland, on July 29, 1945, less than three months after the Allies declared victory in Europe. His parents, Robert and Edith, gave him the middle name "Olivia" as a gesture of peace, their "olive branch," to the world. Having endured two world wars, they hoped their first child would grow up in a world without war. With Europe devastated, they believed that the future looked much brighter in the United States. They viewed America as a dynamic, energetic society that rewarded hard work and valued individual initiative. "My father always raved about America being a country where you can be whatever you wanted to be," recalls Bobby's younger brother, Roger, born in 1947. Although neither parent spoke English, both wanted to move to the United States and share in what they knew of the "American dream." They got their chance in 1950 when Bobby's father was transferred to New York. They packed their bags and told 5-year-old Bobby and 3-year-old Roger that the family was going on a long trip.

Life was good the first few years in the United States. The family settled in New York City, first in Astoria and then in a modest single-family home in Queens. The Swiss manufacturing business that Robert worked for was prospering enough to afford to send Bobby and Roger to private schools. There were lots of family vacations. They skied nearly every weekend during the winter. "Life at that point was pretty good," recalls Roger. Since he was in sales, Muller spent a great deal of time on the road. "I don't have memories of my dad as a kid because he was never home," recalls Roger.

In 1958, when Bobby was in the eighth grade, his father decided to start his own machine tool business. It was a risky move, and Edith opposed the idea. Why give up a dependable income, she asked, especially when the kids were so young? But Robert Muller was ambitious, and he enjoyed the challenge of American capitalism. He was confident he could make it on his own and was willing to gamble. They argued about the decision, but in the end, the father made the decision. "That's when everything really went downhill," recalls Roger. They went from a comfortable middle-class life to near poverty. In order to raise money to start the business, the family sold the house in Queens and moved into a small apartment in the middle-class, and largely Jewish, community of Great Neck, Long Island. There was no more skiing on weekends. At times, the family finances were so bad they had the phone cut off and burned candles to save electricity.

More important, the decision doomed his parents' relationship. "I think when he was home spending more time with my mother they realized that they had really grown apart," Bobby recalls. Now they fought constantly over many things, but money—or the lack of money—was at the heart of most of it. His father had a hot temper, would break dishes, and would physically assault his mom. As the older child, Bobby sometimes got caught in the middle of the fights. He would always stick up for his mother. On a few occasions, he and his father came to blows. At one point Bobby suggested to Roger that they run away. The fighting continued for almost three years. In 1961, when Bobby was 16 years old, his parents divorced, and his father moved out of the apartment.

Childhood friend Per Bang-Jensen remembers meeting Bobby shortly after he moved to Great Neck in 1958. "I think the first thing I noticed was that he showed up in a leather jacket, which wasn't very common in Great Neck." Bobby's Little League team in New York City was sponsored by the Flushing Federal Savings and Loan, and he wore a bright red leather jacket that said "Flushing Federals." When Bobby wore the jacket for the first time in suburban Great Neck, many assumed that this "tough-talking city kid" was a gang member. The class bully decided he needed to protect his turf, so he challenged Bobby to a fight. "So the first day he and I 'got it on,'" Bobby recalls, using his favorite expression to describe a fight. Bobby bloodied his opponent's nose and quickly earned the reputation for being a tough guy. No one ever challenged him again. "I had my reputation from the first day."

Although he spent his first five years in Switzerland, Bobby grew up as the "quintessential All-American kid." Perhaps growing up with parents who spoke better French than English made him want to prove his Americanism more than his native-born friends did. New York Yankee center fielder Mickey Mantle was his hero. One of his favorite activities was to go to Yankee Stadium wearing a uniform with Mickey Mantle's number, 7, imprinted on the back. "When we used to go to Jones Beach as kids, we had to park in the seventh row because it was Mickey Mantle's number," recalls Roger. His other idol was Elvis Presley. "He was totally rock and roll," recalls Roger.

"He was Elvis. We have pictures of him literally with his hair slicked back, the white shirt with the button-down, tight black pants, singing 'You Ain't Nothin' But a Hound Dog.'"

Bobby channeled anger and frustration from home into sports, especially wrestling and track. "Sports defined my life as I grew up," he remembers. Bobby was a star athlete at Great Neck South High School, which had opened in 1956 to accommodate the flood of school-age Boomers. He stood 5 feet 8 inches tall and weighed 130 pounds, although he wrestled at 123 pounds. Bobby was the captain of the wrestling team and the cross-country team. "He was just incredibly gifted," recalls Per Bang-Jensen. "He was not only strong and fast, but he is probably the only person I've ever met in my life who was a cross-country runner and a pole vaulter." Very few athletes possessed the strength, dexterity, and endurance to compete in both events. When he learned how to play lacrosse in his junior year, Bobby's biggest challenge was deciding whether to play right-handed or left-handed, because he was so coordinated.

Although everyone recognized Bobby's great athletic skill, what distinguished him was his attitude: he was always the most determined, the most intense, and the most energetic athlete on the team. "There were people on the cross-country team and the wrestling team who were better athletes than Bobby," his brother observes. "But Bobby always worked harder than everyone else." He trained harder, and he set an example for the other athletes. Bobby was "the enforcer"—the guy who made sure the other athletes were doing their exercises, giving 100 percent to the team. "He was the guy that made sure everyone came to practice," recalls Jensen. Bobby felt that his work ethic gave him an advantage over his competitors in tough wrestling matches. "I would win because I had stamina, endurance, and I would win in the third period when everybody else was sucking wind and dying."

When Bobby entered high school in 1959, America had a new worry: juvenile delinquents. The term, and the worry, did not originate with Boomers so much as their older siblings; between 1948 and 1953 the number of teenagers charged with crimes increased by 45 percent. Yet the Boom fueled the worry. As early as 1953 the federal government's Children's Bureau predicted that the exploding teenage population would soon produce an increase of 24 percent in car thefts, 19 percent in burglaries, and 7 percent in rapes. "Younger and younger children commit more and more serious and violent acts," wrote psychiatrist Fredric Wertham in his popular book, *Seduction of the Innocent* (1953). Movies such as *The Wild One* (1953), *Blackboard Jungle* (1955), and *Rebel Without a Cause* (1955) brought the images of troubled youth to the screen. Tough guy that he was, these popular fears nevertheless bore little resemblance to Bobby's teenage life. While many of his high school classmates were experimenting with drugs and sex, Bobby remained doggedly focused on sports. He referred to himself as "a majority of one." He did not smoke or drink. "We didn't date. We didn't go out with girls. We didn't get high. We didn't get fucked up." On weekends Bobby and his group of friends hung out at the local soda shop. Bobby was not religious, and he rarely attended services on Sunday, but he often attended social events organized by the local church. Although he was one of the most attractive and popular guys in the school, Bobby was shy around girls. He did not have a single date in high school. One evening there was a mixer at the local high school. Bobby was nervous about going and asked his mom to pick him up at 11:00 P.M., insisting that she not be late. When he entered the party, his classmates were drinking beer and playing spin the bottle. Bobby went into the bathroom and stayed locked inside until it was time to go home.

He had one vice: horse racing. He placed his first bet at Roosevelt Raceway on Long Island when he was 16 years old, betting $20 on the trotters. He won and was hooked for life. In high school and college, short of money, Bobby would panhandle. "We would hustle and get together a couple minutes before the race and pull whatever we begged up and make a couple of bets." The race track provided an ideal outlet for an action junkie who loved taking risks.

After graduating from high school in the spring of 1963, Bobby enrolled in the State University of New York at Cortland. The school boasted a strong athletic program, and he planned on wrestling and majoring in physical education. Once he got to campus, however, he grew disillusioned with the wrestling coach. After his sophomore year, Bobby decided to transfer to Hofstra University on Long Island and pursue a degree in business. The straitlaced kid who was always shy around girls also started dating a young, attractive coed named Tracy.

Bobby's college years took place against the backdrop of a widening war in Vietnam. In 1954 the Communist forces led by Ho Chi Minh had overwhelmed French colonials, forcing a temporary division of Indochina at the 17th parallel. Fearing that a Communist victory would produce a domino effect—"You have a row of dominoes set up, you knock over the first one, and what will happen to the last one is the certainty that it will go over very quickly," President Eisenhower declared—the administration propped up a fragile pro-American government in the South, providing economic and military assistance. Kennedy continued pouring money and military "advisers" into the South Vietnamese sinkhole, but failed to deter the Communists or stabilize the regime.

Lyndon Johnson dreaded getting mired in a protracted ground war in Southeast Asia. He told biographer Doris Kearns Goodwin "that bitch of a war" would destroy "the woman I really loved—the Great Society." Having remembered the chastising Truman received when China "fell" to the Communists, Johnson told the U.S. ambassador to Vietnam, "I am not going to be the president who saw Vietnam go the way China went." By the spring of 1965 a steady stream of North Vietnamese troops, often supplied with Chinese weapons, was flowing into the South, undermining a government already weakened by corruption and constant political intrigue. "The situation is very disturbing," Secretary of Defense Robert McNamara informed the president at the end of 1964. "Current trends, unless reversed in the next 2–3 months, will lead to neutralization at best and more likely to a Communist-controlled state."

The same year that Bobby transferred to Hofstra, President Lyndon Johnson made the fateful decision to commit American ground forces to offensive operations combat in Vietnam. In July 1965 the president publicly committed 50,000 ground forces to Vietnam, though privately he assured the military that he would commit another 50,000 before the end of the year. While planning for war, Johnson talked about peace, deliberately misleading the Congress and the American people about his planned escalation of the conflict. While confidently predicting victory in public, privately he feared defeat. In private conversations he recorded on the White House taping system, made public in 2001, the president describes himself as "depressed" and "scared to death" about the conflict. He was convinced that the United States needed to expand the war in order to maintain its credibility, but doubted whether the nation could win a war in Vietnam. "If you let a bully come in and chase you out of your front yard," he said, "tomorrow he'll be on your porch, and the next day he'll rape your wife in your own bed." But he feared that the United States could not defeat the Vietcong "bully" without "kicking off World War III." At one point early in the conflict, he cried to his wife, Lady Bird, "I can't get out [of Vietnam], and I can't finish it with what I have got. And I don't know what the hell to do!" Trying to decide what to do about Vietnam, he told her, is "like being in an airplane and I have to choose between crashing the plane or jumping out. I do not have a parachute."

The size of the Boomer generation helped convince Johnson that he could fight the war with a minimum of domestic upheaval. In 1964 there were 24 million people between the ages of 15 and 24. By 1970 that number had grown to 35 million. Boomers were the first generation in history to grow up in the shadow of a peacetime draft, which Congress created in 1948 as a way of deterring Soviet adventurism after World War II. Hoping to avoid the experience of the British and French, which saw a generation of their "best and brightest" decimated in World War I battles, Congress included a new feature in the conscription law: a student deferment that allowed young men to avoid the draft by attending college and earning respectable grades.

After the Korean War, the Selective Service Board, which administered the draft, realized that it did not need all of the men coming of draft age, so it gradually loosened the rules for exemptions and deferments. Draft boards raised the preinduction physical standards and expanded student deferments to include postgraduate study. As a result student deferments grew by 900 percent between 1951 and 1966. The most significant change was the board's decision to include marriage and fatherhood under the hardship and dependency deferments. By 1966 the deferments for hardship, including marriage and fatherhood, outnumbered student deferments by nearly two to one.

When Johnson suddenly escalated the Vietnam War in 1965, the Selective Service Administration had to scramble to close the loopholes in order to satisfy the demand for troops. Draft boards limited fatherhood deferments to men who had never been granted student deferments and stopped giving deferments to married men and graduate students. Fearing the potential backlash on college campuses, the boards left undergraduate deferments in place. The result was that America fought the longest war in its history with only 6 percent of its eligible population. During the years 1964 to 1973, from the Gulf of Tonkin to the final withdrawal of American troops from Vietnam, 27 million men came of draft age, 2.2 million men were drafted, 8.7 million enlisted, and 16 million did not serve.

While most of his classmates were thinking of ways to avoid service after graduation, however, Bobby wanted to go and fight. "You felt an obligation, at least I felt obligation. When my generation was called, you needed to respond, and you didn't ask why." One of his business professors at Hofstra told him that the service would be a good career move: It was a valuable way to develop leadership skills, and it would allow him to become part of a veterans' fraternity on Wall Street. Bobby remembers thinking it would not hurt to "pump up the volume to get something out of it that would be a career enhancer." With the patriotism typical of an immigrant and without the peer pressure of more socially dependent kids to dodge the draft, fighting for his country came naturally to Bobby.

As early as 1964, during his freshman year in college, Bobby told his father that he wanted to drop out and join the Green Berets to fight in Vietnam. His father pleaded with him to finish college, hoping that the war would be over by the time he graduated in 1967. Tracy opposed the war and pleaded with him not to enlist. "Why risk our life together?" she kept asking him. She wanted to get married and start a family. But Bobby was not ready to get married and settle down. Without telling her or his parents, he enlisted in the marines. "He wanted to join the most athletic organization he could," recalls Bang-Jensen. His attitude was, "If I'm going to be a marine, I'm going to be the best marine. I'm going to be where the action is."

Bobby planned to finish his degree and enter the corps as an officer. As part of his training he joined the Platoon Leaders Corps (PLC) program. In the summer of 1967 he went through the PLC ten-week program in Quantico, Virginia. He graduated first in his class, and was chosen as the "honor man" in his platoon. The experience convinced him that the marines was the right place for him and that Vietnam was the right place for the American military. A few weeks into the semester Bobby had his first confrontation with an antiwar demonstrator who was passing around a petition in the student union. Bobby grabbed the student and threw him up against the wall. "Don't you understand the United States has committed itself to this war? We are in. And all you are doing is giving the enemy encouragement to fight in hopes that we are going to be divided within our ranks and fall apart." When the protesters refused to back down, Bobby hit him in the face. "Fucking fag," he muttered as he swaggered away.

On graduation day in January 1968 a proud Bobby wore his marine uniform under his graduation garb. In a second ceremony he was commissioned as an officer in the Marine Corps. "Very few people from Great Neck wound up going to the military," recalls Bang-Jensen, who served in the army. "This was a period when everyone was trying to figure out how not to go, and if they were to go, how to do it a safe way." Not Bobby. "The marines could not have found a better guy." Bobby even wanted to be in the infantry. He wanted to fight. "My only fear was that the war was going to end before I got a chance to get over there and do the right thing," he reflects. He spent the next thirty-three weeks of intensive training in boot camp and officers' school. When he finished the following fall, he had his choice of assignments. He was one of five men, out of the fifty in his group, who chose the infantry. "I demanded Vietnam, and I demanded front-line infantry," he recalls. Once again, he lied to his parents and to Tracy. "I told them I was assigned to the supply office," he recalls. "I did not want them to be concerned every night I went out in the bush."

Bobby enthusiastically risked his life to fight a losing and unpopular war. By the time he took a commercial flight to Da Nang in September 1968, the military situation in Vietnam had shifted against the Americans, and public opinion at home had turned decidedly against the war. The critical turning point had taken place the previous January, when Communist troops launched an offensive during the lunar New Year, Tet. The Vietcong invaded the U.S. embassy compound in Saigon and waged bloody battles in the capitals of most of South Vietnam's provinces. Television pictures of marines defending the grounds of the American embassy in Saigon shocked the nation. CBS anchorman Walter Cronkite, echoing many other Americans, declared the United States was "mired in stalemate."

Johnson's military advisers recommended that he send another 206,000 troops, which would have brought the total to 750,000, but a frustrated Johnson accepted the recommendation of his civilian advisers, rejecting the troop request. Unable to win the war but unwilling to accept defeat, the president called for a negotiated settlement. At the same time, on March 31, 1968, he announced that he would not seek reelection.

After arriving in Da Nang, Bobby made his way up to the Northern I Corps where he joined the Second Battalion, Third Marines, which was engaged in stemming the flow of enemy men and materiel to the south. He thought that the South Vietnamese would be grateful that Americans were coming to protect them. But even on the first day, he saw evidence that the war was more complicated than he had thought. "I remember getting up to my units, seeing these Vietnamese kids. They would say in broken English, 'Hey GI Number 1.'" Bobby returned their cheer, "Yeah, GI Number 1." Then they would then give him the finger. "Fuck you GI Number 10."

The night before meeting up with his unit, Bobby had a long and memorable conversation with his seasoned African American platoon sergeant. "You've been out there," Bobby began. "You have been around this track. You understand the game. If shit goes down. I'm going to be looking to you for guidance on what to do." The sergeant shot back: "No you're not. You are the lieutenant. You're going to have all those eyeballs looking at you. That is your job. You make the decisions. You fuck up, I'll come and say, 'Sir, you may consider this or you may want to consider that.' But you are in charge." After a few more drinks, the sergeant told Bobby, "With all due respect sir, I hate second lieutenants."

The lesson would come in handy the next day. A helicopter dropped him into a battlefield, where his platoon had just been ambushed. A few guys had been killed in a firefight, and others were wounded. "My platoon had just had the shit kicked out of them and I got to go around and introduce myself," he recalls. Bobby wanted to make clear that he was in charge to instill a sense of command and confidence. The first thing he did was order a medevac helicopter to remove the wounded. To make sure there were no Vietcong in the area who could shoot down the chopper, Bobby called in artillery and jet rounds to pound the perimeter. "These jet strikes and artillery bombardments were fucking awesome," he recalls with some glee. "The ground is shaking. All hell is breaking loose. I've never seen or experienced anything as awesome as that."

Bobby was crouched down in his bunker thinking, "Oh yeah. Oh yeah. We are fucking bad! The Vietcong don't have the balls to fight us and all our firepower." Then the bombing stopped, and the helicopter swooped down and picked up the wounded. They got 30 meters off the ground, and suddenly there was the crackling sound of gunfire from the very places they had just dropped all the bombs. "I watched the chopper go down in the fucking valley. That was my first afternoon!" It would serve as a valuable lesson. "I never would have believed that after seeing this awesome firepower that these people would have had the audacity, the nerve, the balls to respond. But they just said, 'fuck you.' And they took down the chopper."

It did not get much better the next day. After a sleepless night Bobby led a patrol in the morning. "So I understand that this is my first ever patrol, and the guys were shaking because they got whacked yesterday and the day before." As they were leaving the perimeter of the base area, the men were crossing themselves. Bobby was overwhelmed by the sense of responsibility he had assumed: these men's lives depended on him. After spending a few days on patrol, he was told that there were no helicopters available to bring them back to camp. They had to walk back. "How the fuck do you walk out of a triple canopy dense jungle?" he shouted. Eventually they all made it back safely, but this episode made him realize that the military was often disorganized and failed to support the troops in the field.

A few months later, in April 1969, Bobby was working as an adviser to the South Vietnamese army. They were moving through a wooded area when a tank ran over a land mine. Bobby was walking right next to the tank. The experience reminded him of the cartoons he used to watch as a kid. "You get blown off your feet, and you go up in the air in a cloud of dense black smoke." He landed in some bushes a few feet away. He immediately took inventory of body parts: "I got my legs. I got my arms. I'm here, so I guess I'm okay." He walked away with only a small piece of shrapnel in the arm.

A standard tour of duty for a marine was thirteen months, with eight months in the field, before being sent back to headquarters. The end of April marked the end of Bobby's eight months of combat, and the order came for him to leave and be replaced by another officer. On the afternoon of April 29, an army lieutenant approached him: "You Lieutenant Muller?" "Yeah," Bobby responded. "They want you in the rear ASAP," he said. "You're supposed to take the next chopper out of here." Bobby had one more mission to accomplish before he left. "I'll be right with you," he said. "I just got to finish something up."

A few hours later, Bobby led a joint U.S.-Vietnamese operation, including ten marine tanks and a platoon of South Vietnamese troops, against a heavily fortified hill where the North Vietnamese had left a suicide squad to delay their advance. It would be his last mission. Bobby called in heavy artillery on the hill to try and dislodge them. "It was heavy artillery, and it was right on fucking target." He called in jet strikes "that blew the shit out of the hill." And then there were the tanks. Eight of the tanks used half their ordnance hitting the hilltop. One of the tanks, a flame thrower, burned the top of the hill to a crisp. The other tank got stuck in the mud and was disabled. Yet every time the explosion stopped, the North Vietnamese popped up and started firing. The colonel kept shouting orders, "Take the fucking hill. Take the fucking hill." Bobby knew that the South Vietnamese were notoriously unreliable and often ran at the first sound of gunfire, but he decided to lead the charge up the hill anyway. "It had been a long, hot day. I'm pissed, and I want to take the fucking hill."

He did not get very far. "The next thing I know I'm lying on the ground looking up at the sky." His first reaction was, "Oh shit! My girl is going to kill me." After the initial shock, there was a certain mellowness, and a calm settled over him. He felt no pain; he felt alone. *This is what it must be like to die,* he thought. *I'm going to die on this shitty piece of ground. I'm going to die. I don't fucking believe this.* He passed out.

Bobby could have bled to death on the battlefield. A bullet had pierced both of his lungs and severed his spinal cord. He suffered massive internal injuries. He may have inadvertently saved his own life. Right before he started the march up the hill, Bobby had called in a medevac helicopter to help another injured man, who died before the chopper arrived. The helicopter landed just as Bobby got hit. Within minutes they swooped him off the field and rushed him to a hospital ship, the USS Repose, anchored off the coast of Vietnam. The doctors later told him that his life was spared by a matter of seconds.

The first thing Bobby remembers were the bright lights of intensive care at the hospital ship. The doctors had already performed surgery. He was strapped into a striker frame to immobilize him. There were tubes everywhere: in his nose, his throat, his chest, and his stomach. He could not believe that he was alive. "I was ecstatic," he recalls. A few days later the doctors told him they had "good news and bad news." The good news was that they were pretty confident that he was going to make it. Bobby started laughing. "I could have told you that the minute I opened my eyes." Then came the bad news. "We cannot say for sure, but we're pretty sure that you're going to be paralyzed." They were surprised by Bob's casual reaction. "Don't worry about it," he said. "I'm going to be fine."

Bobby spent a few nights on the navy hospital ship before getting transferred to Japan and Guam en route to New York. His first stop was the naval hospital in Queens, where his family came to visit. By now they had learned that he had not been working on supply lines, but had volunteered for infantry. They were shocked. His mom remembers Bobby sending home postcards saying, "I'm safer here than you are, and there's nothing to do." It was hard for her to be angry seeing him helpless in a hospital bed. Bobby allowed only his mother, his brother Roger, and Tracy to visit him in his room. "There was just one bed in the middle of the room. He was lying there and the sheets were pulled up to his neck," recalls Roger. "He had a tracheotomy tube. He looked so young."

The transition to a new post-Vietnam life was incremental. In addition to the loss of mobility, he had to learn how to control his bladder and bowel function. "You had to figure out how you're going to live without shitting your pants every couple of hours and how not to piss on yourself." He had to learn how to perform other basic activities that he had always taken for granted—getting dressed, putting on a pair of shoes, buttoning a shirt. For Bobby the most difficult part was dealing with the loss of all sexual function. "You are 23 years old and you are in the prime and you get cut down." In the late 1960s many Baby Boomers were reaching their peak years of sexual powers, and advertisers were using lots of sex even then to sell their products. Bobby used to hate the commercials for Pepsi featuring young people running on the beach, reaching for a Frisbee, laughing, and throwing the girls around. America was celebrating its youth culture, but Bobby did not feel young.

How should he deal with his girlfriend? It was a question the navy psychologist raised with him. "Do you have a girlfriend?" he asked. "I have a fiancée, and I am going to tell her to find another guy." The psychologist responded: "Do you respect your girl?" "Oh yeah," Bobby said. "Is she smart?" "Yes, she's very smart." "Well, then, why don't you let her make her own decisions." "I couldn't fight the logic in that," Bobby recalls. It was raining on the day that Tracy visited him for the first time. She was carrying an umbrella. "I knew something was up by the look she gave me," he recalls. "She comes over to me and she says, 'I have a few questions for you.' I said okay. 'Were you infantry'? I said yeah. 'Did you volunteer for infantry?' I said yeah.' Then she started to fucking whack the shit out of me with that umbrella. She was pounding me on the head, shouting 'You ruined our lives. You threw our future away. You stupid idiot.'" Finally the attendant and medics came and dragged her out. His relationship with Tracy continued for a few more years, but they gradually drifted apart.

The hospital psychologist told Bobby that he needed to "come to terms" with his paralysis. He said that "what I needed to do was to go in a corner and just cry and acknowledge the loss." Bobby claimed that he wasn't depressed. "You don't get it," he said. "You look at me as a glass that's half empty. I look at me as a glass that's half full." He kept telling them that he was "fucking ecstatic" to be alive. "I have honestly never felt a pang of depression over the loss," he still insists. "I've had frustration. There have been annoyances up the kazoo. But not depression over any sense of loss." The highlight of his six weeks at the naval hospital was when he got his first wheelchair. "My life opened up," he said. "I got out of bed. I was mobile. I could do things for myself."

His long and painful convalescence was only beginning. In July 1969 Bobby was transferred by ambulance from the naval hospital to the infamous Bronx veterans hospital. He remembers looking out and seeing people going about their daily routine. "And I'll never forget how I wanted to scream out of the ambulance, 'People! There's a war going on! Right now, guys are dying in firefights!'" His reaction revealed the anger that was growing inside him about the war, and especially about the way the government had misled people about the American role in the conflict. In the wake of LBJ's retirement, Richard Nixon won the election in 1968 by capitalizing on the

public's yearning for tranquility, promising that he had a plan—
never specified—to end the war in Vietnam. Once in office, he continued the futile pursuit of victory, but by different means. The president hoped to cut the casualties that fueled home-front protest by
reducing the number of combat troops at the same time that he dramatically enlarged the bombing campaign.

For now, however, Bobby had a more immediate battle to fight
with the Veterans Administration (VA). The only time that he cried
through his entire ordeal was the day he arrived at the veterans hospital in the Bronx. Bobby discovered one of the dark corners of neg-
lectful government programs. "It was a large box, crowded, filthy,
smelly, filled with these old farts." Less than 10 percent of all the
patients in the facility suffered from service-connected disabilities.
The overwhelming majority of patients were older indigent veterans
who lacked private health care. It was, in essence, a dumping ground
for aging veterans of previous wars and a warehouse for sick and
indigent vets. Bobby recalls it as a haven for "lunatics, drunks, and
convicted criminals." It was, he said, "the Hyatt Regency of the Salvation Army." Ron Kovic, who lived on the same ward and went on to
write *Born on the Fourth of July*, remarked that "it never makes any
sense to us how the government can keep asking for money for
weapons and leave us lying in our own filth."

The Bronx hospital lacked the staff and the facilities to deal with
the profoundly wounded like Bobby Muller. He was in the hospital
for a couple of hours before he asked an attendant to bring him a
wheelchair. The attendant said he was too busy, and he could not
find one anyhow. "Look, I want a wheelchair," Bobby shouted. "Get
me a wheelchair." He made enough of a fuss that another attendant
brought over a chair. But Bobby still needed help transferring from
the bed to the wheelchair. At the naval hospital, someone would hold
his legs while he grabbed a trapeze bar that hung over the bed, pick
up his torso, and slide into the chair. "Grab my feet. I want to transfer," he said. "I don't have time for you," the attendant responded.
"I'm busy." It was not a good sign.

Later that day his mother came to visit. The doctors at the naval
hospital had warned the family that Bobby would probably never
recover use of his legs but had added that, with proper care, he could
live a normal life. The new physician at the Bronx announced in

front of both of them that given the extent of his injuries, his life expectancy was about seven years. His mother burst into tears and ran out of the hospital. Bobby could deal with a bullet wound and could accept being paralyzed, but he could not cope with seeing his mother cry. He felt guilty. He lay in his bed that night and wept.

After a restless first night, Bobby waited for the doctors to make their morning rounds. When they arrived at Bobby's bed, the lead physician read from a 3 by 5 index card. "Oh, Lieutenant Muller. Well, son, I hope you realize you are hopelessly paralyzed." At the naval hospital, the neurosurgeons had told him that it was difficult to predict the long-term impact of spinal cord injuries, and there was a slim chance he could regain use of his legs. "I remember being completely speechless, just stunned that somebody reading off of a 3 by 5 card after a moment of review would come out with something like that." A psychologist who was part of the team of doctors making the rounds sensed Bobby's discomfort. "You look like you might benefit by talking to somebody," she said. "Would you like to do that?" Bobby nodded and asked her to come back later in the afternoon.

She returned on schedule and sat in a chair next to Bobby's bed. "What do you plan to do with the rest of your life?" she asked, trying to shift his attention to the future. "I think I'm going to become a political assassin and I'm going to kill all the sons of bitches responsible for the stupid fucking war!" he snapped. Startled by his response, she started meeting with him every week, trying to get a better understanding for his emotional state. Applying standard Freudian methods, she tried exploring his relationship with his mother and father. He wasn't buying any of it. His anger did not result from some deeply buried emotional scar. "Don't you understand," he lectured her, "this has nothing to do with my mother. I'm fucking pissed. This is political. This war is wrong." He felt that he had every right to be angry. He, and the nation, had been betrayed by its political leaders. He was lying in a dirty bed at a crowded, understaffed veterans hospital, paralyzed from the waist down, and for nothing, he thought.

In a matter of weeks, Bobby went from being a marine lieutenant leading men into combat to being a paraplegic begging a disrespectful orderly to help him transfer into a wheelchair. As a marine lieutenant

"I was God!" he remembers thinking. "I was determining who lived, who died. I was calling in fire missions. Then you get treated like a piece of shit!" Bobby believed that he had a right to quality care. "I had enough indignation, pride, and rage that I spoke up. I gave expression to how I felt, so I wasn't going to be silenced." Bobby became the resident hell raiser. Most of the complaints were legitimate. The meals were often late and cold. The nurses failed to change bedpans. At night the patients set traps to see how many mice and rats they could catch: they were rarely disappointed. Many of the men developed bedsores from not being moved. Bobby also liked provoking the staff. "He was very much into acting out," reflects his brother, Roger. "He had a beard, and he grew his hair longer." A lot of times he would go down to the waiting area, make noises, and pretend he had no control over his arms, shouting, "Help me, help me."

"Bobby was angry," recalls his physical therapist Jim Ford. "There was always the question 'Why did I get shot? Why was I there?' Ford kept his patients focused on learning the skills they would need to survive in the outside world. Since he would never walk, Bobby had to learn to maneuver in a wheelchair: how to get in and out of it; how to climb back in if he fell out; how to get across the street. He had to learn basic bodily functions: how to catheterize himself, how to apply an enema. Bobby was not always the easiest patient to work with. "Sometimes Bobby would just totally refuse to do anything," he says. Once Ford was teaching Bobby how to balance on two wheels to go up and down curbs. The first few times, Bobby fell backward, landing on the floor. Ford wanted to teach him how to retrieve the chair and mount it by himself. Bobby had lost his patience. "Bring me my chair back," he shouted. Ford refused to back down. It was a few minutes before noon, so he said, "You have to go to lunch and I've got to go to lunch. It's as simple as that. This is your chair. You're going to get into it. If you don't get in that chair, you're not going to lunch." Bobby let out a torrent of curse words but eventually climbed into the chair and completed the exercise.

Bobby got his revenge against the VA by providing information about the miserable conditions at the hospital to *Life* magazine, which published a devastating critique of veterans hospitals in May 1970. The story and accompanying pictures exposed the fallacy of veterans administrator Donald Johnson's claim that veterans received "care second to none." It called the hospitals "disgracefully under-staffed" and "inferior" to an average community hospital. Pictures of a quadriplegic, Marke Dumpert, sitting helplessly and unattended in the shower drew national outrage. "Nobody should have to live in these conditions," he said. "We are all hooked up to urine bags, and without an attendant to empty them, they spill over the floor. . . . I lay in bed on one side from 6 A.M. to 4 P.M. without getting moved or washed. When and if you do get a shower, you come back and you're put into bed on the same sweaty sheet that you started with. It's like you got put in jail, and you're being punished for something." Bobby learned a valuable lesson about the power of the media with that story.

The same bullet that did such violence to his body had also robbed him of his memory. He recalls little about his life before April 29, 1969. During his long and painful rehabilitation in the vet-erans hospital, his mother would sit next to his bed for hours show-ing him old family photographs. "Mother, please help me get my memory back," he pleaded. "Do you remember this day?" she would ask, pointing to a picture of Bobby at his high school graduation. He would stare at the picture, hoping that some light of recognition would go off in his head. It never did.

After a few months, Bobby started to make progress, managed to get passes to leave the hospital, and even bought a car—a 1970 Buick fitted with hand controls. Bobby, physical therapist Jim Ford, and another friend, John Macari, used to sneak out to the track at Aque-duct and bet on the races. Macari was a 17-year-old kid from Brook-lyn when he was shot during a Communist raid on Clark Air Force base in the Philippines on July 4, 1969. Like Bobby he was a fun-loving, athletic guy who was left paralyzed from the waist down. Bobby was the bookie for the second floor of the hospital. John was the bookie for the third floor.

Bobby often stayed up all night studying the racing forms. One night he was convinced that he had found a winning horse named Red Sun that was going to make them all rich. "It came to the day," and Bobby recalls, "I've got to go to the race track. There is a horse running today and I've got to go to the race track today. Jim do you have any money? We're going to make a ton of money today. We've got to get out of here and get to the race track." Ford, who doubled as the driving instructor, borrowed car keys under the pretense of taking John and Bobby out for a lesson. They drove straight to the track, pooling their money, and betting $2,500 on a horse with odds of sixty-two to one. The horse won the race, but as soon as it crossed the finish line, the "inquiry" light started flashing, and Red Sun was disqualified for bumping another horse.

It's easy to point out how different Bobby's life was after Vietnam. But it's also striking how much of his personality remained the same. A bullet may have severed his spine, but it did not sever his ambition. He remained tough, determined, and passionate. Now he refocused his energy and ambition away from making money and toward having an impact in shaping American policy in Vietnam and the government's approach to dealing with veterans. He was convinced that had he not been shot, he would have returned from Vietnam, climbed the corporate ladder and, in his words, become a "supreme asshole." His injury changed everything. "What counts," he came to realize, "is the positive energy of life and of love. It's not about material gain. It's not about things that don't fucking matter. If I'm going to get up and deal with life every day, I need to have a significant purpose. And that purpose is not some trivial inconsequential acquisition shit. It has to be about something that is enduring and meaningful."

After he was released from the hospital, Bobby got an apartment in Great Neck down the street from where he grew up and where his mother still lived. Many of his old high school friends came to visit. Per Bang-Jensen remembers seeing Bobby for the first time in May 1971. Bobby looked smaller to him. He had long hair, and his lifeless legs were having muscle spasms, a common reaction to paralysis. As he sat watching Bobby trying to maneuver his legs to stop the painful contractions, he thought about how unfair the war had been. Most of his friends went to such great lengths to avoid service, and here was the toughest, bravest kid from their high school sitting in a wheelchair for having answered the call of duty. Bang-Jensen by then had joined the army and was finally on his way to Vietnam. Bobby told him not to go and suggested he could have a friend break his kneecap. He would do it cleanly, he promised, so that he would have no permanent disability. Bang-Jensen was struck by how much Bobby went out of his way to stress how happy he was to be alive and how much he was looking forward to the future. "Listen, I'm lucky to be alive," he said repeatedly. "I'm going to be getting a pension from the government for the rest of my life. I have nothing to worry about. If I need a new wheelchair, I'll get it. I'll get a free medical pension."

Lenny Shambon, who, like most of Bobby's peers, did not go to Vietnam, came to visit Bobby shortly after he moved to Great Neck. It was the first time he had seen Bobby since high school. He could not get over the contrast between the thin, frail man sitting paralyzed in a wheelchair and the young, vibrant, athletic man he once knew. "I still can't get used to the image of talking with him at table level and then standing up and towering over him. I'm used to seeing him as an equal in physical stature." The contrast between these two men who grew up in the same town and spent nearly every afternoon together in high school underscored the impact of Vietnam on the Baby Boom generation. Lenny, unscathed, graduated from Yale College and went on to earn a law degree at Yale Law School. "I could walk out, and he was stuck there in his chair," Lenny reflects.

Bobby's small apartment became a crash pad for his antiwar buddies. "We were professional protesters." He directed his anger at the VA, and especially the Bronx facility where he spent a year. He got involved with a new group, Vietnam Veterans Against the War (VVAW), which held a number of high-profile protests against the war. What Bobby found most useful were the extended rap sessions when they got together and talked about their experiences. Like Bobby, many of these men were angry and disillusioned—angry because of the emotional and physical trauma that they had endured, disillusioned because the government they had trusted and had fought to defend had lied to them about the war. "It was a network that you got connected to that allowed you the opportunity to talk through your shit and to vent," he said. "It was a very emotional thing to stand before a group of your peers and say, 'My name is Bobby, and I served in Vietnam.'"

He spent much of his time traveling around the New York City area participating in antiwar events. He spoke to civic groups and religious organizations, and at schools. Bobby had grown up watching television, so he understood the power of the medium to shape public opinion. In 1970 he appeared on a new daytime talk show hosted by Phil Donahue. His message was always the same: "Vietnam is the defining experience of our generation," often referring to it as a "major wake-up call." He had not been very interested in government or politics before the war. "I accepted what the government was saying. But to go and participate in that war and realize that we had been sold a bill of goods, that reality was very different from what we had been told," had radicalized him.

Like many other Baby Boomers, Bobby had been nurtured on the stories of heroism during World War II, raised in a Cold War culture that underscored America's mission to defend freedom around the world, and aroused by the soaring rhetoric of John F. Kennedy. "I believed that Vietnam was invaded by the north. That they were freedom-loving people who were being crushed by the Communist invasion. We were there to liberate them, to be freedom fighters." Once he got there, however, he realized it was very different. "It wasn't an invasion. The people hated our guts. The South Vietnamese were the ones that fucked us over every step of the way. The South Vietnamese army that I wound up working for as an adviser ran every time we had combat. The North Vietnamese fighters were the most dedicated, tenacious sons of bitches you ever wanted to fight. I worked for three different platoons, and they were all worthless." He returned home only to watch the government "continue to lie, to fabricate what was really going on. It just woke you up."

Richard Nixon, however, had effectively disarmed the peace movement with his reassuring plea of "peace with honor" combined with patriotic appeals to what he referred to as "the silent majority." Polls showed that most Americans wanted to end the conflict without losing the war. They wanted to preserve national honor but avoid shedding American blood. By 1969 many white middle-class Americans—even those who opposed the war—were convinced that a willful minority of violent youth, militant blacks, and arrogant intellectuals had seized control of the public debate, showing contempt for mainstream values and threatening social stability. In fact, by the fall of 1969, Americans by a 55 to 31 percent majority called themselves "doves," and nearly 80 percent said they were "fed up and tired of the war." As frustrated as Americans were with the war, they disliked protesters even more. Polls showed that more than half of all those who favored immediate and total withdrawal from Vietnam had negative feelings toward those who publicly advocated this same position. Not only did most Americans resent the organized peace movement's public displays of dissent, they viewed the war itself differently. Antiwar protesters tended to oppose the war for moral reasons and viewed it as an indictment of the entire system. The vast majority of Americans simply saw the war as a mistake and a waste of valuable resources. "We may find out someday that what we're doing in Vietnam is wrong," a Brooklyn bus driver told *Newsweek*. "But until then, it's my country right or wrong."

By the summer of 1971, Bobby was frustrated with the direction of the antiwar movement. That fall, he enrolled at Hofstra University Law School. In his application essay he said that it was time for the antiwar movement to work within the system. He made an effort to remove himself from the public protests, and he stopped returning phone calls from his fellow protesters. The only way for him to disengage was to shut out the world. He stopped reading the newspaper and pulled the plug on his television. He woke up early, drove to school, attended classes all day, and then stayed late at night in the library. "I studied my ass off," and he quickly grasped "the basic concept of what lawyering was about."

During the winter break he relaxed for a few weeks and turned on the television for the first time in months. The images were painfully familiar—the faces of young servicemen killed in combat, the announcement that Nixon was launching a massive eleven-day Christmas bombing campaign. "And I could not deny the reality that the entire fucking world was going crazy. That Nixon had lost his mind. That this was an absolute tragedy." Bobby could not block out the war, or his responsibility to participate in the debate about it. People were dying needlessly every day—people just like him—and he was sequestered in a library cubicle trying to deny it. "I just couldn't do it anymore."

Bobby went to the dean and asked for a leave of absence, but was told that New York law required students to complete the entire first year. He could not get partial credit for the semester: It was all or nothing. Bobby enrolled for the spring term—but never set foot on campus, never attended a class, never took a note. A few weeks before finals in the spring, he popped a handful of amphetamines and crammed for the exam, which were all essays. Somehow he managed to earn higher grades than he had the first semester. He completed his final two years the same way and graduated in 1974.

Instead of attending classes, Bobby threw himself back into the antiwar movement. Most of his anger was directed at Nixon. Now it was personal: For Bobby and many other activists of the time, Nixon embodied everything that was wrong with America. What frustrated and confused them was his continued hold on the American people. Politics as usual would not work; Bobby needed to make a dramatic gesture to highlight the absurdity of Nixon policies in Vietnam. What better place to make a statement than on prime-time television at the 1972 Republican National Convention in Miami. "I went down there, and at that point I had a serious attitude," he admits. "I was very confrontational." It was obvious that Bobby and his fellow protesters were not in Miami to support Richard Nixon. "We had been sleeping in Flamingo Park for five days, we stunk to high heaven, we had these filthy clothes on, and we looked like bums." Bobby was waiting outside the convention center in his wheelchair sitting next to a double amputee. "And these cops come over and look at him and a cop takes his fucking billy club and whacks him right in the fucking head," Bobby recalls.

Bobby and Ron Kovic managed to get tickets to attend the convention on the night of Nixon's acceptance speech. The cavernous convention hall grew quiet as Nixon ascended the podium and began his speech. The plan was to shout Nixon down, to do anything to disrupt the convention and make a scene on national television. At first Bobby felt intimidated by the thousands of Nixon supporters and by the beefy security people who surrounded him. "Then I thought about what it was that brought me here. And all the people that are getting fucked who would never have a chance to be in a position I'm in. I realized that I had to speak about the situation and give voice to it." So he took a deep breath and started shouting. Security people swooped down on him in seconds. Some of the well-dressed, well-behaved, always proper Republican delegates spit on him as he was being dragged out of the hall.

Bobby dropped out after the Miami convention. "I was very depressed," he recalls, "very depressed." He lost all hope that he would be able to change American policy. The organized antiwar movement had fractured into numerous splinter groups. Bobby went to the race track every day, and in the evening, he sat alone in his apartment, getting stoned and listening to music. He had been fighting against the war for more than a year, but had little to show for his efforts. The Democrats had nominated George McGovern on an antiwar platform, but Nixon maintained a huge lead in the polls. American casualties in Vietnam had declined steadily during Nixon's first term, and the president's assurance that America would achieve a peace with honor in Vietnam was closer to what voters wanted than McGovern's call for immediate withdrawal.

Although all the polls indicated otherwise, Bobby remained convinced right up until Election Day that McGovern would pull off a stunning upset. For him the issue was so black and white, the war was so clearly wrong, that he could not understand how people—especially his generation—could go into the booth and pull the lever for Nixon. In his mind Nixon was a war criminal. Like many other activists, Bobby overestimated the sense of political solidarity among Boomers. After young people rallied around Eugene McCarthy in the 1968 New Hampshire Democratic primary, many pollsters predicted the emergence of a powerful Baby Boomer voting bloc. In 1968, when the voting age was still 21, Boomers made up less than 10 percent of the eligible voters. By 1972, with the voting age lowered to 18, Boomers made up about 23.1 percent. Frederick Dutton, a former adviser to Robert Kennedy, predicted that "the impact of this restless new generation will come rolling in with a staggering cumulative effect in this and the next two presidential elections."

It never worked that way. Sharing a common generational experience did not mean that Boomers would all vote the same way. Less than half (49.6 percent) voted, and only 52 percent of those who bothered going to the polls supported McGovern—the only age group to give a majority of their votes to the Democrat. For some years thereafter, politicians, especially liberals, would continue to pursue the mirage of a monolithic Baby Boom protest vote. Boomers shared an appreciation for a style of politics that relied on charisma, media savviness, and a willingness to challenge convention, regardless of party affiliation or political ideology. "What babyboomers look for in a politician is idealism, pragmatism and independence, someone unbeholden to the ideologies and interests of the past," noted the political analyst William Schneider. "In other words, another Kennedy." For Boomers, JFK had come to symbolize a time when the United States stood strong in the world, the nation felt united, and life seemed simpler. Events in the years following JFK's death would shatter that faith, but as their confidence in government diminished, Boomers clung more tenaciously than ever before to a mythic view of Kennedy.

On Election Day Bobby urged his father to go out and vote for McGovern. "Don't believe these polls," he said. "I'm telling you Americans understand who Nixon is." Maybe not. Nixon won by a landslide, carrying every state except Massachusetts and the District of Columbia, for a margin in the electoral college of 521 to 17. Bobby was devastated.

On inauguration day, January 20, 1973, Bobby sat alone in his apartment watching coverage of the triumphant president as he waltzed from one party to the next. His television reception was poor, and dark lines rolled through the grainy picture. It was appropriate for his mood. "I'm sitting there and just fucking crying. I felt totally alone. This guy is a criminal. This guy is a piece of shit. He's insane. He's a lunatic. He's a murderer. Everybody is celebrating him. The world's joyous. I'm here by myself in this apartment with a broken fucking TV." The all-American boy, the child of immigrants who came to this country to pursue the American dream, felt abandoned by his country. No previous generation had experienced anything like it, except perhaps, the defeated Confederacy after the Civil War.

It wasn't just politics that was getting Bobby down. His race track buddy, John Macari, failed to show up at the track one day. For weeks, John had been making comments about committing suicide. "Hey, Bobby," he would say, "what do you think about cashing it in?" John was such an energetic, fun-loving guy that Bobby did not take him seriously. Yet in the winter of 1974, John Macari put a cold gun barrel to his head and pulled the trigger. Bobby began thinking seriously about taking his own life. "You got all these losses, and you got all this pain, why put up with all this sadness," he thought. As a child Bobby had channeled his frustration about his home life into sports. As a young adult he directed much of his anger and frustration into the antiwar movement. Now he could not be an athlete, and he felt like a failed activist. He was stuck: He refused to give up, but he could also not find a reason to go on.

Not even the end of the war, or Nixon's resignation, provided

Bobby with much relief. The Paris Peace Accords, signed on January 27, 1973, officially ended U.S. involvement in the Vietnam War. Nixon told a national television audience that the United States had achieved "peace with honor," but Bobby knew that it had achieved neither. The North Vietnamese had no intention of abandoning their dream of unification. National Security Adviser Kissinger hoped that the treaty would provide for a "decent interval" between the U.S. military withdrawal and the North's complete military conquest of the South. As Kissinger predicted, the North violated the cease-fire within a few months and continued its relentless drive south. By that point, most of the nation was focused on Nixon's struggle to hold onto power following revelations of a White House cover-up of the Watergate break-in. In August 1974 Bobby took little delight in watching a disgraced Richard Nixon became the first American president to resign from office. He thought Nixon got off easy: The president and Kissinger should have been tried as war criminals.

The following month, Bobby finally worked up the courage to visit John's mother in Long Island. He wanted to pay his respects and tell her what a wonderful friend John had been to him. It was 8:00 P.M., and he was sitting outside in his car trying to work up the courage to knock on the door. A new-model Mercedes pulled up and parked in front of him. An attractive woman, dressed in a long evening gown, stepped out of the car. It was John's aunt, Virginia. Bobby had met her before, but she never looked so attractive. She saw him sitting in the car and came up to talk with him. "Hi, bright eyes," she said. "How are you?" Bobby invited her to join him in the front seat. The next thing he knew, they were kissing and groping each other.

It turned out that they shared more in common than just physical attraction. Virginia, who was half Puerto Rican and half Cuban, had fallen in love with an African American man. They had two children together. She had been active in the civil rights movement and, like Bobby, had grown frustrated with the slow pace of change. "So you have two activist types that were disillusioned with our respective movements, who like to get high, and enjoy each other's company," he remembers. "We fell in love. It was that love which really gave me a reason to live."

Bobby and Virginia were married in May 1976. They had a tempestuous relationship: Both had hot tempers and loud voices and seemed to enjoy fighting. While Bobby was partial to pot, which often made him mellow, Virginia enjoyed liquor, which made her aggressive. When Bobby's brother, Roger, met Virginia for the first time, she had passed out after drinking an entire bottle. Roger rushed her to the local emergency room near their house in Huntington, Long Island. The doctor revived her with smelling salts. The first words out of her mouth were, "Get me out of this fucking hospital. I don't want to be in any fucking hospital on Long Island. Take me to the city. I want to be at Columbia Presbyterian."

A few years later she and Bobby rented a one bedroom apartment on West 68th Street in New York City. By this time, both of Virginia's children were grown and living on their own. One day she received a call from her son, Joseph. "Guess what? I'm married. And guess what? You're going to be a grandmother. And guess what? We're coming to town." A week later, Joseph and his wife, Tony, arrived with their new daughter, Kayla. The plan was for Tony and Kayla to stay for a few weeks while Joseph traveled to Texas to look for an apartment. But in Texas, he met another woman and never came back. Now Bobby and Virginia faced a tough decision. They were living in a cramped apartment with a woman they had just met and her infant daughter. Should they let them stay? For Bobby it was an easy decision. Knowing that he would never have a child of his own, he decided to take in Tony and to raise Kayla as his own.

In two years, as the first era in Boomer history came to an end, Bobby had been transformed again: this time from a suicidal loner into a loving husband and father. That love, for both Virginia and Kayla, probably saved his life, replacing despair with hope and turning cynicism into activism. Back in 1972, in the depths of depression, Bobby was angry that most vets came home to a nation that failed to appreciate the sacrifices they had made. A grateful public had greeted World War II vets by saying, "That was a bitch of a war, but we had to do it, and you guys saved democracy and freedom. God bless you and thank you." A disillusioned public responded very differently to Vietnam vets. Young men were sent into a confusing war. Some watched their friends die. Some were haunted by memories of killing innocent civilians. They returned home, and there was "no absolution" from society, no recognition of the horrible conditions they had had to endure. "In fact, society puts the onus of responsibility on the backs of 18- and 19-year-olds who got suckered into fighting the war. So not only do you get mind-fucked by going over to a situation that was totally crazy, but then you come back and get mind-fucked again. Instead of being seen as heroic, you are perceived as a psycho. You're the son of a bitch that killed those women and children. You're a drug addict."

In 1971, the pollster Louis Harris conducted a survey that confirmed many of Bobby's suspicions about the way the public perceived Vietnam veterans. It showed that 62 percent of Americans associated Vietnam veterans with "a war that went bad." Nearly half referred to Vietnam veterans as "suckers," who had been led "to risk their lives in the wrong war in the wrong place at the wrong time."

Many vets came home and felt ostracized from society. They felt little in common with older veterans' organizations like the Veterans of Foreign Wars and the American Legion. Only five years separated those who served in combat in World War II and Korea. More than a dozen years separated Vietnam vets from the Korean War, and nearly two decades passed between the end of World War II and the massive escalation in Vietnam. "We did not want to join our father's organization," reflects a Vietnam vet. The generational and cultural divide was too great to bridge. "We did not want to listen to Glenn Miller on Flatbush Avenue with World War II vets. Our community collapsed inwards because the society outside basically rejected us," reflects Vietnam veteran Michael J. Handy. "We've always helped each other. It started overseas in the combat zone, and it just continued when we came home." Many Vietnam vets tried to forget their experiences and avoid the negative feelings by fading into the background. Many others, however, formed small networks in their communities, their schools, and on the job.

Soon after Nixon's reelection, Bobby wanted to find a way to organize Vietnam vets to challenge the system from the inside. He shed his radical image and his revolutionary rhetoric, shaved his beard, cut his hair, and put on a suit. Having influence, he discovered, required both righteousness and power. He now needed to find a way to reach the broad mass of vets who had never joined the

VVAW or participated in protest rallies. Bobby assumed that most Vietnam vets were ticking time bombs waiting to explode; that, like him, they had been traumatized by the war. He imagined an army of angry, disillusioned vets who could be mobilized into a powerful liberal political force.

The problem was that vets were not of one mind on the war. The majority of veterans, like most Americans, directed their anger at student protesters and the weak-kneed politicians who caved in to their demands. If they were angry at the government, it was because its leaders had forced them to fight the war "with one hand tied behind their backs." They were members of Richard Nixon's silent majority, and while they were willing to mobilize for specific grievances, like an expanded GI bill, they shared little else. The Vietnam generation was the fragmented generation: the war divided those who fought against those who stayed home; it pitted moderate antiwar activists against radicals; and in perhaps the cruelest irony of all, it split many of those who fought into rival camps of hawks and doves.

In 1973 Bobby had started working for the Paralyzed Veterans, helping them to file claims for benefits. He was living in Huntington, Long Island, and commuting ninety minutes each way into New York City every day. In the process of handling cases of veterans, he came to believe that vets were getting a raw deal. "It became stunningly clear that Vietnam vets had gotten shafted." They were getting screwed by large veterans' organizations that were steering money away from younger veterans in need to older veterans receiving nursing care not related to service. "I could sit in the office all day and help individual veterans, but I realized that the basic entitlement structure had to be changed." "We had a generation of guys getting fucked. Nobody was saying anything or doing anything about it." The paralyzed vets were a small group that benefited by cooperating with the VA. Bobby realized that if he was going to develop a more confrontational approach to veterans' issues, he would have to form a new organization—the Council of Vietnam Veterans (CVV). It also meant he had to go "to the belly of the beast": Washington, D.C.

THREE

GROWING PAINS

Marshall in college;   **Fran at high school graduation;**   **having fun in the '70s.**

Traditional histories of postwar America cover certain topics as a matter of course: the civil rights movement and rock and roll, along with Vietnam, Watergate, and other standard political events. The Boomers did not launch rock and roll, much less the civil rights movement. They provided the bulk of the soldiers in Vietnam, but they did not have much say in the war itself. Yet they grew up with all of these influences and more: great wealth, freedom, and unprecedented opportunity. As they moved through the life cycle, the Boomers pulled the cultural center of gravity with them. During the 1950s advertisers pitched them toys and breakfast cereals while encouraging their parents to buy more spacious homes and bigger cars. By the 1960s the nation fixated on the generation gap as boomer teens, now accustomed to being the center of attention, rebelled against their parents' authority.

The nation was in the midst of a youth frenzy in the 1960s. In 1965, *Time* estimated that teenagers possessed $14 billion in purchasing power and spent $570 million on toiletries, $1.5 billion on entertainment, and $3.6 billion on women's clothes. The press wrote articles trying to explain their behavior. The Associated Press declared 1964 "the year of the kid." In 1966 *Time* magazine named the under-25 generation as its "Man of the Year," noting that it was "a new kind of generation" that had been "cushioned by unprecedented affluence" and raised in a "prolonged period of world peace." As a result, the Boomers possessed a "unique sense of control over their own destiny" and a deep distrust of all forms of authority. "No adult can or will tell them what earlier generations were told."

■

Fran Visco graduated from West Catholic Girls High School in the spring of 1965, a year of momentous changes in America. In March U.S. Marines had landed at Da Nang and by the summer, draft calls were increasing. The Rolling Stones' "(I Can't Get No) Satisfaction" hit number one on the charts in July. On August 13, 1965, the Watts section of Los Angeles exploded in a six-day riot, which would help set the scene for Ronald Reagan's election as governor of California the next year. Later that summer Lyndon Johnson signed into law the Voting Rights Act. The Beatles toured the United States, beating Pope Paul's attendance record when they played at Shea Stadium in New York on August 23, 1965.

Like many other teenagers during the decade, Fran Visco watched the evening news stories about civil rights protests, urban rioting, and Vietnam body counts. She read the local newspaper and participated in frequent conversations with family and friends about current events, and she developed strong opinions about most issues. The momentous events of the decade that splashed across the headlines every morning did not, however, influence the daily rhythm of her life. As an 18-year-old young woman, she worried about more practical issues that directly touched her life: finding a job, figuring out a way to attend college, buying clothes, and meeting "Mr. Right."

Shortly after graduation, Fran picked up a job as a legal secretary during the day while attending junior college at night. She continued to live at home with her mother and her grandparents. Most weekends were devoted to meeting men. The women of her generation had more freedom to experiment because of the widespread use of the Pill. Developed in 1957 and licensed by the Food and Drug Administration in 1960, the birth control pill, which quickly became known as the Pill, gave women a greater sense of sexual freedom than any other contraceptive device that had come before. It was an instant success. By 1962 an estimated 1,187,000 women were using the Pill. Ten years later 10 million women were using it. *Time* magazine called it "a miraculous tablet." The Pill divorced sex from the danger of unwanted pregnancy. It gave women the freedom to have sex when and where they wished and made contraception acceptable to the mainstream.

In 1967, while attending a dance at Holy Cross, Fran spied this "incredibly handsome, very tall, very handsome guy" with brown hair and blue eyes. Fran asked her friend Vicki to dance with her. "Let's see if he cuts in," she said. He did.

Bill and Fran dated for a few years. She always had mixed feelings about the relationship, even after she accepted his offer of marriage. A year before the wedding Fran was sitting in the living room of her house when she burst into tears. "What's the matter?" her mother asked. Fran said, "I'm not sure that I want to get married." "Then don't," was the response. A few days later, Fran decided it was time to confront Bill. She told him that she wanted to call off the wedding, and she was about to say, "and I want to date other people." Before she had the chance, however, he interrupted her: "If you're going to tell me you want to date other people, then we're over." Fran could not bring herself to admit that to either him or herself. She really did want the freedom to see other people, but she also enjoyed the comfort and security of a relationship. They stayed together and were married in September 1967.

Most of her friends sensed Fran's ambivalence, even after the wedding. She never seemed completely happy or satisfied. "From day one, I knew she wasn't happy in the marriage," recalls a friend. Bill was attractive—a real "head turner." Fran may have hoped that he would be her ticket to a better life. "I thought he was a rich guy," Fran says. "His parents had a boat." He turned out to be very different from what she had expected. He was not rich, although he sometimes pretended to have money. Initially, he told her that he had earned a degree from Georgia Tech. She later discovered that he had never finished. He then promised that he would go to school at night to complete the requirements for his degree. He claimed to have enrolled and even carried home books at night to study. But that too was a lie. He was just trying to please her.

In an earlier era, Fran might not have questioned her station, but she was restless. There was a part of her that wanted to be married and happy, to have the idealized family life that she had seen on television and read about in magazines but had never really experienced. Yet she did not want to be stereotyped as a suburban housewife. In some ways Fran was trapped between the expectations of two generations. Her mother wanted so desperately to be a good wife that she avoided for years confronting her husband's infidelity and gambling. Even as a child, Fran found that unacceptable, and as a young adult she demanded much more. She wanted to have a career, to go out and enjoy life, and not be tied down in a stale marriage. Perhaps marrying someone with money would have given her more flexibility: she could have gone back to school full time, maybe earned a law degree. Instead she was trapped in the worst of both worlds: tied down in a loveless relationship and forced to continue working as a legal secretary. "I think the best way of describing it is to say that I was on autopilot," she observes. "I don't know that it was ever really working. But it was sort of going along."

After three years of marriage, Fran left Bill. It was personally a very difficult time for her. "I've often thought of myself in this very strange situation, as someone who is not good at being alone. I always had someone. I always had a boyfriend," she reflected, adding, in what could be a slogan for many Boomers, "I'm also not good at marriage and relationships." In an age that emphasized personal fulfillment, self-awareness, and sexual freedom, there was less incentive to remain in marriage. The divorce rate, which climbed almost 100 percent in the 1960s, increased another 82 percent in the 1970s. More than two out of five marriages during the decade ended in divorce. "In the 1950s as in the 1920s, diamonds were 'forever,' " observed the historian Sheila Rothman. "In the 1970s diamonds were for 'now.' " Just as important, Boomer couples that stayed together rewrote the rules of marriage. By the end of the 1970s three-quarters of Baby Boomers said they preferred an "equal marriage," with the husband and wife sharing responsibility. Only 10 percent wanted a "traditional marriage" with clearly defined male and female roles.

Rising divorce rates were just one indication of how Boomers were redefining attitudes toward sex and marriage. Between 1960 and 1977, as the Boomers graduated from college, the number of unmarried couples living together more than doubled. A survey in 1967 found that 85 percent of parents condemned premarital sex as morally wrong. By 1980, as Boomers became parents themselves,

63 percent would condone it. According to the pollster Daniel Yankelovich, the new attitude had become: "If two people loved each other, there's nothing morally wrong with having sexual relations." Eventually a poll in 1983 would find that 44 percent of Baby Boomers felt that living together before marriage was a good idea, 29 percent believed marijuana should be legalized, and 37 percent believed casual sex was acceptable. Many Boomers acted on their developing beliefs. A survey of female sexuality by *Redbook* magazine in the late 1980s would reveal that one-third of women had extramarital affairs, and another 36 percent said they would like to. "Our findings show that women have completely abandoned the role of passive sexual partner," said sociologist Robert J. Levin. "They are now active participants in the sexual relationship."

It did not happen overnight in spite of the Pill. The Boomers reinvented sex quickly, but the institution of marriage took much longer to change. Fran's mixture of political and social views are a case in point. Between working full time and attending classes at night during the '60s, Fran dabbled in politics and protest. Her politics remained decidedly liberal: She supported local Democratic candidates, championed civil rights, and opposed the Vietnam War. She wrote letters and occasionally attended antiwar rallies, but for the most part, she remained on the sidelines of the big political clashes of the 1960s. She was never afraid, however, to voice her opinion, which sometimes caused friction at family gatherings, especially after her brother, Louis, volunteered for the marines in 1968. "He and I had this friction because he was a Marine of the Month and I was in moccasins and a poncho."

The war divided the Visco family. Fran was outspoken and vocal in her opposition; Louis supported the American goal of preventing a Communist takeover of South Vietnam. "It was a job that had to be done, and I did it," Louis recalls. In 1971, when he was about to be shipped to Vietnam as a machine gunner, Fran started raising money to send him to Canada. "That was personal," she said. "It had nothing to do with my belief that the Vietnamese people should make their own decisions or that we were imposing our will on them. This was about my brother." Her mother agreed. "Yes," she declared, they "were going to send him to Canada." Fran's occasionally present father was appalled by the suggestion. The crisis passed: Louis managed to get an early honorable discharge before being shipped overseas.

Fran still stirred controversy when Louis returned home. The family organized a small party for him, hung red, white, and blue balloons, and constructed a big "Welcome Home" sign. Fran decided to use the occasion to make an antiwar statement. She took a large American flag, turned it upside down, and hung it on the wall separating the living room and dining room. It was impossible to miss. Her father walked into the house and ripped the flag off the wall. "How can you do this to your country?" he asked.

Fran was taking full advantage of her single life. On weekends she went out with friends in Philadelphia or to the Jersey shore. During one visit to Avalon, a popular Jersey beach community, Fran met Ron, another tall, handsome man who would soon become her second husband. "Ron was a happy drunk," recalls a friend. "He was one of these people who could drink all night and the next day get up for work as if nothing happened." Before they were married, Fran was still living in Philadelphia and commuting to his home in New Jersey. "I remember her going there with a plate" of cookies, says a friend. "When she arrived, he was out drinking, and she sat outside for hours with this plate waiting for him to come home." There were other warning signs about the relationship. "I remember one time coming back from his apartment and just breaking down in the car on the way back to Philadelphia," Visco reflects. "I remember trying to go through the toll booth and digging for exact change so I would not have to see the toll collector." A toll collector happened to be standing in front of the exact change booth. He saw her, tears streaming down her cheek, and tried to reassure her: "It's not that bad, honey."

After a few months of dating, Ron forced a decision. He had been promoted and was asked to move to Washington, D.C. Would she marry him so they could move together? In March 1976, despite doubts, she went ahead with the marriage. "I knew I should not have married him. But I did." They held a small, informal ceremony in the living room of her mom's house in Philadelphia. Few people who knew Fran expected the relationship to last. "I knew that marriage wasn't going to last because she never bought a dress," recalled a family friend. "Fran was always into clothes. But she never bought a dress for this wedding."

Fran made the move to a Maryland suburb of Washington, stopped going to school, and started working at a graphic arts and printing company. Again she felt trapped. At one point she considered having her tubes tied to make sure she did not have any children. But Maryland law required the husband's permission, and he refused to sign. They were together less than a year.

In 1978, at the age of 30, with two failed marriages behind her, Fran decided that it was time to focus exclusively on her career. "That's it," she declared. "I am going back to school. I want to be a lawyer and I'm just going to do it, and I'll find a way to get the money." She never wanted to be "just a suburban housewife," but that was exactly what she had become. As much as she wanted to be married, she did not want to depend on a husband to provide for her. Without a college degree and with no real skill, she saw herself going down the same dead end road as her mother. "I felt very strongly that I had to take care of myself," she reflects. Fran moved back to Philadelphia and enrolled full time at St. Joseph's College to finish her undergraduate degree. She returned to her old law firm job, where she was promoted from secretary to a paralegal with more flexible hours. Initially, she moved back into her grandparents' house on Simpson Street, but later moved into a house with a recently divorced friend, Felicia, and her young son. Money was scarce. "We ate macaroni and cheese for dinner almost every night," Felicia recalls.

In many ways, Fran is representative of an older generation of women Baby Boomers who were caught in the center of a revolutionary change in social values. She was young enough to absorb the new ethic of self-fulfillment that found full expression among Shadow Boomers who came to maturity in the late 1970s and 1980s. She wanted a mutual marriage where power and responsibilities were shared, an independent and satisfying career, and the free expression that had always been available to men. Yet she could never completely shed the idealized image of marriage passed down from her mother's generation and popularized in film and television during the 1950s. Frustrated by her inability to resolve this conflict, Fran decided to forget about relationships for a few years and focus on her career.

She was moving into a world that provided greater opportunities. By the 1980s, 25 percent of new graduates of law, medical, and business schools would be women, up from only 5 percent in the late 1960s. Between 1960 and 1990 the percentage of women working outside the home jumped from 35 to 58 percent. There was a corresponding change in public attitudes. In 1970, 50 percent of college freshmen and 30 percent of women agreed that "the activities of married women are best confined to the home and the family." Five years later only 30 percent of men and less than 20 percent of women took that position.

The feminist movement won a number of impressive victories in the courts and legislatures during the 1970s. In 1970 California adopted the nation's first "no-fault" divorce law, which allowed a couple to initiate proceedings without first proving that someone was responsible for the breakup of the marriage. Within five years, all but five states adopted the principle. In 1972 Congress passed Title IX of the Higher Education Act, which banned discrimination on the basis of sex in "any education program or activity receiving federal financial assistance." The legislation set the stage for an explosion in women's athletics later in the decade, as well as a backlash at schools that had to cancel men's programs since fewer women wanted to be athletes and the law mandated equal funding. Also in 1972 Congress passed and sent to the states a constitutional amendment banning discrimination on the basis of sex. By the end of the year all fifty states had enacted legislation to prevent sex discrimination in employment. Federal and state laws protecting victims of domestic violence and rape were strengthened. Before 1974, when Congress passed the Equal Credit Opportunity Act, married women were routinely denied credit cards in their own names. The women's movement helped precipitate a revolution in family law. As demands for divorce increased, many state legislatures liberalized their statutes in an attempt to reduce the acrimony and shame associated with the divorce process.

The most dramatic change came in the area of reproductive rights. In a number of states women fought to give doctors more power to perform abortion. A few states revised their statutes. On January 22, 1973, the Supreme Court declared in the landmark *Roe v. Wade* case that a woman had a constitutional right to an abortion. Writing for the majority, Justice Harry Blackmun asserted that the Fourteenth Amendment, which prohibited states from denying "liberty" to anyone without "due process," established a "right of privacy" that was "broad enough to encompass a woman's decision whether or not to terminate the pregnancy." The Court stated that during the first trimester, the decision to abort a fetus should be left to the discretion of a woman and her doctor. Over the next three months, up until the point of fetal viability, the state could establish some limits on the right to an abortion. In the final trimester the government could prohibit an abortion except where necessary to preserve the mother's life or health. It was a ratification of liberalizing abortion laws in many states, though Blackmun's "right of privacy" was a sufficiently novel reading of the Constitution that opponents kept up hope of overturning *Roe* for years. And prolifers would never accept abortion no matter what the statutory argument.

All of these changes in law and politics were reflected in popular culture. Televison viewers watched as family comedies of the 1950s and 1960s were replaced by new shows that dramatized the ambiguity of family and work. *The Mary Tyler Moore Show* starred an over-30 career woman. Other popular television shows—Valerie Harper's *Rhoda* and Diana Rigg's *Diana*—presented strong, independent, and resourceful women. *Maude* starred a loud, opinionated feminist who decided to have an abortion in middle age. Male chauvinism was dealt a major blow in 1973 when 55-year-old former Wimbledon star Bobby Riggs, a self-avowed sexist, challenged the top women's player, Billie Jean King, to a match. "You insist that top women players provide a brand of tennis comparable to men's. I challenge you to prove it. I contend that you not only cannot beat a top male player, but that you can't beat me, a tired old man." Millions of Americans watched the match on television as King dismantled Riggs, winning in three straight sets. In 1976 journalist Barbara Walters broke through the glass ceiling at ABC, becoming the highest-paid television anchor and the first to cohost the evening news.

Feminism, perhaps more than any other social movement, was led by Boomers, and it touched more lives than any other movement. Many Boomer women shunned the term *feminist,* yet they assumed that they should have autonomy unlike any previous cohort.

■

The other arena—both inside and outside the home—that the Boomers wholly occupied in the '70s was that of popular culture, first through rock music, then Hollywood, then television. Marshall Herskovitz's pilgrimage to California is emblematic of the shift. Like many of his fellow Boomers, Marshall had no direct involvement in the dramatic political events of the 1960s. "I was one of the younger members of the Baby Boom generation in that sense," he recalls. "The people who were making it happen in 1966, 1967, and 1968 were my brother's age." Marshall opposed the Vietnam War, and he admired men and women who organized sit-ins in favor of civil rights, but he had no direct involvement with either cause. The one aspect of the 1960s that Marshall identified with most, and experienced firsthand, was the counterculture. In 1967, when he was a sophomore in high school, Marshall took the train from Philadelphia to visit his brother in Brooklyn. While in New York, he decided to explore Greenwich Village, the bohemian epicenter of the counterculture.

"I felt like I had come home," he reflects. Marshall relished the free expression of people who defied convention. He was a sensitive man in a world that placed a premium on masculinity, an intellectual in a world that rarely valued ideas. For him, these people with their long hair, sideburns, and faded jeans were "authentic." Like him they were the ultimate outsiders, but they had come together to create their own alternative community where they could live by their own rules. Marshall was part of the mass of people who shared little more than a general antipathy to convention; however, he felt little in common with hippies, a smaller subset of the counterculture. "Hippies to me had a very particular ideology: love everybody, live communally, live in peace, and take a lot of drugs. None of this stuff made any sense to me. I didn't love everybody. I didn't believe that peace was the only way. I didn't want to live in a commune. And I wasn't particularly interested in taking a lot of drugs."

In the summer of 1967, at the age of 15, he traveled to Europe for a few weeks with his aunt and uncle. When he left, none of his friends had ever tried pot. By the time he returned, they were getting high almost every day. Before he left, none of his friends had kissed a girl. By the end of the summer, they were having "make-out" parties. Music was central to their experience. Every afternoon after school, Marshall and his friends would get together and smoke dope, puff on cigarettes, and listen to The Doors, Jefferson Airplane, and the Beatles. Marshall was especially attracted to the music of Donovan, the English singer-songwriter routinely referred to as the "prince of flower power," who linked traditional folk music and mysticism to the counterculture. "It was like this new world happened," Marshall reflects about the summer and fall of 1967. It was one of the happiest moments of his life. The repressed teen who had been plagued most of his young life with self-doubt had found an outlet for his anxiety and a group of friends who shared his sense of self-discovery.

Music emerged during the 1960s as the language of the Boomer generation, establishing its identity and distinguishing it from its elders. In 1964 rock accounted for 90 percent of the 130 million single records sold in the United States. By the early 1970s it made up 80 percent of all music recorded in the United States, generating $2 billion in annual sales—more than movies ($1.6 billion) and sports events ($600 million). The new music expressed the pent-up frustration and utopian idealism of the young in a language that most adults could not understand. "Don't criticize what you can't understand / Your sons and your daughters are beyond your command," folk artist Bob Dylan warned mothers and fathers of the Baby Boomers. Dylan's music often had an explicit political message, but most rockers were more interested in free expression than radical action. "My music isn't supposed to make you riot," said Janis Joplin. "It's supposed to make you fuck."

The most popular group of the decade, the Beatles captured the hearts of teenage America following a TV appearance on the popular Ed Sullivan television show on February 9, 1964. In the first of three consecutive appearances, the Beatles attracted an audience of 70 million viewers—the largest for a show up to that point. Afterward, Fran Visco went running down the street to her friend's house screaming with excitement. "I used to fantasize about Ringo because I figured there was no way I could get any of the other ones," she remembers. The Beatles' appeal had to do with more than sex, however. Their music seemed to mock the adult world, containing a barely disguised message of freedom and excitement that by the 1967 *Sgt. Pepper's Lonely Hearts Club Band* album added barely disguised references to drugs: "It's all within yourself, no one else can make a change." "When the Beatles told us to turn off our minds and float downstream," recalls one fan, "uncounted youngsters assumed that the key to this kind of mind-expansion could be found in a plant or a pill."

As Marshall and his friends discovered, those plants and pills were more readily available in the 1960s. "Tune in, turn on, drop out," Harvard psychologist Timothy Leary advised the young, promoting the wonders of LSD. The drug was widely available on college campuses, and many of the world's most popular rock groups used it and wrote songs about it. According to *Life* magazine, by 1966 over 1 million people had experimented with LSD. But the drug of choice for the young remained marijuana. By 1969 more than 30 percent of all college students in the United States had smoked pot.

Marshall and his close friends were more interested in trying to figure out how the world worked than they were in debating who would win the next World Series. During many long, often pot-induced bull sessions, Marshall and his friend John Morse developed a unique philosophical view of the world, which they called "The Dialectic," a fusion of Marx and pop Freud. In an effort to understand himself, Marshall had read most of Freud's writings. He was struck by his notion of "reaction formation," which said that people will exhibit the opposite of what they're really feeling. Someone who was kind and soft-spoken was probably concealing inner rage. It was the perfect counterculture thesis, since, by extension, the counterculture must be the only true culture. It also explained so much about his own emotional makeup and his sense of alienation. Most of the world, he believed, was shaped by unconscious emotions and desires. Things happen that don't make sense because people have an inner life that is often disconnected from their external actions. This insight would provide the intellectual underpinnings of his later writing.

In addition to Freud, Marshall for the first time was exposed to books and other forms of culture that reflected his own ironic sense of the world. In his junior year in high school he read Joseph Heller's *Catch-22* (1961), the darkly comic novel whose title became a universal metaphor for life's madness. The novel was about a bombardier named John Yossarian who discovered that military rules require anyone who is declared insane to be excused from flying death-defying missions. The "catch" was that anyone who was smart enough to show "rational fear in the face of clear and present danger" was obviously sane and must continue to fly. More than thirty years later Marshall could quote passages from the novel. He became infatuated with the Marx Brothers, who he believed were always "tweaking authority." He loved spy movies, especially James Bond films, and television shows like *The Man from Uncle* and *Secret Agent*, whose plots revolved around men who were "not bound by rules." They were independent thinkers who trespassed as they pleased, were always on the right side, and, perhaps most important, always got the girl.

Marshall's hopeful and liberating summer of 1967 quickly turned into a dark and brooding winter and summer of 1968. The most difficult moment came during summer camp when he had a bad experience smoking pot. "I got massively stoned one night and just became terrified. I was in a state of terror for about two hours." Smoking pot never had the same appeal after that night.

The world also seemed like a darker place. In April Martin Luther King, Jr., was gunned down in Memphis. His death touched off an orgy of racial violence. Rioters burned twenty blocks in Chicago where Mayor Richard Daley ordered police to shoot to kill. The worst violence occurred in Washington, D.C., where seven hundred fires burned and nine people lost their lives. For the first time since the Civil War, armed soldiers guarded the steps to the Capitol. Nationally the death toll was forty-six. Two months later came Bobby Kennedy's assassination. In July the Democratic convention in Chicago turned into an orgy of violence, all captured for broadcast on the evening news. Through it all, the war in Vietnam ground on with no end in sight. "The world was exploding," Marshall recalls. "It wasn't changing. It was exploding. We literally were afraid the world was coming apart. That we were going to have anarchy or civil war. It was frightening."

As he moved into his senior year in high school Marshall had to decide what college to attend. An excellent student with impressive SAT scores, he aimed high, applying to Harvard, Amherst, Cornell, the University of Pennsylvania, and Brandeis. He was accepted at Cornell and Penn but was placed on the wait list at Brandeis—his first choice. His family was puzzled about the Brandeis decision, so his grandfather, who was active in the Jewish community, contacted a friend on the admission committee to see why Marshall had not been accepted. He was told that the committee was "worried that he's too radical." The university trustees were putting pressure on the administration to crack down on student protesters. The response was to keep them out in the first place.

Marshall did not consider himself a "radical." In four years of high school he had never participated in a protest of any kind. He smoked a lot of dope and listened to Donovan and the Beatles, but that hardly qualified him as a troublemaker. He assumed that he said something during his campus interview that gave people the wrong impression. His grandfather managed to schedule another interview for him with some "old guy in Philadelphia." Marshall went out of his way to assure him that he "was a good boy that wasn't going to make trouble." An acceptance letter showed up in the mail a few weeks later.

In April of Marshall's freshman year, Richard Nixon announced that he was sending American combat troops into neutral Cambodia. The next day, in a national televised address, a visibly nervous president explained his decision to a war-weary public. Claiming that an American defeat in Vietnam would unleash the forces of totalitarianism around the globe, he insisted that the invasion of Cambodia was a guarantee of American "credibility." "The most powerful nation in the world," he said, could not afford to act "like a pitiful helpless giant." At home the invasion reinflamed antiwar sentiment and eroded support for Nixon's policy. College campuses erupted in marches and protests. On May 4, at Kent State University in Ohio, panicked National Guardsmen fired into a crowd of student protesters, killing four and wounding nine. A week later at Jackson State College in Mississippi, two black students were killed and eleven wounded when police fired indiscriminately into a dormitory. After the Kent State killings, in what Columbia University president William J. McGill called "the most disastrous month of May in the history of American higher education," over 400 colleges canceled some classes and 250 campuses were closed as young people expressed their outrage.

Always the outsider, Marshall opposed both the blindness of American policy and the superficiality of its critics. He had little sympathy for Richard Nixon, and he opposed the war in Vietnam as both wrong-headed and immoral. But he found something shallow and superficial about the radical critique of American society that was emerging in response. After Kent State, Brandeis students created the National Strike Information Center. The organization's headquarters were in the building next to Marshall's dorm so he saw them coming and going every day. "I just felt like everybody was having much too much fun." His biggest problem was that the radicals oversimplified the state of the world, often repeating the tired Marxist view that the war was a manifestation of the evils of the capitalist system. Marshall had a hard time oversimplifying anything. They could not appreciate that the capitalist system, which they were so eager to overthrow, was the same system that provided them with designer clothing, cars, and the money to pay for their education.

It was finally the draft that brought the reality of the Vietnam War home to Marshall, his friends, and his two older brothers. There were many family dinner conversations about avoiding the war; and there was never any doubt they would find a way out of service. The oldest brother, Rick, drank ten cups of coffee minutes before going for his physical. His blood pressure was so high he was forced to spend the night in the hospital. It also won him a 1-Y deferment. By the time Marshall was ready to be drafted, the government had instituted a lottery system. On December 1 draft officials drew from a large container with capsules containing every day of the year. The first numbers drawn had the highest likelihood of being drafted. Marshall's brother Bart pulled a low lottery number and decided to go to medical school to get a student deferment. Marshall drew a high number and was confident that he would never be called.

The activities in the Herskovitz family were not unusual. The federal government reached out and touched millions of Boomer men with the draft. For many, especially those who were white, middle class, and living outside the South, the draft was their first personal experience dealing with Washington. The draft, and how to avoid it, was a constant topic of conversation in the school cafeteria and around the family dinner table. Many made key decisions about their future in an effort to avoid it. Do I have a child? Do I major in English or engineering? Do I become a doctor or accountant? In 1968, for example, when the New York City draft boards announced that teachers qualified for deferments, the city received nearly 20,000 more applications for a teacher's license than the year before. The following year city universities experienced an 800 percent increase in draft-age men taking teacher education courses.

That 1969–1970 academic year proved emotionally difficult for Marshall. The stress of being away from home for the first time, the anxiety associated with the first year of college and getting good grades, the tension on campus over the war, proved too much for him. "I just couldn't cope," he says. "I just couldn't handle it." His friend John Morse, who went to Haverford College, was having similar feelings. "Of all the people I know," Morse wrote his friend, "half I don't want to see and the other half I am afraid to see." Marshall said the sentence captured his state of mind perfectly. Morse believed that Marshall was overwhelmed by the social chaos that surrounded him. "It was a cultural time in which the entire society was experimenting with freedom," he recalls. "The larger social clash was a reflection of his own internal turmoil and reminded him of his own complex feelings."

By October of his freshman year Marshall developed an ulcer. He continued to attend classes and study for exams, but he was miserable. It seemed to him that everyone was miserable that year. Bob Dylan was his constant barometer. "Whatever you felt, you would listen to his songs and realize that Dylan was in the same place." The song that resonated with him at the time was "Desolation Row," released in 1965 as part of the *Highway 61 Revisited Album.* "You listen to the words of 'Desolation Row' and that's what it means to be so miserable and depressed."

Marshall sought escape through reading about exotic times and places. In high school he had spent hours listening to mellow music and reading J.R.R. Tolkien's *The Lord of the Rings.* "I was able to be in the world and take enjoyment from the world, but there was a huge part of me that just lived inside myself," he recalls. His escapism took him to medieval times when he was in college. For his senior project at Brandeis, he wrote a screenplay of *Beowulf,* the oldest extant epic in the English language. Written in the tenth century, it tells the story of the hero Beowulf, who travels to Denmark to slay the monster Grendel, who was terrorizing the kingdom of Hrothgar, protector of the Danes. "Marshall came to the story with the great sympathy for the monster," reflects Morse. "At the same time he enjoyed the great fantasy of being the slayer of the monster. It's a storyline that let Marshall become whole again." More than anything else, writing the screenplay provided him with an emotional outlet for his anxiety and a path for channeling his talent and his ambition. "It's the key to understanding how that gawky tormented adolescent really became this successful creator of film and television," says Morse.

In May 1973 Marshall graduated from Brandeis *summa cum laude* with a degree in English. He had anguished over what he should do after graduation. He had an obvious love of the arts but wondered whether he could make a living as a writer or working in the theater. He also had this notion that suburban kids from Philadelphia did not become artists: they worked in their father's business or became accountants or lawyers. He assumed that he needed to do what his father did: get up every morning, leave for work, and return at the end of the day. During his junior year he started seeing a therapist in suburban Newton, Massachusetts. In the classic Freudian approach, the analyst limited his role to asking questions, rarely offering advice. When Marshall told him he was not sure what he would do after graduation, the therapist suddenly responded: "Well, one thing that seems clear is that whatever you do, it will be something in the arts." The observation stunned and moved Marshall. "It was literally like a switch being thrown," he said. "It was like he gave me permission to do what I wanted to do. From that moment on there was no question that I would do something in the arts."

After graduation he traveled briefly in Europe, where he watched an American political spectacle—from a British perspective. Marshall remembers being in the lobby of a cheap London hotel watching a special Senate Committee chaired by Sam Ervin (D, North Carolina) as it investigated allegations that President Nixon had covered up a "third rate burglary" at the Democratic headquarters, housed in the Watergate hotel, during the 1972 presidential campaign. The British bystanders seemed "absolutely dumbfounded" that Americans would make such a public display of bad behavior. "What's wrong with your country?" they asked him. "Why on earth would you put this on television?" What they were watching was the slow, public unraveling of Nixon's grip on power. The first blow came on June 25, when White House counsel John Dean told the committee of the president's personal involvement in a scheme to cover up the Watergate burglary. Nixon professed innocence, but only 17 percent of the public believed him.

Marshall returned from Europe later that summer and settled into a large house in West Newton, Massachusetts, which he shared with four women, including his girlfriend and future wife, Susan Shilliday, and a few stray cats. He watched intently as Nixon suffered from a series of body blows: revelations that he kept a secret taping system in the Oval Office, the resignation of Vice President Spiro Agnew, and IRS charges against Nixon of financial impropriety. The Supreme Court delivered the crowning blow on July 24, 1974, when it ordered Nixon to turn over secret tapes, proving that he had personally intervened to stifle an FBI investigation and authorized payments of more than $460,000 in hush money. On August 8, 1974, facing certain impeachment, a disgraced Richard Nixon became the first American president to resign from office. Despite all its sordid details of government lying and intrigue, Watergate actually inspired Marshall's faith in government and in the criminal justice system. "It was quite amazing to me that a bad person, even one in such a high position, could be punished."

Marshall was less interested in Nixon losing his job than he was in finding one for himself. The fall of 1974 was the worst time for a recent college graduate, especially one with a degree in English, to be looking for a job. "It was quite a shock that there were no jobs to be found, and no interest in me as a bright young man who had just graduated summa cum laude from Brandeis. Nobody could give a shit."

The generation's size worked against itself in the 1970s. The nation had constructed new grade schools to accommodate young Boomers in the 1950s, and colleges and universities built new dorms and classrooms for them in the 1960s. The economy created 28 million jobs between 1964 and 1980, but it was not enough to satisfy the demand from the massive numbers of Boomers entering the workforce. In 1965 there were 75 million Americans in the workforce. By the end of 1979 the labor force had swelled to 104 million. The number of new workers entering the American marketplace surpassed the total labor force of France.

Included in those numbers were two groups that previous generations of white men did not have to compete against: women and African Americans. In 1960, 30 percent of married women between the ages of 20 and 24 worked outside the home. By 1975 that figure had soared to 57 percent. At the same time, new affirmative action policies, given official sanction by the Supreme Court in the *Bakke* case (*Bakke v. University of California,* 1978), which allowed schools to consider race as a "plus factor" in admissions, increased the number of African Americans who were attending college and competing for jobs after graduation. By 1977 more than 1 million blacks were attending college, a 500 percent increase since 1960. The Bureau of Labor Statistics reported that every year during the '70s, colleges and universities produced an average of 400,000 graduates who could not find jobs commensurate with their education. Boomers in the 1970s were twice as likely to be unemployed as their parents were in the 1950s. The average income of 25- to 29-year-olds who were lucky enough to find jobs dropped from $12,658 to $12,387.

Marshall joined the swelling ranks of the underemployed. He enjoyed his first job in a bookstore but could not survive on the $2 an hour salary. He switched to a part-time catering job, which was miserable but paid reasonably well. Working part-time gave him the freedom to enter a film competition sponsored by Brandeis. In his spare time Marshall wrote a script about a young man who inherited his father's business. Somewhere along the way, the prize money for the competition dried up, so Marshall ended up with a script but no competition and no reward for his effort. Yet he enjoyed the process so much that he wanted to keep going. He made an appointment to talk with a film professor at Brandeis. "I want to be a director," he told him. "How do I do it?" The professor gave him two pieces of advice: produce a film that he could use as a calling card and get out of town. "You've got to go to Los Angeles," he said.

He had a script, so why not turn it into a film? Brandeis gave him the equipment and an assistant, an aspiring freshman film major named Jeff Silver. There was only one problem: neither Marshall nor Jeff knew what they were doing, and Marshall thought Jeff was something he wasn't. Jeff's only experience was sneaking onto the set of a TV show in Florida where he grew up. On the first day, Jeff confidently explained to Marshall how it was done. "Well, basically, you have a slate and it tells you what shot it is and then the actor does the line of dialogue," he said. An incredulous Marshall asked, "Do they have a different slate for every line of dialogue?" Without hesitation, Jeff responded, "Oh yeah, of course." So for the first few days of filming, Marshall turned on the camera, slated it, and the actor would repeat one line of dialogue. Marshall would then shout, "Cut." They would reset the slate and film the next line of dialogue. It took him two days to work up the courage to tell Jeff that he thought they were doing it the wrong way. "Jeff," he said, "I think we could do the whole scene and then cut it later in editing."

Marshall spent more than a year working on the film and spent his bar mitzvah money, about $6,000, producing it. "It was all the money I had in the world," he reflects. "I had no money left after that film." After a few frantic final weeks of editing, Marshall was ready to show the result at a special screening at Brandeis. Everyone would be there: his friends, the crew, the people at Brandeis who supported his effort. His parents came up from Philadelphia. It was Marshall's "coming-out" event, his way of communicating to his parents that he was now an artist, a filmmaker. He had already made plans to move to California. His parents had reservations. His father was adamant that Marshall was making a big mistake—that it would be impossible for him to make a decent living in Hollywood. He arranged for Marshall to talk with a distant friend who had once dreamed of making it big in Hollywood, only to fall flat on his face. He serenaded him with "one horror story after another."

The movie was well received, but for Marshall the evening was a disaster. His father claimed to be "embarrassed" by Marshall's "amateurish" effort. Marshall was devastated. He respected his father, genuinely valued his opinion, and was eager to gain his acceptance. "It was a very difficult moment for us," he remembers. "It was the first time in my life he ever doubted me. And this was the most important thing I'd ever done." In the past a confrontation of this magnitude would have sent Marshall into an emotional tailspin. "I was anxious and I wanted people to like me, and I would maybe listen to what people said too much." This time it was different. He had gained a certain confidence and maturity. He had also discovered what he wanted to do with the rest of his life. On this issue he did not care what other people thought.

In 1975 Marshall packed his bags and moved to California to launch his career in Hollywood. The decision, made against the wishes of his family and the advice of many of his friends, replayed a common minidrama from generations past. Yet there were Boomer tinges. It was not fair for Marshall to ask Susan to quit her job and move with him unless he was ready to get married, and he wasn't. He was moving to young and vibrant California, and he wanted to experience the freedom of the single life, so he left to pursue his new career, and perhaps his new life, alone. He lasted four days in Los Angeles by himself. He hated being alone, and he missed Susan, who quit her job and joined him the following week. Like many other men in their early 20s and like many of the characters he would later create, Marshall was torn between his need for commitment and his desire to be independent.

Marshall was part of a massive migration taking place from the Rust Belt, which extended from Massachusetts down to Delaware and across to Illinois and Michigan, to the Sun Belt, the bottom half of the country extending from North Carolina to southern California. During the 1970s the Sun Belt accounted for 90 percent of the nation's population growth, and by 1980 claimed a majority of Americans. Just three states—California, Texas, and Florida—accounted for nearly 40 percent of the nation's population growth and controlled nearly 25 percent of the electoral votes needed to win the presidency.

During the '50s and '60s popular culture depicted southern California as the promised land for Baby Boomers. In 1960 most teens, when asked by *Look* magazine what they would do if they had an unlimited amount of money, said they wanted "a sports car and a big house in California." Popular songs such as "Surfin USA" and "California Girls" by the Beach Boys highlighted the association with beautiful people, sunny beaches, and a carefree lifestyle. The Mamas and the Papas lured people west with the lyrics of "California Dreamin'"—"I'd be safe and warm if I was in L.A." Much of the youthful innocence, however, had disappeared by the mid-1970s, smothered in a haze of green metallic smog, clogged freeways, and soaring taxes.

California may have fallen on hard times, but Hollywood was experiencing a renaissance as new directors challenged the industry's aging leadership by producing films that appealed to younger viewers. "The 70s was the first time that a kind of age restriction was lifted, and young people were allowed to come rushing in with all of their naivete and their wisdom and all of the privileges of youth," observes Steven Spielberg, one of the Boomer "movie brats" who came to prominence during the decade. Beginning in the late '60s, the new Hollywood produced memorable and innovative films that reached across the generation gap to attract younger audiences. *The Graduate* (1967), starring Dustin Hoffman as a confused 20-year-old college graduate searching for his place in the artificial—"plastic"—adult world, was the highest-grossing film of 1968, scoring seven Academy Award nominations. The success of *The Graduate* and, also that year, *Bonnie and Clyde,* boosted theater attendance for the first time since the end of World War II, and opened the door to a host of new films dealing with youthful themes of alienation, including *Easy Rider* (1969), Dennis Hopper's road trip classic, which cost $300,000 to make and grossed more than $19 million at the box office.

Hollywood's decision to pursue young audiences forced television executives to follow suit. By the mid-1960s the networks were still relying on a stable of shows that appealed to older audiences—ABC's *Lawrence Welk Show,* CBS's *Ed Sullivan Show,* NBC's *Bonanza.* With movies now making a direct appeal to the expanding Boomer market, network executives feared that a generation nurtured on *The Mickey Mouse Club* would outgrow television and spend their millions on other forms of popular entertainment. The result was a Hollywood arms race to attract the biggest arsenal of hip, youthful products to win over the hearts and minds of the Boomer generation. The networks dropped popular shows and touted their new "with-it" schedule. *The Mod Squad*, which premiered in 1968, showed three hippies turned cops—Pete, Linc, and Julie—collaring adults preying on the young. The same year, *Rowan and Martin's Laugh-In* debuted and quickly catapulted to number one in the ratings with its youthful style and antiestablishment humor. "You know, we only went into Vietnam as advisers," said co-host Dan Rowan. "Last week we dropped over 400,000 tons of advice." *Laugh-In's* success paved the way for *Saturday Night Live*, which premiered in 1975 as part of NBC's effort to reach young viewers. Once again Boomers, simply because of their size and extraordinary wealth, produced a shift in popular culture. And it worked. According to the Hollywood Chamber of Commerce, TV, film, and recording industry production reached a record $13 billion in 1979.

Marshall would soon play a major role in Hollywood's effort to reach the lucrative Boomer market, but for now he had more mundane issues to contend with—finding an apartment and getting a job. He and Susan found a small apartment in West Los Angeles near the beach community of Santa Monica. It was hardly a glamorous start. All their furniture came from the local Goodwill. He had no job and no leads. They had no income. Marshall spent hours every day combing through the Yellow Pages calling production companies. One of the first people he called was a distant family friend named Stanley Kallis, a television producer who had agreed to look at his film. "You know," he told Marshall, "there's a certain primitive passion in this film, but you really don't know what you're doing." He suggested that Marshall purchase "one of these newfangled things called a video tape recorder" to tape television programs so he could review them scene by scene to understand their structure. Marshall, who fancied himself a moviemaker, was disdainful of the suggestion that he could learn anything from television.

After a few months of rejections, Marshall came across an ad in a magazine about a film school in Beverly Hills. At this point, without contacts or experience, film school made sense, though he couldn't afford it, and was forced to turn to his father. His father reluctantly agreed to pay the tuition, perhaps hoping that his son would get this film bug out of his system and move on to a real career. To help pay the bills Susan picked up a job working for a pornography distributor. Her company's big hit was *If You Don't Stop It, You'll Go Blind,* followed by the unforgettable sequel, *Can I Do It Until I Need Glasses?*

In the fall of 1975 Marshall enrolled at the American Film Institute (AFI), a remarkable place, with twenty-six directors, twenty producers, and fifteen writers and a tough and demanding curriculum. "It was the first time in my entire academic life anyone had ever expected something of me that I wasn't sure I could do. It was like boot camp." One of the most memorable classes was on how to provide direction to actors. One teacher declared that the key to successful acting was "idiosyncratic contrapuntal juxtaposition"—in short, irony. An example she used was how actors play a drunk. The person who is drunk is usually trying not to appear drunk. In order to play a convincing drunk, a sober actor needed to pretend to be a drunk who was trying to appear sober. One day Marshall and a few friends decided to test the theory at a pool by pretending to fall into the water by accident. They lined up like Olympic judges, giving scores to the most convincing displays of intended accidental falling. When it was his turn, Marshall intentionally fell into the water by trying not to fall into the pool and won the highest score. It was a valuable lesson for someone who had always looked for authenticity yet been fascinated by irony.

Marshall enjoyed most of the students in the class, but there was one who initially rubbed him the wrong way. Ed Zwick talked too much in class and seemed too eager to please the teacher. "He wore saddle shoes, which he thought was hip at the time, but I didn't think was hip." One day in class the teacher asked them to bring an object with which they had a strong emotional attachment. The goal was to have them talk about the object as a way of understanding how an actor connects with events or people. The exercise was called partnering. Marshall brought in a ruler that his grandfather had used as a cabinetmaker. Ed talked about his grandfather's pocket watch. After class they got together and talked about their grandparents. It was the beginning of a deep personal and professional relationship.

In 1977, while still enrolled at AFI, Marshall was offered a freelance job as a writer for the television show *Family,* which chronicled the life of the Lawrence family. Marshall presented the producers with about a half-dozen story ideas. They rejected them all. Later he wrote a script that tried to add new dimensions to one of the main characters, Willie.

In Marshall's script, Willie is forced to confront a moral dilemma: he learns the whereabouts of a close friend who had been involved in terrorism and had been living underground. Does he protect the friend or turn him in to the authorities? The producers hated the story and had it rewritten. Marshall bounced around for a few months. He had completed the program at AFI and directed another film, *Cambridge Nights,* which examined the ambivalent feelings of a young man torn between his love of a woman and his hatred for the Vietnam War. In January 1978 Marshall ended up back again writing for *Family.* This time he had reason to believe they would be more receptive to his ideas: his friend Ed Zwick was the new story editor.

Marshall had a few of his scripts accepted, and he managed to pick up other small writing jobs as well. It paid the rent but provided little emotional or professional satisfaction. "I was really struggling," he remembers. Ed was having more success in television, but he shared Marshall's frustration with the movie business. Together they made a pact: Television, they agreed, would be a means to an end: "We can't be brainwashed into thinking that this is what we're going to do. We're always going to remember that we're filmmakers." "We understood," Marshall reflects, "that the way of the world was that we had to work in television." But it did not mean they had to respect it.

Marshall may have disliked the tube, but he was joining an interlocked group of entertainment industries that were collectively skyrocketing—not just movies and TV but also music. Los Angeles housed a third of America's total employment in film production and distribution. More than 90 percent of the world's music was recorded within five miles of the intersection of Hollywood Boulevard and Vine Street. In the affluent '60s and '70s, with Americans freed from duties at home (thanks to appliances) and blessed with unprecedented amounts of money to spend, the entertainment industry exploded into a global power. British rock and French films were still powerful, but an increasing percentage of the global business came from California and New York. Marshall believed that his generation was evolving, facing new worries as it settled into adulthood, but popular culture seemed fixated on Boomers as rebellious teens. Marshall wasn't sure how, but he knew that he wanted to provide a more authentic view of his generation's mind-set.

FOUR

FINDING GOD

Alberta, strung out.   Alberta's daughter, Kentina.

In the early 1960s much of the nation's attention focused on the plight of African Americans in the South and the dramatic protests to overturn nearly a century of legal segregation and disenfranchisement. Martin Luther King, Jr., mesmerized Americans with his "I Have a Dream" speech at the Lincoln Memorial in 1963, and over the next few years, Congress responded to public outrage at televised images of police dogs and fire hoses used against African Americans by passing two of the most important pieces of legislation in the nation's history: the Civil Rights Act of 1964, which banned segregation in public places, and the Voting Rights Act of 1965, which ensured blacks access to the ballot box.

Yet these dramatic victories did little to improve the lives of African Americans living in northern cities who faced their own problems of overcrowding, unemployment, and crime. In August 1964 the black section of North Philadelphia exploded in violence after an angry confrontation between a police officer and a black motorist escalated into widespread looting. Before it ended the following day, two people were dead, hundreds wounded, and more than 600 businesses, many of them owned by Jewish merchants, had burned to the ground.

The Philadelphia explosion was a harbinger. Between 1964 and 1968 the United States experienced the most intense period of civil unrest since the Civil War. In August 1965, five days after Johnson signed the Voting Rights Act into law, violence broke out in the Watts section of Los Angeles, leaving thirty-four dead, nearly four thousand arrested, and property damage reaching $45 million. In the summer of 1966 thirty-eight disorders destroyed ghetto neighborhoods in cities from San Francisco to Providence, Rhode Island. The result was seven deaths, four hundred injuries, and $5 million in property damage. The following year Newark erupted, leaving twenty-five dead and some twelve hundred wounded. In Detroit forty-three were killed, and more than four thousand fires burned large portions of the city. President Johnson's National Advisory Commission on Civil Disorders, known as the Kerner Commission, created to investigate the causes of the riots, speculated that despair, black militancy, and white racism combined to create a combustible situation. Boomers were at the forefront of the riots. In Detroit 61.3 percent of the rioters were between the ages of 15 and 24. Ominously, the commission warned: "Our nation is moving toward two societies, one black, one white—separate and unequal."

Alberta Haile's neighborhood was torn apart not only by summer racial riots but by the daily threat of violence. "Barrett Junior High was like a gladiator's arena," she reflects. While the media focused on the lawbreaking antics of white middle-class, student protesters, the nation was caught up in a deadly crime wave. The rate of serious crime soared between 1961 and 1974: robberies (255 percent), aggravated assault (153 percent), and murder (106 percent). The problem was especially bad in African American neighborhoods. Although they represented only 11 percent of the population, blacks accounted for more than half of all murder victims. There were many reasons for the crime surge, but most criminologists believed that the Baby Boom had increased the number of teens and young adults who were most likely to commit crime. In 1950 there were 24 million people in the prime age group of 14 to 24. By the mid-1970s it was 44 million. Forty-four percent of convicted murders were under age 25; 10 percent were under age 18. Baby Boomers were not only swelling college campuses, they were filling jails.

Alberta joined one of the local gangs and eventually emerged as its leader. Her school day no longer revolved around math and history, but after-school riots and brawls. "I could no longer get in touch with that nice little girl that loved school and wanted to be a doctor someday," she says. Instead she was marching around the neighborhood, stick in hand, looking for a rival gang. She still bears the scar on her nose from being struck with a stick during one melee. "I was ready to go to war," she remembers. "I was angry."

In later years Alberta could not finger a specific cause of her hostility. She was neither desperate nor destitute. Although she was not raised in a loving family, her parents provided for her every physical need. In part, being angry and fighting seemed like the thing to do in the mid-1960s—all of her peers were breaking the law, joining gangs, fighting against the police. But the violence was also an expression of outrage. Like Marshall Herskovitz and Fran Visco, Alberta grew up on promises of a better life: more freedom, more choices, more possessions. Marshall was able to embrace the new opportunities; Fran could at least dream of becoming a lawyer. But Alberta felt trapped, growing up in a world that seemed to be closing in on itself. Martin Luther King was a great man, but what had he done for blacks in Philadelphia who watched as whites fled to the prosperous suburbs, leaving behind empty industrial factories and a declining tax base? "The Negro masses are angry and restless," observed the author Louis Lomax, "tired of prolonged legal battles that end in paper decrees."

Alberta's home life, which had disintegrated into a daily ritual of beer, offered no refuge from the chaos. She had started experimenting with alcohol by the time she entered junior high school in 1965. There was rarely milk but always a cold beer in the refrigerator. Once in a while when she was thirsty, she would sneak into the kitchen and take a few sips. Over time she found herself craving the taste. By junior high school a few sips turned into a few bottles a week and, soon, a few bottles a day. There was no stigma attached to drinking beer in her family: "It just seemed to be another beverage that quenched her thirst."

In 1968 she graduated from junior high school and enrolled in South Philadelphia High School. In many ways it was a typical urban high school. Constructed in 1958, the five-story building at Broad and Snyder in a small Italian-American section of the city was designed as an educational laboratory. By building one large school for over 3,000 students, the school board hoped to promote interaction among the city's sharply segregated ethnic and racial groups and provide a broad range of subjects and extracurricular activities while also guaranteeing a safe and secure setting with plenty of adult supervision and direction.

The experiment was a miserable failure. For one thing, the school board had underestimated the demand. By 1968 the school was packed with more than 4,000 students attending classes in staggered shifts. The board had also failed to anticipate how their massive numbers allowed teens to develop a separate culture that resisted adult supervision and rebelled against the very middle-class values the school was designed to instill. More than anything else, the board was blindsided by the intense racial clashes that would tear apart the city and the rest of the nation. In 1968 the school was 50 percent white, 49 percent black, and 1 percent Hispanic. Stabbings, muggings, and street brawls between whites and blacks became almost a daily ritual at the school and in the surrounding neighborhood.

In October of Alberta's freshman year, school officials were forced to close the school for two days in order to stem the violence. By this time, Alberta had lost all interest in learning. Not only was she tired of the violence, but the subjects she studied seemed to have no relevance to her life outside the classroom. "I never really understood why history was so important anyway. All of the folks we were talking about were already dead. They had no relationship at all to me, nor were they the same color." Most days she stayed home, often with her mother's permission. All Alberta had to do was say she had a headache, and her mom would let her stay home. She never saw a doctor or a school nurse. She missed so many days that she failed the tenth grade twice. When the truant officer came to the house, her mother, on the rare days when she was home, would cover for her. Her father had no idea that Alberta was missing school until she was left back for a second time. "He knew that I was about to drop out, but his hands were tied," she reflects. "My mother had him convinced that I was too sick to go to school." When the school year began in September 1970, Alberta failed to register.

Now that she was no longer a student, Alberta considered herself an adult. "I was about 15 years old and 'calling my own shots' and 'doing my own thing.' I was ready to explore the world and find out what 'living was all about.'" She was not alone. Three of the four girls on her block dropped out of school at the same time. Since she had lots of free time on her hands and needed money, she started babysitting for Mrs. Tina, a neighbor with two small children. Mrs. Tina also had a teenage son, Donnell, nicknamed "High Bomb" because of his basketball shots. Alberta had been attracted to Donnell for some time, so she leaped at the chance to spend time at his house, babysitting his younger brothers. "I spent more and more time at Mrs. Tina's house than I did at home," she recalls. "I was the cook, the housekeeper, and the babysitter, all in one."

In addition to her household chores, Alberta spent lots of time in the upstairs bedroom with Donnell. She was an unemployed high school dropout whose only goal in life was to get pregnant and have a baby. She had been sexually active since she was 12 years old. Like many other lonely teenage girls, Alberta believed that a child would provide her with the unconditional love she had always wanted but never received. "I would finally have someone of my very own. Someone who would love me for myself and I could love them back and they wouldn't go away." Perhaps even more surprising, her mother encouraged her efforts to get pregnant because she wanted to be a grandmother. Her father, as usual, was clueless.

Many other African American women of her generation were making the same decision. By the start of the 1980s almost 55 percent of all black children were born out of wedlock, compared with 15 percent in 1940; 85 percent of black teenage mothers were unmarried; and 47 percent of black families were female headed compared with 8 percent in 1950. In 1965 Daniel Patrick Moynihan, then an assistant secretary of labor in the Johnson administration, suggested in a controversial report, "The Negro Family: The Case for National Action," that culture had as much a role in the breakup of the family as did poverty. But Alberta's case underscores the difficulty of trying to separate culture from poverty. Alberta's family was not poor, but she grew up in a community torn by rising expectations and diminished opportunities. Her neighborhood was more segregated in the 1970s than it had been in the 1950s. Racial tensions had pushed whites and blacks further apart and accelerated the flight of jobs from city to suburb. Like most other Boomers, Alberta looked to her peers for guidance, and most of them had dropped out of school and were pregnant. Within her increasingly insular world, having babies was "the thing to do."

There were no home pregnancy tests at the time, so Alberta

made regular trips to the prenatal clinic at Pennsylvania Hospital. They would draw blood, and a few days later Alberta would call for the results. Occasionally her mother went with her to the hospital to quiz the doctors about why Alberta was not getting pregnant. One day in the spring of 1970 she finally received the results she wanted. She was thrilled, as was her mother. Her father was not. He told her that she had just ruined her life. More important, the baby's father, Donnell, was not happy about the news, although it could not have been a surprise. He enjoyed the sex but had no interest in the consequences and gradually withdrew into a world of heroin. "During my pregnancy, while babysitting his brothers, I would go into his bedroom and find him so high that he still had the needle in his arm with the blood return still in the syringe," Alberta recalls. "He was out." The relationship ended before the baby was born. Donnell would die years later from a heroin overdose.

On February 19, 1971, Alberta gave birth to daughter, Kentina. Like many other teenage mothers, she believed that having a baby around would improve her life. She had not counted on the demands of infant care or the expense. Since Alberta had no income, she went on welfare, which seemed like the natural thing to do. "Almost everyone on my block was dependent" on a welfare check, she says. "We would actually borrow money from each other until check day." In the past women like Alberta had to depend on extended family or local charities for support in difficult times. Boomers were the first generation to expect—and often demand—that the federal government would provide welfare benefits. Alberta's check came from the Aid for Families with Dependent Children (AFDC) program, created by Franklin Roosevelt as a minor, noncontroversial addition to the Social Security Act of 1935 that allowed widows to stay at home and raise their children. The program was transformed in the 1960s after Lyndon Johnson launched the war on poverty as the centerpiece of his ambitious plan to create a "Great Society."

Like many of the other social programs of the 1960s, the war on poverty was characterized by grand ambition and limited gains. Johnson had promised that his program would offer people jobs, not relief. "We want to offer the forgotten fifth of our people opportunity and not doles," Johnson said in the signing ceremony. During the 1960s the unemployment rate was cut in half, but the number of AFDC recipients increased by two-thirds, and the cost of the program doubled. Between 1965 and 1975 the number of recipients of AFDC more than doubled, from 4.4 to 11.4 million. Although a majority of people on welfare were white, a growing proportion were black, adding a racial dimension to public perceptions of the program.

The failures of the Great Society marked an important turning point in the evolution of the Boomer generation and further distinguished them from their parents. The alphabet agencies that made up the New Deal had only limited success in rescuing the economy from global depression, limiting economic misery, and providing secure jobs. In 1939 the unemployment rate was still 17 percent. But Roosevelt's modest efforts inspired confidence in a generation that had come to expect little from government. The Great Society, on the other hand, represented an ambitious effort that fell short of satisfying a generation that had grown up expecting Washington to solve social wrongs. Instead of inspiring confidence, Johnson's reforms contributed to an erosion of faith in government and its leaders. At the same time that the war in Vietnam divided the generation over America's proper role in the world, the unrealistic expectations of the Great Society forged a split over the proper role of government. Ironically, the Greatest Generation sowed the seeds of prosperity that would provide the Boomers with unprecedented opportunities and the freedom to pursue their own ambitions. But in their postwar hubris—believing the nation could win an undeclared war abroad and a declared one at home—they also planted the seeds of discontent and debate.

For many Boomers, Vietnam and the war on poverty would become metaphors for government ineptitude. Liberals blamed the amorphous "military-industrial complex" for perpetuating the war in Vietnam and entrenched conservative interests for neutering the war on poverty. Conservatives, for their part, charged that student protesters had prevented the military from waging all-out war in Vietnam, while their liberal allies pushed for an ill-conceived war against poverty at home. The lesson everyone learned was that government could be swayed by well-organized groups. The government's response to both the Depression and World War II had raised hopes among Boomer parents that Washington could serve as a powerful arbiter of the public good. Vietnam, the war on poverty, and, later, Watergate shattered those hopes. In fact, they revealed just the opposite: government responded to those who had the most power and made the most noise. Whether they moved to the left or the right after the polarizing 1960s, Boomers learned how to mobilize support and make noise, and they also learned to be highly cynical of government.

Although she was living at home and had few expenses, Alberta had trouble living off a weekly welfare check. She was constantly buying Kentina new toys and clothes. Ironically, she established the same relationship with Kentina that she had with her mother: she substituted toys and gifts for affection and attention. "Her first Christmas looked like the local toy store housed their inventory at our house," she recalls. "There was nothing that she didn't have . . . except me." In order to make money, Alberta started working two jobs, leaving much of the child care to family, friends, and babysitters. "Isn't it ironic, the very one that I wanted so much, was the very one that saw me so little?" she noted years later. "I was so busy trying to give her things because I thought that was how I loved her."

Alberta was starting to resemble her mother in other unflattering ways. After working two jobs all week, Alberta spent the weekend at the bar unwinding. It wasn't long before she started drinking every day. Alcohol was only one of her addictions. She smoked two packs of cigarettes a day and, constantly struggling to control her weight, she fed on diet pills. To escape the drudgery of everyday life she snorted cocaine and smoked pot. Her life became a merry-go-round of work, alcohol, drugs, and sex. "There was so much ugliness," she reflects. "My girlfriend and I would go down to Eighth Street. We were dating these two brothers and we would be drinking Thunderbird in the alley and getting sick. I was snorting cocaine. I was smoking marijuana. I was going with married men. This man that I was dating was married, had a wife and kids. And I was dating other people while I was dating him."

Between work and play, Alberta had little time for Kentina. If there were no babysitters available and Alberta could not be found, her mother would drag the baby with her to the local bars. Having a baby was not as much fun as Alberta had once imagined. And there was another problem: Something was "not right" with Kentina. She did not respond to her mother's voice and seemed strangely detached from the world. Around her first birthday, Alberta took Kentina to the hospital for tests. The physicians confirmed what she had suspected but had refused to admit: Kentina was deaf. "I was not prepared for this, nor did I, at such a young age myself, know how to deal with it, or understand it." At first she tried to avoid the problem, thinking that Kentina would grow out of it. Of course the problem only grew worse as Kentina became frustrated with her inability to communicate. Alberta dealt with the problem the same way her mother would have: "I found myself drinking more and more."

Alberta lived in a neighborhood where it was acceptable to escape into a world of promiscuity, drugs, and alcohol. There was no structure to her life. Most of her role models were alcoholics or drug addicts. It was arguably worse than America's infamous urban ghettoes of past eras, from Five Points in 19th-century New York to Hooverville, the Depression-era tent city in Washington. Alberta was drowning in freedom. Finally, as she approached her 20th birthday, she decided to go back to school and get her high school diploma. It was a first step on what would prove to be a long, complicated journey.

In 1972 Alberta signed up for the Neighborhood Youth Corps (NYC), a program created in 1965 as part of Lyndon Johnson's Great Society to provide low-income youths with jobs and career counseling. It also helped her to earn a high school degree. One of the teachers in the program was a Muslim who talked to her about Allah and the Koran. She was intrigued and started going with him to the mosque. The Nation of Islam, led by Elijah Muhammad and catapulted into national prominence by his most famous convert, Malcolm X, gave African Americans a voice and a sense of pride. Islam, it was often said by converts, was "more than a religion, it was a lifestyle." As one put it, "In many ways, our community operated as a subculture with its own value system and customs. There was an emphasis on good health, self-discipline and financial independence. Dressing as a Muslim woman meant never exposing more than your face, hands and feet in the presence of any man except your husband. . . . By embracing the notion of living in submission to the will of Allah," recalled former Muslim Jana Long, "we could somehow face down fears and insecurities."

Although she professed loyalty to the Koran, Alberta was more radical than religious. Her life was so undisciplined, so devoid of authority, that she needed it to impose order on chaos. "I think it was the discipline that appealed to me about Islam," she says. Her life changed almost overnight. "I stopped drinking alcohol, stopped going to the bars, stopped dancing, stopped everything!" She adopted the traditional Muslim dress, wearing skirts and dresses that went to her ankles, and keeping her head wrapped in public. Because she was spending less time drinking, she had more time to spend with Kentina. Like many other young converts, she bonded to the Nation of Islam's hatred of white people and its strong nationalist message. Alberta found herself agreeing with H. Rap Brown who said about the white man: "Don't love him to death, shoot him to death." "Day after day we were told that 'the white man' was the devil. The more I attended the Mosque, the more I became full of this poisoned hatred," she observed. "I began to hate Caucasians."

As she traveled down the road from Muslim to militant, Alberta became infatuated with the Black Panthers. Radicals Huey Newton and Bobby Seale created the Panthers in 1966 to embody Malcolm X's doctrine of community self-defense. Above all, the Panthers believed that the black community needed to arm in order to defend itself from the brutality of the white police: "Only with the power of the gun can the black masses halt the terror and brutality perpetuated against them by the armed racist power structure." Black people constituted a colony in the mother country of the American empire, he said, and like all victims of oppression, could legitimately resort to revolution—meaning guns. "The heirs of Malcolm X," Newton rejoiced, "have picked up the gun." True to their word, Newton, Seale, and thirty followers armed with shotguns and M-16 rifles marched into the California state legislature in Sacramento in May 1967 in order to protest a bill that would have made it illegal for people to carry unconcealed weapons. By 1970 the Panthers had killed eleven police officers.

For perhaps the first time in her life, Alberta had a role model: Angela Davis, the heroine of the Black Panther movement. Davis had been fired from her job as a philosophy professor at the University of California for being a member of the Communist Party. With her big afro hairstyle and black power salutes and her run-ins with the law, she became a symbol of the growing militancy and nationalism among African Americans.

The Panthers provided Alberta with a scapegoat to explain the hardships of her life. She had grown up in an entirely black world. The nation was fighting a battle to desegregate the South, but she lived in a segregated world in the North. She had no white friends. She grew up bombarded by images of success but was struggling to survive. Her childhood ambitions of becoming a doctor had fallen by the wayside. The Panthers gave her an enemy: She had failed to live up to her expectations because white people had oppressed her.

Over time she turned away from the Muslim emphasis on self-denial and became attracted to the cultural expressions of black nationalism. For many African American leaders Black Power was not about confrontation and violence but about pride and assertiveness. In order to overcome racism, they argued, blacks must close ranks. African American parents pushed school boards to approve teaching black history and culture courses. College students pressured administrators to recruit black teachers and students and create Afro-American cultural centers and black studies classes and departments. James Brown declared, "Say it loud, I'm black and I'm proud." Perhaps the most well-known, and loquacious, advocate was heavyweight boxing champion Cassius Clay, who proclaimed his membership in the Nation of Islam and changed his name to Muhammad Ali in 1964.

Alberta stopped wrapping her head and wearing long dresses, and now sported a large afro, leather jacket, and jeans. In the most dramatic gesture of her new militancy, she wore shotgun shells as bracelets. She hung on the living room wall of her family's house a life-sized picture of Huey Newton, the defense minister of the Black Panthers, with a machine gun strapped across his chest. When the insurance man, who was a Caucasian, came to collect every other week, her father was too embarrassed about the picture to allow him in the house. "My dad thought that I had gone crazy," she recalls, but, as usual, he did nothing to intervene.

Eventually hatred and radicalism proved a phase, just as the Nation of Islam had been. "The discipline and the hatred that I learned from the mosque, and the militancy of the Panthers, created a greater yearning inside of me for freedom," she reflects. "I just wanted to be free. I wanted to be free from rules, free from hatred, free from this 'ghetto' mentality, free from everything, even myself!" For many people freedom meant casting off rules and restrictions, opening up opportunities, and providing greater choices. For Alberta freedom meant something different: she wanted structure and order. She needed freedom from chaos.

Her search brought her to Rittenhouse Square, a quiet residential neighborhood that also served as the center of Philadelphia's hippie movement. "I remember painting a flower on my face and cutting little square windows all up and down the legs of my jeans," she recalls. It was her first introduction to white people. They were more open, loving, and accepting than the Muslims, but she realized that she did not belong. Most of the hippies were middle-class white kids with whom she had little in common.

In less than a year Alberta had experimented with Islam, militancy, and free love. None of it helped her make sense of her life. In 1973 she completed her general equivalency diploma and signed up for another government program for unwed mothers, which allowed her to enter a training program at the Philadelphia Naval Hospital. Kentina's life was also improving, thanks to the dedication of a young social worker who became her surrogate mother. Carol Moore worked at the day care center that Kentina attended. Alberta dropped Kentina off in the morning and Carol looked after her, took her to doctors' appointments, and learned sign language so she could communicate with her. Alberta enrolled in signing classes but rarely attended. Her relationship with Kentina disintegrated as the communication gap widened. "She tried so hard to tell me things," she recalls. "I was just as frustrated because I wanted so badly to know what she wanted to tell me."

By 1976 she was almost back where she started. After her brief flings with Allah, militancy, and free love, she had settled back in her old routine of sex, drugs, and alcohol. She was dating an older man, Jimmy, who also worked at the naval hospital. Still married and living with yet a third woman, he was not exactly a model citizen. She guessed that he had fathered as many as two dozen children. Alberta, amazingly, wanted to marry him and settle down. He said he loved her, but there was always an excuse: He needed to get a divorce; he could not leave the woman he was living with because she had mental problems and he needed to care for her.

Her means of escape proved to be another man, unlike any of the others. Norman Bishop was a confident born-again 16-year-old African American student at Tuskegee University who was working at the naval hospital for the summer. Alberta came to work most days tired, miserable, and hung over. Norman was always refreshingly upbeat and content. "He had a certain joy in his life that just radiated from his face," she observes. "He truly looked happy. He was always smiling and singing a song. Whenever I saw him, he had his

Bible. At lunchtime, he would listen to Christian music." She would joke with him, "Norman, why aren't you out partying?" "But that wasn't my purpose," he says. She would complain that "my life was a mess." She was drinking, eating, and working too much. She was also having trouble making ends meet: she was spending a fortune on booze and on sending Kentina to private school. "She asked about what heaven was like," recalls Norman. "What happens when a person dies." Norman sat for hours in the lunchroom telling her how Jesus Christ had changed his life. She was skeptical and always found an excuse to turn down his invitations to attend his church.

Finally one day in July 1976, she went with him to the Deliverance Evangelistic Church. Pastor Benjamin Smith packed the converted movie theater on Sunday mornings with more than 6,000 people, many of them watching the ceremony on television screens in adjacent rooms. "The very first time that I went there, I sensed this same joy on the faces of many others in that congregation." She had listened to preachers many times in the past, but this day was different. She found inspiration listening to a verse from the Bible, Romans 5:12: "Therefore, just as sin entered the world through one man, and death through sin, and in this way death came to all men because all sinned." That overpowering message that day changed her life permanently as she came to the realization that she was a sinner. "Whatever text he used showed me that the reason my life stunk so bad was because I was a dirty, rotten, stinking sinner! There was nothing good in me or about me! I was in need of a thorough cleansing and the only one that could do it was Jesus."

When Pastor Smith gave the invitation for everyone who wanted to be saved to come to the altar, Alberta leaped to her feet. "I almost ran up the aisle. Tears were streaming down my cheeks. This was different than anything that I had ever known." She had been through many different conversions over the past few years, but only this one would stick. "I knew I wanted to turn away from my old life. I wanted this 'new life' that the Scriptures talked about. I knew that I wanted to be saved!" She stood at the altar. Pastor Smith asked her, "Do you believe you are a sinner?" "Yes!" she shouted. "Do you believe God sent Jesus to die for your sins?" "Yes, I believe that," she responded. "Would you like to turn toward him and repent," he asked. "Yes, I want to turn, I believe, and please save me because I am lost," she said. She returned to her pew a different person. "I felt such peace."

Alberta's experience with finding religion was not unique. *Newsweek* called "the emergence of evangelical Christianity into a position of respect and power" the "most significant—and overlooked—religious phenomenon of the '70s." Between 1970 and 1978 the number of people saying that religion was "increasing its influence on American life" tripled from 14 percent to 44 percent. Weekly attendance at church services increased, reversing a downward trend that had started in the late 1950s. The most obvious change was in the number of people who, like Alberta, had a "born-again" experience. Polls showed nearly 50 million adult Americans, including half of all Protestants, claimed to have been born again. After reviewing all the evidence, pollster George Gallup concluded that 1976 should be considered the "year of the evangelical."

Perhaps the most well-known born-again Southern Baptist was Jimmy Carter, the former Georgia governor who openly professed his faith during the 1976 campaign for president. As a boy growing up in rural Georgia, Carter attended church services several times a week, including twice on Sunday. At age 11 he was baptized by total immersion. Later, while serving on a navy submarine, he conducted Easter services in the torpedo room. Carter told reporters that he prayed "about 25 times a day" and ended each day by reading a chapter of the Bible—in Spanish. "I could do it [in English] in three minutes," he said, but "it wasn't a challenge." Throughout the campaign, he seemed to offer a religious salve for the nation's wounds, reassuring audiences that they deserved a government as "decent, honest, truthful, fair, compassionate, and as filled with love as our people are." A columnist at the liberal *New Republic* groused that with all the talk of religion, "I don't know whether the country is having a presidential election or a religious revival." Carter's politics of piety played well in a nation looking for forgiveness in the aftermath of Vietnam and Watergate. Even Republican Gerald Ford, burdened by his pardon of Richard Nixon, presented himself as a devout Christian, claiming that he read the Bible every day and often prayed in the White House. "This is the first time in 200 years that the leading Presidential candidates have made public profession of their faith," noted an observer.

Many Boomers who had turned away from organized religion in the '60s and '70s were turning their attention again to things spiritual. Two-thirds of all Boomers raised in religious households found churches irrelevant and dropped out during the rebellious 1960s and 1970s. The mainline Protestant churches were the hardest hit. Slightly less than half who dropped out never returned to church, but those who did return changed the face of religion. "This is a generation of seekers," wrote the historian Wade Clark Roof in a book on Baby Boom attitudes about religion. Regular church attendance among the older Baby Boomers (those born from 1945 to 1954) climbed steadily from 32.8 percent in 1975 to 41.1 percent in 1990. Many were tempering the rebelliousness of their youth, starting families, and searching for what Daniel Yankelovich called a "culture of commitment."

Unlike their parents, Boomers moved across religious boundaries, often trying out different churches before settling into some form of nondenominational setting that combined elements from different traditions. The majority subscribed to a mix of spirituality and self-help philosophy. Many congregations multiplied their membership by going light on theology and offering worshipers a steady diet of sermons and support groups that emphasized personal fulfillment. "It is practical and personal, more about stress reduction than salvation, more therapeutic than theological. It's about feeling good, not being good," *American Demographics* noted about the new spirituality. "Baby boomers think of churches like they think of supermarkets," noted a church marketing consultant. "They want options, choices, and convenience. Imagine if Safeway was only open one hour a week, had only one product, and didn't explain it in English."

In many ways, the born-again religious phenomenon appealed to the Boomers' individualistic and antiauthority streak. What united born-again Christians was their belief that a highly personal spiritual experience had changed their lives. Most Boomers, even those who called themselves born again, were more likely to describe themselves as "spiritual" instead of religious. They were reluctant to profess belief in a single doctrine or belong to a single denomination, and instead pulled selectively from traditions that satisfied their emotional and spiritual needs. Baby Boomers "want the à la carte menu instead of buying the whole experience," said the executive director of the Evangelistic Association of New England. "They're picking and choosing according to what meets their needs." Nearly one-third, for example, said they believed in reincarnation and astrology. Nearly half agreed that "a married woman who doesn't

want any more children" should be allowed "to obtain a legal abortion." "Choice, so much a part of life for this generation, now
expresses itself in dynamic and fluid religious styles," observes Roof.
Modern religion adapted to contemporary society, dulled its ideological edges, and emphasized the role of religion in making people
feel whole and fulfilled. "People are looking at the role faith and spirituality can play in making them a better, more effective, and more
fulfilled person," observes sociologist Alan Wolfe.

By some estimates over 100 megachurches were springing up every
year by the 1990s. Most followed a similar formula, toning down doctrine and turning up lifestyle programs for the busy members of the
congregation. Most offered a smorgasbord of Bible classes, self-help
sessions, and counseling. The model for many megachurches was Willow Creek Community Church in South Barrington, Illinois, thirty
miles northwest of Chicago. Pastor Bill Hybels preached in a business
suit from a lectern, using contemporary music instead of a choir. Realizing that most people needed the church to help with their earthly
problems and not just with eternal salvation, he established a wide
range of social service programs for nearly every age group: children,
teenagers, older singles, adults, and the elderly. His efforts were
rewarded by increased attendance and larger contributions. Willow
Creek attracted nearly 14,000 people to its weekend services and nearly
6,000 to its Wednesday evening services.

The upsurge in religious feeling in the 1970s was part of a
broader cultural shift toward finding meaning and self-fulfillment in
a confused and chaotic world. Alberta's gradual evolution from black
Muslim to born-again Christian was not as dramatic as it may
appear. She was searching for a personal experience that would liberate her from despair, authority that would impose order and rules,
and a sense of community with those with whom she shared some
common interests. Religion filled all of those needs for her.

Millions of other Americans were undergoing a similar search
but finding different answers. Many Americans looked to Eastern
religions "to get in touch with their feelings," with others, and with
the forces of nature. America in the mid-1970s, observed countercul-
tural historian Theodore Roszak, launched "the biggest introspective
binge any society in history has undergone." By the middle of the
decade, more than 80,000 Americans had sought enlightenment in

"Est" seminars run by former used car salesman Werner Erhard. The most popular fad, transcendental meditation (TM), required two twenty-minute periods daily of repeating a word or phrase called a mantra. In 1977 George Gallup reported that some 6 million Americans had tried transcendental meditation, 5 million had tried yoga, and 2 million had tried one variant or another of Asian religions. "From 1971 to 1975, I directly experienced est, gestalt therapy, bioenergetics, Rolfing, massage, jogging, health foods, tai chi, Esalen, hypnotism, modern dance, meditation, Silva Mind Control, Arica, acupuncture, sex therapy, Reichian therapy—a smorgasbord course in New Consciousness," former '60s student radical Jerry Rubin wrote in 1976.

Alberta joined the millions of other Baby Boomers who returned to religion later in life as a source of comfort and security. Like the majority of her peers, she considered herself born again, but her faith remained fluid and flexible. She spoke in vague spiritual terms but had not integrated religion into her daily life, which continued to revolve around drink, drugs, and sex. As committed as she was to building a new relationship with God, Alberta's life did not change overnight. After her conversion experience she attended church services regularly and read the gospel. "I'm going to church and Kentina is going to church and we are praising the Lord," but she never officially joined the church and she refused to be baptized. She knew that the Bible condemned sex outside marriage, but she did not break off her relationship with Jimmy. "I told him I didn't want to see him anymore because I have to stop fornicating. It's not right. I would try to stop seeing him and stop fornicating, but then I would get right back into it." Jimmy was not the only one she was dating. She also was having an affair with Clyde, a cook at a local restaurant.

She may not have been pure in her commitment, but that did not stop her from spreading the word to anyone who would listen and a few who would not. "I was a fanatic. I went off on the deep end," she admits. At work when she stepped on the elevator, many people would get off because they did not want to hear her preach to them. "They would take the stairs because they knew I was going to talk to them about Jesus."

Her faith was about to receive its biggest test. January 1977 was the coldest month in Philadelphia in 187 years. During the last few days of the month the temperature dipped below zero for the first time in 14 years. Alberta's father bought a space heater, which he used to keep the living room warm during cold evenings at home. On January 29 Alberta fixed Kentina her favorite dinner of chicken wings and french fries. Kentina had a birthday coming up and her mom had promised to buy her a television for her room. They both went to bed early that night. At 11:30 P.M. Alberta woke up to the sound of her father screaming from the first floor. The house was on fire. Police speculated that the space heater had ignited some of the furniture in the living room and quickly spread through the top two floors. "It was a miracle that I heard him because I was on the third floor, sound asleep." By the time she opened her eyes, the flames were shooting up the stairs and smoke was filling the third floor where she was sleeping. She assumed that Kentina had been sleeping on the second floor and had already escaped. With the smoke filling the bedroom, she went to the window and looked down, hoping that the fire department had arrived and would be able to rescue her. No one was there. "The three-story building seemed to be a skyscraper when I looked down," she said. "I tried to wait as long as I could, but nobody came. Finally, I had no other option. I had to jump."

She tumbled three stories, smacked hard against the pavement, and passed out. When she woke up she was surrounded by people. "Where is Kentina?" she asked. Someone told her they thought she had been on the third floor with her. No, Alberta said; she wasn't with her. "As I lay on the ground waiting for the ambulance, I saw Kentina standing in the doorway with her nightgown and robe holding her favorite doll. She told me she was okay." By this time Alberta was in excruciating pain: both ankles were broken, she had compressed a disc in her back, and a deep gash over her eye was bleeding. Emergency workers strapped her onto a gurney and rushed her to the hospital.

She was being treated in the emergency ward when her father walked into the room and leaned against the back wall. "I will never forget his expression in a million years. His hat was lopsided, he had smoke and ashes all over his clothes and his face. He opened his mouth, and the words that he said will forever ring in my ears. 'We couldn't get Kentina out . . . she's gone.'" Alberta screamed at the top of her lungs. Kentina had not been on the second floor. She had been sleeping on the floor just a few feet away from Alberta. Her father reassured her that her daughter had not suffered. She died in her

sleep of smoke inhalation less than one month from her sixth birthday. Alberta realized that the image she had seen of Kentina on the
steps was a vision, "God's way of giving me the comfort of knowing
that she was with Him." A few days later Alberta was taken by ambulance to the funeral home, where she was escorted in by the two men
she was dating at the time. Kentina's father, Donnell, was nowhere in
sight. Kentina lay in a closed casket with a portrait on top. Alberta
kept asking, "If Kentina had died of smoke inhalation, why is she in a
closed casket?" No one answered the question.

Not only was Kentina gone; the family had lost their house and
all of their belongings. "We had nothing but the clothes on our
backs. We didn't have any money saved up anywhere." Her father had
allowed the insurance policy to lapse. The family was forced to split
up: her father lived with relatives, her mother moved in with one of
her drinking friends, and Alberta stayed with friends after being
released from the hospital. Some of the local churches rallied and
raised money for the family. That money, combined with the insurance money Alberta received for Kentina, allowed the family to purchase a new house in the same neighborhood for $3,500.

Shortly after the funeral, Jimmy took Alberta on a ten-day trip to
Florida and Atlanta. She was deeply in love with him and was no longer
willing to wait for him to marry her. "Come on, you say you love me,"
she told him. "Let's get married." But he refused to make a commitment.
Gradually she slipped back into her old habits. Her weight ballooned to
225 pounds. She started smoking, drinking, and spending more nights
on the town. "We partied from Wednesday to Sunday," recalls drinking
friend Joan Fortune. While working at the naval hospital, Alberta picked
up an evening job at a local record store, the Harmony Hut, which got
her invitations to every new record party. "Alberta never missed a party,"
Fortune remembers. She would drink a few brandy Alexanders and
then spend the entire night dancing to her favorite disco songs. But it
was not fun anymore. "I need to get my life straightened out," she would
say, often after a long night of dancing and drinking. "She knew she
shouldn't have been out there," says Fortune. Her friends would often
tease her. "I thought you were saved!?"

Alberta was miserable. She felt trapped in an unfulfilling relationship with a man who did not love her. "I think it was because of this man
and my love for him and the fact that I couldn't get that fornication

under wraps" that led her back to drinking. She became deeply depressed. On New Year's Eve 1978, when Jimmy was unable to spend time with her because he had to be with his wife, Alberta took a knife and cut her arm in a half-hearted suicide gesture. "I remember being miserable in the relationship because I was saved now. I belonged to God now." She knew that her lifestyle was wrong and immoral, but she lacked the conviction and discipline to change. "I'm trying to turn away from Jimmy so that I can find a husband. I'm convinced that if I get married, I can stop the fornication. If I stopped the fornication, I can avoid this stuff that comes along with fornication." She prayed that God would give her the strength to break off her relationship with Jimmy. "I would cry and say, 'God deliver me and help me not to drink anymore.' "

At one point she was rushed to the hospital in intense abdominal pain. Although she did not know it at the time, Alberta was pregnant with Jimmy's baby. But there were complications: her appendix ruptured and she had a cyst on her ovary. The surgeons aborted the baby and removed her ovary, tubes, and uterus, making it impossible for her to have more children. "We still do not know whether the tubal pregnancy caused the other problems or the cyst infected my appendix," she recalls. "In any case, I have a baby in heaven along with Kentina."

Kentina's death, and the loss of her baby, both tested and strengthened Alberta's faith. Why would God punish her just as she was trying to straighten out her life? "I thought I was to have fullness of joy forever and ever. I had a new life now," she thought. "This can't be happening. I was saved." At the same time, her faith lessened her guilt and provided a way to explain the tragedy. Kentina did not die because of anyone's negligence; she died because God willed it. "God makes no mistakes," she assured herself. Although she may not be able to understand the reason, Kentina's death had a purpose: "No matter what happens, God is still in control." Alberta had spent most of her life searching for an integrated worldview and had finally found one. Many Boomers accompanied her, but others struggled.

TV Guide announces the arrival of America's most famous Boomer baby. In January 1953 more than fifty million Americans tuned in to see Lucy give birth to "little Ricky." *(AP/Worldwide)*

A 1955 baby derby—one of the ways that parents kept themselves, and their babies, occupied during the peak Baby Boom years. *(Getty)*

Television became a daily ritual for many young Boomers. Here parents and children gather in the living room to watch their favorite show in 1954. *(AP/Worldwide)*

Boomer children flooded school classrooms during the 1950s. California built a new elementary school every week during the decade. *(Getty)*

Well-groomed Boomers and their older siblings crowd onto the dance floor of *American Bandstand* in 1958. *(AP/Worldwide)*

Boomers swelled college campuses during the 1960s, providing much of the energy for the campus protests that followed. This free speech demonstration at Berkeley in 1964 helped set the tone for the decade. *(AP/Worldwide)*

The deadly protests at Kent State in 1970 polarized both the nation and the generation. *(Corbis)*

Goldie Hawn on *Rowan and Martin's Laugh-In,* which premiered on NBC in 1968. Like Hollywood, television was pulling out all the stops to attract Boomer viewers. *(Corbis)*

The Graduate, the 1967 classic starring Dustin Hoffman, was the first of a spate of movies that catered to the taste of disillusioned youth. *(Corbis)*

The 1976 blockbuster movie *Jaws,* directed by Steven Spielberg, signaled the rise of the Boomer generation in Hollywood. *(AP/Worldwide)*

Boomer Bruce Springsteen, perhaps the most popular singer-songwriter to emerge in the 1970s, performs in New York City in 1979. *(AP/Worldwide)*

As this 1981 rally suggests, the struggle over the ERA stirred passions among both supporters and opponents and exposed a deep cultural divide among members of the Boomer generation. *(Corbis)*

Many of the names on the AIDS quilt displayed in New York's Central Park in 1988 were of gay Boomer men who "came out" during the 1970s. *(AP/Worldwide)*

This 1998 Promise Keepers rally showed how middle-aged Boomers looking to reconnect with their faith helped to produce a religious revival in America. *(AP/Worldwide)*

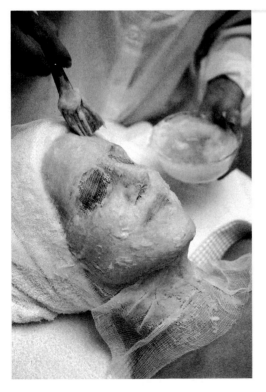

As they moved into middle age in the 1990s, Boomers searched for new products and procedures that would maintain their youthful image. *(Corbis)*

Dan Quayle, the first Baby Boomer on a national ticket, after his 1988 vice presidential debate with Lloyd Bentsen. Quayle lost the debate, but he and his running-mate won the election.
(AP/Worldwide)

Bill Clinton, America's first rock 'n' roll president, plays the sax with friends.
(AP/Worldwide)

America's queen of self-reflection gets a kiss from its first Boomer Republican president.
(AP/Worldwide)

PART II

THE GREAT SHIFT:
1978–1992

Republican versions of recent American history stress the election of Ronald Reagan as a great turning point. Not only did the economy begin a long boom after Reagan's first few years, as inflation finally came under control, but the Cold War end game began, with an American arms buildup along with simultaneous negotiations over nuclear reductions. To some observers, the conservative groundswell that elected Reagan came out of nowhere, since Barry Goldwater's similar prescriptions had been repudiated in 1964. Historians have looked for the other side of the '60s, in a grassroots California conservative movement, along with the growing student organizing by Young Americans for Freedom (YAF), the conservative alternative to the radical Students for a Democratic Society (SDS).

There is a simpler answer: the Boomers entered high-earning, high-spending adulthood in the late 1970s. By the mid-1980s, they were responsible for half of all U.S. personal income, and they were ready to spend it—and more. They produced a boom in the housing market that would continue for the next two decades. In the 1970s, to meet the rising demand, homebuilders constructed 1.3 million new homes annually. In popular places like Los Angeles the average price of a single-family home doubled—to $100,500—between 1975 and 1981. Having purchased their new home, often in the sprawling suburbs, Boomers furnished it with the latest gadgets. Between 1983 and 1988 they purchased 62 million microwave ovens, 57 million washers and dryers, 105 million color television sets, 46 million refrigerators and freezers, 63 million VCRs, and 31 million cordless phones. "There's a message in these numbers," observes the economist Robert Samuelson. "In the 1980s Americans went on a spending spree unlike anything since the late 1940s." The problem was that personal spending outpaced income. The government had the same problem, resulting in massive private and public debt.

Evidence of a new culture of consumerism was everywhere. Awards of law and business degrees climbed through the mid-1980s. *Money* magazine watched as its circulation soared from 800,000 in 1980 to 1.85 million in 1987. Merger mania on Wall Street, fed by lax government regulation and new tax laws, produced unprecedented wealth for a handful of financial insiders. "Never have so many unskilled twenty-four-year-olds made so much money in so little time as we did in this decade," confessed Wall Street broker Michael Lewis. Successful businessmen enjoyed celebrity status. Real estate tycoon Donald Trump became one of the most recognizable men in America. Chrysler chief Lee Iacocca's self-serving autobiography, appropriately titled *Iacocca*, sold more than 2 million copies in hardcover. Victor Kiam joined the business celebrity ranks with his television commercials for Remington electric shavers. "I liked the shavers so much I bought the company," he told audiences. Popular culture reinforced the infatuation with wealth and status. *Dallas*, the most successful prime-time soap opera of the decade, chronicled the wealth, infidelities, and outrageous behavior of Texas oilman J. R. Ewing. In Oliver Stone's film *Wall Street*, Michael Douglas, playing Gordon Gekko, a ruthless corporate raider who relies on inside information to make his deals, tells stockbrokers: "Greed, for lack of a better word, is good. Greed is right. Greed works."

Many observers dismissed the generation as Yuppies, an acronym for "young, urban, upwardly mobile professionals." Yuppies aspired to become investment bankers, not social workers. "Much of the energy and optimism and passion of the '60s," *Newsweek* observed, "seems to have been turned inward, on lives, careers, apartments and dinners." "The name of the game," declared *The Yuppie Handbook,* "is the best—buying it, owning it, using it, eating it, wearing it, growing it, cooking it, driving it, doing whatever with it." Of course, the vast majority of Boomers were not Yuppies. By some estimates, less than 5 percent of Boomers met the definition of Yuppies; the vast majority were struggling to make ends meet. Boomers were competing against each other for a limited supply of houses, jobs, and quality schools. They could not afford the houses of their parents. A typical Boomer who purchased a home in 1984 had to pay 44 percent of gross monthly income to cover the mortgage. Just ten years earlier that figure had been 21 percent. Although they saw family income grow by 280 percent in the two decades after 1965, the federal tax bite, despite all the political rhetoric about cutting the size of government, soared by 542 percent.

At the same time, Boomer struggles with parenthood inspired a national debate about "family values." The former "rock and roll" generation led the charge against sex and violence in the 1980s. A 1991 poll showed that three in five Boomers wanted their children to have less sexual freedom than they had enjoyed as teens. Books with titles such as *Getting Your Kids to Say No in the '90s When You Said Yes in the '60s* and *Raising Self-Reliant Children in a Self-Indulgent World* filled bookstores. "The parenting motto of the baby boom generation seems to be: 'Do as I say, not as I did,'" noted the columnist Ellen Goodman. Advertisers jumped on the demographic bandwagon, appealing to the family values of Baby Boom parents. Canada Dry sold its ginger ale featuring young parents with a couple of kids: "For when your tastes grow up." VH1, the Baby Boom cousin of MTV, featured ads of young parents nestling a child. Their goal was to appeal to the priorities of the aging Baby Boomers, which consisted of "family and work."

Prosperity, advances in medical science, and a growing interest in health and nutrition distinguished Boomers from their parents. By the time the Boom marked its 40th birthday in 1985, the average Boomer ate a lighter diet that included more fish and low-fat milk and less red meat. They smoked less. They were the best-educated generation in history, averaging 12.9 years of school. More than 84 percent had completed high school, 44.5 percent had attended college for at least a year, and 25.1 percent had graduated. They were five times as likely to be divorced than their parents. They were more likely to work in a service-related job than their parents. In 1947, 51 percent of workers were employed in manufacturing or production. In 1985, 70 percent were employed in service industries. They were more racially tolerant and cared more about the environment. Only 15 percent of women were housewives compared with 70 percent in the 1950s. The average 40-year-old female Baby Boomer stood 5 feet 4.2 inches and weighed 140 pounds. She weighed as much as her mother but was almost an inch taller. The average man weighed the same as his father—173 pounds—but at 5 feet 9.6 inches was more than an inch taller.

Perhaps the single biggest change caused by the Boomers' aging was a political Great Shift. Here, predictions of the Boomers have been remarkably wrong. Many people assumed that the youthful protesters of the 1960s would become the liberal Democrats of the 1970s and 1980s. As Boomers moved through the life cycle from teenage protester to adult breadwinner, however, their politics evolved with them. Nothing forces a reexamination of priorities faster than a monthly mortgage payment or a dirty diaper. Not only did their politics become more fiscally conservative, they added a strong independent flavor to the mix. Not surprisingly, the Boomer gravitational pull carried the political system with them as they moved to the right. The Boomer ascendancy contributed to the shattering of the New Deal coalition, the end of the solid Democratic South, and the rise of ticket-splitting independents. Republicans benefited most from the changes, but by the late 1980s, nearly every major politician was repeating the middle-aged mantra of smaller government, lower taxes, and family values (although they often disagreed on exactly what those "values" were).

FIVE

THE PROLONGED ADOLESCENCE OF DONNY DEUTSCH

Donny in high school;

in college;

with his father.

Sexual intercourse began in 1963," wrote British poet Philip Larkin as he watched the Boomers come of age. It was almost true, as traditions of restraint from premarital sex began a collapse that would accelerate into the 1980s. The younger the Boomer, the more likely he would lose his virginity in college (if not earlier) and smoke pot along the way. For some, high school and college were one extended party. Yet despite the hand wringing of cultural critics, the Boomers proved themselves in the work world when they grew up.

By all accounts Donny Deutsch was a bright, outgoing kid, very popular in his middle-class Queens neighborhood. "We never wanted for anything; we were very comfortable." His father ran a midsized advertising agency and his mother worked as a teacher. Because both worked long hours, Donny spent lots of time alone in front of the television. "I remember being so profoundly connected to TV growing up," he recalls. He watched his favorite television shows, like *I Dream of*

Jeannie, every day. He not only could repeat dialogue from the show, he had watched the credits roll by so many times that he knew the names of the producers and crew. Years later he would enjoy watching reruns of the shows he had watched as a child. "When I go to the video store, I'm 99 percent more likely to rent a movie I've already seen." There was something reassuring about the consistency of watching the same show over and over again. It would be a pattern in Donny's life. For someone who had such a bold and creative mind, he was personally wedded to tradition and routine.

For Donny, the most memorable year of the very memorable decade of the 1960s was 1969. He was in the sixth grade at P.S. 188, a middle-class, predominantly Jewish elementary school. It was the year that we landed a man on the moon. The Mets won the World Series. A group of hippies gathered at Woodstock. It was during the sixth grade he realized that he was "a cool dude" for the first time. Sixth grade represented a transition between childhood and adolescence—it was the first year in which boys and girls went to parties together. "That was the year that girls suddenly liked boys." One day during school he intercepted a note sent between two girls. It had a question on it. "Who do you think are the five cutest boys in the class?" Donny was ranked number 1.

In 1972 Donny went to Martin Van Buren High School, which swelled to over 4,000 young Boomers. Like many other high schools built during the 1950s, Van Buren was not constructed to accommodate the tide of Boomers, so students were required to attend school in shifts: tenth graders went to school from 12:30 to 5:30, while eleventh and twelfth graders did the morning shift from 8:00 to 12:30. For his last two years in high school Donny was home alone most days by 1:00 P.M., which gave him plenty of time to watch television and hang out with his friends.

These are always difficult years for young teens, but they were especially tough for Donny. Puberty was not kind to him. He experienced what his friends now refer to as "the ugly years." He developed bad acne, wore corrective braces, and gained lots of weight. Since his hair was kinky, he decided to tease it into an afro style. He was very self-conscious about his appearance. Once he overheard a conversation between a male and female friend. When his name came up, she said, "Oh, God, Donny is so gross looking." That moment would stick with him. Because he felt so unattractive, he overcompensated by developing an outgoing, gregarious personality. He ran and won election as president of the senior class. He came home one day and told his parents that he had the lead in the senior class musical. "Donny, how could you have the lead—you cannot even sing?" his mother asked. "I can't sing," he agreed, "but I love being on stage."

Donny was a good student but was not part of the academic crowd in high school. "He wasn't the studious type at all," recalls friend Perry Shore. In his senior year, his mother convinced him to apply to the University of Pennsylvania. He managed to get accepted off the waiting list and traveled to Philadelphia in the fall of 1975. It was the first time he had ventured far from his neighborhood in Queens, and the experience instilled new confidence. His fellow students were better educated, probably naturally smarter, but he sensed that they lacked street smarts. "I couldn't wait to play cards, take their money, drink their beer, and steal their girlfriends," he says. "Because as bright as they were, they didn't have that kind of street perspective you just grew up with in Queens."

He also knew how to have fun. At a comparable age, many members of his father's generation were worried about fighting a global war, perhaps getting married and starting a family. Donny and many other Boomers (especially those born after 1950) had the benefit of an extended adolescence. "We were the lucky generation," Donny recalls. "We had a lot of wind at our backs," he said. Like most of his peers, he was in grade school while the Vietnam War was raging, and he was out of college before AIDS emerged as a major health crisis. For Donny there was a brief window between these two tragic events when he and other middle-class men enjoyed "fun without the pain."

His generation also had the advantage of using education to extend their adolescence. More Boomers went to school in larger numbers, and stayed there longer, than any previous generation. In 1900 only 13 percent of teenagers attended high school. By 1940 that number grew to 40 percent, and by 1965 to 95 percent. More than half of Boomers attended college, meaning they were able to push back adult responsibilities—getting a job and surviving on their own—until the age of 20 or 21. According to one scholar, Boomers marked the transformation of children from "a family asset as labor to a family liability as student-consumer."

Donny had no major responsibilities other than to study (occasionally) and attend classes (when convenient). He devoted most of his time to having fun, something that came naturally to him. Like many other younger Baby Boomers, Donny experimented with drugs. "I get high with a little help from my friends," the Beatles informed their fans. Most Boomers followed their advice. A 1971 survey at the University of Kansas revealed that 69 percent of students smoked marijuana. A Gallup poll the same year noted an eightfold increase in four years in the number of college students who smoked pot. Donny smoked pot for the first time in 1970 when he was in the seventh grade. Like many other first-timers, he told people he got high, but he faked it. Quaaludes, not pot, was his drug of choice. "It was a love drug," he recalls. "You just loved everybody. It was like truth serum. You ended up sleeping with whoever you're with, and the next morning when you woke up you were fine." During college Donny and his group of friends found a doctor in Philadelphia who was generous with prescriptions for popular recreational drugs. "What's the problem?" the doctor would ask. Donny would respond: "My back hurts. I can't sleep." They would walk out of the office with a legal prescription and then sell the pills to friends.

These were the disco years, and Donny and his group of friends became regulars at local discos in Philadelphia and New York. Despite all the scorn heaped on it, disco preached a message of inclusion. It started out as club music in largely Hispanic, black, and gay nightclubs in New York and San Francisco. In 1978 it emerged as a national sensation after the release of the hit movie *Saturday Night Fever*, starring John Travolta as a bored Brooklyn youth who finds excitement on the dance floor. The movie's soundtrack by the Bee Gees became the biggest-selling record in history. By the end of the year, *Billboard* magazine estimated that 36 million people had danced to the beat at 20,000 clubs across the country—more than 200 in New York City alone. And it wasn't just big cities. Fennimore, Wisconsin (population 1,900) housed a $100,000 disco. The music moved millions of young people to dance, while the lyrics, which one critic described as "simple and repetitive to the point of absurdity," left their consciences unscathed.

On Saturday nights Donny and his friends would put on their floral polyester shirts, load up with hairspray and perfume, and spend hours gyrating beneath the swirling lights to the beat of Gloria Gaynor's "Never Can Say Goodbye," K.C. and the Sunshine Band's "Get Down Tonight," Thelma Houston's "Don't Leave Me This Way," and Donna Summer's "Bad Girls." One of the most popular groups, the Village People, presented themselves as cartoon homosexual pinups—a cowboy, construction worker, leather man, Native American, policeman, and soldier—who appealed to largely straight audience with suggestive gay lyrics of songs like "Macho Man," "I'm a Cruiser," and "YMCA" ("They have everything for young men to enjoy / You can hang out with all the boys").

Drugs played a key role in the whole disco experience, but for Donny they provided an added benefit: the confidence to approach women. "We used to love to go out to clubs, get hammered and meet girls," reflects Richard Thal. Weekends consisted of "a lot of quaaludes and women." "I told Donny that quaaludes made up about 60 percent of his personality," joked Thal. "When they took those off the market, that's when he really started to run into trouble dating."

Donny actually had little trouble dating, and, unlike previous generations, there was no social stigma to having sex; in fact, it was a moral imperative. In 1970 a presidential commission to investigate the pornography industry discovered there were 830 adults-only bookstores, 200 theaters showing sex films, and about 45 million pieces of sexually explicit material sent every year. By the time they reached age 18, nearly 80 percent of boys and 70 percent of girls had been exposed to images or descriptions of sexual intercourse. Polls showed that up to 25 percent of the public watched porno films. The pornographic movie *Deep Throat,* released in 1972 and starring Linda Lovelace, gained critical acclaim and emerged as one of the year's most popular films, earning more than $25 million in sales.

You did not have to sneak into an X-rated movie theater to be exposed to sexual themes, however. Off-Broadway plays featured frontal nudity, magazines displayed centerfolds, and dinner table conversation revolved around previously taboo subjects such as birth control and abortion. The *Joy of Sex* (1972), which billed itself as "the first explicitly sexual book for the coffee table," sold more than 3.8 million copies in its first two years. Explicitly sexual messages permeated popular culture. Disco queen Donna Summer moaned her way through "Love to Love You Baby" and followed up that hit with "More, More,

More." Among the most popular television shows were *Get Christie Love!, Love, American Style,* and *The Love Boat.* Not surprisingly the decade witnessed a sea change in attitudes about sex. In the 1950s less than 25 percent of Americans thought premarital sex was acceptable; by the 1970s more than 75 percent found it acceptable.

The liberalization of all things sexual helped bring the gay rights movement out of the closet and into the mainstream of American life, at least in large urban areas. The modern gay rights movement was born on Friday night, June 27, 1969, when a group of Manhattan police officers raided the Stonewall Inn, a gay bar in the heart of Greenwich Village. Such raids, and the police abuse that frequently followed, were routine affairs. Not this time. As one reporter noted, "Limp wrists were forgotten. Beer cans and bottles were heaved at the windows and a rain of coins descended on the cops." The confrontation—what one gay group called "The Hairpin Drop Heard Around the World"—ignited a nationwide grassroots "liberation" movement among gay men and women. Over the next decade the number of gay organizations in America grew from fewer than 50 to more than 1,000. In many large cities gays and lesbians created support networks, newspapers, bars, and travel clubs. American society, noted an observer, witnessed "an explosion of things gay." The gay rights movement received a psychological boost in 1973 when the American Psychiatric Association reversed a century-old policy and stopped listing homosexuality as a mental disorder. Although they continued to face discrimination—thirty-two states designated homosexual practices as crimes—gay Boomers grew up in a world of openness and freedom that previous generations could only have imagined.

For Donny sex was not about gaining rights but about having fun. Along with knowing how to have a good time, Donny also had a flair for getting attention. During his junior year at Penn a TV news crew came to school to interview second-year M.B.A. students about their plans after graduation. "Unfortunately, the TV correspondent got the same kind of answers from these well-educated adults that most eighth graders write in the back of their school yearbooks," Donny recalls. "America's best and brightest said they wanted to 'live life to the fullest.'" Donny stood on the sidelines growing annoyed. He realized that what a reporter really wanted and needed was a provocative sound bite. Although still an undergraduate, Donny stepped up to the microphone and gave them what they wanted to hear: "I plan to play a lot of basketball and meet girls."

After graduation Donny accepted a job at the advertising agency of Ogilvy and Mather. He hated it. He was not ready to settle into a twelve-hour-a-day job working his way up the corporate ladder. He enjoyed being the center of attention, and at Ogilvy he was one of thousands of employees. He resented the corporate culture. More than anything else, he was restless: he did not want to be tied down in either a relationship or a job. "After less than two years there I realized I hated the way that a big organization operated."

Instead of turning in his resignation, Donny just stopped going to work. He disappeared for a week to travel to California, where he appeared as a contestant on the *Match Game.* He won $5,000. He was excited and called all of his friends and family to make sure they tuned in to watch the show. On the day that it aired, the host, Gene Rayburn, announced his name: "Welcome Donny Deutsch." The camera caught Donny for only a second before a news bulletin flashed across the screen. The rest of the show was preempted by news about the Iranian hostage crisis: Donny had been upstaged by a group of militant Islamic students.

Donny returned to New York and took a series of aptitude tests to help him identify his interests. The scores were unambiguous: Donny was "supposed" to be a salesman. In 1981 the elder Deutsch announced that he was looking for someone to buy his business, although he would have preferred to have Donny inherit it. While he realized he was not ready to settle down, Donny started working at the firm, assuming that he could learn enough to run the business eventually. "I acted too much like the owner's son from day one," he wrote in an unpublished autobiography. "I kind of treated people as if I was already their boss, as if I was marking time until my father retired." The other employees did not respond well to taking orders from a brazen kid with no advertising experience. When they complained about Donny's behavior, his father fired him. "At the time, I was pretty ticked off about it," Donny reflects. "And I was really embarrassed." His father had chosen "his other employees over me, his own flesh and blood! Later, I realized that he was just trying to be a good businessman—and he was also trying to be a good father, but that was a lesson that took a hell of a long time to sink in."

Donny bounced around for months after being fired. He sold jeans at the Aqueduct Raceway Flea Market. He made enough money to survive and had a good time, but he realized that he had greater aspirations than to be a jeans junkie and to spend his time drinking, taking drugs, and having sex. He realized how remarkably privileged he was and what a great opportunity his father had given him. "I was being a really immature, stupid shmuck, who did not know a good thing when he had it. So I tucked my tail between my legs and asked my father for a job again. I convinced him that I had, through my experience in the real world and some real thought, learned my lesson. I offered to start at the bottom and work my way up, if he'd still have me. Lucky for me he agreed."

David Deutsch & Associates was a small design-driven shop that produced understated print ads. When Donny joined his father's business, it was booking about $12 million per year. Instead of taking a position as an account executive, he asked his father to give him "an office over in the corner" so he could think about ways of expanding the business. He had to prove to his father, to the employees, but most of all to himself that he had the ability to run a business. I had "to show everyone that I had more to offer than a big mouth, a rebellious streak, a last name, and a degree from Penn." Once Donny decided that he was going to work for his father and take over the business, he threw himself into it. "He devoted 100 percent of himself to the business. He worked long, hard hours," recalls Perry Shore.

In 1984 Donny put together the "What Excites You?" campaign for tristate Pontiac dealers. It was the firm's first television ad campaign, comprising a series of commercials that asked celebrities and common people the same question: "What's the last exciting thing that happen to you?" The answer, of course, was that only purchasing a Pontiac offers real excitement. Pontiac dealers in New York, New Jersey, and Connecticut said their sales grew by 29 percent at a time when sales across the nation increased by only 9 percent. After the Pontiac ads, the firm won a number of new accounts, including People's Bank, Samsung electronics, and RCA Global Communications. An ad for Japanese Samsung electronic products was named one of the year's best by *Advertising Age* magazine in 1986. It showed a young man in his loft apartment who discovered that his TV remote control changed the channel on the Samsung billboard outside his window. The voice-over announced, "Samsung: field of power."

Donny's style and ideas were having a clear impact on the firm. Father and son were emblematic of two generations: David as the understated, hard-working representative of the Greatest Generation; Donny as the fun-loving, outgoing, television-addicted Boomer. "We're two generations, and we are as different as two people can be," said David. Donny agreed: "I think we both came along in the right generation. My dad had to build something from nothing. He was a grinder." David had put his head down to work seven days a week, twelve hours a day and laid the foundation for his business. "Never in one million years could I have ever scratched out and started an agency," Donny admitted. David had hit a wall, however, and the business, while profitable, remained stuck at $12 million annually, lacking television. "My father was from a generation that was very task oriented. He had to do everything himself. He would never delegate. He was not good at hiring people smarter than him. I've always been very good at that. The key to success is to surround yourself with people who are smarter than you are. I think I've been a good table setter." More than anything else, Donny had an instinctive sense of the power of television. In the firm's first five years of television work, ending in 1989, it started with $12 million in print campaign billings and ended with more than $70 million worth of ads, mostly on television.

In July 1989 the agency used a brochure to announce, "David Deutsch Associates is letting David and the associates go." It was the firm's way of letting people know that the agency had changed its name to "Deutsch." The change signified that Donny, at the age of 31, was assuming creative control. "Donny has made a contribution over the last five years that has changed the face of this agency," the 60-year-old senior Deutsch told the *New York Times*. "Donny has attracted clients who are bigger. Donny has attracted talent I could not have brought in." To mark the change and the agency's growth, it moved from its cramped quarters on 42nd Street to a larger suite of offices on Park Avenue South.

In 1989 Donny made another wise decision when he offered a job to Linda Sawyer. She was moving to New York City from Washington, where she had worked for a small agency that handled the account of the Swedish furniture company IKEA. IKEA had decided it needed a larger firm to handle its planned expansion into the U.S. market and wanted her to keep working on the account. When she met Donny, "I thought either I'm going to just love this person or hate him," she recalls. "He had an edge which was appealing but also could be polarizing." She accepted his offer, and IKEA became a Deutsch client.

Deutsch's main task was to create an image for the 270,000-square-foot Elizabeth, New Jersey, store that would be IKEA's flagship. The company, which opened its first U.S. store in 1985, had planned to expand operations by opening at least five or six stores in each region of the country. Its style stressed functionality over fashion, and most of its goods came ready to assemble. Donny and Sawyer believed that young Boomers were the ideal market for IKEA. Its core U.S. market in 1989 consisted of urban adults between the ages of 25 and 35 with a household income of about $50,000. These tail-end Boomers perceived themselves as being "early adopters." They liked to think of themselves as progressive, smart, and savvy. "It was the same person who first responded to Honda and who were the first ones to use money machine cards. They were going to be the first people to go to a furniture store where there was no sales help and where you had to take it home and put it together yourself."

It was a challenge. Consumers had to travel long distances to one superstore to buy items that were not advertised on sale, pick them out without sales help, and then take the merchandise home and assemble it themselves. Sawyer spent months looking over consumer and demographic data about Baby Boomers. There were mountains of studies analyzing every aspect of their attitudes. Ultimately Sawyer broke down the entire Boomer generation into five consumer segments. "Creative starters" were excited about expressing their new maturity and establishing their own adult space. "Midscale utilitarians" were married with children, and their needs were driven by family concerns, primarily comfort, practicality, and durability. "Wannabes," in their late 20s and early 30s, were dual-income couples trying to move up the economic ladder. They were confident in their tastes and had "high-style aspirations." "Upper reaches" were established and successful consumers who could afford to spend whatever they needed to make their home look good. They tended to be older empty nesters, often creating a new workspace out of a child's bedroom. The final category, "starting over," consisted of people going through a major life change, often a divorce, who needed furniture to reflect their new status. They needed basic furnishings but also wanted to feel empowered to make their own decisions.

These categories, driven by life-span segments, reflect the Boomer era in subtle but unmistakable fashion. Boomer consumers were driven by self-image and by lifestyle choices as a reflection of self-image. Furniture was not simply about quality and craftsmanship; it was about status. Ironically, IKEA appealed to status seekers even at low prices.

How could you translate these findings into a series of 30-second television ads? IKEA was a three-phase campaign that extended over twelve years. The first campaign turned perceived negatives—there was no sales force—into a positive. The ads shot real furniture salespeople and delivery guys casually talking about damaged goods and backlogged deliveries, making IKEA's self-serve system seem attractive by comparison. Title cards read, "We don't want you to have to pay for these guys." The ads underscored the point that "you don't have a slimy salesman climbing all over you," recalls Deutsch executive Cheryl Green. They also turned the store's remote location, across the street from the Newark International Airport, into an advantage. For three weeks leading up to Memorial Day, Deutsch ran radio spots and posted ads on billboards, buses, and subways declaring: "On May 23, find a place to crash on the Jersey Turnpike." Deutsch took out a double-page ad in *New York* magazine that read: "Why thousands will spend their Memorial Day vacation on the Jersey Turnpike." That ad initiated the signature slogan for the campaign: "It's a big country. Someone's got to furnish it."

Boomer lifestyle, according to the IKEA campaign, was hip. This was not the furniture store that your parents dragged you to as a kid. This was a store that understood how much the world had changed. Deutsch casually wove into the ads some controversial themes that would get people's attention without distracting from the product. An ad featuring a newly divorced woman with an infant daughter shopping for furniture underscored the anxiety associated with starting over. As she browses the store, she talks about moving into a new apartment and having nice furniture so "I can have guys over maybe in, like, ten years." Another ad showed an interracial couple shopping for furniture while discussing having a child.

Perhaps the most provocative ad dealt with a gay couple who reached the point in their relationship when it was "time for a serious dining room table." The commercial shows the two men in their 30s shopping at IKEA and later sitting at the table in their home:

Steve: Well, you know, we went to IKEA because we thought it was time for a serious dining room table, and . . .

Steve's roommate: We have slightly different tastes. I mean, Steve's more into country. It frightens me, but at the same time I have compassion.

Steve (laughing): We've been together about three years.

Roommate: I met Steve at my sister's . . .

Together: . . . wedding.

Roommate: I was really impressed with how just well-designed the IKEA furniture was.

Steve: He's really into craftsmanship.

Roommate: These chairs are really sturdy.

Steve: This table included a leaf.

Roommate: A leaf means . . .

Steve: . . . commitment.

Roommate: Staying together. Commitment. We've got another leaf waiting when we really start getting along.

The commercial ran in large urban markets with significant gay populations. Given the popular perception that gay men have good fashion sense, one columnist suggested that the commercial intended to give the shop "the Gay Housekeeping Seal of Approval." Both IKEA and Deutsch downplayed the social significance of using a gay couple in the ad, although they welcomed the controversy that ensued. "Our goal wasn't to make a statement about gays or the gay market, but instead we wanted to show two men who are living a gay lifestyle who happen to be IKEA customers," said the head of marketing for IKEA. Donny explained it in simple marketing terms: "Show me another group that's at least 10 percent of the population that is not represented in advertising. We wanted to show that IKEA is for everyone."

At that time, 1989, only a few large companies—Apple Computer, Philip Morris, and Time Warner—had run ads in gay publications. American Express had run advertisements for joint accounts using the names of a sample couple "Robert Stevenson and Matt Howell." The Gap had shown portraits of gay men and women in jeans. But the IKEA ad was the first to include a gay couple in a mainstream lifestyle campaign. Gay rights groups applauded the commercial. "We are usually portrayed as a controversial issue rather than as people who are incorporated in American life," said Ellen Carton, executive director of the New York chapter of the Gay and Lesbian Task Force. "There is nothing more ordinary than buying furniture together." Left unsaid was that young gay men are excellent home outfitters. This was not just an appeal to a market segment, but also a signal that the best and most discriminating customers choose IKEA. It was the commercial's understated style that made it so remarkable. "What makes this advertisement a cultural milestone is that it avoids heavy stereotyping," observed the London *Times*. "These table-buyers are far from the half-naked narcissists with perfect bodies that sell aftershave and underwear in the pages of *Esquire* and *GQ*. The IKEA commercial is more homely than homoerotic."

These risky ads made a bold statement about both the brand and the agency. By featuring ads that touched on interracial marriage, divorce, and gay couples, Deutsch wanted to convey a clear message to Boomers that it understood their lives and how their values and lifestyles differed from those of their parents. Donny believed that this added element of realism was the key to tapping into jaded Boomers like himself who had been bombarded with television ads their whole lives. Boomers had an instinctive skepticism about advertising, and the only way to get around it was to use real-life dialogue, images, and situations. "If I see characters that sound like me, I'm going to pay a lot more attention," he reflects. "If I see a situation that I can relate to, or emotion that I might relate to, it's going to forge a connection." Donny said that Baby Boomers, who grew up with advertising, "can't be fooled by the old three-second song-and-dance." IKEA claimed that its store traffic increased by 30 percent following the Deutsch advertising campaign.

The ads also revealed an important generational change taking place on Madison Avenue. While many of the older, more established firms were struggling, young upstarts like Deutsch were thriving. They shared a youthful spirit, a sense of creativity, and a desire to distinguish themselves in style and content from the traditional firms that had dominated advertising for the previous generation. "They are the first generation of agency founders bred entirely on television," observed journalist Randall Rothenberg. Many of the established firms, created in the 1940s and 1950s, had developed a style based on print and on the first generation of television viewers. They used direct sales pitches. Rosser Reeves, one of the early pioneers of television advertising, described this approach in his book *Reality in Advertising* (1961): "The consumer tends to remember just one thing from an advertisement—one strong claim, or one strong concept." The key to a successful ad was to keep the message simple: "Buy this product, and you will get this specific benefit."

That style no longer appealed to a generation weaned on skepticism of authority. By the 1980s widespread remote control had given this generation of cynical and jaded viewers the power to use their thumb to change the channel. That, along with the rise of cable networks, put added pressure on advertisers to develop quick, entertaining spots that could hold viewers' attention. In 1966 viewers in New York City could choose among four stations; twenty years later there were thirty-seven channels, and studies showed that most viewers regularly switched channels during commercials. Deutsch had another advantage: most of the senior management at the firm were Boomers themselves and knew instinctively how to reach their peers. "The agencies with the older management did not all catch on as quickly as we did," observes Cheryl Green. "The mission of the agency was to launch an attack on the institution of advertising, which we viewed as stagnant, condescending, and insulting to consumers," reflects Greg DiNoto, former creative head at Deutsch. "Whenever we did advertising we asked what would appeal to us," and they knew that a generation raised on television had become immune to traditional approaches to selling products. "We were very conscious of what we did not like about the existing world of advertising. We were very cynical about how we were being spoken to by the television set." The differences in their ads were obvious: "You never hear a jingle coming out of Deutsch," said DiNoto.

For Paul Goldman, a copywriter and director who worked at Deutsch until 1992, the difference appeared in the voice of each ad. Much of the advertising by other firms in the late 1980s had a "romantic American" quality. Donny was very conscious of trying to develop a unique voice, to produce ads that would speak to consumers in a different way. "We would come to Donny with what was considered at that time to be mainstream good work." He would always dismiss it. "This is terrible," he said. "I have seen this a thousand times before . . . I want to do something different." While Ronald Reagan ran for reelection in 1984 with simple, patriotic ads touting that it was "morning in America," Deutsch could not stand to produce anything similar. Irony, he believed, was the common language of Boomers, so he gathered around him younger creative types, in the early days primarily men, who understood how to speak to a jaded generation. "To have an ironic voice in advertising was to say: 'We're not really an ad. We're just like you guys,'" recalls Goldman. "We grew up watching TV too. We're not going to take ourselves seriously." In their ads, "The voice is simply saying to the consumer: we're like you—we have the same problems, attitudes and desires. We understand."

All of Deutsch's ads were distinctive and instantly recognizable. Older ads were smooth and polished; Deutsch's were rough and often low budget. He replaced catchy jingles with seemingly spontaneous dialogue. He used subtle, often ironic humor instead of a direct hard sell. He used a candid and quirky documentary style with choppy editing. Many of the ads featured real people, not actors. An ad for Filene's Basement showed the hyperkinetic chairman, Sam Gerson, walking through the store talking about clothes. They would tape dozens of hours of spontaneous conversation and edit it down to a few seconds. An ad for the Pontiac Bonneville featured on-the-street interviews with Yuppies, asking them to compare it to expensive imports like BMW. "I guess I blew it on the Beamer," reflected one disenchanted Yuppie. They avoided big-name personalities and celebrities. One of Donny's favorite approaches was to use references to classic TV shows, the ones that he watched while growing up. There are clips from *Bewitched* for Bank One. There are images of *Gilligan's Island* and the *Brady Bunch* with their huts and homes decorated by IKEA. The *A-Team* sold Mitsubishi.

There were times when Donny stepped over the line in his efforts to appeal to emotions. In 1989 smaller, more fuel-efficient Japanese cars had flooded the market, suppressing domestic car sales. In response, Donny put together an ad campaign for Pontiac dealers that played on both patriotic spirit and anger toward the growing economic clout of the Japanese. The ad suggested that if Americans continued to buy Japanese cars, they might see a bonsai tree in Mitsubishi Center on Christmas rather than the traditional evergreen at Rockefeller Center. Another ad featured a background of a rising red sun while a narrator read the copy that scrolled across the screen: "Recently, a leading JAPANESE politician described American workers as: 'a work force too lazy to compete with Japan.' . . . '30% can't even read. WELL, excuse us. But the new Pontiac Grand Am has better fuel efficiency, a larger engine, and costs thousands LESS than a Honda Accord or Toyota Camry. Maybe THEY need a reading lesson." Donny felt that he had walked the delicate line between patriotism and prejudice. "This is not screaming Yellow Peril," he said. "It's just smart marketing." But he paid a long-term price: "Not a single Japanese company invited us to pitch an account for almost ten years."

The reality that Deutsch has attempted to capture is a self-reflection of the Boomer sense of self as both sophisticated consumer and cosmopolitan citizen. Buying furniture at IKEA won't make shoppers any more sophisticated than smoking Marlboros once made them tough, but what Deutsch understood is that Boomers longed for a sense of authenticity and reality, even if that reality is contrived and artificial.

The office atmosphere at Deutsch in the '80s and '90s reflected its youthful and informal style. The *New York Times* said that Deutsch looked "more like a set of *Saturday Night Live* than a New York advertising agency." There was rock music blaring from one office; in another suite the employees were singing songs from vintage television programs. *Newsweek* commented that Deutsch offices had "a cast of employees straight out of a *thirtysomething* rerun." If the reporters had been in the office in the evening, the offices would have resembled a scene from *Animal House*. "It was like a boys' club," recalls a former employee. There were no rules. Employees worked long hours and often let off steam after dark by drinking, smoking pot, or having sex. For those who were unfortunate enough to be working after midnight, there was a woman in an apartment directly across from the Deutsch Park Avenue offices who used to parade through her living room naked at the same time every night. Little did she know that the windows across the street were lined with telescopes.

Professionally Donny was thriving: the business was flourishing, he was getting the media attention he craved and making lots of money. He cultivated his image as the "Madison Avenue Bad Boy" by wearing cowboy boots and jeans. He courted journalists, carefully practicing punchy sound bites that would keep his name in the papers. He took full advantage of his extended adolescence. He spent most summer weekends with friends at the fashionable Hamptons on Long Island. They spent their evenings drinking and doing drugs, going out to clubs, dancing and picking up women and their days sleeping off the wild nights. During the week Donny was out most nights for dinner. "I'll never forget the first time I met Donny," recalled fashion designer Stephanie Greenfield, who had been set up with Donny on a blind date. He left a message on her answering machine. "Babe, it's Donny Deutsch. I hear you're going to be my wife so I should at least buy you dinner." (His other favorite line was: "How would you like to be the mother of my child?") She showed up at the restaurant, sat down, and waited for her mystery date to appear. "I'm this fashion girl and this guy comes in and he's wearing a camel cashmere coat and suspenders that had dolphins on them."

Although he dated often, Donny found himself spending more time with an old friend, Jody. Donny had met Jody in 1982, when her first marriage was breaking up and he was on a hiatus with a long-term girl friend. Over the next few years, they ran into each other at various events, but she remarried, and he continued to date other women. In 1988, after her second marriage ended, they went on a date. Shortly afterward, they moved in together. Commitment has always been a serious issue for Donny. Part of him longed for a traditional family—the type of family in which he was raised. Most of his friends were married and had children, and Donny was every-one's favorite uncle. But he was reluctant to give up his freedom and take on the responsibility of starting a family. "His single life was a huge part of who he was for a long time," recalls a friend. Getting married involved making a commitment and changing his lifestyle, and, in Jody's case, becoming a stepfather to her daughter, Chelsea.

He agonized over the question for months. Many of his closest friends advised him against it. "If she were right, you would know it,"

Perry Shore told Donny. Others were far less generous. But Donny went ahead with the wedding, reluctantly. The night before, Donny went out to dinner with his close friend Richard Thal. "He was very quiet and depressed. I think he knew from the beginning that it wasn't right, but he made a commitment and went along with it." Richard was adamant that Donny was making a mistake. Right up to the hour of the ceremony, he urged Donny to back out. Reflecting his own ambiguous feelings, Donny scaled back on the wedding plans to a small, informal ceremony in Jody's apartment. "They didn't even have a wedding," recalls a friend. "They had a couple people over to the apartment for bagels." The relationship would only get worse.

The difficulties in the relationship reflected a clash of personalities, but it also highlighted an important problem for Boomer relationships: the traditional husband-wife roles no longer worked. Boomer mothers may have joined the workforce, but they rarely threatened their husband's status as the principle breadwinner or questioned their own responsibility for raising children and taking care of the house. Boomer women grew up with more egalitarian notions about relationships and marriage. But Boomer men, while accepting the idea of an equal partnership, often had trouble shedding cultural assumptions of manhood. By the 1990s Boomer men, especially white heterosexual men, found themselves under assault from assertive women, gay men who openly mocked traditional notions of masculinity, and African Americans who benefited from affirmative action policies that threatened their dominance in the workplace. "The Angry White Male" became a popular topic for discussion and debate among psychologists and pundits. In 1992 Robert Bly's best-selling *Iron John* urged men to get in touch with their inner maleness, and the following year, Michael Douglas played a frustrated white man who lashes out at fast food restaurants and convenience stores in the movie *Falling Down*.

Ironically, in Donny's marriage, it was Jody who insisted on a more traditional role. She wanted to stay at home and raise her daughter while Donny served as the breadwinner. She wanted him to come home after work, sit down for a family dinner, and spend the evenings watching television with her. But Donny was too restless and did not want to be tied down. It was becoming painfully obvious to both that the old rules governing relationships had changed, and they, like most other Boomers, were struggling to find a replacement.

SIX

THE WAY WE WISH WE LIVED NOW

Liz at Yale, early 1970s;   Seaside, Florida. © Steven Brooke Studios

Boomers were the first generation to grow up in the suburbs. Though suburbs are as old as the commuter railroad, dating back to the 1850s, and such towns as Garden City (New York) and Riverside (Chicago), the Serviceman's Readjustment Act (1944), popularly known as the GI bill, made the suburbs accessible to the middle class by requiring smaller down payments and providing lower interest rates. In the past, prospective home owners had to produce a 30 percent down payment and pay off the rest of the loan in less than ten years. Now they could put down as little as 10 percent and pay off the mortgage over thirty years at a much lower interest rate.

Young couples looking for added space for their growing families took advantage of the new government program. In 1944 there had been 114,000 new houses built in the United States; by 1950 that number soared to 1,696,000. In 1949 builder William Levitt bought 4,000 acres of potato fields in Hempstead, Long Island, and transformed them into the model of modern suburban life. Completed at the rate of thirty per day, each house was identical: one story high, with a 12 by 16 foot living room, a kitchen, two bedrooms, a Bendix washer, or 8-inch television, and a tiled bathroom. The price: $7,990, or $60 a month with no money down. Buyers snapped up 1,400 houses in the first three hours after sales began in March 1949. "Our best prospect," recalled one developer, "was the guy walking down the street with his wife and family. He was holding the hand of a 5-year-old, she had hold of a 2-year old, and she was pregnant. The guys used to say, 'There goes a man who has just screwed himself out of his apartment.'" Similar developments sprang up in suburban Philadelphia, Detroit, and Los Angeles.

At the time, social critics complained that the new suburbs, with row after row of identical homes and well-manicured lawns, were a cookie-cutter wasteland lacking the culture of the city or the beauty of the countryside. The physical monotony was supposed to be synonymous with conformity and repression. "For literally nothing down," wrote critic John Keats, "you too can find a box of your own . . . inhabited by people whose age, income, number of children, problems, habits, conversations, dress, possessions, perhaps even blood types are almost precisely like yours." Everyone in the suburbs, a hostile observer noted, "buys the right car, keeps his lawn like his neighbor's, eats crunchy breakfast cereal, and votes Republican." Critic Lewis Mumford denounced Levittown as an "instant slum" and suggested that it represented the worst vision of America's future: bland people, living in bland houses, leading bland lives.

Of course, then as now, even modular housing can be customized in small ways, and city tenements or housing projects were hardly more individualized. Boomers ignored the critique and had little choice since their demand required supply. They moved farther away from the central city, plowing under millions of acres of farmland along the way. In 1950 one in four persons lived in suburbia; forty years later one in two lived there. In the 1950s the issue was conformity; in the 1980s it would be identity—the fear that suburban sprawl was an outgrowth of unchecked individualism that was eroding community life and corroding civil society. Instead of producing a generation of conformists, critics would worry that the new suburb was breeding a generation of social misfits.

It is hard to imagine that a quaint town nestled in the sandy beaches of northwestern Florida could be ground zero for a powerful Boomer cultural movement, but Seaside, a resort town designed by the husband-wife team of Elizabeth Platter-Zyberk and Andres Duaney, embodied the response of many Baby Boom architects, city planners, and social thinkers to the problem of suburban sprawl. Ironically, the Boomers' freedom and self-expression has engendered their own Boomer response, which reveals how certain classic American values survive generational upheaval. With the creation of Seaside, many Boomers looked to the past to shape the future.

■

Elizabeth Platter-Zyberk was the first American-born child of wealthy Polish immigrants forced to flee their homeland by encroaching Soviet troops near the end of World War II. They came to the United States with little more than their ambition and their faith in the American dream. In a matter of a few years they had gone from European royalty to American paupers. "We lived off the goodwill of those distant family members and friends who befriended us," recalls oldest brother Bob. Liz's father, Josaphat (Joe), a talented architect, immediately got a job as a draftsman, took his exam to be an architect, and started working for the Philadelphia Saving Society. Her mother, Maria, worked in the family garden and took care of the children.

Both parents felt a deep sense of kinship to Poland, and they were determined to instill in their American-born child a deep respect for tradition and a strong faith in religion. Liz's mom was determined that her daughter would never forget about the past: the family's deep roots in Poland, their long journey to America, and the divine guidance that successfully transplanted them in America. Liz was raised on a steady diet of respect for self-control, tradition, and history. Both mother and father were reserved, keeping a careful check on their emotions. During their summer vacations, the children had to spend a few hours every day sitting on the sofa getting Polish history and language lessons from their mother. The entire family gathered for dinner at the same time every night. Everyone had to be present. There were evening prayers every night.

Much of Liz's later work as an architect would revolve around trying to capture the small-town feel and community warmth of her childhood in Paoli, an inner suburb of Philadelphia laid out along the local commuter train rail. It was suburban enough to allow people to live in detached single-family homes, urban enough to foster a sense of community, and close enough to the train to allow residents to commute to the city for work. "Part of living in Paoli," she reflects, "was walking to the corner store, walking to the train station, or just walking to school." When she was very young her mother would take her shopping by pushing her in a small cart. It would be an all-day trip, because along the way, they would stop and chat with neighbors sitting on their front porches. "You could walk everywhere perfectly safely," recalls her sister Rosemary. "You never locked your door. I remember enormous snowstorms and going out sledding and everybody in the neighborhood being out, including adults," Liz reflects.

Like Fran Visco, Liz received conflicting messages from her mother. Despite her reverence for tradition, Maria was in some ways a closet feminist. She had earned a college degree in agriculture in Poland and was an accomplished horse rider and skier. She resented the way America relegated women to second-class citizenship, and she pushed Elizabeth to work hard and set high standards for herself. "She was full of contradictions," Elizabeth admits. "Her words and her actions often were different."

Elizabeth started high school in 1964, the same year that the Beatles appeared on the *Ed Sullivan Show*. Insisting that Liz receive a traditional education, her parents enrolled her at Sacred Heart Academy, a conservative Roman Catholic high school for girls founded on the belief that girls deserved an education equal to that of boys. Not only did the nuns at Sacred Heart provide her with a rigorous education, they instilled a sense of achievement and social responsibility. "They believe that you change the world one heart, one mind at a time," observes a fellow graduate. In one assignment, the nuns asked students to put together a book about the false media images of women.

The most dramatic events shaping Elizabeth's world were not civil rights demonstrations or antiwar protests, but rather the most sweeping reforms of the Catholic church in 500 years. In 1963 Pope John XXIII called for the creation of the Second Ecumenical Council, also known as Vatican II, which enacted many changes in liturgy and the sacraments. The reforms had a direct impact on the daily lives of most Catholics. During mass, the priest now faced the congregation and spoke in English rather than Latin. Confessions, once held in dark closets, were renamed "acts of reconciliation" and now often took place in an open space. Folk guitars replaced Gregorian chants in some churches, as music was freed to more local decision making. In addition to these physical changes in the church, Liz noticed how the reforms seemed to stimulate many of the young nuns who taught at Sacred Heart: "It represented a breath of fresh air for them." She speculated that they may have seen the changes as the first step in more significant changes that would expand their ability to participate in church life. For Liz the reforms were successful because they allowed the church to retain its older traditions—it continued to perform some Gregorian chants—while adding new features that made the services more welcoming.

After graduating from high school in 1968, Elizabeth wanted to go to college to study architecture, but her mother insisted that she attend Manhattanville College, a small Catholic College run by the Sacred Heart nuns. Liz had spent most of her education at Sacred Heart schools, and while she believed they provided a nurturing environment for young women, she was ready to break out and try a different approach. There was something too restricting, too confining, about Manhattanville. Part of the problem was the limited range of classes and the lack of any offerings in art and architecture. But the bigger problem was that it was socially and intellectually cloistered. She used to escape on Saturdays by taking the bus into New York, where she enjoyed strolling around the artsy SoHo district and going to museums. Her weekend junkets reinforced her love of architecture and accentuated her growing disenchantment with Manhattanville. After two years, Elizabeth was looking for a way out.

Manhattanville had an Asian studies program that allowed students to take their junior year at Princeton. Elizabeth wrote to Princeton to see if it had a similar one-year program to study architecture. The university did not, but responded that she could apply to transfer. For a young woman, going to Princeton was almost unheard of. It was only in January 1969 that the university had announced that it had "approved in principle the university undertaking the education of women at the undergraduate level." On September 6, 1969, 148 women, including 100 first-year students, enrolled at Princeton for the first time. Although she was about to become part of this pioneering group, undermining centuries-old traditions of sex segregation in higher education, Liz had little interest in sexual politics. Her deeply conservative and traditional education simply inspired her to seek out the best education. It was Princeton's strong academic reputation and its conservative atmosphere, not the opportunity to strike a blow for sexual liberation, that inspired her.

Her mother did not see it that way. She opposed the move, fearing that Elizabeth might be exposed to radical ideas. She believed that most of the faculty at institutions like Princeton were Communists who used their positions to recruit future revolutionaries. Because Elizabeth was her only American-born child, the only one who had no personal memories of the family's roots in Poland or the "miracle" of its journey to America, her mother always feared that she would lose touch with her roots—become too American, too independent. Elizabeth's older siblings spent hours trying to change her mother's mind. It was time to let Elizabeth go, they said, trusting that she would do the right thing. Reluctantly, she relented and gave Elizabeth her blessing.

Elizabeth entered Princeton in the fall of 1970, living in the Princeton Inn, an old hotel on campus that was converted into the university's first mixed-sex dorm. She was one of a handful of women who transferred in as juniors, and she was the only female in the architecture program. When she received her summer package of information, it included a map showing which bathrooms had been converted to women's rooms. She had to carry the map with her at all times. Most of that first generation of students had a difficult time adjusting to a university that took pride in its male culture and only superficially embraced the presence of women. Many women in those early years felt isolated from the largely male culture of the institution and even ostracized by the men. Indeed, that male culture was changing as well, toward greater permissiveness. "There was something lonely and depressing in seeing roving bands of boys inebriated with beer who knew that they did not have to show their glazed eyes and staggering walks to a housemaster or waiting father anymore," observed Jane Leifer, one of Liz's fellow students.

It was the first time that Liz was really on her own, the first time she was free of her mother's often oppressive control. Liz enjoyed her new freedom and quickly immersed herself in Princeton's rich intellectual life. There was only one aspect of campus life that made her uncomfortable. Liz disliked Princeton's deeply embedded sense of entitlement and elitism. She was conservative, but a daughter of immigrants and, now, a pioneer herself. Princeton was a refuge for upper-middle-class WASPs. Although the Platter-Zyberk family had been a part of Polish royalty before the war and her mother constantly reminded her of the connections to the past, Liz understood what it was like to be an outcast. She found distasteful the way some of her classmates mocked American middle-class culture. Her Sacred Heart education had instilled in her a sense of social responsibility and humility that seemed to be lacking on the Princeton campus. "On the one hand, you can fit into the American elite," reflects friend Joanna Lombard. "On the other hand, you know that you are different."

Princeton exposed Elizabeth to a wide range of people from different backgrounds, but it did little to change her in either style or temperament. Some of her classmates were serious and studious; others liked to smoke pot, listen to loud music, and throw wild parties. Elizabeth never completely loosened up; she remained disciplined and focused. "Liz was a very quiet person," recalls her senior-year roommate, Jan Howard. "Very attractive, well liked, but also very shy." She observed but did not participate in the sexual revolution (despite a male-female student ratio of forty to one). She remained conservative in style and taste. She always sat straight, spoke in full and complete sentences, and maintained a low-key, serious demeanor. She joined Cap and Gown, one of Princeton's famed eating clubs, which were similar to social fraternities, and one of the first to accept women.

More than anything else, it was during her Princeton years that she discovered her love of architecture. After graduating in 1972, she decided to enroll in a master's program at Yale. Her father supported her decision; once again, her mother argued against the move. Although she herself had earned a college degree in a man's field—agriculture—she believed that a woman's place was in the home. She wanted Elizabeth to settle down, get married, and start a family.

Yale University was located only a few hours north on I-95 from Princeton, but the schools were worlds apart in temperament and appearance. Princeton was nestled in a bucolic rural setting in New Jersey; Yale sat at the center of the poor, gritty industrial city of New Haven. Although Princeton had been forced to shut down in the tumult of student strikes following the killings at Kent State in May 1970, it remained insulated from much of the political turmoil sweeping the nation. New Haven, in contrast, was swept up in it. "There was a sense of change in the air," recalled classmate Patrick Pinnell. "There was a sense of discovery and change [even] in the architecture business." In May 1970 Yale students went on strike— "Skip class, talk politics" was the motto—to protest the New Haven trial of Black Panther Bobby Seale, one of the original Chicago 8 accused of inciting a riot at the 1968 Democratic National Convention. The prospect of violence forced the governor to call out 2,500 National Guard troops and the attorney general to dispatch 4,000 marines and paratroopers to nearby military bases. There was no violence, but the protest politicized the university's outspoken president, Kingman Brewster, and its student body. Over the next few years, Brewster led delegations of students to Washington to lobby for an end to the war and helped raise funds to elect antiwar candidates to Congress.

Liz had never been politically active, and as a graduate student, she was even less engaged in campus activities. For her, the spirit of change and reform could be found in the architecture school, where Yale's most inspiring lecturer, Vincent Scully, railed against modernism—the Greatest Generation's contribution to architecture. In the years after World War II, modernists used steel frames and glass curtains to construct sleek, unornamented buildings. Modernists believed that buildings should be isolated objects, like sculptures on pedestals, that were unconnected to the surrounding community. Because they could be constructed cheaply and quickly, urban reformers and city managers turned to modernist designs for their urban renewal projects, so public housing, run by bureaucrats, soon appeared in the form of Soviet-style ugly towers. Scully believed that modernism, especially in the guise of urban planning, was destroying community life. In his book *American Architecture and Urbanism* (1969), Scully urged every American citizen to "share an active and critical responsibility for the future of the American city, as for that of the American community as a whole." For Scully the United States was on the verge of a crisis; the old brownstones and shingled houses of urban communities awaited the wrecking ball that modernism was swinging in the name of progress.

Although Scully was an intimidating presence on campus and known for being mercurial, Liz wanted to work for him and soon became one of his teaching assistants. She sat in the front of the lecture hall every week, mesmerized by his lectures. It all seemed to make sense to her. Architects placed such a premium on the new and the original, but Elizabeth was raised to respect the old and the traditional. At Princeton the emphasis was on constructing individual buildings, but she knew from her warm memories of growing up in Paoli that the space between the individual buildings formed the connective tissue of community life. As part of her work Elizabeth led Yale undergraduates through some of New Haven's older neighborhoods. She fell in love with the nineteenth-century vernacular houses, with their front gables and porches built close to the streets. There was something warm and inviting and a real sense of neighborhood. "Perhaps most of all," Scully later reflected, she "saw in the modest streets with cars parked on them that not everything needed to be given away to the automobile."

Liz, and her future husband and fellow graduate student Andres Duaney, and many of their classmates at Yale, were drawn to Scully and found themselves becoming critical of the modernist faculty members. One dismissed Liz and her cohorts as "the worst class in the history of the Yale architecture school." Scully often hosted Friday afternoon lunches with his teaching assistants. Afterward they would walk through the local neighborhoods. Liz and Andres started pacing the streets to see how far back the houses sat and measuring the porches. Her classmates nicknamed her "Liz Planning-Zoning" because of her interest in "the machinery" that made up mixed-use neighborhoods. "We were never taught these things in classes," recalls Patrick Pinnell, "but they were essential to understanding how cities evolve, or don't evolve."

After her first year living in New Haven, Elizabeth was having doubts about her profession. For one thing, she had no women role models. At Princeton she had been the only woman in the program; at Yale women made up only four of the twenty-five students in the school. There were no female faculty members and no successful women architects. Also, her strong religious training and her deep spirituality made her uncomfortable focusing so much of her attention on physical things like buildings. She was also turned off by what she considered the high-handed intellectualism of the profession. It was not reassuring that most architects she met struck her as arrogant and self-important. "Yale was at the forefront of the idea of architects as heroic figures, remaking cities by tearing them down," she remembers, and most of the faculty were uninterested in ordinary housing for the middle class.

Classmates recall a shy and reserved but attractive and exceptionally bright student. She would occasionally let loose with a loud laugh, but for the most part, she remained tightly controlled and disciplined. "Liz is nothing if not a concentration of controlled energy," recalls Pinnell. "She is the classic iron fist in the velvet glove." She and her roommate often hosted small dinner parties at their cramped apartment, but there was never enough food, recalls a classmate, so "we would stop at the local hamburger joint and eat before going."

Elizabeth graduated with a master's degree in 1974, just as the oil crisis and stagflation shocked the economy into recession. She could not have picked a worse time to enter the job market. No one was constructing new buildings; architecture firms were laying people off by the dozens. She traveled briefly in Europe before returning to Philadelphia. Unable to get a job, she moved back in with her parents and interviewed with insurance companies and management firms. On the side, she helped design a house for her brother.

She spent most of her time working at a women's clothing store in a local suburban mall. The store was going bankrupt and since there was not much traffic, Liz had lots of time to spend with the store's eccentric owner. At the time Liz met her, she was in her mid-50s, married with grown children, and ready to start a new life. She divorced her husband and started dating another man, who was still married at the time. Elizabeth was fascinated by this woman: she was smart, independent, and living a life that was far different from anything Liz had ever experienced. Liz had ignored the Boomers' new lifestyles at Princeton and Yale, but now, with an older woman, she finally faced in a tangible way the larger social and cultural changes that were transforming the nation. The shy, introverted little girl from Sacred Academy met a liberated woman of the 1970s. "She was leading this exotic life that I had not encountered in my sheltered life," Elizabeth recalls. "She was the first woman I encountered who was totally independent and autonomous. She was not attached or dependent on a man or in any way on her family. She was out there making her own judgments and having a good time, and she was very forthright."

While working at the store, she received a call from Duaney. After leaving Yale, Andres had accepted a teaching position at the University of Miami and started a renovation project in the Florida Keys. He invited Liz to come to Florida to help with the project, but that was not his only reason for calling. They had been friends since their junior year at Princeton, but during their last year at Yale, Andres fell in love with Liz. A few months earlier, he had sent a long letter on yellow lined paper proposing marriage. At the bottom of the letter he drew an engagement ring. She refused his offer. "I was still uninterested and unconvinced," she says. Liz found Andres "too stiff" and "too serious"—in essence, too much like herself. "I thought he was a bit dry," she recalls. "I wanted someone with more humor." Andres pleaded with her to come to Miami and give both him, and the project, a chance. It was a big move for her: leaving her family, going to a part of the country where she had never lived. Perhaps influenced by her boss, she agreed to come to Florida—but only for one month and only for the work. "I needed something to do because the store was closing," she reflects. She was tired of looking for jobs and fed up with the cold. So she thought to herself, "Let me take a month and go someplace I have never been before with a friend."

Andres Duaney had grown up in a wealthy Cuban family that had moved freely between Cuba and the United States. Both his father and grandfather were Princeton-educated land developers who designed and developed most of the pre-Castro French-influenced town of Vista Alegre, Cuba, where Andres grew up. Andres was destined to follow in their footsteps. In 1949 his mother traveled to the United States to give birth to her son so that he would be guaranteed American citizenship. When he was only a few weeks old, he and his mother returned to Cuba, where he spent most of his childhood.

Around his tenth birthday, he started hearing the crackle of gunfire in the distant hills. His parents, neighbors, and friends talked enthusiastically about the revolution. Although his family was wealthy, they considered themselves progressive reformers who hated the corrupt and inefficient American-supported Batista regime. They rallied around the young nationalist Fidel Castro, who promised to end corruption and aid the poor. "He was a great reformer and extremely charismatic," Andres remembers. "Everybody was on his side." As a child, Andres played with "revolutionary cards" the way American youth swapped baseball cards. They were packaged similarly, sold in packs with a strip of bubble gum, with pictures and important information about key players.

It soon became clear when he started seizing control of private property that Castro was more Communist than reformer. Feeling betrayed, the family fled to the United States in 1960, where they moved into a waterfront mansion on Long Island owned by one of his father's friends from Princeton. Andres was in the sixth grade and was immediately enrolled at the exclusive Buckley School, a disciplined and rigorous private prep school where his father had gone. For the last few years at Buckley and for his four years of high school at the exclusive Choate School in Connecticut, his parents lived in Barcelona, Spain. As soon as each year ended, he boarded a ship to spend his summers in Europe with them.

He and Liz were both raised in strict Catholic families that had been forced to flee Communist persecution in their home countries. Their parents retained a deep and emotional attachment to those countries along with a desire to assimilate into their adopted land. Both Liz and Andres straddled their family traditions and heritage and their identity as Americans. Both attended traditional, formal schools—Liz at Sacred Heart, Andres at Buckley and Choate. At home and at school there were proper rules of behavior that had to be observed, and a heavy premium placed on discipline and order. Both shared a nostalgia for their childhoods, and especially for the neighborhoods in which they were raised.

Yet they were very different in personality and temperament. She is quiet and unassuming. He is outspoken, gregarious, and mercurial. He exaggerates; she understates. Liz is methodical and patient, often taking on long-term projects. She enjoys the give-and-take of debate and discussion. Andres is impatient with dissent. He's emotional and excitable; she's detached and calm. "They are fire and ice," recalls a friend. "She is not cold, but she is unbelievably reserved, self-controlled, and poised." "It is like the difference between opera and serious classical music," reflects architect Walter Chatham. "They are both high art forms but they find expression in different ways."

They have succeeded together because they complement each other. His strengths are her weaknesses, and vice versa. Andres is the visionary, the polemicist, the abstract thinker who embraces the unconventional. Liz is the practical-minded and skeptical planner who helps realize his often wild schemes. "He has immediate reactions, and I think about things," she says. He is deductive; she is inductive. She works from the facts up; he starts with the theory and finds the facts to support it. Andres overwhelms you with the power of his intellect and his enthusiasm for ideas; Liz is the patient teacher who walks you through a series of logical steps. Their styles clashed so often in the early years that they agreed never to work on the same projects. If they did work together, one or the other would have the final decision.

As planned, Liz stayed in Florida for a month, returned home to Philadelphia, and quickly found a job with a local architectural firm. What she had not planned on, however, was getting engaged to Andres. "We had more fun than I thought [we would]," Liz recalls. "We enjoyed working together." In the months before Liz arrived, Andres had spent lots of time in the company of a group of female Cuban students who had decided that it was unacceptable that he was "such a stodgy Cuban." They took him under their wing and taught him about Cuban culture and music. "They loosened him up," recalls Liz. At some point during the month, he decided to propose again. This time Liz accepted. Over the next few months they visited each other and made plans for a June 1976 wedding.

They are a very attractive couple, and many associates believe they possess a certain sex appeal that has added to their celebrity status in the architecture profession. "They almost have movie-star qualities," observes a former colleague. "You have no idea how many people come up to me and say, 'I have always been in love with her, or I have always been in love with him.' " Andres is well built with chiseled facial features, a dark complexion, and a mop of graying black hair. "He walks into a town meeting and the women swoon," notes a friend. Some people compare Liz to Grace Kelly: "Although she would never allow herself to be glamorous enough, you can imagine it if she put on a pair of $40,000 diamond earrings."

They joined with three other partners to create a small storefront business, Architectonica. "In the beginning it was deck and kitchen renovations," recalls a young intern in the office. They had to take just about everybody who walked through the front door. One of their early clients was Mr. Big, a very obese and very flamboyant nightclub owner from Liberty City. "I remember so clearly Mr. Big would come to the office with these two very attractive young women on either arm whom he referred to as his 'hostesses.'" He would come in and take off his shoes and socks, exposing long multicolored toenails. "They would all be sitting around having a serious discussion about architecture while he sat wiggling his toes." At one point, during a heated discussion about fees, Mr. Big reached into his back pocket and pulled out a .38 magnum snub-nosed revolver and placed it conspicuously on the table. "You want to negotiate," he said. "Let's negotiate."

It was during that first year in Florida that they met developer Robert Davis, who was planning to build an "alternative" community on the Florida Panhandle. To Andres he was from "the late bell-bottoms crowd," though in truth there was nothing late about it. Raised as a liberal Jew in the conservative South, Davis always perceived himself as an outsider. He had been active in the peace movement and was a member of the Socialist Workers Party as an undergraduate at Antioch College in the early 1960s. Uncertain about what he wanted to do after college, he followed his roommate and enrolled in Harvard Business School. After graduating in 1965 he became a successful developer in Florida, although he never abandoned his radical politics or his counterculture style.

As a child Davis had spent many summer holidays on the beaches in Florida, where his family stayed in simple wood frame cottages with big porches and high ceilings. When he inherited eight acres of land near Seagrove Beach on Florida's northwest coast, he wanted to re-create that community. "To a great degree what I was really initially concerned about was reminding people of the sheer sensual delight of living by the sea in contact with nature, the smell in the air and feel of the sea breezes," he says. The group of people who were attracted to his vision of a beachside community were far more ambitious. They saw this eight acres and wanted to create a utopia. Seaside, as the town would be simply named, would be a refuge from the crass commercialism of the modern world, a place that counterculture leftovers of the 1960s could call home. The town would welcome people from all walks of life, and special provisions would be made to allow workers to buy houses. "They wanted to build a wonderful beachfront town where the families could get together with sand in their toes, no pavement, just little seaside shacks," recalled Andres.

The desire to create an alternative community that rejected the crass materialism and rampant individualism of contemporary society was a prominent goal of the 1960s counterculture. No one knows for sure how many people fled the pressures of modern life to live in self-contained alternative communities. In 1969 *Newsweek* estimated there were 500 communes scattered around the country housing more than 10,000 residents, but most estimates are much higher. The historian Timothy Miller put the number of communes in the thousands and the number of people who lived there in the hundreds of thousands. The promise of drugs attracted people to LSD guru Timothy Leary's Millbrook in upstate New York, while the members of Trans-Love Energies commune in Ann Arbor, Michigan, enjoyed flouting social prohibitions against free love. Despite their individual makeup, most communes rejected private property and insisted on sharing food, housing, work, drugs, and even sexual partners.

While hippies gravitated toward communes, most young people satisfied their desire for community by attending rock festivals. In 1967 a crowd of 50,000 turned out at the Monterey International Pop Festival. Over the next few years rock fans flocked to star-studded festivals in Miami, Newport, and Atlanta. The biggest celebration of "peace and love and music" took place on August 15, 1969, when 500,000 young people gathered at Max Yasgur's 600-acre farm near Bethel, New York. "Woodstock," as it came to be referred to, included a stellar lineup of musical talent that included Jimi Hendrix, the Who, the Grateful Dead, Joe Cocker, Janis Joplin, and Sly and the Family Stone. Whether they attended the concert or not, the generation that came of age during the 1960s embraced Woodstock's freedom-espousing spirit. "Everyone swam nude in the lake," recalled one participant, "balling was easier than getting breakfast, and the 'pigs' just smiled and passed out the oats."

Woodstock emerged as a symbol of youthful rebellion, but it also underscored the problems plaguing alternative communities. Since most of the people attracted to rock festivals and communes were trying to escape society, they resisted all form of authority. The result was often anarchy. Woodstock organizers, for example, were overwhelmed by the size of the crowds. There was such a severe shortage of water, food, and medical and sanitation facilities that New York governor Nelson Rockefeller declared a state of emergency. "I went to Woodstock and I hated it," recalled singer Billy Joel. "I think a lot of that community 'spirit' was based on the fact that everybody was so wasted." The problems of maintaining order were made abundantly clear a few months later at a concert near Altamont, California, when members of the Hell's Angels beat a number of spectators, leaving one dead.

Davis was too shrewd a businessman to fall into the trap that destroyed so many '60s experiments in communal living. He wanted to combine his counterculture sensibility with accepted business practice to create an alternative community that rested on a foundation of market capitalism. The paradox, he believed, was that it took an authoritarian hand to mold a truly egalitarian community and clearly defined rules limiting behavior to guarantee individual expression.

Andres was attracted to the idea and spent much of his time talking with Davis and his partners about their utopian ideas. Initially, Liz showed little interest and almost no tolerance for Davis and his "stoned hippie friends," as she called them. The firm did some initial drawings, but Davis believed they did not fully grasp his vision. Since his vague ideas were based on communities he remembered from his past, he decided the best way to communicate his ideas was to take Liz and Andres on a road trip. In 1979 Elizabeth and Andres, along with Robert and his wife, spent days driving between Miami and Seaside and along the coastal areas of South Carolina and Louisiana in a 1975 Pontiac convertible. They took pictures, made a few sketches, and paced off dimensions. In addition Robert and his wife spent time traveling the Mediterranean looking at coastal towns in France and Italy.

Like archeologists trying to uncover ancient ruins, Andres and Liz unearthed an optimistic vision of an American city before it was overrun by the automobile and buried in suburban sprawl. During evenings in Miami, they organized "architecture patrols," traveling around to discover the remnants of the original Miami neighborhoods—bungalow houses from the 1920s, old streets and sidewalks. They realized that the architecture that they had learned at two of the finest schools in the country, Princeton and Yale, had done little to explain the way the vast majority of people actually lived their lives or the responsibility architects shared for ruining it. They became acutely aware of "this disconnect between what they were trained to do and what society needed them to do," their friend Lombard observes.

Liz and Andres's critique of suburban sprawl reflected their generation's increased concern about limited resources and the need to use them wisely. Boomers coming of age in the 1970s had very different views of the environment from their parents, who had been nurtured on promises of unlimited resources. The birth of the modern environmental movement dated to the publication in 1962 of marine biologist Rachel Carson's book *Silent Spring,* which documented evidence that the widely used insecticide DDT was killing birds, fish, and other animals that ate insects. Andres remembers reading the book shortly after it was published during one of his long boat rides back to Spain at the end of the school year. The book led to a ban on DDT and, more important, underscored to a generation of Baby Boomers the fragility of the natural environment and the costs of living in a technological society. A clear indication of the sea change in public attitudes took place on April 22, 1970, when the nation celebrated its first Earth Day. Twenty million people gathered in local events across the country to hear speeches and see exhibits and demonstrations promoting environmental awareness in what the *Christian Science Monitor* called "the largest expression of public concern in history over what is happening to the environment."

A series of events in the 1970s underscored concerns about the environment. When people living in the Love Canal housing development near Niagara Falls, New York, reported abnormally high rates of illness, miscarriages, and birth defects, investigators learned the community had been built on top of an underground chemical waste disposal site. In March 1979 an accident at the Three Mile Island nuclear power plant in Pennsylvania heightened public concern about the safety of nuclear power and led to calls for tighter regulation of the industry. The incident at Three Mile Island took place less than two weeks after the release of the popular movie *The China Syndrome,* which dealt with the consequences of a nuclear meltdown. Public attitudes turned decidedly against nuclear energy at just the time that the nation was struggling with soaring oil prices. For many Boomers the clear implication of OPEC embargoes, chemical contamination, and fear of nuclear meltdowns was simple: they were living in a world of limited resources in which the natural environment had to be protected and preserved. "We recognized that there was a planet that needed stewardship," Liz reflects.

Nestled on the Florida Panhandle far away from other beach communities, Seaside provided an ideal setting for a new social experiment. There were no existing homes nearby and few zoning laws to limit the imagination. It became a tabula rasa for two Baby Boom architects who had been looking for an opportunity to challenge the profession's conventional wisdom. The width of the sidewalks, the front yards, and the distance between the street and the front porch were up to them. Behavior, they believed, followed form. People who lived in small towns acted and lived like people in small towns: they walked the streets, sat on their porches, talked with their neighbors, and visited friends.

The key breakthrough for Andres and Liz was to focus on building codes, the often complex set of rules that serve as the genetic code governing construction. Especially after World War II, conscious government policy on both the local and federal levels produced a patchwork of laws that led to suburban sprawl. The federal government paid for 90 percent of its new interstate highway system under Eisenhower, giving rise to four- and eight-lane rivers that made commuting possible for millions. The downside was new housing far from town and working parents who never walked anywhere in their community. The government also provided mortgage programs that made it easier to buy a new house than to pay rent for an apartment. The result was that people tended to buy new homes farther from the city center. Local authorities used zoning codes to separate houses from factories and to segregate residential neighborhoods by income. Codes were often complicated regulations written by lawyers for lawyers. Their end result was that big houses tended to be clustered in one area, smaller homes in another, and rental property in still another part of town. Everyone had to get in their cars to drive to the local commercial area, usually a shopping mall. Zoning laws did not make small towns illegal, but they placed enough obstacles in the way to discourage potential builders and buyers. The result is etched across the land in strip malls, beltways, and the constant chauffeuring of suburban kids by their moms.

The challenge for Seaside was to develop an alternative code that allowed for the traditional architecture Liz and Andres admired without imposing a sterile uniformity on the community. "Andres and Liz had the great common sense to realize that in order to recreate the small town you had to go after the zoning laws," observes Pinnell. The codes needed to be specific and detailed enough to create the small town feel they were looking for but general enough to invite a variety of structures. The "new urbanism" code was simplified, designed to make it easy for prospective builders to understand the specific architectural requirements. "Typical zoning code consists of hundreds and sometimes thousands of pages of prescriptions and our code consists of two large sheets of mainly graphic prescriptions," recalls Davis.

There were a few basic rules that needed to be followed. First, the town needed to be built around public buildings. Civic buildings like churches, schools, and libraries should be given preferential positioning near the center of the town. Second, towns needed to be constructed for pedestrians, not cars. "The suburban ideal is based on the idea that cars have a constitutional right to be happy," Andres quipped. Third, there had to be distinct neighborhoods that were compact, on a small scale, and with a diversity of building types. The neighborhood needed to have well-defined edges and a clear center. An average person should be able to walk from the center of the neighborhood to the edge in less than five minutes. Fourth, the neighborhood needed to mix people of different incomes, and it should blend residential and business properties. There should be enough shops and offices integrated into the neighborhood to supply the daily needs of a family. No one should have to get into the car to buy milk. Finally, while houses could be individualized, they needed to have front porches, and the porches needed to be at least 8 feet deep to encourage people to use them. Each front yard had to be enclosed by a picket fence, with no more than 16 feet separating the fence from the front porch. This would encourage people to sit on their porches in the evenings while engaged in conversation with people passing by. In their own way, Liz and Andres were creating an astonishingly restrictive model, forcing a particular kind of community on all residents.

Building in Seaside started in 1983 and progressed slowly. By December 1984 there were about a dozen buildings, mostly houses, stretched along a single street. By 1990 there were 150 pastel clapboard homes, clustered around the local post office, a gourmet food market, a bookstore, and the neighborhood pool. The town became a media sensation, and for a time, Andres and Liz were heroes. Most of the press coverage focused on the aesthetics of Seaside: the cozy, narrow streets and mandatory front porches. In 1988 an *Atlantic Monthly* cover story christened Seaside "the most celebrated new American town of the decade. . . . It looks like a fanciful turn-of-the-century town that has been cleaned, painted, and planted to perfection." In 1990 *Time* declared, "Seaside could be the most astounding design achievement of its era, and one would hope, the most influential." A few years later *Newsweek* would call it "the most influential resort community since Versailles." Andres and Liz were hailed as "the first radical critics of modern sprawl" who knew enough about "the nuts and bolts" of suburbs "to mount an effective campaign of subversion."

Seaside was "Bobo" paradise, the term that the journalist David Brooks coined to describe "highly educated folk who have one foot in the bohemian world of creativity and another foot in the bourgeois realm of ambition and worldly success." It was a perfect symbol of Boomer values, representing a mixing of the bourgeois desire for self-discipline and order with the bohemian celebration of self-expression and creativity. It was profoundly nostalgic. They were all searching for their lost childhoods. Davis wanted to re-create the summer homes of his youth; her childhood home of Paoli was never far from Liz's mind as she designed Seaside; and Andres's reference point was Barcelona. The result was an odd mix of nostalgia and reform, of utopian idealism and architectural formalism. The codes, which prohibited picture windows and glass doors, even enforced individual privacy.

The intense media attention increased public interest, and property values soared. "The first group of people [who purchased houses in Seaside] were school teachers, postmen—normal people," observes Lombard. The original lots sold for as little as $25,000, and houses were going for $75,000. As the place became more fashionable, many of the original owners sold their lots for huge profits, often to far wealthier people, who constructed large houses. By 1988 most houses were selling for between $130,000 and $500,000. A typical three-bedroom house in Seaside sold for about $325,000. By comparison, in the adjacent town of Seagrove, which had larger lots, an identical house was worth less than $85,000.

Ironically, Seaside's commercial success guaranteed its failure as a social experiment. Both Liz and Andres hoped that Seaside would be a middle-class mecca, an alternative to sprawl that characterized so many suburban developments, and an affordable way for children growing up in the 1980s and 1990s to experience the same sense of community that past generations had known. They discovered, however, that it was impossible to build a utopia completely isolated from larger social forces. "We didn't tell people they couldn't fulfill the American dream, which is to make a lot of money by selling your house," reflects Davis. The result, lamented Andres, was that they developed "Kansas and got Oz" instead.

Since there was little they could do to prevent owners from selling their home and making a profit, Liz and Andres decided that the only way to make communities like Seaside affordable for the middle class was by using the market against itself. Seaside became an affluent resort because it was unique; if they increased the supply and gave people more alternatives to choose from, the prices would decline and more people would be able to afford to live there. By the end of the decade, both Liz and Andres, convinced that Seaside was the prototype for a new model of community, set out to spread the gospel of the new urbanism. They left their small Miami firm and formed their own company, DPZ, so they could pursue projects that would promote the new urbanism, even if they were not always profitable. "We always felt that advancing the work was the first priority and not bringing in money to the firm," says Liz. Andres agrees: "We are very interested in the great goal of changing the world, not just building communities."

Andres aspired to be the Fidel Castro of the architectural revolution: a preppie version of the firebrand guerrilla challenging the staid and self-satisfied establishment. He began with a simple but important step: rewriting major code books. "What we are proposing is to get hold of the radio transmitters of America, of the architectural radio transmitters, and do it that way," he told Yale graduates in 1987. Andres volunteered his services to revise the codes, always being sure to include a traditional neighborhood development (TND) ordinance, a generic document that local governments could use to replace the hodgepodge of regulations that produced suburban sprawl. "Andres Duaney's great insight in this matter was to realize that while it was nearly impossible to persuade people to design things better, even if they stood to profit from it, they would happily follow instructions just to save themselves from the pain of thinking," wrote James Howard Kunstler.

While Andres spread the word, Liz focused on paying the bills and training a new generation of architects. The success of Seaside did not produce an immediate financial windfall for the couple. During most of the decade, they supported themselves largely through Liz's salary at the University of Miami and by designing individual houses. "One house at a time," remembers Andreas. "One $4,000 check at a time." Liz shared her husband's passion for the new urbanism, but she did not share his love of the limelight. Cautious and understated, she felt more at home in the academic world. Andres was impatient to lead a revolution, but Liz took a longer view of the process. She saw the university setting as an ideal laboratory for refining her ideas. Andres never doubted the wisdom and righteousness of his ideas; Liz, in contrast, was constantly tweaking and refining, trying to find common ground with critics. She also believed that the key to institutionalizing the new urbanism was to establish a foothold in major architecture schools and to train the next generation. Over the next decade, she helped transform the architecture school at the University of Miami from a sleepy second-rate institution into a dynamic and energetic pioneer of new urbanist thinking.

Their calls for a new urbanism ran into numerous practical problems. Local fire departments complained that the streets were too narrow for their trucks. Builders were afraid their houses would not sell as standard suburban models did. "The development industry is full of legends about people who tried something different and went broke," said a Sacramento County planner. Banks and insurance companies that lent money for projects specializing in either retail, office, or residential were reluctant to fund projects that required mixed uses. Many large retailers shied away from investing in an area that lacked a sprawling parking lot for the convenience of their customers. The biggest problem, however, was that while many people admired neotraditional towns, most still preferred to live in the suburbs. To build in an existing neighborhood, said a senior vice president at Del Webb, one of the nation's largest home builders, was to "run against the market, instead of with it." Many people associated the suburbs with good schools and less crime. "Fear of crime is a great motivator for development," asserted a Phoenix planner. "Everybody wants to be on the far side of the freeway."

By the end of the 1980s, despite the problems, a number of new urbanist projects were sprouting up in cities and suburbs across the country. DPZ started work on Kentlands in Gaithersburg, Maryland. At the same time, it started helping a developer in Mashpee, Massachusetts, who wanted to "retrofit" a standard suburban shopping mall as a town center, complete with a post office, bank, library, church, municipal buildings, offices, and stores. More important, other planners and architects in cities such as Houston and Los Angeles were experimenting with many of their ideas. "The newest idea in planning is the 19th-century town," Andres crowed.

Nevertheless, the Boomers have used their unprecedented wealth to build and buy bigger houses, on more land, with longer commutes than ever before. The typical American family has shrunk from 3.6 to 2.7 people since the end of the Baby Boom, but the size of the American home has continued to grow. According to the U.S. Census Bureau, a typical boomer grew up in a 583-square-foot house. By the time Boomers started buying their own houses in 1970, the typical house had grown to 1,595 square feet. As they started trading up to second and third homes, it expanded to 1,905 in 1990 and 2,310 in 2000. Most Boomers grew up with a large family room, two bedrooms, one bathroom, and a one-car garage. By 2000 they were demanding a minimum of a two-car garage, three bedrooms, two and a half bathrooms, including a master bathroom suite, and expanded kitchen. "We've forgotten what we lived in when we were kids and now we want something always better," reflected a Boomer.

Although they expressed frustration with traffic, Americans showed little desire to abandon their cars. Instead, they chose to arm themselves with bigger, more powerful vehicles to intimidate the opposition. In 1993 there were 7 million sport-utility vehicles (SUVs) on the road. Five years later there were 20 million. The typical SUV owner was a white dual-income Boomer living in the suburbs with two children. As the *Washington Post* observed, "Just as each American age has adopted its signature vehicle—the '50s land yachts, the '60s muscle coupes, the '70s rice-burners, the '80s luxo-sedans—this decade has chosen its own wheels: the sports utility vehicle." Although SUVs were advertised for their ability to climb mountains and cross streams, less than one-tenth of 1 percent of SUV buyers ever take their vehicles off paved road. "You don't buy a $30,000 sport utility vehicle to take it off-road," said a Dodge salesman.

The lesson of Liz and Andres is that Boomers long for community and love nostalgia, but they remain individualists at heart. "If today's suburbs are so awful, why do 60 percent of Americans choose to live in them?" asked architect Witold Rybczynski. "The simplest explanation is that people like living this way." "A large part of what some people call sprawl," said Daniel Fox, president of the Milbank Memorial Fund, "is what other people call affordable housing, jobs, highways that go somewhere and get you there."

SEVEN

THE NEW POWER POLITICS

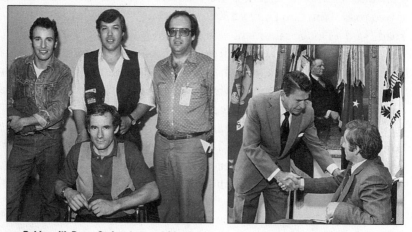

Bobby with Bruce Springsteen and friends;   Bobby with Ronald Reagan.

From Eisenhower to George H. W. Bush, eight straight American presidents were World War II–era veterans. At one level or another, it was the Greatest Generation that entered government after the war and shaped American politics for the next quarter-century. The oldest Boomers could not vote until 1966, and even as they gained a larger share of the electorate in the '70s and '80s, rarely did their vote sway elections. Nor did they have a big impact as candidates The Boomers were not eligible to be senators until the 1970s or president until the 1980s. Yet as Boomers emerged as a major electoral force, they managed to shape the tone, style, and substance of American politics in dramatic ways. Boomers spent their entire lives in the postwar era of television and of national interest group politics. In many ways Bobby Muller and Fran Visco embody the new Boomer political activist.

■

By 1978 there were a number of hopeful signs that the nation was ready to deal with the legacy of the Vietnam War. In Congress a group of eleven members formed the Vietnam-Era Veterans to focus on issues related to the war. The release of two blockbuster movies, *Coming Home* and *The Deer Hunter,* signaled a shift in popular culture. *Coming Home* told the sentimental story of a marine captain who returned from Vietnam a paraplegic. His love for his wife, played by antiwar activist Jane Fonda, allowed him to overcome his bitterness and to heal the war's emotional wounds. *The Deer Hunter* traced the impact of the war on three men from a western Pennsylvania steel town. The trauma of the war transforms the main character, played by Robert De Niro, from a violence-prone loner into a compassionate man who is at peace with himself and his surroundings.

Arriving in Washington in January 1978 as head of the Council of Vietnam Veterans (CVV), Bobby planned to take full advantage of the public's growing interest in the war. He was a master at garnering media attention for himself, his organization, and his cause. "From the moment a TV crew stuck a microphone under his nose, Muller discovered he had a gift for articulating what was on his mind," wrote the historian Gerald Nicosia. "Bobby was a genius in dealing with the media," recalls a colleague. "He was not always the person who framed the issue, but no one was better at selling it than Muller." When he was at his best, "Bobby could sell Madonna on the virtues of being a virgin." Major newspapers ran stories about him. The *Washington Post* greeted his arrival in Washington with an op-ed piece headlined, "Vietnam Veteran Advocate Arrives." Over the next year it published a regular series of pieces supporting Bobby and his cause. But the key to his success was television. He appeared on both network and local television across the country lobbying for an extension of GI bill benefits, including a "tuition equalizer" to help veterans attend college, a tax credit for employers who hire and train Vietnam vets, and an increase in funding for counseling for drug and alcohol abuse. His favorite forum was the daytime television talk show hosted by Phil Donahue. Bobby held the record for the most number of appearances on the show, as Donahue invented the genre that would eventually lead to Oprah and be a powerful force in shaping public opinion.

Bobby's efforts gained a great deal of media attention but failed to produce a single piece of legislation. The indifference inside the Beltway puzzled him. "I believed that if somebody could get the story out and focus attention on the injustice, the government would make it right," he reflects. "I still naively believed that if you simply got the story out, a caring and values-based society would respond." It did not. At the end of the year he had dinner with the editor of the *Washington Post* editorial page, Phil Geyelin. "Bob, what I've done with Vietnam veterans on your behalf is unprecedented," he said. "I have never conducted an editorial campaign as I have for you, and the response has been total, absolute silence. The agencies that we've gone after haven't called. The White House hasn't called. The public hasn't called. Nobody has called." Geyelin suggested that Bobby switch focus, moving away from the specific needs of the veteran and instead "talk about Vietnam in a broader sense, talk about Vietnam in a way that every American, whether they are a veteran or not, can relate to the discussion."

The advice came just as Ronald Reagan was beginning his presidential campaign, emphasizing patriotism and a military buildup. The public was ready to talk about Vietnam as never before. Geyelin's opinion was seconded by a group of opinion makers who met with Bobby in New York to talk about his efforts. Among those attending the meeting were McGeorge Bundy, the former Johnson aide who was then president of the Ford Foundation, and Winston Lord, who headed the influential Council on Foreign Relations. At the end of a long discussion Bundy summarized the opinions of those gathered around the table. Trying to organize Vietnam veterans was laudable and meritorious, but it was doomed to fail. "Vietnam is something that makes powerful people in this country nervous and uneasy," he said. "And they're basically not going to come to you." Bundy suggested that he broaden his agenda to deal with Vietnam-era issues like civil rights and the environment but avoid becoming an advocate for a specific group.

Ironically, the organized veterans' groups were the most vocal opponents of Bobby's efforts. A clear generational power struggle was taking place in Washington among veterans. By 1978 there were more than 30 million veterans in the United States. World War II accounted for 13 million, followed by Vietnam (8.7 million), Korea (6 million), and World War I (689,000). And there were still 333 survivors of the 1898 Spanish-American War. The older established organizations, veterans in Congress, and the VA formed an iron triangle that fought to preserve its turf. The American Legion, with 2.7 million members, was the largest veterans' group. Chartered by Congress in 1919, it included honorably discharged veterans of World Wars I and II, Korea, and Vietnam. The Veterans of Foreign Wars (VFW), organized in 1899, claimed 1.85 million members drawn from those who served overseas during wartime. Unlike the American Legion, which took positions exclusively on veterans' issues, the VFW pursued a broad conservative stance on national security and foreign policy matters. The 575,000 million members of the Disabled American Veterans (DAV) had suffered a service-connected disability. Like the American Legion, the organization limited its lobbying to issues directly related to veterans' benefits. There were other smaller groups, including Paralyzed Veterans of America, with about 14,000 members, and American Veterans of World War II, Korea and Vietnam (AMVETS), with about 200,000 members.

Many Vietnam vets felt unwelcome in the older organizations. "The old line organizations were not very welcoming of Vietnam vets because we did not win the war," recalls Vietnam vet Bernard Edelman. "They looked down on us because we lost." Many returning vets had experiences similar to Rick Weidman, who grew up in New York City and graduated from Colgate University. He opposed the war and once worked as a campaign organizer for Allard Lowenstein, the mastermind of the "dump Johnson" movement in 1968 and later a congressman from Long Island. But when his time came and his school deferment ended, he traded in his khakis for combat fatigues. "I opposed the war, but I believed it was a responsibility of citizenship to serve in the military," he recalled. "Why was my life more important than anyone else's?" After serving a tour of duty as a medic, he returned home and served as a dean of students at a college in Vermont before coming to work with Bobby Muller in 1978. He was shocked at the reception he received, especially among the older vets. Their attitude was that "you didn't fight a real war. We won our war and we didn't kill any babies." He and many of his fellow vets claimed they were excluded from VFW halls.

The older organizations pointed out that there was no policy of discriminating against Vietnam veterans and wrote off the complaints as gripes by a small handful of disgruntled vets. The number of Vietnam vets who joined the American Legion and the VFW dwarfed the CVV membership. In the words of a veteran familiar with the situation: "You know the World War II veterans didn't come out with a World War II group, and there wasn't a Korean group. . . . They used the traditional service organizations and finally [assumed] leadership roles in them."

While there was no open policy of discriminating against Vietnam vets, the fact was that the organizations did little to bring them into the fold. Fewer than 100,000 of the 9 million Vietnam-era veterans had joined these organizations by the end of the 1970s. Differences in style and approach also divided older and young veterans. Muller viewed the split in generational terms. "There has been a generation gap, to say the least," he said. "Their control, their outlook, is still a very conservative, very traditional one. We are not the knee-jerk militarists that they are." Vietnam veterans shared the same heightened expectations, skepticism of authority, and sense of entitlement of their fellow Boomers who had not served. Like many of their peers, they had been influenced by the counterculture. They wore their hair long, smoked pot, and listened to rock music. Ironically, by the 1980s, Vietnam veterans sounded much like the antiwar protesters of the 1960s. They distrusted the government, expressed frustration with the VA, and skillfully used the media to get out their message. Older veterans' groups, which were heavily entrenched in Washington, were more trusting of government, less likely to criticize the VA, and more conservative in their views.

There were clear generational experiences dividing Vietnam vets from older veterans. The average World War II veteran was 26 years old when he was drafted. He returned home to a grateful nation and a growing economy. The average Vietnam veteran was only 19 and returned home to a disillusioned nation and a stagnant economy. World War II vets immediately became a force to be reckoned with, using their wartime service to run for political office. They won a virtual badge of honor that often promised preferential treatment from landlords and employers. Vietnam vets faced a very different world. Five years after the end of the Vietnam War, only eleven Vietnam-era veterans served in Congress. In the words of sociologist Wilbur Scott, the Vietnam veteran "virtually disappeared from public view."

Although they often dismissed Vietnam vets as "crybabies," those who fought in World War II and Korea received benefit packages that were far more generous. The housing and education provisions of the GI bill allowed them to buy their first homes in the suburbs and go back to college to earn a degree. The original GI bill paid tuition directly to the university and provided each veteran a monthly allowance of $75 in living expenses. During the 1947–1948 academic year, veterans made up 59 percent of the students enrolled at Harvard University and filled many of the seats at the nation's finest private universities: 85 percent of the student body at Notre Dame, 54 percent at New York University, and 44 percent at Stanford, for example. Congress reduced the payment provisions for veterans of Korea and Vietnam. Korean veterans received a single lump sum of $110 a month. In 1966 payments to Vietnam veterans were reduced to $100 a month. By 1977 that figure had increased to $310 a month, but it represented a significant reduction in real purchasing power. The soaring price of a house and a private college education meant that Vietnam vets couldn't do much with that. During the 1971–1972 academic year, for example, Vietnam veterans on the GI bill made up only 1.5 percent of the Harvard student body, 1.7 percent at Notre Dame, and 1.6 percent at Stanford.

The biggest issue dividing Vietnam vets from older vets was health care. The VA, the nation's largest health care provider, catered to the needs of the 12 million veterans of World War II. In 1978 the average World War II veteran was 57 years old. As they looked toward retirement, older vets pushed for expanded benefits for non-service-related disability, essentially turning the VA into an alternative health care system for older veterans without private insurance. "The VA hospital system is becoming nothing but glorified nursing homes," said John Terzano, a navy veteran who worked with Bobby. The older organizations flexed their legislative muscle to guarantee cost-of-living increases for veterans receiving compensation and pensions. Vietnam veterans just back from combat, for their part, wanted the VA to respond to their service-related problems and feared that aging vets would compete for their benefits.

Bobby argued that Vietnam vets had a series of health issues that were directly related to their service in Vietnam. There were numerous studies, but definitive figures were hard to come by. A 1977 study at Cleveland State University found that as many as 500,000 veterans could be suffering from posttraumatic stress disorder. In 1977 more than 60 percent of the Vietnam veterans treated at veterans' hospitals suffered from psychiatric problems. Vietnam vets suffered from higher rates of both suicide and alcoholism than their nonservice peers. One of the biggest issues was forcing the VA to recognize that exposure to the herbicide Agent Orange was directly linked to their numerous health problems. Between 1965 and 1971 the United States had sprayed approximately 11 million gallons of Agent Orange in Vietnam as a defoliant in the dense jungle. Although it estimated that as many as 2.4 million vets had been exposed, the VA maintained there was no scientific consensus about the health consequences. In 1979 the CVV sponsored a bill that would have provided compensation for veterans exposed to Agent Orange, and Bobby made regular appearances on Capitol Hill to testify in favor of it. The battle would drag on for years in Congress and the courts.

The CVV adopted its philosophy from a report prepared in 1956 by General Omar Bradley. The central question the Bradley commission report addressed was what a society owes its veterans. It argued that there should be two main principles. First, the highest priority should go to programs that provide medical care for service-connected injuries or illnesses and ease reentry into civilian life. Second, if there's a doubt about a claim, the veteran should be given the benefit of the doubt. The CVV interpreted the Bradley commission Report to argue that the VA should provide first-rate medical care to Vietnam veterans with service-related disabilities. They should essentially have a credit card to be able to see whatever doctor they wanted to see and not be tied to the VA hospital system. That was their top priority. Second, they interpreted the report to say that it was the responsibility of government to bring those who served on parity with those who did not serve. But once that parity was achieved, then government responsibility disappeared. The older groups, Muller complained, "are exploiting the nation's willingness to help veterans to create a massive welfare system."

This position put them at odds with the iron triangle. The VA existed to provide lifelong support to veterans. Every year a member of Congress would introduce legislation to provide a new program for alcohol and drug abuse treatment and readjustment counseling for Vietnam veterans. Every year the American Legion and the VFW would lobby against the measure, claiming they would support it only if the money "shall not be taken from existing funds." As one official observed, veterans were faced with a stark choice: "Hold back the growth of programs for older veterans, or block the development of Vietnam veterans programs. The veterans administration budget pitted the generations against each other and major veterans organizations chose to favor older veterans over younger veterans. That choice condemned Vietnam veterans to a history of neglect."

In November 1978 the older veterans' organizations pushed through Congress a bill calling for a 50 percent increase in pensions paid to disabled veterans. The new system guaranteed veterans a minimum annual income. The catch was that all veterans age 65 and older were automatically considered "permanently and totally disabled." The Congressional Budget Office estimated that the cost of the program would add $2 billion to the $3.4 billion program by 1983. Bobby viewed the legislation as a massive transfer of resources from service-connected disabilities to nonservice disability or, indeed, even to perfectly healthy men and women. "When you broadened the program to include hundreds of thousands of nondisabled retirees into a special assistance benefit, you are severely limiting how much assistance you can afford to provide the catastrophically disabled veteran with dramatic needs." If passed, the program would have meant that 70 percent of all pension beneficiaries had no war-related disabilities. "The VA, more and more, is America's welfare agency in disguise," he wrote in Stars and Stripes.

Initially Bobby had high hopes that Jimmy Carter, who spoke eloquently about the need for reconciliation during his 1976 presidential campaign, would support his cause. But Carter had a different kind of reconciliation in mind. Less than six hours into his presidency he told aides that he wanted to issue an executive order granting "full, complete and unconditional" pardons to anyone who had peacefully resisted the draft or who had never registered during the Vietnam War. It did not extend to military deserters. The move delighted the thousands of largely white, middle-class men who had fled to Canada, and angered just about everyone else. Senator Barry Goldwater (R, Arizona) called it "the most disgraceful thing a President has ever done." Bobby could not understand why Carter would use his symbolic first act as president to honor those who had dodged the draft and not those who had answered the call to duty. "He could have done something different, but his first official act as president was to honor those who did not serve by announcing his draft pardons," Bobby complained to the Washington Post in 1979. The CVV was also disappointed that the president appointed only five Vietnam vets to the top 700 positions in his administration. Bobby urged the White House to veto the massive veterans pension legislation. Although the *Wall Street Journal* and the *Washington Post* supported Bobby, President Carter was in no position politically to oppose the powerful veterans' lobby on Capitol Hill. White House aides complained that the CVV, which they dismissed as "essentially a two-man lobbying team," had "leveled many false charges" against the bill.

The dismissive comment about the CVV revealed another aspect of the administration's view of Vietnam vets. The VA argued that the vast majority of vets adjusted to life at home, and most of the complaints were coming from a small, vocal minority. "These guys are probably the best readjusted veterans of any war we've been in," a VA representative said. "There is an element of guys with trouble readjusting, a relatively small group, and they just don't trust the establishment." The administration cited figures showing a higher percentage of Vietnam vets using their GI educational benefits than the total for World War II and Korea combined, and that those who served had both a lower unemployment rate and higher median income level than nonvets. Bobby complained that the administration downplayed the serious adjustments issues faced by combat vets by including the nearly 90 percent of veterans who served in various noncombat support positions.

Carter signed the legislation into law, and as a consolation prize the administration announced support for a Vietnam Veterans Week beginning May 28, 1979. "No steps we take can undo all the damage done by the war," he said. "What we can do is to acknowledge our debt to those who sacrificed so much . . . and to repay that debt fully, gladly, and with a deep sense of respect." Bobby had given only half-hearted support to the idea, believing that veterans needed to focus on getting basic benefits, not on symbolic gestures. As part of the Vietnam Veterans Week, New York City planned a ceremony to honor veterans on May 29. There had been a series of perfunctory speeches until Bobby wheeled onto the stage and grabbed the microphone. He started slowly, talking about his background, and why he had felt an obligation to fight in Vietnam. His voice became crisp and firm as he related how the government had turned its back on veterans who had risked their lives to preserve American honor. America, he said, had turned its back on Vietnam War veterans because of "guilt, hang-ups and uneasiness." For many people in the crowd it was the first time they had heard Muller speak. "I was standing in the back of the crowd in City Hall Park. You could hear the pigeons fluttering. It was that quiet. Spooky," recalls CVV organizer Rick Weidman. "It was mesmerizing." New York mayor Ed Koch, a former World War II infantryman, was so overcome with emotion that he could not speak (a rare moment for the loquacious Koch).

Although he had not supported the idea, Bobby used the week to emerge as the leading spokesman of Vietnam vets. The *New York Times* ran a front-page story the following day about Bobby's speech. The next week *Time* magazine profiled him. Even when he was trying to avoid the limelight, he still found himself on the front pages. There is a famous picture of Bobby reaching up and shaking Jimmy Carter's hand from that period; the only reason that Bobby got so close to Carter was that he had planned to boycott the affair because he disliked Carter so much, but at the last minute, other CVV members talked him into attending the ceremony. Carter entered the room just as Bobby was wheeling in, and a photographer snapped a shot of the two men.

Despite his increased visibility, Bobby still had no effect on policy. Many in Washington saw the CVV as an outgrowth of Vietnam Veterans Against the War, which by this time was a largely ineffectual group of left-wing veterans with little credibility in Washington. The point was underscored for Bobby when he was testifying before the House Veterans Affairs Committee. The chairman, Democrat Sonny Montgomery of Mississippi, held up the *New York Times* editorial page expressing support for Vietnam veterans. "You know," he said in an exaggerated southern drawl, "some people don't get it. I'm from Mississippi. In Mississippi we tend not to run in harmony with *New York Times* editorials. As a matter-of-fact we tend to run in opposition to *New York Times* editorials." Bobby got the point: Generating free media did little good if he was unable to apply political pressure at key points. He needed to do more than win over the opinion makers. He needed to go into local congressional districts and apply pressure. Five members of the Veterans Affairs Committee were from Ohio, Bobby went to Ohio. He appeared on local radio shows and did interviews for local papers. And those Ohio representatives started moving in his direction. "It wasn't about editorials in the *New York Times*," he realized. "It was about editorials back in the papers in their districts."

In the summer of 1979 he changed the name of the organization to Vietnam Veterans of America (VVA). It was a public relations move: CVV sounded too much like their former enemy, the Vietcong (VC). "It was the same organization with a different name," recalls John Terzano, who would serve as Bobby's right-hand man for more than two decades. The big difference was that it would now be a membership organization. The key to exercising power, Bobby recognized, was having a constituency. He had a board of directors but no membership list, so people questioned his ability to speak on behalf of the 8.7 million Vietnam veterans. During one contentious session testifying before the Senate Veterans Affairs Committee, the chief of staff dismissed Bobby's pleas for changing the VA: "What do you represent, nine people?" Bobby decided that if he was going to have an impact, he had to take his struggle to the grassroots.

All this cost money, and the VVA was drowning in debt. Bobby took out a second mortgage on his house to pay the monthly office rent. To save money, they borrowed photocopier paper from friendly staffers on Capitol Hill. They kept one step ahead of the phone bill by switching long-distance carriers every few months. "The only reason you want me to travel with you," Rick Weidman told Bobby, "is because I am the only one with a functioning American Express card." By 1981 Bobby was ready to throw in the towel—when a series of unrelated events boosted his fortunes and moved the organization in a direction he had never anticipated.

In January, on the same day as Ronald Reagan's inauguration, the nation welcomed the return of fifty-two American hostages held in Iran for 444 days following the overthrow of the American-sponsored government in November 1979. Millions of people turned out for a ticker-tape parade in New York City featuring twenty-three of the hostages. The city hosted a dinner for them on top of the World Trade Center. In addition to their regular salaries, Congress provided each of the hostages with $200 for each day spent in captivity. Vietnam veterans were shocked by the contrast between the way the nation received the hostages and the way it had greeted them after the war. The phones at the VVA office in Washington rang nonstop during the day of the parade. Bobby's mother, who was traveling in Houston, Texas, called. "Nobody ever did anything at all for you when you came back," she says. "And we have one of these hostages here and they gave him a Cadillac. They gave him lifelong passes to the ball games." Terry Austin, an air force veteran in Portland, Oregon, who was in Vietnam from 1969 to 1971, put it bluntly: "What did these 53 people do? They're not heroic. They sat on their cans. Here they come in, they get a ticker-tape parade. No Vietnam vet got that kind of reception. He took the abuse from the American public. People called him a baby-killer, spat on him when he came off the boat."

One of the people who called following the hostage release was the manager of pop singer Bruce Springsteen. The drummer in his original band had been killed in Vietnam, and Springsteen wanted to do something to help the cause of Vietnam veterans. He invited Bobby to travel to New Jersey where he was performing at the Meadowlands. After the concert they sat down for about ninety minutes. At the end of the meeting, Springsteen offered to do a benefit concert for Vietnam vets. The concert took place on August 20, 1981, at the Los Angeles Forum. It began with Springsteen walking onto the stage alone, without his guitar. He told his fans in the packed arena that before he played, he wanted them to listen to his friend Bobby Muller. Bobby wheeled out onto the stage and gave his standard stump speech about how the people who started the war now refused to stand up for those who fought. He asked those in the audience to support the Vietnam vets. It would be ironic, he said, if rock fans, the symbol of the counterculture, would be the ones to "apply the healing salve." Bobby wheeled off while Bruce broke out in a rendition of "Who Will Stop the Rain."

The concert gave the organization a much needed financial boost: a check for $100,000 arrived a few weeks later. "There would have been no organized Vietnam veterans movement had it not been for Bruce Springsteen," Muller reflects. "Without him we would've burned and crashed." He went on to raise hundreds of thousands of dollars and generated tons of media. "Suddenly it was cool to be a Vietnam vet." Within thirty days, Pat Benatar dedicated a concert in Detroit for VVA. Charlie Daniels performed for them. Suddenly money was pouring in. They received funds from the Combined Federal Campaign (CFC), a United Way for federal employees that distributes money to needy causes and organizations. In 1982 they received over $1 million and eventually received more than $2 million by 1987.

During his 1980 presidential campaign Ronald Reagan had referred to Vietnam as a "noble cause," an altruistic attempt to help a "small country newly free from colonial rule" defend itself against a "totalitarian neighbor bent on conquest." Like many of his conservative supporters, the president believed that the "liberal media," antiwar protesters, and incompetent Washington bureaucrats were responsible for America's defeat because they forced the military to fight with "one hand tied behind their backs." Alexander Haig, who served briefly as Reagan's secretary of state, argued that the war could have been won at any of several junctures if American leaders had been willing to "apply the full range of American power to bring about a successful outcome."

The new conservative revisionism of Vietnam found its way into the popular culture of the decade. During the 1970s Hollywood and television often portrayed the military as self-serving, inept, and corrupt. "The bullshit piled up so fast in Vietnam you needed wings to stay above it," Captain Willard complained in *Apocalypse Now* (1979). By the mid-1980s Hollywood was producing a rash of movies about heroic "rescues" in Indochina. A few, such as *Missing in Action I* and *II* and *Uncommon Valor,* performed well at the box office, but none came close to the popularity of Rambo films starring Sylvester Stallone as a tormented former Green Beret who returned to Vietnam to rescue American soldiers trapped in bamboo cages. The superhuman Stallone managed to knife, shoot, electrocute, or blow up a large number of Vietcong and their Russian overlords. In addition to battling these foes, Rambo had to contend with a cowardly Congress, an unpatriotic media, and antiwar protesters who fought "a war against all the soldiers returning." The clear message was that individual soldiers in Vietnam were brave and heroic. America lost the war because of misguided peace activists and spineless politicians in Washington. At the end of the first movie, Rambo tells his commanding officer: "It wasn't my war—you asked me, I didn't ask you . . . and I did what I had to do to win—but somebody wouldn't let us win."

The Rambo movies perpetuated the myth that Americans were still being held prisoners in Vietnam. A 1976 Congressional Select Committee reported that "no Americans are still being held as prisoners in Indochina," and a later presidential inquiry by Jimmy Carter reached the same conclusion. Yet the issue of prisoners of war (POWs) and those missing in action (MIAs) was more about politics than policy. There were 2,477 officially listed MIAs in Vietnam. By 1980 there were 78,751 American soldiers still missing from World War II and 8,177 from the Korean war. Realizing they had found another political fault line in a generation already deeply divided over the meaning of the war, the Reagan administration announced that it would give the search for MIAs "the highest national priority," and it designated April 9 as a national day of recognition for POWs and MIAs.

Beginning in 1982 the Reagan administration brought all the family members of POW-MIAs to Washington every spring. They held private meetings with the secretary of defense and the secretary of state, and the president always addressed them. It was all too much for Bobby. Not only did he see it as a cheap political ploy, but he resented the excessive attention being devoted to prisoners who didn't exist when many of the needs of the real heroes of the war were being ignored. "I don't mean to be callous, and yes, they went through some hard times and I respect that, but never before in war have the people who were taken prisoners been considered to be the fucking heroes," he complained. "It was the guys that went down in a blaze of glory who were the heroes. That all got reversed with Vietnam."

However cynically, the POW-MIA issue worked for the administration. By the early 1980s polls showed that a large percentage of the American public was convinced that thousands of American servicemen were trapped in Vietnam. More important, many Vietnam veterans—Bobby's constituency—responded to Reagan's call. Bobby understood the appeal. He felt that his fellow soldiers were desperate for acknowledgment and absolution, believing they were finally getting the recognition they had been denied when the war ended. The renewed interest in Vietnam brought a flood of new members into the organization. Between 1979 and 1981 membership grew to 2,800. Beginning in 1982 membership increased to 8,500, much of it organized in local chapters. By November 1982 there were over sixty local chapters.

Increased membership was a double-edged sword for Bobby. Vietnam veterans agreed on few issues other than perhaps expanded benefits. "Get any four Vietnam veterans around a table and they'll get into an argument," says John Terzano. "They all relate to that patch of ground, but they all relate to it differently." They disagreed whether the war was right or wrong, whether the United States could have won, and what lessons should be learned. Not only could they not agree about the one experience they shared in common, they were as divided as the rest of the nation by race, region, religion, and a host of other factors. Overall, however, Reagan's rhetoric and the renewed interest in Vietnam brought into the organization many vets who had originally come home and tried to forget their experience. Very few had been involved in Vietnam Veterans Against the War or had participated in "rap therapy" after the war. Many still bore some resentment about how they had been treated, by both the government and society in general, but they had buried much of that resentment and readjusted to civilian life. They joined the organization as a way of getting in touch with other vets and, more than anything else, to fight for benefits that would be of tangible help: expanded GI benefits and better health care. Many were "Reagan Democrats." They questioned the government and may have had different views about America's role in the world, but they were a soft touch to patriotic appeals. "The majority of the organization is made up of working class Democrats," recalls Weidman.

That put them at odds with Bobby and with many of the other national leaders who founded the organization. Bobby not only wanted to lobby for concrete benefits for Vietnam vets, he wanted to address a host of other issues, from limiting American adventurism in the world to pushing for reconciliation with North Vietnam. "Nobody is in a better position to address the question of how to meet military manpower needs or to commit U.S. soldiers anywhere in the world than those who responded when there was a call the last time and have paid the price since then," Bobby told the *Washington Post* in 1980. He had hoped that Vietnam vets would be a "natural check against rampant militarism."

Bobby reflected many of the doubts of the post-Vietnam generation, which questioned America's global foreign policy commitments at the same time that the Reagan administration was reviving 1950s-style Cold War rhetoric and policies. Reagan believed Moscow was to blame for most of the trouble spots in the world, especially in Central America. "Let us not delude ourselves," he advised the American people. "The Soviet Union underlies all the unrest that is going on. If they weren't engaged in this game of dominos, there wouldn't be any hot spots in the world." For Reagan and his advisers, any leftist victory in Latin America would threaten the possibility of another Cuba that could serve as a staging ground for Soviet expansion in the Western Hemisphere and produce a flood of political refugees. Since the administration viewed relations with Central America as an extension of the superpower conflict, it relied heavily on military aid and covert warfare to prop up friendly regimes and help overthrow unfriendly ones. In El Salvador Reagan spent nearly $5 billion in military and economic aid to the beleaguered anti-Communist government. In Nicaragua Reagan committed the United States to overthrowing the Marxist-led Sandinistas. Beginning in 1982 the CIA organized, trained, and financed the contras, a guerrilla army based in Honduras and Costa Rica. Infiltrating Nicaragua, the contras sabotaged bridges, oil facilities, and crops. In 1983, when a leftist government friendly with Cuba assumed power in Grenada, Reagan ordered 6,000 marines to invade the island and install a pro-American government.

Bobby believed that the Reagan administration was making the same mistake that Kennedy and Johnson had made in Vietnam: turning nasty local political struggles over power and wealth into a superpower conflict. He wanted VVA members to travel as neutral observers into Central America, along the Nicaraguan border with Honduras and even into controlled zones in El Salvador. He began to see just how different the organization had become when he published an article entitled "Fools Rush In" in the VVA monthly newsletter. It criticized the Reagan administration for recruiting Vietnam veterans to serve as mercenaries to fight with the contras in Nicaragua. The article generated tons of mail, but it wasn't the mail Bobby had hoped for: His membership wrote to see how they could sign up to go in and fight against the Sandinistas. "That's when I realized that we were clearly losing the battle for the ideology within the organization."

Almost immediately friction emerged between some of the local chapters and the Washington office. The new members and the local chapters wanted to have a greater voice in the organization. Although Bobby wanted their votes, he did not always listen to their voices. He believed that the antiwar movement had failed in the 1960s because it was too democratic and was determined not to make the same mistake. Another name for Vietnam Veterans Against the War should have been "anarchists united," he complains. "We were so fucking democratic that anybody who wanted to say anything was going to be afforded the opportunity to say it." Bobby saw the Vietnam veterans organization as a guerrilla operation that would respond largely to his demands and to his agenda. One of its greatest assets was its ability to move quickly. "If the White House did something, we'd be the first organization to respond. We put out a press release. I'd be available to do media interviews. It was the guerrilla nature of the organization that made it successful." He resisted any effort to give the chapters a voice in the decision-making process.

Bobby was no longer temperamentally suited to the give-and-take of organizational politics. "Bobby is pretty autocratic," recalls a colleague. He had a strong streak of self-righteousness. He knew that he was right and everybody else be damned. He was always the marine charging up the hill. "He simply would not lose," says a former associate. "He was ruthless." He survived on a "controlled rage" that made him more competitive and more driven than anyone else. Once he made up his mind, there was nothing that was going to change it. He had unintentionally created a grassroots democratic organization, and he was no longer relevant. "He was our biggest asset and our biggest liability," reflects Weidman. "He is a great man, and like many great men, he has great strengths and great liabilities."

While most of the membership rallied around Bobby's fight for expanded health benefits and better treatment from the VA, his efforts to push for reconciliation with North Vietnam exposed deep divisions within the organization. On December 13, 1981, the Vietnamese government extended an invitation to Bobby and three others to visit Hanoi. Their goal was to discuss Agent Orange and the American servicemen who were missing in action. The United States and Vietnamese had held informal discussions but no formal governmental meetings about the MIA issue since the end of the war. It was his first time back to Vietnam since that day in April 1969 when he lay on the ground near death from a gunshot wound. As the plane landed, he wondered what his reaction would be. Would he be angry at the people who left him a paraplegic? Surprisingly, the visit produced more empathy than anger. "I was rocked by how desperately poor and stunned by the suffering of those people over there," he says. "The war was over but we were continuing the war through diplomatic and economic isolation of North Vietnam. It was unconscionable how these people were suffering." The vets were warmly received by the people of Hanoi and Ho Chi Minh City (formerly

Saigon). "After all the stuff we dumped on them—20 millions tons of bombs and ordnance—I was stunned at how friendly they were," he said.

On the last night in Hanoi, Bobby told the foreign minister that he needed something to bring back so the trip would be perceived as a success. They organized a final meeting with members of the Foreign Ministry service. Bobby and the other three members of his delegation sat across a large table from about half a dozen Vietnamese representatives. "We need some progress on the MIA and POW issue," Bobby told them. They explained that they had brothers and fathers and friends who were also missing from the war. "Each one of the six guys opened his shirt and showed us their scars from shrapnel or other war-related injuries," Bobby recalls. "We realized that we had so much more that was in common having gone through the reality of that war than we did separating us because of the ideology of our countries." The meeting ended with members of both delegations tearfully embracing each other. "It was a brotherhood," he says. The Vietnamese officials gave Bobby the news he wanted to hear: They promised to return any remains of American soldiers. But there was one provision: They refused to work with the Reagan administration and instead offered to make contact directly with VVA. Bobby thanked them but pointed out that as private citizens, they had no authority to deal with the issue. He told them to work through the government, and they took his advice.

Bobby thought the trip was a big success. That changed when he arrived home to a storm of criticism from other Vietnam vets who accused them of betraying their country by talking to the enemy. On December 28 they held a press conference in New York City, but it was attended by hostile representatives of other veterans' groups. "As a Vietnam veteran, I feel you're a total disgrace," said Albert Santoli, who said he represented seven veterans' groups, including the VFW and the American Legion. "These gentlemen are a fraud," said the president of Agent Orange Victims International. What gave particular offense to some was a wreath-laying ceremony at the tomb of Ho Chi Minh, which one veteran called the equal of "urinating on the American flag." An Indiana VVA chapter withdrew from the organization. Said one local member: "The only thing I want to see in Vietnam is Hanoi from a B-52."

Bobby was typically unrepentant. "We have no apologies," he told reporters at the time. "We know we've got people who want to continue this war for decades. We felt there was nobody more appropriate to end it than four guys who shed blood over there and have the biggest grudge."

While playing up its concern for POWs and MIAs, the Reagan administration was cutting programs for vets. Compared with their peers who did not see combat, Vietnam vets had higher divorce and unemployment rates, were more likely to get arrested, and had a greater chance of suffering drug and alcohol abuse. In 1979 Congress had approved Operation Outreach, providing $12 million to provide counseling for troubled vets. By 1980 there were ninety-one storefront centers offering counseling to vets. Although the centers had a mixed record and had been approved only as a pilot program, they were of enormous symbolic value to many veterans. Yet David Stockman, head of the budget-cutting Office of Management and Budget, referred to the vet centers as "dispensable expenditures," and the Reagan administration announced that it planned to allow the program to lapse. Bobby blasted Stockman, calling him "a 34-year-old draft dodger." There was nothing he hated more than a "chickenhawk"—that breed of animal that was chicken when it was their time to serve, but a hawk when it came to sending other people to fight for their causes. "When I was doing what my country asked me to do, he was safe in Harvard Divinity School."

Reagan's attempt to cut the centers convinced Bobby that Reagan was using the vets as political pawns. "It was all designed to pump up the volume," he reflects. "And it was all a charade." A key symbolic moment took place with the dedication of the Vietnam Veterans memorial in November 1982. The 247-foot granite wall cradled in a grassy knoll of the Mall in Washington, D.C., was inscribed with the names of each of the 58,022 Americans who died or disappeared in the war.

Bobby was at a White House meeting with Reagan a few weeks before the dedication. As Reagan passed by, Bobby reached out and grabbed his hand. He held on tight so Reagan could not get away. Nervous Secret Service agents moved in, but the president signaled them that it was okay. "You know, Mr. President, we're going to have a dedication of the Vietnam Memorial and you've got to come." Reagan never lost his composure. "Well, you know," he said, "I guess you didn't hear but my wife's father died and we're going to have a memorial service." Bobby did not back down. "This is the national Memorial. This is for our war. You need to be there."

More than 150,000 people attended the parade and the dedication. President Reagan was not among them. Yet it was the first time that vets reunited as "a critical mass" that could "do something," Bobby told *Newsweek*. He took full advantage by organizing a series of events extending over the entire week to educate vets and increase the profile of his fledgling organization. The VVA scheduled hearings on post-traumatic stress syndrome and Agent Orange. They came together on a Saturday morning to produce the largest Veterans Day parade in decades. Many paraded openly as Vietnam vets for the first time. Jan Scruggs, who organized the memorial activities, reflected the feeling of most vets: "Thank you, America, thank you for finally remembering us."

By the time the organization held its first national convention in Washington, D.C., in November 1983, it had 14,000 dues-paying members in 126 chapters and a budget of $1 million. More than 200 delegates attended the four-day convention to draft a constitution, pass resolutions, and elect officers. "It was pure chaos," reflects VVA member Ned Foote. There were no by-laws, so initially the meetings consisted of unstructured debate over a wide range of resolutions. Eventually a delegate from a Wisconsin chapter who was versed in Robert's Rules of Order took over as parliamentarian and imposed order on the convention. No one would have confused the VVA with the VFW. Not only was the meeting disorderly, but the delegates wore long hair, some had beads around their necks, and many wore their combat fatigues. "We don't have hats," recalls a member.

The convention elected a national board and voted Bobby Muller as president. The *Washington Post*'s Coleman McCarthy applauded Bobby's election, saying that "no one has spoken out more, traveled more and cajoled more on behalf of those Vietnam veterans who were left behind without jobs, health care, education and—perhaps the deepest need of all—a few words of national thanks." Prophetically, he warned that Bobby's greatest challenge was "to avoid getting too far in front of his membership by turning the group into a left-wing version of the American Legion."

Bobby only reluctantly agreed to call the convention, but once he did, he worked hard to build political support for his election as president. He had wanted to get the convention to pass resolutions opposing U.S. intervention in Central America and supporting normalization of relations with Vietnam. But he knew they would not pass. Many of the chapters tried to push through a resolution that would have limited the organization to veterans' issues. Bobby fought against it and won the debate. Instead the VVA passed a resolution giving its board of directors permission to write position papers on those topics to be made public at a later date. Bobby appealed to conservative members by promising to improve the VVA's relations with the American Legion and the VFW.

The convention was a turning point for the VVA. It legitimized the organizational structure and provided Bobby with the credibility he needed to speak on behalf of Vietnam veterans. A number of prominent Washington insiders attended, including the powerful House Veterans Committee chair, Sonny Montgomery (D, Mississippi). The gathering provided emotional support and a sense of brotherhood to a generation that felt marginalized by society and unwelcome in traditional veterans' organizations. "It was magical," observes Rick Weidman. When not debating resolutions and writing by-laws, groups of veterans traveled together to the Vietnam Veterans Memorial and spent evenings huddled in the rooms watching the PBS airing of Stanley Karnow's series on the Vietnam war. For most, the dramatic moment came when Congressman David Bonior (D, Michigan) told the delegates that they must vow to "never again allow one generation of veterans to abandon another." It was as if the frustration and anger building since the end of the war were released by those words. "The place erupted," recalled Weidman. "Vets stood, stomped their feet, hooted and hollered." That phrase of generational abandonment and defiance became the unofficial motto for the organization.

For the next few years, Bobby focused his efforts on getting a congressional charter to acknowledge the VVA as the recognized spokesman of Vietnam veterans. In January 1984 Sonny Montgomery promised to support the effort in the House. The Senate proved more difficult. When Alan Cranston (D, California) sponsored the bill in that chamber, conservatives established a lobby group to fight it, some dismissing Bobby's group as the "Vietnamese Veterans Association." They were attacked because their constitution prohibited discrimination based on sexual orientation. The VFW opposed them and circulated among members of Congress an article from *Soldier of Fortune* that made unsubstantiated claims that VVA was financed by "strange bedfellows" with Communist connections. In addition the VFW national commander sent a letter charging that "the VVA has done nothing of substantive benefit for the Vietnam veterans that it purports to represent."

Cosponsors in the Senate started dropping off. They needed sixty votes for cloture to break any filibuster and didn't have enough. The bill was reintroduced in 1985. Bobby and a few staff members from his office sat down with the new Delaware senator, Joseph Biden, who told them a story of when he first came to the Senate as its youngest member. He wanted a seat on the Appropriations Committee, and went to Russell Long to plead his case. At the end of every day Long would break out a bottle of bourbon and hold "office hours." "Well, son," he said behind a cloud of blue smoke from his cigar, "you count." Biden wasn't sure he heard him correctly. "What was that, Mr. Chairman?" "You count," Russell repeated. Biden still did not understand what he had said. "I'm sorry, Mr. Chairman. What did you say." Annoyed, Russell spat out: "Can you count son? You know—one, two, three, four. Count! You go count and then come back and we will finish this conversation." Biden explained to Bobby and his cohorts, "You boys need to go count."

They went from office to office, meeting individual senators and their staffs. They rallied their members in states to write and pressure from the bottom. They flooded congressional offices with postcards and telegrams. "I lived on the hill for two years," says political director Rick Weidman. Bobby went to Capitol Hill almost every Tuesday to meet with Jeremiah Denton (R, Alabama), a former POW who sat on the powerful Judiciary Committee. They referred to it as the "Tuesday afternoon rap session." Slowly the tide began to turn. They got their sixty votes for cloture, and the bill made it out of the Judiciary Committee. Senate conservatives John East and Jesse Helms (both from North Carolina) led the opposition on the floor, but it passed overwhelmingly nonetheless.

Bobby was hoping that he would get the legislation passed

before the organization's convention meeting in Detroit. He needed all the political support he could get because he was facing a revolt from the membership. For the first time, he faced two challengers in his run for president. Although only one candidate had a significant following, together they threatened to siphon off enough votes to prevent Bobby from gaining the absolute majority of delegates he needed to win. The challengers tapped into a deep reservoir of bad feeling among many of the members that Bobby was too liberal and too outspoken and that he refused to listen to them. The POW-MIA issue and Bobby's push for reconciliation with North Vietnam were the stickiest issues. "We had some very radical POW-MIA activists," recalls Ned Foote, and they went after Bobby in 1985.

There were also charges of financial impropriety. Bobby had set up the Vietnam Veterans of America Foundation to raise money and fund many of the VVA's activities. Like everything else in the organization, he kept tight control over the foundation, using the money to pay for a wide range of causes. He also used the money to reimburse himself for the money he had lent the organization over the years, including paying off the second mortgage he had taken out on his house to keep the organization alive during the early days. His critics seized on perceived accounting irregularities to charge him with stealing money. The delegates spent hours poring over incomplete and distorted accounting reports to find some evidence of financial impropriety. "We didn't have any money to begin with," recalls a member, "so I don't know how he could have stolen money." The bigger problem was one of credibility: many of the members resented Bobby's autocratic leadership so much they did not trust anything he said.

There was intense lobbying in the months leading up to the convention, and the meeting itself was explosive. On Saturday afternoon, after hours of heated debate and personal attacks, came the showdown. David Christian, a highly decorated Green Beret captain, had been an original vice president of the VVC and a former veterans official in the Carter administration. His willingness to criticize the president cost him his job, but it earned him the respect and support of many working-class veterans. He and Bobby had repeatedly clashed over issues. They were temperamentally similar: both had large egos, loved playing to the media, and were rigid and uncompromising. Christian had left and formed a separate organization, but he still cared deeply about VVA. He came marching into the hall with all of his medals pinned down the side of his uniform—seven Purple Hearts, two Bronze Stars, two Silver Stars, the Distinguished Service Cross, and two Vietnam Crosses for Gallantry—and threw his support for Bobby. "He provided an emotional punch," recalls Weidman. Bobby needed 181 votes for a majority. He squeaked by with 183.

In 1985 Bobby realized the organization was much different from what he had hoped. At the annual convention he pushed through a resolution limiting the organization to dealing only with veterans' issues. "I had created a Frankenstein. I knew that my days were numbered." He announced that he would stay on as president for two years.

The last two years were among the most difficult of his life. Bobby and Virginia found themselves victims of an organized harassment campaign, which peaked in 1987. Bobby kept an apartment in Washington, where he worked most weekdays, and he spent weekends in New York with Virginia. Beginning in 1986 Virginia found death threats slipped into her morning newspaper. She would walk down the street and men would walk up to her, say they were going to kill her children, and then walk away. She got phone calls from people who had intimate knowledge of her private medical records. Bobby could not figure out who had targeted him or why, but he suspected that members of the Reagan administration may have tried to "tune him up." At one point Bobby hired a private investigator, a former Vietnam vet, to uncover the source of the campaign. He ran into one roadblock after another, finally reporting back that the campaign had all the markings of a government intelligence operation.

In 1987 Bobby stepped down as president of VVA, but before leaving he contacted fellow Vietnam vet and Massachusetts senator John Kerry to ask for help in ending the harassment campaign. Since Kerry was heading the Foreign Relations Committee's investigation into the contras, Bobby assumed that he would have good contacts in the intelligence community. The senator organized a meeting between Muller and a deputy director of the FBI. The day the FBI agreed to investigate the problem, the harassment stopped. "Now I'm not saying that the FBI was doing this," he recalled, "but it's pretty obvious that when the word went out to knock it off, whoever was involved knocked it off." Nevertheless, it had a devastating impact on Bobby, and especially on Virginia, who was so distraught by the threats and the invasion of her privacy that she suffered a breakdown and ended up spending weeks in a psychiatric hospital. "She was suicidal," Bobby recalled. "She was very depressed and she cracked." Bobby spent most of 1987 and part of the following year at home in New York nursing Virginia back to health.

■

The conflicts within the VVA underscored the confused legacy of the Vietnam War. Even among those who had fought, there were wide variations in experience. Those who fought early in the war were more likely to have positive views of the American effort; those who went to Vietnam after 1969 were more likely to see the war as a mistake. Some have speculated that those who saw combat tended to be more critical of the war than those who served in a supporting role, but there are no surveys to support the claim. Some Vietnam vets were permanently radicalized, participated in protest demonstrations, and became convinced that America needed to curtail its international adventurism. Some became pacifists, believing the United States should fight only if it were attacked. Still others, perhaps a majority, emerged as hawks, believing that the nation needed to maintain a strong presence in the world.

While they may not have agreed on the lessons, all members of the Vietnam generation came away with a profound skepticism of government. Vietnam accentuated the Baby Boom's instinctive skepticism about authority. Those who refused to fight believed the government had deceived them all along about the nature of the war. Those like Bobby Muller who went to Vietnam believing in the cause were disillusioned by the contrast between the optimistic government reports and the harsh military realities. Later they felt betrayed when many of the same government officials who were so eager to send them off to battle refused to stand by them when they returned. Even veterans who supported the war effort believed the government lied to them about fulfilling the nation's commitment to defeating communism.

The failure in Vietnam, the Johnson administration's duplicity in explaining it, and the exposure of Nixon's illegal behavior in the Watergate affair combined to erode public faith in the integrity of its elected leaders. The journalist Tom Wicker wrote that many Americans had come to look on their government as "a fountain of lies." "All during Vietnam, the government lied to me," declared the journalist Richard Cohen. "All the time. Watergate didn't help matters any. More lies. . . . I've been shaped, formed by lies." A 1976 study revealed that 69 percent of respondents felt that "over the last ten years, this country's leaders have consistently lied to the people." Pollster Daniel Yankelovich noted in 1977 that trust in government declined from 80 percent in the late 1950s to about 33 percent in 1976. More than 80 percent of the public expressed distrust in political leaders, 61 percent believed something was morally wrong with the country, and nearly 75 percent felt that they had no impact on Washington decision making.

For better or worse, Vietnam made the American political process and institutions more responsive to public pressure. It was the cause of Congress's new assertiveness toward the presidency. The most important sign of that changed relationship is the 1973 War Powers Act, which prevented the commander in chief from sending U.S. troops into combat for more than ninety days without congressional consent. Congress expanded the personal staffs of individual senators and House members, enlarged committee staffs in both houses, and increased the research service of the Library of Congress. These steps, though little noticed, represented a significant change in the relationship between the two branches. In the wake of Watergate, Congress passed the Ethics in Government Act, launching an age of limitless investigations—generally but not always of the executive branch—by "special" and "independent" prosecutors. The result has been a chain of expensive and lengthy investigations, from the Keating Five to Iran-contra to the Starr Report. The irony is that American politics has never been cleaner, so free of corruption and graft. But the sensationalized reports of scandal have eroded faith in the integrity of government and politicians.

Changes in the structure of Congress contributed to a new decentralized political system that made it more responsive to pressure from well-organized interest groups. Noted the journalist Robert Samuelson, "Fragmentation. In a word, that is what has happened to American politics during the past 30 years." Corporations and trade associations opened Washington offices, hired Capitol Hill law firms, and retained legions of political consultants to keep track of pending legislation and develop strategies for promoting favorable policies and killing those considered bad. By 1980 nearly 500 corporations had Washington offices, up from 250 in 1970, and the number of lobbyists had tripled. Trade associations opened national headquarters at a rate of one per week, increasing from 1,200 to 1,739 during the decade. "Washington has become a special-interest state," said a government official. "It's like medieval Italy—everyone has his own duchy or kingdom."

The rise of special interests further eroded the power of the political parties to forge consensus among competing factions. "The rise of special interests is directly related to the loss of trust that people have had in the traditional political institutions, parties specifically," noted the Republican pollster Richard Wirthlin. The turmoil of the 1960s, especially race riots and the Vietnam War, loosened the loyalties of many Democrats, while Watergate undermined the Republican claim of being the party of good government. Interest groups moved in to fill the void, but they had little interest in compromise and consensus.

Most Boomers have been turned off. Yet for those who lead a group or care passionately about a particular issue, the new politics can be intense and deeply meaningful.

EIGHT

THE "SECOND STAGE" AND OTHER STRUGGLES FOR WOMEN

Fran with young son David;   and at a 1991 Washington, D.C., rally.

In August 1980 the *New York Times* editorialized that "the battle for women's rights is no longer lonely or peripheral. It has moved where it belongs; to the center of American politics." The movement's success was recorded in education, the workplace, and changing public attitudes. But the movement also faced a spirited assault from conservatives, who blamed it for a rising divorce rate accompanied by soaring numbers of illegitimate births, which doubled between 1975 and 1986. Opponents of the Supreme Court decision legalizing abortion in *Roe v. Wade* mobilized, protesting at local clinics where abortions were performed and pressuring Congress to restrict public funding for the procedure.

The struggle for a constitutional amendment favoring equal rights was, for a time, the single most contentious political issue for women. In 1972 Congress overwhelmingly approved the equal rights amendment (ERA) to the Constitution, which declared in simple but powerful language that "equality of rights shall not be denied or abridged . . . on account of sex." The amendment then went to the states for ratification. Throughout the ratification process, polls showed large majorities of the public supported the measure. The support, however, was broad but shallow. Nearly half of those who supported the amendment said they could not vote for a qualified woman for president. Conservative activist Phyllis Schlafly, the "Sweetheart of the Silent Majority," campaigned tirelessly against the ERA, calling it "anti-family, anti-children, and pro-abortion," and charging that it would promote lesbianism, require women to serve in combat roles in the military, and roll back protective legislation that housewives and female workers cherished. Schlafly's attacks whittled away at support for the amendment and for feminism in general. On June 30, 1982, the deadline for the amendment passed with only thirty-five of the required thirty-eight states having ratified. The equal rights amendment was dead.

The women's movement split on how to respond to the conservative climate. In 1981 Betty Friedan, who had issued a call to arms to the Boomers' mothers with publication of *The Feminine Mystique* in 1963, now spoke directly to their daughters. The women's movement, she argued, needed to move into a "second stage." The goal of the "first phase" was "full participation, power and voice in the mainstream." The "second phase" needed to focus on "embracing the family in new terms of equality and diversity." The movement, she argued, had presented Baby Boomers with a false choice between womanhood and motherhood—between having a career and having children. Boomers benefited from the "first wave," but they were unwilling to settle for one or the other. "From the daughters, working so hard at their new careers, determined not to be trapped as their mothers were, expecting so much and taking for granted the opportunities we fought for, I've begun to hear undertones of pain and puzzlement," she wrote. Many feminists branded Friedan a traitor for giving credence to conservative criticisms that the women's movement threatened family stability. In fact Friedan understood that the Boomers were demanding more freedom and, unlike their mothers, wanted both a rewarding career and a fulfilling home life.

Fran Visco's life was finally shaping up in the early 1980s. After two failed marriages, she went back to school full time, earned her bachelor's degree, and then went directly to law school. In May 1983 she graduated from Villanova Law School and began working as a litigator at the Philadelphia law firm of Cohen, Shapiro, Polisher, Sheikman and Cohen. Fran had always dreamed of being a civil rights or civil liberties lawyer, but at this stage of her life, corporate law made more sense to a struggling single woman with thousands of dollars in student loans. Her personal life was also showing signs of improving. She started dating Arthur Brandolph, a lawyer and old acquaintance. He would soon be her third husband. They were married in November 1984. In June 1986 Fran gave birth to a son, David. At age thirty-nine Fran had a career and a family, after many years of mistreatment and bad choices.

Fran's gynecologist suggested that she have a baseline mammogram when she finished breast-feeding David. On September 17, 1987, Fran had her first mammogram. Later that afternoon she went downstairs to watch a parade celebrating the two hundredth birthday of the Constitution. When she went back upstairs, she found an urgent message from her gynecologist. When she called, he told her that the radiologists had found something on her film. "They're fairly certain it's malignant," he said. He gave her the name of the surgeon and suggested that she contact him immediately, but she could not get an appointment for another two weeks. She called her husband, who represented a number of doctors, and one of his clients agreed to see her the next day and perform a biopsy.

After the biopsy Fran was sitting in the recovery room with Arthur. The nurse walked in, looked at Fran, and started crying. "Oh, I'm so sorry I don't know how to tell you," she said, her words muffled by sobs. Fran's first thought was that this woman was in the wrong job. But her behavior was also alarming. "If she's acting this way, I must be going to die." Afterward she met with the surgeon, who seemed optimistic about her recovery, but Fran had been convinced of the worst by this time. "I didn't think I was going to live to see 40," she remembers. And why now? She had never really had the chance to enjoy life. "I was happy," she recalls. Now she spent every day learning to live with the fear of dying. Her greatest fear was that she would not get to see her son grow up, that he would never know her.

Fran was careful to hide her fears, especially from her family. Once again she was the big sister who needed to protect her siblings from a bad situation. She told each of them one at a time, reassuring them that everything was going to be fine. The last and most difficult person to tell was her mother, who had remarried and was living in Florida. She waited until her mother made a planned trip to Philadelphia, and then Fran gathered the entire family around for added support before breaking the news. "Do you remember when I went to have a mammogram a few weeks ago?" Her mother said, "Oh yes. I was meaning to ask you about that. How did it go?" As gently as possible, Fran responded, "Well, there was a problem. I went to have a biopsy. The biopsy was positive, and I will have surgery on Monday." A trained nurse, Lucy knew exactly what her daughter was up against, but Fran tried hard to reassure her. Always the caregiver, Fran worried as much about everyone else's reaction as her own disease.

Like other women who faced breast cancer, Fran confronted an intimidating array of choices. There had been some modest progress in the treatment of the disease in the years before Fran was diagnosed. At the beginning of the twentieth century the brilliant surgeon and cocaine addict William Stewart Halsted had pioneered the radical mastectomy. Believing that cancer spread to surrounding tissue before entering the bloodstream, Halsted advocated the removal of the breast, surrounding lymph nodes, and chest muscles. The procedure saved countless lives but left its patients with a flattened and sunken chest wall. By the 1950s a handful of surgeons experimented with a modified radical mastectomy, which removed the breast and surrounding lymph nodes but left the pectoral muscles intact. By the time Fran was diagnosed, surgeons tried to remove as little tissue as possible. For smaller tumors they performed a lumpectomy, in which only part of the breast containing the cancer was removed. Surgery was often followed by six weeks of daily radiation and chemotherapy—treatment that feminist surgeon Dr. Susan Love referred to as "slash, burn, and poison." Despite these advancements in treatment, the death rate for breast cancer had changed little.

Fran opted for the less invasive lumpectomy. During surgery the doctor found that the cancer had spread to her lymph nodes, so it was too late to catch it all in its original spot. Doctors were divided about what to do. Oncologists at Jefferson Hospital in Philadelphia recommended a toxic form of chemotherapy, which would cause her hair to fall out. She went to Memorial Sloan-Kettering Cancer Center in New York City for a second opinion, where the doctors suggested a less toxic form. She also had to make a choice whether to start with chemotherapy and then try radiation, or radiation followed by chemotherapy, or both at once. Fran chose to do both at once. "I just wanted to get it over with," she recalls. The dual treatment took its toll. Although she tried to keep working, she was too sick and too tired to make it to the office every day. She needed to take time off. In addition to the cancer treatment, Fran was having trouble with carpal tunnel syndrome, a painful inflammation of the tendons in the wrist. Her friend Rosemary Clark remembers meeting Fran for lunch one day. "I had to cut her food for her because she wasn't able to use her hands. She was helpless." Clark wondered: "Is she going to make it?"

Even after her diagnosis and surgery, Fran had a difficult time thinking of herself as a "cancer patient." She was disciplined and focused enough to keep her mind occupied on the daily rituals of life. But there were occasional, and powerful, reminders. She remembers the doctor telling her that chemotherapy would cause premature menopause, and she would not be able to have more children. "Now I knew what it meant when someone says that my knees buckled. I had never known what that phrase meant." Perhaps the most difficult moment was when she came home from the hospital after her surgery. She sat on her living room sofa and her husband, Arthur, handed David to her. "That was the low point for me," she reflects. Fran had always been careful to keep her emotions in check, to maintain "this facade of the strong, independent woman," recalls Arthur. For the first time in her life, the emotions overpowered her will. She sat for hours crying. She had never been so vulnerable. But it wasn't until she was about to walk into the cancer treatment center at Jefferson Hospital and she looked up at the sign above the door that read "Bodine Cancer Center" that it finally struck home: she was a cancer patient.

She came to realize what millions of other cancer patients and thousands of doctors already knew: the medical profession had few answers for cancer. They did not know why some people developed cancer and others did not. Why some people survived and others died. They had many treatments and studies, but there was no cure, as there was for polio, the scourge of the early 20th century, and there was no containment as there had been for such infectious diseases as malaria, the scourge of the Third World until the 1950s. She started volunteering at the Linda Creed Foundation, named after a songwriter-victim and dedicated to the early detection and treatment of breast cancer. Since it was a new organization, she had the chance to get involved in its early stages. She organized the foundation's visiting business program. Representatives from the foundation, often breast cancer survivors and female health care professionals, volunteered their time to talk to local companies, churches, and social organizations to teach women about the importance of early detection and demonstrate how to perform a breast self-examination. The foundation also provided free mammograms to poor women.

Fran was learning a painful lesson: Medical science had spoiled Baby Boomers. During their lifetimes they had seen scientists solve diseases that had perplexed their parents' generation—not just malaria and polio, but tuberculosis, measles, mumps, rubella (German measles), diphtheria, whooping cough, and tetanus. Cancer nevertheless stood defiant. They had also grown up in a society that emphasized youth and beauty. The treatment for breast cancer threatened to destroy a woman's sexual identity and to rob her of her youthful appearance. It was also the randomness of breast cancer that made it so difficult to accept. Baby Boomers had learned about the connection between diet and exercise and their health. They could reduce their risk of heart attack by exercising and eating right. They could cut down on lung cancer by not smoking. But there seemed no such direct connection between food or exercise and breast cancer. The one clear connection was between breast cancer and age: as they got older, their chances of developing breast cancer increased. Women over age 50 accounted for about 78 percent of all breast cancer cases. Similarly, men were learning that they faced accelerating odds of developing prostate cancer as they aged. Medical science was allowing men and women to live into their 80s and 90s, which, for many, simply meant that cancer would be more likely to catch up to them.

Boomers became adults with dashed hopes about curing cancer. In 1971 President Richard Nixon declared "war on cancer." The National Cancer Act, passed in 1971, called for a $100 million appropriation to launch a cure for cancer. "This legislation," Nixon said, "can mean new hope and comfort in the years ahead for millions of people in this country and around the world." Over the next ten years the budget of the National Cancer Institute grew from $230 million to over $940 million. Nonetheless, the breast cancer death rate increased. "It's really very depressing," a scientist told the American Cancer Society in 1986. "After all this work we don't know much more about the causes of breast cancer than we did twenty years ago."

Until the 1970s women were forced to exchange information on how to deal with surgery, chemotherapy protocols, and diet and develop methods to help each other manage their feelings, with or without professional guidance. The American Cancer Society was the oldest organization devoted to helping cancer survivors. Created in 1952, it established the Reach to Recovery program that provided emotional support to survivors; members visited women after their mastectomies to assure them there was life after the operation. During the 1970s, however, many feminists began clamoring for more professional attention and questioning the traditional assumptions about the way the medical profession dealt with the disease. The women's health movement, which started as hippie free clinics in the 1960s, grew into a national movement in the 1970s as female health activists disseminated biological knowledge, questioned doctors' control over reproductive decisions, and conducted "self-help gynecology" seminars. What bothered them most of all was that medical research was being done primarily on men, largely for the benefit of men. All of the large, expensive studies on cancer and cardiovascular disease had been done predominantly on men or on male laboratory animals. Funding for cancer research showed little being spent on cancers that were of concern to women, such as breast and ovarian cancer. Breast cancer, for example, represented 15 percent of all cancers diagnosed every year but received only 6 percent of the National Cancer Institute's research budget.

Just as women demanded the right to choose in decisions of reproduction, they also wanted a wider range of choices when it came to breast cancer treatment. As was often the case, the seeds of reform were planted by an older generation of women and institutionalized by their Boomer children. In 1977 Rose Kushner wrote a book called *Why Me?* which questioned the widespread practice of having breast cancer diagnosed and a mastectomy performed at the same time. A freelance journalist who bragged that she had once "told off" General William Westmoreland, Kushner decided to challenge the conventions of the medical profession. Diagnosed in 1974, she insisted on a modified radical mastectomy. She became a public advocate for abolishing the one-step procedure and for forcing doctors to consider less invasive approaches to the disease. It was the paternalism of the medical profession that seemed to bother her so much. "No man is going to make another man impotent while he's asleep without his permission," she wrote. "But there's no hesitation if it's a woman's breast." In 1986 Kushner joined with other breast cancer activists to create the National Alliance of Breast Cancer Organizations (NABCO), an umbrella organization for groups seeking information about the disease.

Kushner was often forced to fight alone against the medical establishment, but she found kindred spirits among younger breast cancer survivors. Boomer women were not content with "managing their feelings." They were the first generation of women to attend college and enter the professions in large numbers and were not willing to be treated as second-class citizens. "We were the antiwar advocates of the '60s. We were in the woman's rights' movement in the '70s. We're now getting breast cancer and were not used to being quiet," declared Visco. Boomer expectations of medicine clashed with the practices of a profession that remained aloof to patient opinion. "Unlike their parents who were reverential toward their doctors, boomers will walk into the doctor's office not altogether trusting," said Bruce Clark, cofounder of a consulting firm that studies the impact of generational change on business and medicine. Boomers, he said, make up a group of "tens of millions of irreverent, and cranky, angry and demanding people." Boomer women demanded the same rights in the doctor's office that they had come to expect in the boardroom. "They have created a system in which, whether you call it patient activism, or patients' rights, or informed consent," observed medical historian Barron Lerner, it "now dominates the medical mindset."

In addition to its roots in the women's health movement, breast cancer advocacy looked to another group for inspiration: AIDS activists. The gay rights movement, born at the Stonewall Inn in 1969, continued to gain momentum during the 1970s. Homosexuals flooded into cities such as San Francisco and New York in the '70s and established a variety of support organizations. Between 1974 and 1978 more than 20,000 homosexuals moved to San Francisco, many of them living in the city's Castro District. Many gay Boomers coming of age in the 1970s viewed sex as a political act, an expression of individual freedom that society had denied them. "The belief that was handed to me was that sex was liberating and more sex was more liberating," observed the activist Michael Callen. "[Being gay] was tied to the right to have sex." Tragically, sexual promiscuity helped spread a deadly virus, human immunodeficiency virus, which could lead to acquired immune deficiency syndrome (AIDS). By 1989 gay men and intravenous drug users made up the bulk of the 60,000 people killed by the disease. Nationwide, AIDS was the second leading cause of death among Boomer men ages 25 to 44, topped only by unintentional injury. In San Francisco, with its large gay population, it accounted for 61 percent of deaths among Boomer men.

As the death toll mounted, gay leaders organized to educate the public and to pressure government to find a cure. In New York, the Gay Men's Health Center spearheaded the effort, raising millions of dollars, offering services to the sick, and lobbying Washington. The Human Rights Campaign Fund, founded in 1980, raised millions of dollars to support gay-friendly politicians. At the same time, radical groups like the AIDS Coalition to Unleash Power, or ACT UP, staged highly visible demonstrations to garner research budgets, experimental drug approvals, and greater public awareness. Their slogan, "Silence = Death," underscoring a pink triangle on black, became a trademark for late-1980s protest. Its members picketed Food and Drug Administration (FDA) meetings, brought the New York Stock Exchange to a halt, disrupted Catholic masses, and chained themselves to the doors of major drug companies. They understood that science was funded through a political process and the only way to change the system was to organize and apply public pressure at key points in the process.

Their tactics, though controversial, worked: AIDS activists had changed the way the government responded to public health, accelerated the review process for new drugs, and forced health officials to share power with patients and their advocates. By 1992 the government spent $2 billion a year in federal research, prevention, and treatment programs for AIDS, roughly the same that it spent on all forms of cancer, a disease that killed twenty-two times more people.

AIDS activists had forced disengaged scientists to take into account the anguish and pain of the people they were supposedly trying to help. It was "a new form of constituency advocacy and activism," said Dr. Anthony S. Fauci, director of the National Institute of Allergy and Infectious Diseases, "a phenomenon that clearly will be carried forth with other diseases of the 21st century."

If the women's movement helped identify the problems, AIDS activists provided a strategy for change. "We looked at what the AIDS community had done to get increased funding and increased attention for that disease," Visco recalls. "We wanted to do something similar for breast cancer." Breast cancer advocates believed that their cause would be an easier fight because it was a "more acceptable" disease than AIDS. Therefore their strategy could be more mainstream and avoid the risky, high-profile tactics of groups like ACT UP. But they learned from AIDS activists that they had to shock the public in order to get its attention. Fran's method for getting that attention was to refer to breast cancer as an epidemic, arguing that one woman will be found to have breast cancer every three minutes and one would die from it every twelve minutes. Most startling of all, she claimed that women had a one in eight chance of developing breast cancer. "It's inappropriate to say there's an epidemic," complained the head of the American Cancer Society, who argued that the figure of one in eight was a lifetime risk based on the assumption that a woman would live to be 95. The risk for a 40-year-old woman was much lower—probably 1 in 200.

Many of the early leaders of the breast cancer movement had been directly involved in either the women's movement or the gay rights movement. They were people like Susan Hester, an organizer for the National Organization for Women (NOW) who created the Mary-Helen Mautner Project for lesbians with cancer. She named the foundation after her partner, who died of breast cancer in 1989, and modeled it after the AIDS buddy programs, which provided counseling to AIDS victims and their families.

Another pioneer was Dr. Susan Love. The oldest of five children, she grew up in a Catholic family in suburban New Jersey and entered a convent in the 1960s, but soon realized that medicine was her true calling. She went to medical school, becoming the first female general surgeon on Boston's Beth Israel faculty. Although she wanted to avoid being confined to women's medicine, doctors at Beth Israel kept referring breast cancer cases to her. In 1988 Love opened the Faulkner Breast Center in Boston. Her strategy was always to try to save the breast: "You're born with two and it's nice to die with two." In 1990, she published *Dr. Susan Love's Breast Book,* which became the bible for breast cancer patients.

As Love went on her book tour, she came to appreciate just how angry many breast cancer survivors were and how ready they were to take action. She believed that the middle-aged white men who were making most of the decisions about how money should be spent focused on the disease that scared them the most: heart disease. "The reason we don't know more about breast cancer is that the people making the decisions didn't care enough about finding out those answers," said Love. During one televised debate a doctor suggested mastectomies for healthy women, saying that the breast tissue be removed while leaving a small envelope of skin stuffed with silicone as a preventive measure against potential breast cancer. Love countered that doctors might remove men's testicles and replace them with Ping-Pong balls to remove the threat of testicular cancer. She became annoyed when people told her that she was politicizing research. "That's baloney. It's always been political. It's just a matter of whose politics was calling the shots. People are upset because now the women are getting angry and may want their politics reflected in where the research dollars are spent. I think that's totally appropriate."

Amy Langer, a graduate of Yale College and the Harvard Business School, was a vice president at Lehman Brothers in 1984 when a routine mammogram revealed a small tumor in her breast. Since she was only 30 at the time, doctors recommend that she leave it alone. "Don't be hysterical," a doctor told her when she insisted on having the lump removed. After the surgery, the surgeon came to her room and while staring down at his shoes, mumbled the words *malignant* and *mastectomy.* It was only through a conversation with a friend who lived in Paris that she discovered that European surgeons were routinely doing lumpectomies. After the surgery she applied her research skills to learning as much as possible about the disease. "I was extremely surprised at how little information there was about how to cope with it. There seem to be a lot of drama and personal stories, but very few information resources," she recalls. While volunteering a few days a week at NABCO, she realized there were hundreds of local grassroots organizations floundering around trying to get information about breast cancer.

In December 1990, Amy, Susan Love, and Susan Hester met in

Washington and decided to start laying the foundation for a new organization that would coordinate these local groups into a national coalition to serve as a political voice. Langer used NABCO to contact local
breast cancer groups. "We had the organization and we had a postage
machine. We had a phone and a fax." She sent a letter out to 52 member
organizations and 412 individuals who had recently contacted them.
She said it was time that women organized a movement to change
breast cancer treatment in the United States. She spent $37 on the mail-
ing. Within ten days she had received over $9,000 in contributions. She
took the money and used it for administrative help, calling for a meeting in Washington, D.C., in May 1991.

Fran took the Amtrak down to Washington for the day on Thursday, May 16. She had no idea what to expect. There were probably 100
women at the first meeting, each with brochures from their groups.
For people who were used to struggling alone, it was empowering to
see so many other women dealing with the same issue. That meeting
was to women's health what Rosa Parks's defiance on December 1,
1955 was to the civil rights movement. "I don't remember if I ate that
day," said Barbara Balaban, director of the Adelphi University breast
cancer hotline and support program. "I just remember that room, a
posh lawyer's office where the table goes on like the Atlantic Ocean
and that every quarter jammed people standing, 3 and 4 deep." It was
"like this epiphany," Visco recalls. "I walked into the room, and I said,
'This is where I need to be. This is where my soul is, my heart is.' And
I got involved in the very beginning." It was the birth of the National
Breast Cancer Coalition (NBCC).

They decided that the first twenty organizations that agreed to
be part of the new coalition would make up the members of the
board. Fran had little doubt that she was going to participate. The
coalition hired Joanne Howes, a professional lobbyist, to represent
them on Capitol Hill. Fran helped organize the coalition's first major
effort: a petition drive in Washington. By the end of the year, they
delivered 600,000 letters to President George Bush and Congress
asking that more tax dollars be spent on breast cancer. Fran carried
the boxes of petitions to the White House. She got as far as a locked
gate, where she was forced to load them onto a conveyor belt. At the
time she joked that the boxes would go right through the White
House and directly into an incinerator.

They delivered the petitions on the same day that a previously unknown University of Oklahoma law professor named Anita Hill testified before the Senate Judiciary Committee, alleging that Supreme Court nominee Clarence Thomas had sexually harassed her when he was her boss at the Equal Employment Opportunity Commission. She said that Thomas, a conservative African American, had repeatedly asked her on dates, bragged about his sexual prowess, and made explicit references to pornography. Conservatives on the Senate committee successfully transformed Hill from victim to villain, characterizing her as part of a liberal conspiracy to sink the nomination. Although many wavering senators believed Hill's testimony and voted against Thomas, his nomination survived by a 52 to 48 vote—the narrowest margin for a Supreme Court nominee in the twentieth century.

The public debate over Hill's charges raised awareness about sexual harassment in the workplace. Politically, the affair alienated many moderate women who were outraged by the way many senators dismissed and mocked Hill and angered by the administration's unwavering support for Thomas. "Women will remember where they were when Anita Hill began speaking," declared feminist Naomi Wolf. After the Senate, made up of ninety-eight men and two women, voted in favor of Thomas's nomination, a small group of women demonstrated on the steps of the Capitol chanting, "We'll remember in November." A leader of the National Organization for Women declared, "Women across this country saw in a visceral way that we are not there and they don't represent us." For Fran Visco, the Anita Hill hearings confirmed her desire to organize women as a political force. Shortly after the hearings, members of the coalition had a private meeting with Senator Arlen Specter (R, Pennsylvania), one of the members of the Judiciary Committee who had voted in favor of confirmation. "And we all hated him so much," remembers one member. "But we had to just stick to breast cancer and treat him nicely."

The growing political ferment among women was already being heard in Washington and in medical circles. "This thing was like wildfire," a veteran congressional aide told the *Washington Post*. "It just caught." President Bush responded by creating the first government office of women's health and by directing the National Institutes of Health (NIH) and the Food and Drug Administration to include women in all clinical trials. The NIH chose a woman director, Dr.

Bernadine Healy, for the first time in its history, and the government pledged to spend $600 million over fourteen years for a women's health initiative. A year later more than a thousand of the nation's hospitals established programs specializing in treating women's health concerns. The nation's first peer-reviewed woman's medical journal, the *Journal of Women's Health,* made its debut in spring 1992.

After the successful petition drive many members looked to Fran to provide the fledgling organization with direction. While some board members found her abrasive and aggressive, a majority felt that the organization needed a leader who would be willing to make waves. Visco and her generation of Baby Boom activists understood the new politics of direct action and grassroots protests combined with the sophistication and organization of powerful Washington lobbying groups. The phrase that Visco used over and over again to describe her philosophy was that she deserved "a seat at the table." "We're talking about a disease that affects me. And it's not as though I'm going to just stand aside and trust that what you're doing is in my best interests." There was no one in the scientific process who was advocating on behalf of the victim. "Hell, I am just not willing to trust my life, to turn it over to scientists and doctors. I'm not! So I believe very strongly that I have a right to have a seat at the table to help, to help steer what they're doing."

In the spring of 1992 she received a call from a member of the board saying, "There's a group of us who would like you to run for president." Fran laughed: "That's very nice, but there's no way." By this time she was a partner in the law firm, she was raising her son, and she was working for the breast cancer coalition in her spare time. "It's ridiculous. I can't do it. I don't have that kind of life." But the calls kept coming. Finally Fran said, "I will do it if you promise me it won't interfere with my law practice." Their supporters agreed: "Okay, fine. We will structure it that way." Fran worked out an arrangement with her law firm that allowed her to work half-time and take a 50 percent salary cut. The other half of the time she would devote to coalition work. In fact, she was agreeing to do two full-time jobs. "We didn't see Fran very often," recalls Arthur. "There were many nights when she did not come home until one or two in the morning." She worked most weekends. "It was tough on David and it was tough on me," he says. Some of her partners at the firm also questioned whether the arrangement was working. A senior partner approached her and said, "You have to decide. You're either going to do law, or you are going to work for the coalition. You can't do both."

The decision to leave the law firm was made easier by the generosity of Carol Wall, a philanthropist and breast cancer survivor. Wall and her entrepreneur husband had established the Vance-Wall Foundation to fund programs that focused on women's health and childhood development problems. She thought it was essential that breast cancer advocacy groups work together under an umbrella organization that could provide direction and increase leverage. She was convinced that Visco was both smart enough to provide the vision and tough enough to impose order. "We think the best thing we could do for breast cancer is to convince you to leave your law firm and do this full-time," Wall told Visco. "And we will give a grant to the organization to allow you to do that because we know you're not wealthy. You can't do it on your own." Fran gradually phased out of the firm but did not officially depart until 1994.

In April 1992, the board overwhelmingly elected Fran president, and she moved quickly to consolidate control. At the time the organization was small and fractured, with little central direction. Initially the Washington office consisted of a few rented cubicles in an office near Dupont Circle. Most of the major decisions were made by the large, self-appointed volunteer board. Visco's task was to strengthen the power of the executive while trying to get people who supported her agenda on the board.

The leadership shared a common view that women needed to be more active, but they disagreed over style and strategy and were distrustful of one another and their agendas. "Do you work within the system or do you demonstrate noisily?" asked Sharon Green of Y-ME, a breast cancer support group founded in 1978. Do you lobby in order to achieve incremental change, or follow the model of ACT UP, taking to the streets and forcing change from the outside? Some people believed that the organization should focus on the environmental roots of breast cancer. Some wanted to broaden their base by lobbying for funding for all forms of cancer. A few wanted to address other women's issues like abortion. There were divisions between those who had breast cancer and those who did not.

The disagreements reflect larger differences within the women's

movement. The National Organization for Women (NOW) best exemplified the reform tradition of working within the system. Formed in
1966 to lobby the government on behalf of issues of special concern to
women, and modeled after the NAACP, NOW announced that its purpose was to "take action to bring women into full participation in the
mainstream of American society now, exercising all the privileges and
responsibilities thereof in truly equal partnership with men." NOW
had called for the equal rights amendment, which it believed would
help women win other benefits: equal employment, maternity leave,
child care, and the right to choose abortion.

But NOW had been formed by an older generation, and its
Boomer inheritors kept up that tradition. Younger feminist leaders
by and large rejected NOW's moderate approach and advocated
bolder measures. Many had worked with the Student Nonviolent
Coordinating Committee (SNCC) during the Freedom Summer of
1964 or in one of the student protest movements, where they had
shaped their beliefs about politics and protest. Like others in the
New Left, these women's liberationists, or radical feminists, distrusted establishment political tactics and instead sought ways to
change American culture and build a society based on participatory
democracy. They were not Boomers either, but they were the siblings
of Boomers rather than their parents. Irreverent and eager to challenge prevailing beliefs, they used the tactics of mass protest, direct
action, and political theater characteristic of the civil rights struggles. Some African American feminists joined these predominantly
white groups, but many believed that their white counterparts
underplayed the importance of race.

Whether they were more mainstream or radical, Fran and the
NBCC members shared a common identity as outsiders in a medical
world dominated by men. "The real fights were about power and
process, not about issues," Visco recalls. "There was no trust." But
over the next few months, after a series of bruising battles, she managed to get a number of her supporters placed on the board.

Having consolidated control of the board, Visco started applying
pressure on members of Congress. If the coalition elected Visco
because they wanted someone who was direct and confrontational,
they did not have to wait long to see her in action. On July 29, 1992,
she was scheduled to testify on behalf of the coalition before a sub-

committee of the Senate Committee on Labor, Health and Human Services. It was what she called "disease day" on Capitol Hill. Representatives of various groups paraded before the congressional committee, thanked members for all their support in the past, claimed they recognized that times were difficult, and begged for them to spare a little money for the future. As she sat on the train from Philadelphia to Washington that morning, Visco looked over her prepared testimony, which followed the same model. She also looked at newspaper stories describing how Congress was able to find billions of dollars for the Gulf War. It found billions of dollars to bail out the male heads of the savings and loan scandal. It was, in her mind, "such a male thing." Hundreds of thousands of women were struggling with this disease and they were being patronized by Congress. Visco rewrote her testimony.

Visco decided that it was important for her to make the connection between the women's movement, breast cancer, and Congress's responsibility to provide funding. As she walked to the witness table, she was having second thoughts about taking such a confrontational approach. Hers was a new organization, and most of the senators did not know her. But she wanted to make clear that her organization was different and would not abide by the old rules of decorum. "I wanted to make certain that they understood that this wasn't business as usual." This was a woman's issue, it was a serious issue, and they had better pay attention. "You've found billions of dollars for the benefit of white men in suits who've wrecked the savings and loan industry," she told the committee. "You've found billions to fight a war in the Persian Gulf. Well, we have now declared war on breast cancer and you'd better find millions of dollars to save women's lives." She threw down the gauntlet to senators. "We will no longer be passive," she declared. "We will no longer be polite." For Visco, the testimony was about empowerment. "It means being taken seriously. It means having the ability to be heard. Having the courage to say what you believe should be said. It means having a seat at the table. It means all those things. It's about power. It's having the ability to effect change. Believing you can effect change." The *Washington Post* took note of Visco's confrontational approach, pointing out that she personified "a new generation of breast cancer activists" who abandoned an old "hat-in-hand" approach for more confrontational "in-your-face" style.

The moment was ripe. The Cold War had ended, and many politicians were calling for shifting funding from military to domestic programs. Pundits had declared 1992 "The Year of the Woman," and many politicians were eager to show their support for women's issues, especially after the Clarence Thomas debacle. The coalition's board assembled a few weeks later to consider its next step. How much money should it ask for? The discussion that followed focused on the politics of funding. How much would Congress be willing to provide? Do they ask for a larger amount, knowing that it would be scaled back, or should they ask for a realistic sum? During the conversation someone raised an interesting question: "How much money would it actually take to get rid of breast cancer?" No one knew the answer. So the coalition decided to hold hearings in Washington, D.C., to ask the scientists who worked on the issue to answer the question.

More than a dozen scientists attended the hearings, telling them about the areas of breast cancer that were most promising but underfunded. After the hearings, the coalition decided that the federal government should spend a minimum of $300 million or more a year on breast cancer research. They approached Senator Tom Harkin (D, Iowa), who served as head of the Health and Human Services Subcommittee in the Senate. Harkin had been trying to shift $3 billion in defense spending to pay for domestic programs that would benefit women and children, but there was never much of a chance that his amendment to the budget would pass. A firewall amendment required a two-thirds majority to transfer money from defense to domestic programs. Harkin decided to pursue a clever end run by asking for the Department of Defense to budget $210 million for breast cancer but leave the money under department control. Since the army already spent money on mammography and health care for enlisted men and women and their dependents, this amendment would represent an expansion of an existing program and therefore required a simple majority to pass.

Most Democrats supported the legislation, but the coalition also found itself picking up the votes of previously uncommitted Republicans worried about a potential backlash at the polls to the Anita Hill episode. The House of Representatives passed the amendment on July 2, 1992, by a vote of 328 to 294. The Senate followed on September 23 by a lopsided vote of 86 to 10. While the Senate was debating whether to fund breast cancer research, Fran was in Philadelphia working at her law firm preparing for trial. Late at night her husband called and said he had been watching C-SPAN. She had won: The proposal passed 89 to 4. The coalition had scored its first victory.

The coalition set up a meeting at the National Cancer Institute (NCI), the largest of the National Institutes of Health's seventeen divisions, nestled in a sprawling 300-acre campus in Bethesda, Maryland. Created by a special act of Congress in 1937, the NCI's mission was to perform basic research. Most of the scientists resisted the plea for specialized research, believing instead that diseases would be solved by amassing general information about the way the human body works. "Patience, scholarship and quiet determination are really what matter," declared its head, Samuel Broder. "Cancer cells, I think, are unimpressed by rhetoric, bravado, slogans or hype." Visco argued that the coalition was responsible for getting millions in additional funding and had earned the right to challenge Broder to develop a specific plan for dealing with breast cancer. "We feel we have for the first time ever gotten a significant amount of money for breast cancer research," she said. "What are you now going to do differently?" In a very patronizing voice, Broder said to her that the coalition needed to understand that the NCI was like a large battleship that could not be turned around on a dime.

A few weeks later Fran and other representatives of the coalition went to Fort Dietrich, Maryland, to meet with General Richard Travis, head of research and development for the army. Fran had low expectations. She was a former antiwar liberal who was asking the Defense Department for funding and research for breast cancer. "Who trusted the army?" she asked. "Our position was the Army and the Defense Department have to show women they can do this right. They have something that they have to prove to women and here's a wonderful opportunity for them to do that." Unlike Broder, who came across as a classic bureaucrat, General Travis rose to the occasion. "Ladies," he told them, "I'm going to lead you into battle and we are going to win this war."

Most of the scientists at NIH believed that the new money that had been allocated to the Defense Department would eventually make its way to them. Visco was now determined to see that that did not happen and found herself in the odd position of lobbying on behalf of the Defense Department. Broder's words kept ringing in her ears. She did not want to have to turn a battleship on a dime; she wanted to construct a new battleship. Bureaucracy was part of the problem. Much to the surprise of NIH, the money stayed in the Defense Department budget.

In July 1993 the army started soliciting applications for research projects. It made clear its priorities: the training of new doctors and scientists, new infrastructure for further research, and specific research projects. A small amount of money was set aside for innovative awards for more speculative projects. The big battle for Fran was to get coalition representation at both stages of the review process. In the peer review stage a small group of scientists reviewed proposals in their specialty and made recommendations. In the integration stage, a committee attempted to equalize the scores and establish overall priorities.

On March 29, 1994, the integration panel assembled for the first time in a conference room at a hotel near Fort Dietrich. The army had appointed Fran and Kate Dickerson, who had a Ph.D. in public health from Johns Hopkins, to the integration panel, but they insisted that advocates needed to be included on the peer review phase as well. Most of the scientists resisted the move. "Well could you have them on the peer review panels but they don't get a vote?"asked an army representative on the panel looking for a compromise. "They get to participate but not a vote." Visco was not in a compromising mood. "No way," she declared. "They have to vote." It was a breach into the temple of science, unheard of among past generations who trusted elites to make decisions for them. "It's the people's money and the people have a right to say how it's going to be spent," Visco declared. Hers was a generation that wanted immediate gratification and, in this case, quick answers to a vexing medical problem. They had no choice: Their lives depended on it.

Boomer women were impatient with claims that science was a slow, deliberative process that should not be shaped by interest group politics. "It's the Institute of Health, it's not the Institute of Cell Biology," said political consultant Joanna Howes. They rejected the theatrical approach of AIDS activists, but their underlying premise was the same: "We're looking at issues that are being discussed, and we say, OK, yes that's wonderful, that's elegant science, but what is it going to mean for women with breast cancer? How important is that?" observes a

NBCC leader. Scientists needed to focus on the human toll of the disease. "I think I bring to the table the perspective of someone who wants to get rid of breast cancer," Visco stated. "I don't want to get a particular person funded. I'm not worried about making certain that scientists have jobs. I want to make certain that the money that we fought very hard to get for the scientific community is very well spent and is spent on moving questions about the disease forward."

Their success was registered in the increased support for breast cancer. NIH spent $90 million in 1990. That figure jumped to $155 million in 1992, even without the army money. The coalition lobbied for an additional $210 million for fiscal 1993 budget from the Department of Defense and played a role in increasing NIH's budget by $80 million. The government was allocating over $400 million in research dollars, triple what it had spent in 1992.

Baby Boomer women, who had been raised on the feminist movement of the 1970s, brought a new style and new ideas to the political process. Whether liberal or conservative, they shared an impatience with bureaucracy, a skepticism of authority, and a desire to find quick solutions. They were unwilling to take a back seat, and they demanded a place at the table. For Visco breast cancer advocacy became the women's movement of the 1990s. Like reproductive rights, it was another way for women to have control over their bodies. Viewing breast cancer as a political issue rather than a medical problem gave them a sense of control over their destiny. "You cannot control getting breast cancer," Visco declares, "but you can control the political process."

By focusing exclusively on breast cancer, Visco steered the organization through the turbulent waters of gender politics of the 1980s. In many ways she had helped create the ideal feminist political organization. At a time when the nation was mired in emotional debates over abortion and "family values," the NBCC avoided controversy by blending feminist ideology with a mainstream style. It increased federal spending and oversight during a time of conservative resurgence and government retrenchment. Most of its leaders had been shaped by the antiwar movement of the 1960s and the women's movement of the 1970s, but they built coalitions with the Defense Department and with powerful conservative men on Capitol Hill. The daughters of the first generation of feminists had grown up, and they were flexing their political muscle in ways their mothers would never have imagined.

NINE

THE NEW FUNDAMENTALISM

Alberta and Mom;   with husband Woody.

Political and cultural historians have often simplistically characterized the Boomers as liberal. They are not. They are both liberal and conservative, but united in other ways: they are insistent on freedom, suspicious of government, and, when engaged in politics, extremely energetic.

Not surprisingly, memories of the 1960s are as polarized as the decade itself. Hollywood often presents romanticized images of idealistic youngsters rising up to confront the evils of racism and imperialism. Conservatives, in contrast, demonize the student uprising, complaining that it initiated an erosion of individual responsibility and respect for authority. "The free-sex, free-speech, free-drugs movement [was] profoundly wrong historically, and in the long run it's an important explanation of how American was weakened," declared former House speaker Newt Gingrich (R, Georgia). Both perspectives oversimplify the decade and, more important, miss the thread connecting the New Left and New Right. "The truth is that everyone today, the right as much as the left, stands on the ground of the sixties," observed sociologist Todd Gitlin.

While they pursued very different agendas, both shared a moralistic style, a disdain for Washington, and a desire to transform the culture. Ironically, both used antiestablishment rhetoric even as they became part of the establishment. They appealed to the same group, but at different stages in the life cycle. Rebellious Boomers and their older siblings provided emotional support to '60s protesters even if they did not always participate in their demonstrations. The same was true in the 1980s. Now older, with mortgages to pay and young mouths to feed, Boomers who never considered themselves members of an organized conservative movement often sympathized with their critique of big government. Alberta Haile demonstrates how this can be true from both the left and the right of center.

■

Since her born-again experience in 1976, Alberta had been looking for a way out of the cycle of sex and drugs that had defined her life since high school. As much as she wanted to change, she lacked the willpower. She was often overcome with grief at the thought of her daughter. Alcohol seemed to dull the pain. She was in a relationship with a man who was incapable of providing her with the emotional support that she needed, so she found herself sleeping with other men, trying to fill a vacuum of intimacy. She desperately wanted to meet someone who would help set her on the right track.

In the spring of 1980, Alberta spotted Woodrow "Woody" Wilson, a navy boiler technician on shore duty at the Philadelphia Navy Yard. A native of Pittsburgh, Woody had joined the navy in 1974, just a few years after graduating from high school. After spending five years in San Diego, he asked to be transferred back to the East Coast to be closer to his family. He had been working security for just a few months at the naval hospital when Alberta spotted him eating in a local restaurant with a couple of female friends. He showed little interest. "I wasn't hurting for women," he recalls. But Alberta did not give up. When he left the restaurant, she noticed that his hair pick had fallen out of his pocket. She put the pick in an envelope with a note asking him for a date and had it delivered to him at his office in the hospital.

Woody accepted, and they decided to meet at Zabers, a popular Philadelphia nightspot. There was only one complication: Woody brought along his girlfriend. Alberta was undeterred. Over the course of the dinner she overwhelmed Woody with her warmth and her personality. After dinner, Woody asked Alberta if he could give her a ride home. She accepted, and Woody asked her to sit in the front seat next to him. His girlfriend exploded in tears and refused to get into the back seat, insisting instead on taking a bus home. Woody had arrived with one girlfriend and returned home with a different one.

After their first date, word spread around the hospital that "Jimmy's woman" had been out with another man. Jimmy, who stood nearly 6 feet 5 inches, was waiting for Woody the next morning when he showed up for work. "I don't want to have to take you out of here," he warned, and stormed away. Jimmy went directly to Alberta and said they needed to talk. "He got me in his car and beat me up terribly," Alberta recalls. While speeding along the expressway, he gripped the steering wheel with one hand and used the other to punch her with a closed fist. She tried forcing her way out of the car, but he grabbed and pulled her back. "My face was so swollen and bruised that I was unable to work for two weeks," she recalls.

The incident ended her relationship with Jimmy. Alberta obtained a restraining order to keep him at a distance while she pursued her relationship with Woody. They were together almost every night. Three months later they were engaged. On Christmas Eve 1980, they married in a small wedding in the chapel at the Philadelphia Naval Hospital. Alberta wore a baby blue gown, because she did not feel deserving of virgin white. After the wedding they moved into an apartment in Yeaden, a working-class, racially mixed suburb of Philadelphia. She was 26 years old and finally lived in her own apartment. Woody had saved a bit of money, so they bought new furniture, including a bar and stools.

Over the next few years they moved from suburban Philadelphia to San Diego, where she joined the Mount Erie Baptist Church. It was during those years that Alberta became serious about her "walk with the Lord." Much of her life revolved around the church. During the day she worked at the naval hospital, but her evenings and weekends were devoted to church activities. Wednesday evenings were devoted to Bible study and prayer groups. On other nights she sang in the choir or participated in a women's group. On Saturdays she participated in church outreach programs, often going into poor black neighborhoods, knocking on doors, and trying to "spread the word." Her Sunday evening Bible classes had the greatest impact. Pastor Greg Morgan formed the Bible Training Union, a small group of local ministers, usually less than a dozen, who met every week in a small classroom at the church to talk about theology. Alberta attended the sessions every week, actively participating in the discussions. "Alberta was more studious than some of the ministers in the class," recalls Morgan.

In Bible class, Alberta expressed interest in the practical aspects of theology. She was constantly trying to take abstract discussions about salvation and grace into practical situations. "How do we live our lives day in and day out?" was the question she returned to over and over again. "How do I fit the Bible into my life?" It was a hard question for someone still going out on Friday and Saturday nights, drinking heavily, occasionally dabbling in drugs. The more she studied the Bible, however, the more difficult it was for her to justify the way she was living her life. "I just can't keep living this way," she told Pastor Morgan.

Finally, after years of abuse, she changed. She stayed home on the weekends. She stopped drinking and doing drugs. The problem was that Woody was not changing with her. "Part of her struggle was her love for Woody," reflects Pastor Morgan. "They were not only husband and wife, they were buddies. They were party buddies. They were drinking buddies. And now, one of the partners was saying 'I am no longer going to do this. And not only that, but you should not be doing it either.' " Woody resented that he lost his drinking buddy and that she was preaching to him that he had to change. He assumed that religion was just another one of Alberta's flings. She had been a Black Panther and a flower child. How long could this "religion thing" last?

Since his job required him to travel on navy ships for six months at a time, Woody hoped that when he came back, she would have "snapped out of this thing." She did not; if anything, she grew more committed and more intense. She was spending all of her spare time on church activities—singing in the choir, teaching in the youth fellowship. She wanted to quit her job as a clerk at the naval hospital and devote herself full time to studying the Bible, but it was financially unfeasible. When he was home, Woody went out on weekends by himself. Emotionally they were growing apart. "All of a sudden she broke away from me," Woody reflects.

By 1988, Alberta had become deeply suspicious that Woody was having an affair. He was away half the year, and when he was in town, he stayed out late at night, often stumbling home early the following morning. She would wait up for him. It got to the point where most of their time together was spent fighting. One day when she went searching through his drawers, she found proof: a letter from a mistress. The relationship had apparently been going on for years. She confronted him and began proceedings for divorce. She gave him an ultimatum: either he turn his life over to God, or their marriage was over. Reluctantly, he agreed; he started attending church and gradually tamed his social life.

By this time Alberta and Woody had moved from San Diego to Virginia Beach, Virginia. Alberta wanted to return to the East Coast to be closer to her parents. Her father's health was declining, and she was hearing rumors that her mom's drinking had grown worse. She wanted to return to Philadelphia, but Woody preferred Virginia Beach. "Without discussion, Woody chose Virginia and I am so glad that he did," she later recalled. Alberta decided that she was ready to quit working and attend Bible college full time, so she enrolled at Tabernacle Baptist Bible College. She continued to attend services at the First Lynn Haven Baptist Church, a predominantly African American church in town. There was something missing from the church, however. People showed up on Sundays for services, but they were not interested in reading the Bible or necessarily living a Christian life during the week. The students at Tabernacle would tease her, "What are you doing at that liberal church?" The point struck a nerve when Virginia faced a referendum to decide whether to allow legalized gambling. Tabernacle opposed the measure, viewing gambling as a moral vice that would undermine families. She appealed to the church pastor at First Lynn Baptist to take a stand on the issue. Instead, on the Sunday before the vote, the pastor spoke about a referendum on the environment. Alberta sat in her seat realizing that she no longer belonged in the church. "I had to do everything I could to stay seated and not walk out during the service." She came to understand that being a good Christian meant also being a good citizen. When the referendum passed, she blamed Christians for not mobilizing against it. Shortly afterward, she left the church and joined Tabernacle.

The move to Tabernacle was a dramatic step. For one thing, it was a predominantly white church. Historically, black and white Baptists have read the same Bible and worshiped the same God, but rarely did they share the same pews. The predominantly white Southern Baptist Convention, the largest Protestant denomination in the nation, was formed in 1845 by southerners whose support of slavery provoked a North-South split among Baptists. Most black churches belonged to the National Baptist Convention, U.S.A. Then there were dozens of independent Baptist churches like Tabernacle that refused to join any conference. Alberta had spent her entire religious life in black churches in Philadelphia, San Diego, and during her first year in Virginia. Her San Diego pastor was surprised when he learned that Alberta had joined a white church since she had always expressed a love for the style of black preaching.

Not only was Tabernacle predominantly white; it practiced a rigid form of fundamentalism that had developed at the end of the nineteenth century in response to liberal efforts to reconcile the Bible with scientific truths. In 1902 a group of conservative theologians set down their unwavering belief in scriptural truth in twelve volumes called "The Fundamentals." They identified five "essentials of the faith": acceptance of the infallibility of Scripture, belief in Christ as God, recognition that Christ died for our sins, and acknowledgment that Christ died on the cross and that he will return in the Second Advent. By the 1920s fundamentalism had gained broad appeal in its challenge to secular humanism. In 1925 the battle culminated in "a one-horse Tennessee village," as H. L. Mencken described it, when John Scopes went on trial for teaching evolution at a local high school. Scopes was found guilty and fined $100 in the first trial ever broadcast live on radio, but fundamentalism was the big loser. Famed attorney Clarence Darrow, who defended Scopes, made a monkey out of perennial Democratic presidential nominee William Jennings Bryan, who opposed him.

In a dramatic moment, Darrow called Bryan to the witness stand as an expert on science and religion and humiliated him by getting him to declare that a big fish had swallowed Jonah, that Eve was literally created from Adam's rib, and that all the fish and animals in the world had escaped on Noah's ark in 2348 B.C. The hundreds of reporters who covered the trial mocked Bryan's literal interpretation of the Bible. Embarrassed by the episode, fundamentalists shunned the public arena for the next fifty years. Withdrawing from the mainstream, they built their own schools, churches, clubs, and recreation centers. Believing the world was corrupt, they adopted a separatist approach, believing they should be in the world but not of the world.

No one embraced that philosophy more passionately than Tabernacle's founder, Pastor Rod Bell. Born in a coal mining region of Appalachia in West Virginia in the early days of the Depression, Bell grew up in a family troubled by poverty and alcohol. In 1953 he married his high school sweetheart, but his life soon fell apart after their first child died shortly after birth. In the midst of his personal crisis, a minister came to his house and preached "the Gospel story." "And that night," he recalled, "I accepted Christ as my Savior." The following year, in 1958, he enrolled at Bob Jones University in Greenville, South Carolina. The first Bob Jones (there would be three, with Bob Jones III still running the school today), the evangelist son of an Alabama sharecropper, had founded the university in 1927, a few years after the Scopes trial, to combat "all atheistic, agnostic, pagan . . . adulterations of the Gospel." Under the leadership of Jones and his three children, the university served as a bastion of militant fundamentalism. Rejecting secular influences and refusing to compromise its doctrinal integrity, it lashed out at Catholics, liberal evangelicals, and secular politicians who challenged the infallible wisdom of the Bible. Students attending the university abided by strict rules governing behavior, including a ban on interracial dating.

In 1967 Bell moved his family to Virginia Beach and established the Tabernacle Baptist Church, which he expanded over the next few years to include a day school, a high school, a Bible college, and a seminary. "I feel I must reproduce myself," he exclaimed. "That is why I have my own school, my own Bible college, my own seminary." Practicing the biblical teachings of separation as stated in Ephesians 5:11—"Have no fellowship with the unfruitful works of darkness, but rather reprove them"—independent churches refused to participate in associations with Protestants, Catholics, or other church groups that did not share their belief in the "inerrancy" of the Bible. They interpret every word in the Bible literally: The garden of Eden was a real place where Adam and Eve had lived; all animal life descended from Noah's Ark. Bell fought numerous battles with Southern Baptists who objected to having an independent church in the area, with Catholics who objected to his criticism of the pope and his close friendship with Irish Protestant leader Ian Paisley, and with popular evangelicals like Billy Graham. Bell condemned Graham's "ecumenical compromise with the Liberals, Charismatics, and New Evangelicals" as a "curse" to biblical Christianity.

Bell reserved most of his ire, however, for gay rights activists and ERA supporters for perverting God's word and undermining the traditional structure of the family. The problem was that these issues intersected in some way with government power: gay rights activists applied to the city of Virginia Beach for recognition of Gay Pride Day, which put them in the political arena; ERA supporters were trying to pass an amendment to the Constitution mandating equal rights for women. Bell believed in the absolute separation of church and state, but liberal reformers were now using the state to encroach on religious turf. When in 1978, Virginia passed a law requiring all schools, including private religious schools, to apply for a licence to operate, Bell declared war. Over the next decade he spearheaded a legal battle to have the statute overturned.

Bell's growing political activism reflected the massive movement of conservative fundamentalists into politics. At the same time that Virginia was requiring that independent Baptist schools submit to state regulations, the federal government began clamping down on the tax-exempt status of church-operated schools. In their mind the federal government, and the liberals who staffed it, had declared war on religious freedom in America. The opening salvo had been fired in 1962 when the Supreme Court outlawed prayer in the schools, and it continued with decisions legalizing contraception and abortion. Paul Weyrich, a conservative political strategist, described the battle between the conservative pro-family forces and liberals as "the most significant battle of the age-old conflict between good and evil, between the forces of God and the forces against God, that we have seen in our country."

Despite their doctrinal disagreements, most fundamentalists shared a common political agenda, insisting that only religion and a return to "traditional values" could repair America's moral fabric. At the same time that Bell was organizing independent churches into the Congress of Fundamentalists, conservatives were leading a coup against the moderate leadership of the Southern Baptist Convention (SBC). "Moral and social disintegration surround us on every side, produced by the profound moral and sexual revolutions of the past three decades," said the SBC's Richard Land. "The family in America is increasingly dysfunctional as it reels under the impact of societal blows and pagan parental behavior." Fundamentalists blamed themselves for the problems, claiming their withdrawal from public life created a moral vacuum that the liberals filled. "The withdrawal for too many years by too many evangelicals from society and political engagement has led to many of our nation's problems," he said. "I believe that if there was more hell preached in the pulpits, there would be less hell in our schools, and less hell in the streets and less hell in the homes," Land told his fellow ministers.

Religious fundamentalists found common ground with prominent neoconservative intellectuals, mainly ex-liberals who had soured on government activism. A neoconservative, observed the social critic Irving Kristol, was a liberal who had been mugged by reality. Although they were often funded by wealthy philanthropists and well-connected conservative think tanks, neoconservatives fashioned themselves as intellectual rebels assaulting the citadel of liberal orthodoxy. At the heart of their critique was the charge that many governmental programs of the '60s, designed to alleviate poverty and assist the working poor, had backfired. "Our efforts to deal with distress themselves increase distress," observed the sociologist Nathan Glazer. In an influential essay, "The Limits of Social Policy," Glazer argued that government welfare programs too often preempted the function of family, church, school and neighborhood organizations, and thus perpetuated the social dependency they sought to resolve. "I am increasingly convinced," he wrote, "that some important part of the solution to our social problems lies in traditional practices and traditional restraints."

In addition to New Right disciples and disgruntled former liberals, the conservative revival of the 1970s included millions of Americans angry over rising taxes. "You are the people," declared Howard Jarvis, a seventy-five-year-old curmudgeon who led the crusade for California's Proposition 13 in 1978, "and you will have to take control of the government again or else it is going to control you." Proposition 13, a referendum that voters approved by a two-to-one margin, cut local property taxes by nearly 60 percent and prevented the easy passage of new taxes. "This isn't just a tax revolt," insisted

President Carter's pollster, Pat Caddell. "It's a revolution against government." The success in California emboldened tax reformers in other parts of the country. A dozen states followed California's lead, though most chose more moderate measures. Only two states—Idaho and Nevada—passed Prop 13 look-alikes.

Two powerful currents carried the tax revolt. First, between 1960 and 1980, federal, state, and local taxes increased from less than 24 percent to more than 30 percent of the gross national product. The burden often fell heaviest on traditional Democratic constituencies—working-class families and elderly people on fixed incomes. Second, while taxes kept rising, Americans were losing faith in government and the way it spent tax dollars. Poll after poll showed that a majority of Americans believed that government was wasteful and inefficient. By the 1970s many Democrats showed their anger by abandoning their party and joining forces with conservatives.

Losing faith in government did not necessarily translate into increased faith in God, but the antigovernment message was a powerful way for religious believers to rally against political immorality. The best known of the politically active preachers was Jerry Falwell. By the late 1970s Falwell decided that it was no longer possible for Christians to stay out of politics. In 1979 he formed the Moral Majority, a broad coalition of "Catholics, Jews, Protestants, Mormons, Fundamentalists" united by the common goal of returning the United States to "moral sanity." For Falwell the political possibilities gained by forging an alliance with conservative Catholics, Jews, and Mormons outweighed the doctrinal differences that separated them. To spread the word, Falwell combined old-time religion with the most sophisticated computer technology, targeting potential contributors and lobbying for political candidates who shared his conservative views. "Get them saved, baptized, and registered," Falwell advised his ministerial colleagues. Abandoning any pretense of nonpartisanship, Falwell became a regular visitor at the Reagan White House, prayed at Republican meetings, and helped draft the party's 1984 platform. He called Reagan and Vice President Bush "God's chosen instrument for the regeneration of the country."

Rod Bell and other members of the Tabernacle community agreed with Falwell on just about every major public policy issue, but they disagreed on tactics. Bell refused to compromise his doctrinal purity to build political coalitions with members of other faiths, especially Catholics. "We will not do anything to build the one world church of Rome," Bell declares. Falwell, like Billy Graham before him, allowed his politics to get in the way of his religion. "He overstepped his bounds," Bell complains. "You don't compromise your beliefs in order to build coalitions." Not only did Falwell reach out to other faiths, Bell believed that he softened his views on issues like homosexuality in order to make himself more acceptable to the public. What angered him most of all, however, was Falwell's habit of referring to people of little or no faith as "brother." "If a man doesn't believe in the virgin birth of Christ," Bell declared, "I am not going to call him brother."

Alberta found in the strict fundamentalism of Tabernacle the certainty and structure that had always been absent from her life. She discovered rules to live by and clear guidelines of right and wrong behavior. For years, Alberta had been overwhelmed by choices. Traditional institutions that provided people with guidance—family, church, school—had been absent in her life. Her mother was rarely home and sober; her father was physically present but emotionally distant. She grew up in a culture of alcohol and drugs. In her search for escape she had tried militancy, sex, and drugs. In 1976 she had turned toward the church, and now her religious devotion was evolving from a vague belief to a literal reading of the Bible. She sacrificed her freedom in order to be free from chaos.

For fundamentalists, the assault against secular humanism was a war against the manifestations of Boomer culture—the emphasis on individualism and self-fulfillment and the expansion of individual rights, often sanctioned by government power. At the heart of the fundamentalist critique was a belief that modern culture blurred the line between right and wrong. The problem with Boomers began with the child-centered parenting of their parents. Dr. Carl Bieber, principal of the Tabernacle school, claimed there were two schools of parenting. The first and only acceptable one was the "philosophy of indoctrination," which "is the acceptance of a system of beliefs or values which is deemed worthy to be instilled involuntarily into the next generation." For Christians, these values came directly from God and were written in the Bible. The other approach, the "philosophy of choice," represented "the acceptance of the belief that there are no absolute values or beliefs." Satan was its chief advocate. Raised on the doctrine of choice, Boomers grew up demanding more choices and a wider range of individual rights, ignoring biblical rules for individual behavior. The women's movement and gay rights, perhaps the Boomer's most significant social contribution, were in clear violation of biblical teachings. Fundamentalists cited Ephesians 5:22–24—"The husband is the head of the wife, even as Christ is head of the church"—to prove that women's liberation went against holy writ. Passages from Leviticus supported their contention that homosexuality was a sin.

As much as fundamentalism represented a backlash against the Boomer culture, however, it also accommodated many aspects of modern culture. For one thing, fundamentalists abandoned their long-standing policy of distancing themselves from politics and mobilized for change, developing grassroots organizations and media strategies that were the envy of Washington interest groups. Although fundamentalists called for the reassertion of authority, they viewed themselves as revolutionaries fighting against the entrenched bureaucracy of both established religious denominations and liberal political elites. Like the counterculture they despised, conservative preachers viewed themselves as a persecuted minority outside the mainstream of American society. Their goal was not just to change institutions but to transform the culture.

While pleading for a return to traditional cultural values, they often preached a prosperity theology that promised both material gain in this world and eternal salvation in the next. "You sow it, God will grow it," Oral Roberts told his flock. "Instead of preaching for a better people or a better world," noted a critic, television preachers "pander to the worst excesses of consumerism." Robert Schuller called his church "a shopping center for God" and told audiences that "God wants you to succeed." Most fundamentalists lived austere lives, but a few of the television preachers made millions off their congregations and lived extravagantly with luxury houses, cars, and airplanes. Before being sent to prison for defrauding investors, Jim Bakker owned six houses, including one with gold-plated bathroom fixtures and an air-conditioned dog house.

In their never ending search for self-fulfillment and dogged expansion of individual rights, Baby Boomers blurred the line separating private and public behavior. During the 1970s feminists argued that the "personal was the political," forcing a reluctant public to address previously taboo subjects: rape, domestic violence, and abortion. Fundamentalists took that approach one step further, claiming that morality was also political. Liberals had used government power to "democratize" morality, allowing abortion by choice and ending mandatory school prayer. The left had breached the wall separating church and state. Now religious conservatives had to overcome their own distaste of the political to repair the damage.

Religious conservatives created powerful pressure groups to further their agenda. By 1982 Falwell's Moral Majority bragged a mailing list of 850,000 households. In 1989, the same year that Falwell shut down the Moral Majority, 31-year-old Ralph Reed built the Virginia-based Christian Coalition from the ruins of televangelist Pat Robertson's failed presidential campaign the previous year. Over the next few years, he transformed the group into the premier conservative lobbying group, boasting 1.7 million members in 2,000 local chapters. He expanded the organization by appealing to the anxiety of suburban Baby Boom couples who, in Reed's words, "probably went through a period of youthful rebellion, or youthful exploration, and drifted away from their church or synagogue and chased their career. Then they fell in love and they got married and they had babies. And then all of a sudden, one day they wake up and their kids are asking them questions about sex. And right then, their whole value system changed."

As Reed's observation suggests, the culture war of the 1980s was in many ways a Boomer war—the outgrowth of a generation at war with itself. The conflict between individual expression and moral righteousness, which had deep roots in the nation's past, found expression in the 1980s in battles over family values, abortion, and gay rights. Just as Vietnam had fractured the generation into numerous groups, the response to the cultural upheaval of the 1960s divided Boomers into rival camps of the nonreligious, the vaguely spiritual, and the religiously committed. The historian Wade Clark Roof divided Boomers into three categories. "Dropouts," who made up about one-third of the generation, were often raised in religious households but left behind any religious preferences in their early adult years. They tended to be highly educated and married but without children. "Loyalists," an even smaller group, were often raised in strict families, had avoided the social protest movements of the '60s and '70s, and never wavered in their commitment to their church. The largest group, the "silent majority" of Boomer religion, were "Returnees," who professed a general belief in spirituality but refused to commit to a particular faith or denomination. They believed that religion was important, even if they rarely attended church services.

By the 1980s the gap between Loyalists and Dropouts had widened into a deep cultural divide on a wide range of social issues. Dropouts, who often identified with the civil rights and feminist movements, were three times more likely than Loyalists to favor legalization of marijuana and twice as likely to support a woman's right to choose. These divisions found expression in politics as Republicans, beginning with Ronald Reagan, lured white evangelical voters away from the Democrats by speaking an explicit language of spirituality. The challenge for Republicans was to win over the religiously committed Loyalists without alienating the vaguely religious Returnees. They needed to develop a vocabulary that stressed the importance of spirituality and morality without appearing to favor a specific group or denomination. "The truth is that politics and morality are inseparable," Ronald Reagan declared in 1984. "And as morality's foundation is religion, religion and politics are necessarily related." His Democratic opponent, former vice president Walter Mondale, accused the Republicans of "moral McCarthyism," claiming "most Americans would be surprised to learn that God is a Republican."

Reagan's appeals worked, and white religious voters, especially those in the South, defected from the Democrats and became a mainstay of the modern Republican Party. Reagan crushed Mondale, sweeping the nation except for Minnesota and the District of Columbia and winning 58.8 percent of the popular vote. His victory solidified the alliance between the Republican Party and white evangelicals, who gave him 80 percent of their votes. In 1980, 29 percent of Southern Baptist ministers identified themselves as Republicans and 41 percent as Democrats. Just four years later, those numbers had switched: 66 percent were Republicans and only 26 percent Democrats.

Reagan's successor, Vice President George Bush, hammered home the same cultural themes during his two campaigns for the presidency. Under the tutelage of campaign manager Lee Atwater, Bush turned the 1988 campaign into a battle for the cultural legacy of the 1960s, accusing his Democratic opponent, Massachusetts governor Michael Dukakis, of being a big government tax-and-spend liberal who was soft on crime, antifamily, and unpatriotic. When Dukakis responded meekly that "this election is not about ideology but about competence," Bush retorted that "this election is about the beliefs we share, the values that we honor and the principles we hold dear." Not even the controversial selection of the gaffe-prone Indiana senator Dan Quayle as his vice-presidential nominee, the first Baby Boomer on a national ticket, slowed Bush's momentum. White evangelical Christians provided Bush with his margin of victory, giving the Republican 71 percent of their votes.

By the time Alberta arrived on the Tabernacle campus in 1986, the school was already deeply involved in these intense political and theological debates. Her mentor, Dr. Carl Bieber, served as district chairman of the Republican Party and encouraged his students to get involved in local issues. "The Bible-believing people got lulled to sleep on this idea that politics is dirty and therefore we need to leave it alone," he complained. Alberta was less interested in politics than in theology, however. She worked the phone banks, encouraging people to get out and vote for conservative Republican candidates, and she handed out information sheets on candidates on Election Day. But Alberta's real passion was reading and interpreting the Bible and trying to figure out what it meant to her and the way she was living her life. At this point, she was more concerned with adjusting her own life to the dictates of the Bible than she was with telling other people how they should live. Believers like Alberta were a stronger force than their political leaders wanted to admit.

Alberta was busy enough maintaining a rigorous schedule of classes. A former high school dropout, she found herself immersed in classes on Latin and Hebrew, in addition to the standard courses in math, history, and biology. Tabernacle, however, was not just another liberal arts college. All of the classes, from biology to history, were Bible centered, focusing on basic truths as revealed in Scripture. There was no mention of Charles Darwin in biology class. Instead, students wanting to know about the origins of life on earth read the Genesis account of Adam and Eve. A standard American history survey began by revealing the faith of the founding fathers and continued by showing American history as the unfolding of God's plan. "We teach that history is HIS story," Bieber remarked. "History is the story of God working through men and women and carrying out his purpose." It just so happened that God's plan seemed strikingly similar to the Republican agenda. Bieber, who taught a popular survey class in American history, dismissed the New Deal as a "socialist blueprint," praised Douglas MacArthur as "a hero," and concluded that Joseph McCarthy was a "bully" who was right on most issues. Martin Luther King, Jr., was a "great speaker" who had "a lot of the wrong associations."

By 1988 Alberta was teaching Bible and typing classes in the Tabernacle day school while finishing her degree at night. She was certainly a unique presence on campus. The majority of the school's administration were white, middle-aged, southern men. An occasional Asian, Latino, or black could be spotted on campus, but they were usually visiting from one of the college's foreign missions. Few people would describe Tabernacle as a warm and fuzzy place. It was a serious institution where stern and severe men fought a daily battle to save the world from Satan. Alberta was the only African American on staff and one of only a handful of women who worked at the school. Everyone on campus knew her. She not only looked different, she also acted differently. In an environment that placed a premium on a practiced and cool reserve, Alberta was unreservedly passionate and expressive. At Sunday morning services, most of the congregation sat silently listening to the weekly sermon. Alberta, raised in the more expressive style of the African American church, would often shout "amen" to underscore her agreement with a particularly important point. A large women with a booming voice, she overwhelmed peers and students with her warmth and openness. Perhaps because of her own background, she seemed less judgmental and more interested in winning souls than in condemning sinners.

One of the hardest parts of the job for her was having to discipline students. The school had a paddling policy. Some offenses required the student to go to the principal's office, bend over, and get paddled by a teacher. "I remember the first time she spanked a kid," recalls Bieber. "She had both hands on the paddle." Bieber showed her how to handle the paddle, and encouraged her to use it. Each strike seemed to hurt her more than the student.

Not surprisingly, she was one of the most popular teachers on campus. Students also felt comfortable coming to her with their problems, knowing that she would be more sympathetic and understanding. One day a student approached her after class. "I don't know why I can't go to the prom with Bob," she said. The student was white; Bob was Chinese. Alberta checked and discovered that the school handbook prohibited interracial dating. Since all of the school's rules and regulations were supposed to be drawn from the Bible, she asked Dr. Bieber to cite the appropriate biblical reference that banned interracial dating. "They're going to a homecoming dance," she complained. "They are not getting married." When Bieber refused to change the policy, Alberta appealed to Dr. Bell, the overseer of the Bible college and seminary and president of the Fundamentalist Baptist Fellowship of America. He too dismissed her complaint. Alberta was furious that the policy remained in place and that the administration had so casually dismissed her. She refused to back down, even threatening to resign. Either provide biblical justification for the policy or abolish it, she demanded. Shocked by her emotional commitment to the issue and perhaps fearing a political hailstorm, the institution relented, removing the prohibition against interracial dating from its handbook.

Alberta earned a bachelor's degree in religious education in 1990 and went on to get a master's degree in 1993. She wanted to stay on to get a doctorate, but before she could enroll, the Tabernacle administration needed assurances that she had no intention of becoming a preacher. "She came to train to be a woman preacher, but of course we don't train the women to preach," says Bell. "That is for the men." Alberta agreed. "Okay," she said, "then I will be a teacher." Reassured that she was not challenging doctrine, Tabernacle admitted Alberta as the first women to enroll in the doctorate program.

She continued teaching at the day school while writing her dissertation, which examined the biblical view of women's proper place in the home and society. Completed in 1996, the work offered a point-by-point fundamentalist attack on the modern women's movement. The "early" women's movement had "noble goals such as the right to vote and equal pay," she wrote, but in recent years it had "become the tool in which Satan has distorted God's truth, and caused the Word of God to become compromised for the sake of egalitarianism." The Bible provided clear guidelines about the proper role of women. "The primary place of woman as well as her primary role," she wrote, "is at the side of her husband as his helpmate." Her secondary role was to be a mother. A woman "is never to neglect her family or her home for the sake of fulfilling career goals."

She can pursue her career only if "she can balance the two" and her "loving husband" encourages and supports her. For someone who had spent so much of her life surrounded by chaos, Alberta now knew that "God's universe is a universe of order."

The irony was that Alberta's actions still occasionally contradicted her beliefs. She had spent most of her years since her born-again experience in 1976 trying to reconcile biblical belief with practical living. Although she sincerely believed that women should be subservient to men, she was also a wife who prepared papers to divorce her husband if he did not change his ways. She confronted the male hierarchy of Tabernacle and threatened to resign if they did not change their policies. As much as Alberta looked to the Bible for specific instructions about living a Christian life, she could not completely purge the streak of independent thinking that had been planted in her early days as a Black Panther and flower child.

As she thought about life after Tabernacle, Alberta decided that she would devote herself to "spreading the word" through Christian education. Before graduating, she wrote and self-published her autobiography, *From the Ghetto, by Grace, to Glory,* which told the story of her journey "from the heart of the inner city to the Throne Room of the Almighty." Alberta was determined to spread the word.

TEN

BOOMER CULTURE

Marshall with Ed Zwick;

Marshall receiving Emmy Award
for *Special Bulletin*.

In Hollywood in the 1970s, the Boomers came
of age and demonstrated that they weren't necessarily interested in
politics as much as in themselves. Suddenly Boomers were control-
ling the supply, not just driving the demand. The key moment came
in 1980 when 31-year-old Brandon Tartikoff assumed control at
NBC. Tartikoff, the youngest person ever to head a network entertainment division, surrounded himself with fellow Boomers to create shows that would appeal to their generation. "It's not a reach for
me as a programmer—or my staff, who are primarily in their late
20s and 30s. They only have to look to their peers and friends to
develop shows," he said. *Newsweek* went so far as to say that Tartikoff
"reinvented network television, keeping baby boomers glued to the
box." He developed a series of hits that pushed NBC to the top of the
ratings: *Hill Street Blues, Miami Vice, Cheers, The Cosby Show, L.A.
Law,* and *Seinfeld*. He consciously sought young, educated audiences. "Just as a whole generation was having kids and staying home,
he gave them something to watch," gushed *Newsweek*.

Movies were no different from television in their growing

Boomer focus, and both formats offered plenty of fare both by and about Boomers. In 1980, *The Return of the Secaucus Seven* looked at the reunion of high school friends in New England. In 1983 *The Big Chill* and its 1960s soundtrack hit the big screen. Television shows like *Baby Boom,* a comedy based on the movie of the same name, dealt with a high-powered career woman forced to deal with motherhood when she inherits a child. When she looks up the word *guilt* in the index of "A Guide to Working Mothers," it says, "See pages 11–307." *Almost Grown* showed a young couple who met during the Cuban missile crisis while in high school in 1962. They get married during the 1970s and divorced in the 1980s. *The Wonder Years* revealed the world of the 1960s through the eyes of a 12-year-old suburban kid. It was a time "when a kid could still go for a long walk alone at dusk without ending up on a milk carton." A number of shows including *Tour of Duty, China Beach,* and *Vietnam War Story,* dealt with the Vietnam War. Nostalgic Boomers could tune into Nickelodeon's *Nick at Nite* and watch reruns of *Rowan and Martin's Laugh-In, My Three Sons,* and *Mr. Ed.* In 1989 VH1 tried to boost ratings by appealing directly to Boomers with '60s music, nostalgic video clips, and features named *Woodstock Minutes* and *My Generation.* The advertising campaign featured a slogan: "The generation that dropped acid to escape reality is the generation that drops antacid to cope with it."

The '80s would also prove to be big for Marshall Herskovitz. In 1983 Marshall and Ed Zwick worked together on a TV-movie script called *Special Bulletin* that addressed two issues of interest to Boomers: the conventions of television news and Reagan's policy on nuclear weapons. A classic Cold Warrior who once called the Soviet Union an "evil empire," Reagan called for massive increases in defense spending, including the development of new weapons systems, both conventional and nuclear. Reagan's tough Cold War rhetoric revived the nascent peace movement. A nationwide poll in the spring of 1982 showed that 57 percent of the respondents favored an immediate freeze on the testing, production, and deployment of nuclear weapons. Americans crowded into movie theaters in 1983 to watch *War Games,* which showed a teenage computer hacker accidentally launch a nuclear war. (Computer: "Shall we play a game?" Teenager: "Let's play Thermonuclear War.") The following year, over

100 million people anxiously watched a docudrama, *The Day After*, that portrayed the effects of nuclear war on Kansas.

Marshall strongly opposed Reagan's nuclear buildup, but he wanted to avoid writing a simple morality play. As he was during the Vietnam War, Marshall was as distrustful of the antiwar activists as he was of Defense Department planners. Both sides distorted the truth and oversimplified a complex issue in an effort to sway public opinion. Marshall was more interested in making a cultural statement about how television shaped our understanding of events than he was in making a political statement about nuclear weapons. *Special Bulletin* told the story of a group of antiwar activists turned terrorists who threatened to blow up Charleston, South Carolina, with a nuclear bomb unless the government turned over some of its warheads. The terrorists, led by a former Vietnam veteran and Pentagon nuclear strategist, kidnap a local television reporter and use him to broadcast their demands to the nation. Through network news bulletins, viewers learn about the terrorists' demands, watch interviews with "people on the street," get updates from Congress and the White House, and even hear a psychoanalyst discuss the terrorists' motives. The script concluded as the terrorists were ambushed by government commandos, but not before the nuclear device explodes, destroying Charleston. The script highlighted the fanaticism of the left and the ineptitude of the government. But more than anything else, it revealed television's power to define reality and shape events.

Tartikoff sat expressionless through the pitch meeting, never giving any hint as to whether he liked the idea. "His face was like a mask," Marshall recalls. When he finished his presentation there was a moment of awkward silence. Marshall was convinced that he had bombed, that Tartikoff hated the idea. Without even acknowledging that Marshall was in the room, Tartikoff turned to an assistant and started discussing how they would produce the picture. "He was just off and running."

Production moved quickly, but its content raised concerns among other NBC executives, producing a massive turf war just days before the movie was scheduled to air in March. Tom Pettit, the former news correspondent and now president of NBC News, tried to kill it, believing that it would reflect poorly on *NBC News* and that it could produce the type of hysteria that followed broadcast of the

War of the Worlds in 1938. "He went ballistic," Marshall recalls. At the last minute they reached a compromise: the show would air but with disclaimers at every commercial break pointing out that the events were fictional. In addition, during key moments, especially in the second half of the movie, the network would run disclaimers at the bottom of the screen.

The movie aired on March 20, 1983. NBC inserted thirty-one messages throughout the broadcast assuring viewers that the drama was fiction. Nonetheless, many people interpreted the movie as reality. NBC said that its switchboard received more than 700 calls following the program. Most complained that viewers were not given adequate warning that the program was fictional. Despite the complaints, the movie drew a large audience, even while competing against *Archie Bunker's Place* and *Trapper John M.D.*, and rave reviews. *TV Guide* called *Special Bulletin* "a thinking man's thriller involving nuclear disaster," saying there was "an impressive grit, an evenhandedness and a frightening sense of actuality to the drama." The movie received the $25,000 Humanitas prize, awarded to the show that has "a humanizing influence" on television. The award cited *Special Bulletin* for "its courage to raise moral questions about the use of media in our media culture" and "for its mold breaking dramatization of the central moral issue of our time—the use of nuclear weapons—and the evil absurdity of continuing the arms race."

The success of *Special Bulletin* transformed Marshall from a struggling screenwriter to a Hollywood player. For weeks his answering machine was clogged with congratulatory messages. "I felt like the proverbial fat girl in high school who loses all the weight and [whom] all the boys want to go out with" but never learned to say no. "I had worked on the theory before that you just say yes to everything. So I continued to say yes to everything, and it took two years to work my way out from all of the projects I said I would do."

He had little time to savor his success. Not only was he swamped with new projects, but on March 1, just a few weeks before *Special Bulletin* aired, Susan had given birth to their first child, Lizzie. While enjoying the demands of fatherhood, Marshall had to contend with his own father's declining health. In January 1983 his father had been diagnosed with a brain tumor. Surgeons removed as much of the tumor as they could and began an intensive regiment of radiation. His condition improved for a few months, but by March he began a slow and painful decline. By the summer, when it was clear that his father was dying, Marshall was commuting between Los Angeles and Philadelphia almost every weekend. In September the family made the decision to remove his father from life support. He lived for eleven more days, died on a Thursday, and was buried the next day, according to Jewish tradition. On Saturday Marshall flew back to Los Angeles, where he won two Emmys—for best writing and best movie—the following day for *Special Bulletin.* It was a bittersweet moment: symbolically, the Boomers were not just taking over, they were burying their parents. "Dad, this is for you," he said, while holding the Emmy for best picture above his head.

In 1985 Marshall and Ed created the Bedford Falls Company, named after the town in the movie *It's a Wonderful Life.* Having spent so much time together, they decided to formalize the relationship with a business. Shortly afterward, MGM offered them a production deal: The studio would provide them with a guaranteed salary, an office, and an assistant. They asked for little in return. "You guys can do whatever you want," they were told. "You can do TV movies. You can do a miniseries. Your only responsibility to this company is that you have to develop a television series." Both Marshall and Ed had already pledged not to work in television, so they figured they would accept the deal and use the time to develop movie ideas. Their biggest fear was that they would produce a successful series and get stuck in television their whole lives.

The MGM deal complicated Marshall's family life because, for the first time, he had to leave home and commute to work. On his second day at the office, his wife called around noon. His precocious 2-year-old daughter had something to say to him. She handed the phone to Lizzie. "Daddy doesn't love me anymore," she said. "He's not bad. He just doesn't love me anymore." Marshall dropped what he was doing, hurried home, and spent the rest of the afternoon with her. The next day he took her to work with him, explaining that he was away because he was working and not because he did not love her anymore. Family dynamics, especially the tension between work and family, would be a constant theme in Marshall's writing, and many of the examples were drawn from his own life. "There is a way in which fundamentally work does not acknowledge or understand family, and family does not acknowledge or understand work," he claims. "So when you're pulled away from one by the other, you are sort of on your own in some deep and primitive way. So that's been a problem, and I think is a problem for millions of people of my generation."

At the beginning of the spring season, an executive from MGM contacted Marshall and Ed to arrange a meeting with ABC to discuss their ideas for the upcoming season. There was only one problem: They had not given any thought to developing a television show. It was their only obligation to MGM, but they had been caught up in large-screen fever. With only days before the meeting, Marshall and Ed started brainstorming. Nothing seemed to work. Not only were they facing an impossible deadline, but they were ambivalent about the task. "You understand if we sell one of these, we will have to make it," Marshall complained. "And this would be disastrous." The compromise they reached with themselves was that they would propose a show that would have very little chance of working.

Marshall suggested they do something about their generation, which he believed was underrepresented on television. They started talking about people they knew and the types of issues they were facing. They realized a lot of dramatic things happen to people during their thirties. Parents die. Relationships with friends are redefined. Careers evolve. Children are born. They had no trouble finding issues, but they could not find the hook. Television shows needed to belong to a particular genre. Was it a detective story? Was it going to be about doctors, or about lawyers? Their idea for a show revolved around relationships, not a particular genre. "Why don't we just drop the pretense and just write about these people?" Marshall asked. Neither was totally convinced, so they left the office and went to Ed's house. They sat around that evening talking it over. Ed's wife, Liberty, started naming all the people she knew in their thirties and the different issues they confronted.

Marshall and Ed spent the next twenty-four hours at the typewriter sketching some of the possible storylines. The next day they sat down with three ABC executives. As they were introduced, it occurred to Marshall that everyone in the room was a Boomer in his or her thirties. Marshall and Ed made their case for a show that would revolve around relationships and the changes people experienced at that age. "Let us think about it," the executives told them.

Feeling rejected, they walked out of the office and were on their way to the parking lot when Ed realized he had left his keys on the coffee table in the office. They walked back to get the keys and just as they were approaching the office, the head of development came out and said: "I was just going to call you guys. Let's do it."

It was their nightmare come true. "Writing for me was very tortuous, difficult, and anxiety provoking," Marshall confessed. "I would basically go into the office, sit down in front of the computer screen, and just fall asleep." After two weeks he had written one act. Ed came in and without a word of discussion sat down at the desk, and they started working on it together. "We never talked about it. We just did it. We wrote the rest of it together and had a great time." *Thirtysomething* was the product of an ongoing conversation between two Baby Boomers about their lives and the lives of their family and friends. It made developing story plots fairly easy. Marshall and Ed would invite some of the other writers into their office and talk about issues in their lives: conflicts with spouses and parents, clashes with children, professional frustrations. Either Ed or Marshall would be at the typewriter taking notes.

The central characters were all bright, college-educated friends in their thirties. Nancy was a full-time housewife and mother whose husband, Elliot, was a partner in an advertising agency. Michael, his wife, Hope, and their new baby daughter were the central characters. Michael's cousin Melissa was a freelance photographer. Hopes's best friend Ellyn worked as an administrator at city hall, and Gary was an English professor. Each of the characters struggled to balance the new demands of adulthood with his or her youthful expectations of life. Since Michael and Hope had a child, they could not be as carefree as they had been in the past. "We have responsibility now," Hope intones. Ellyn, an old friend, felt marginalized because Hope was so preoccupied with her child that she could not pay attention to her. Michael felt guilty because he was attracted to other women. He resisted, but his partner, Elliot, cheated on his wife and destroyed their marriage. At work, Michael and Elliot's advertising business was constantly on the edge of failure. They wanted to remain independent and not sell out to a large corporate agency. When they were asked to copy the work of another agency, Michael complained: "What are we doing here? Why did we start this business?" Elliott responded: "To do our thing. Two wives, three kids, four cars, two mortgages, a payroll. . . . That's life. You be the breadwinner now."

"Why is this so hard?" Michael asks Hope at the end of the pilot, confessing that he was having trouble at work and at home. Hope responded: "Because we expect too much. We've always gotten too much. I think that our parents got together in 1946 and said let's all have lots of kids and give them everything they want so they grow up and be totally stressed out and not able to cope with real life." It was Marshall's outlook in a nutshell and a Boomer insight that their expectations of happiness were out of line. "It was the first time on television that I heard us—Baby Boomers—addressed seriously," recalls then thirtysomething *USA Today* television critic Robert Bianco. "It offered a real insight into how our generation perceived the world."

"What Marshall and Ed tried to do with *thirtysomething* was something that Seinfeld tried to do in a half-hour comedy—essentially to say that a show about nothing could be a show about something," observes Richard Kramer, who wrote and directed for the series. "Marshall had the necessary insight and arrogance to say that his life, our lives, were worthy of spending an hour on television once a week." Drama did not have to be about melodramatic peaks and valleys. Life was not always about touching and dramatic moments; it was about the constant tension between expectations and reality and the daily interplay between unconscious thought and practical reality.

Initially many of the actors found the characters too self-involved. There was no one for the audience to identify with and root for. That was true, but it was also exactly what Marshall had intended. His favorite criticism was "fakey." If a scene seemed too contrived, he would say it was "fakey" and demand that it be rewritten. "He hates the false emotions and false moments that popular culture has taught us to be true," observes one of the show's writers. There was a creative edge, a certain defiance to the show. "We said: Fuck you, we know the way to do television better and we don't care if you like us or not," says Kramer.

Especially in the first season of *thirtysomething*, Marshall took an active role in every aspect of the show. "There was not a word or an image that he did not directly approve or greatly influence or create himself," recalls a writer. Those who did not share his perspective or his sensibility often found Marshall arrogant. Nearly everyone found him complicated, and often moody. "He is a man of contradictions," observes Kramer. "A natural leader who hates being in charge; a brilliant writer who hates writing; a successful director who would prefer never to direct again as long as he lives." Marshall could produce inspired ideas, but he would prefer to spend most of his days playing video machines. "He is the most complicated guy I have ever known, but with the simplest soul," reflects Kramer.

For Marshall the show's Baby Boom sensibility revolved around three themes: irony, the lack of formality, and the tweaking of authority. Like Marshall, all the characters were caught between their expectations of what they thought life was going to be like and the reality of bringing up families, dealing with relationships, and juggling job responsibilities. Referring back to the philosophy that he developed in high school with his friend John Morse, he called the conflict "the dialectic of life." Everything was in opposition to itself. "You want to have a career, but you also want to be lazy. You want to play around, but you want to be married. You want to pursue your dreams, but you also want the security of a job." It was these tensions and contradictions, he believed, that "characterized this moment in time and this generation."

Neither of its creators had high hopes for the series. Ed thought it would be yanked off the air in six episodes. Marshall expected it to last thirteen episodes. "It never occurred to us that we would succeed." But it quickly became apparent that they had struck a nerve. Marshall realized it within minutes after the pilot had aired. He'd been watching ABC, and it went from the end credits to the eleven o'clock news. The local newscaster, who had been watching the show, was crying. Before she started talking about the news, she said: "I can't believe that show."

Over the next few seasons the show dealt with a number of Boomer issues, many of them drawn from the personal experiences of the thirtysomething writers and producers. To come up with the story plots each week, the writers never consulted polls or conducted focus groups. They just talked among themselves. "What do you find interesting? What are you struggling with?" For Marshall, the story about Michael's father dying was the most autobiographical in the series. In the episode, Michael's father has stomach cancer and comes back home to die. Some of the dialogue is taken directly from

Marshall's own experience. At one point Michael says, "I don't know how to be a father. I'm just a kid."

Marshall, who had spent much of his life in one form of therapy or another, played the role of the therapist Fred Nicholson in a show that examined the problems in Nancy and Elliot's relationship. "This kind of episode that would delve into the smallest, most intimate details, the most incredibly boring and utterly fascinating corners of a marriage, was exactly the kind of show that Ed and Marshall had hoped they would be able to do on *thirtysomething*," reflected the episode's writer, Susan Shilliday. They fight about sex and money (not enough of either), but they discover through gentle prodding that their real problems are much deeper: their unrealistic expectations of marriage and of each other. Over the course of the hour, the audience gets drawn into the subconscious thoughts of both characters. When Elliot complains that Nancy never wants to have sex, she responds: "I'm so tired at the end of the day, I don't even remember that I'm a sexual person." Nancy feels that Elliot does not understand how demanding it is to spend all day with their two children. And he is angry that she questions his decision to start his own company. "I'm taking this chance on something I dreamed about and she doesn't trust me at all."

The airing of "The Therapist" marked a milestone in television. Perhaps never before, or since, had a network devoted an hour in prime time to the psychological musings of two characters. At its core, the episode showed how two basically good and decent people get trapped in their own pain and are unable to change their self-destructive behavior. "It was like nothing that had ever appeared on television before," reflects Kramer. The day after the episode aired, Marshall went to his office. His assistant buzzed him and told him that Brandon Tartikoff was on the phone. Marshall had not spoken to him since *Special Bulletin* four years earlier. Marshall picked up the phone and Tartikoff did not even say hello. "Last night's show was the best hour of television in the history of the medium." Stunned, Marshall managed to mutter thanks before Tartikoff hung up.

The show tackled another controversial issue that came out of the closet during the Boomer years: homosexuality. While Donny Deutsch was trying to develop realistic advertising for IKEA by showing a gay couple shopping for furniture, *thirtysomething* became the first prime-time television show to put homosexuals in bed together. The network scheduled the episode to air at midnight following election coverage. To Marshall the show was not about homosexuality but "about how physical love, for two people, can be both a window and a wall." The show had depicted the relationship problems of straight characters. Why should gay relationships be treated any differently? Apparently, many of the show's sponsors did not agree with the logic. Half of the regular advertisers pulled out, and ABC lost an estimated $1.5 million. The response did not scare off the writers. In the 1991 season one of the gay characters tested positive for AIDS. Richard Kramer, who wrote the episode, said that they were inundated with mail following the episode.

Most critics praised the show, but even the critical reaction had a strong generational split. "It was usually praised by thirtysomething critics, not so widely praised by older critics," recalls Robert Bianco. Every year the networks parade their new lineup before television critics. In 1987, Marshall, Ed, and many members of the cast attended the meeting and answered questions from nearly 400 critics representing media outlets from around the country. "We had no idea what was going to hit us," Marshall says. "It seemed like everybody hated the show. They not only hated the show, they hated us, and hated what we were doing." The session started with a critic shouting, "You act like you are the first generation to raise kids. On your show the spaghetti pot boils over and it's a crisis." It went downhill from there. "They were the most contentious press conferences that I have ever seen," says Bianco.

The major critics were more positive than negative. "The new season's most talked about new show," *Newsweek* exclaimed in the first season. "Watching *thirtysomething* every week gives me the satisfied sensation of reading a good novel," said *TV Guide* critic Dan Wakefield. The *New York Times* said the show was "as gripping as gangsters, as addictive as soap opera, and as memorable as a full-length feature film." Another critic referred to *thirtysomething* as "the most imaginative and rewarding effort on prime time television." Marshall's efforts were rewarded with Emmys for best dramatic series and best writing in a dramatic series, along with a Golden Globe, a People's Choice, and a Peabody award. Dissenters argued that "Hope, Michael, et al. were so smug, so obnoxious, so utterly, incredibly '80s, they made the rest of us feel better," observed the *San Francisco Chronicle.* "No one ever came home from work too tired to eat, let alone make dinner. Paying bills was never a problem, homes were in a permanent rumpled state but no one yelled about piles of clothes or unpainted walls, child care wasn't an issue, and kids never got sick." Another critic dismissed the show as "a weekly diet of yuppie whining, nagging and complaining."

Marshall and Ed had decided that the fourth season would be their final one. Marshall felt he had nothing left to say; they were repeating the same psychological dynamics that had occurred in previous shows. "I kept having this image in my mind: Willie Mays stayed around one season too long, and there was this horrific game ... where he dropped a ball and later fell running from third base to home. It just broke my heart to see him not be able to do it anymore. I kept thinking, let's quit while we can still feel good about it." They wrote a script in which Michael and Hope split up. He accepts a job in California, and she decides to move to Washington, D.C. They submitted the script to the studio and the next morning received a letter threatening legal action. It made clear that they had forty-eight hours to amend the script in such a way that it did not automatically convey the end of the series. Marshall called a lawyer and asked what to do. "You don't have a legal leg to stand on," the lawyer said. He told them to get back to work and to send a letter back saying that they stand ready to perform their services and act in good faith. So that's what they did. They changed the script so that Michael and Hope decided they would stay together in the end.

The show was a unique generational phenomenon that could have been successful only in the late '80s and early '90s when the bulk of Baby Boomers were experiencing many of the same travails as the characters. Boomers were the most self-involved, self-aware generation in history. By the 1970s and 1980s, the "consciousness revolution," once confined to members of the youthful counterculture who wanted to "raise consciousness" about Vietnam or the women's movement, mushroomed into a mass movement particularly among the white middle class. During the 1980s the personal became public. Many Americans could identify with characters who exposed their inner thoughts because many of them were doing the same. Nearly 40 percent of Americans belonged to a support group (including one for "channelers" who needed support in their efforts to speak with the dead). By the 1990s more than 15 percent of adults and 21 percent of children visited mental health professionals. There were over 400,000 psychiatrists, 65,000 family therapists, 125,000 psychologists, 10,000 psychoanalysts, and 150,000 social workers.

There was another dimension of *thirtysomething* that made it unique to its time. It came about during a period of tremendous change in the television industry as upstart cable networks started draining viewers and advertising dollars away from the networks. In the past, the three networks—ABC, NBC, and CBS—were able to divide the television audience into large chunks and command loyalty. With the proliferation of cable, however, networks were forced to narrowcast, searching for smaller and smaller, better-defined demographic segments. During the 1980s cable television grew from a presence in fewer than one in five homes to 56.4 percent of television homes. By the end of the decade, the average television household received more than twenty-seven channels. As viewers' choices grew, the spoils went increasingly to the programmer that could cater to a special interest and offer advertisers a small but well-targeted cluster of consumers. "*Thirtysomething* was not just the creation of demographic trends, it was a creation of the very idea of demographics in television," reflects Bianco. What kept it on the air was the new ratings technology that allowed the networks to break audiences down by age groups. They discovered that while *thirtysomething* was not popular with a large number of people, it was very popular with a small, but influential, segment of Baby Boomer women. It allowed advertisers to target that audience. "It is one of the first demographic hits on the networks."

Thirtysomething broke with television conventions in fundamental ways. During the 1950s Desi Arnaz referred to sitcoms as "television's happy problems, for happy people, with happy endings." Marshall rewrote the formula, making *thirtysomething* television's little problems for self-involved people with ambiguous endings. The show revolved around subtle moments of personal interaction, not dramatic turning points. Notes writer Richard Kramer, "We set out to find out how little space you could cover in a dramatic hour." It left many issues unresolved. "Ambiguity and ambivalence are as much a part of life as resolution," Marshall observes. The characters were often indecisive and insecure. Some therapists used the show to help their patients work through relationship issues. "The reason therapists and people in therapy relate to our show," Marshall says, "is because we deal with ambivalence, we deal with inner conflicts."

The show also reinforced the public impression that being a Boomer was synonymous with being a Yuppie—young, urban, upwardly mobile professional. Marshall went to great lengths to present the main couple, the Steadmans, as members of the downwardly mobile white middle class. His income ranged between $50,000 and $100,000 a year and they paid $120,000 for their house in 1986. "In truth we were trying to write about the downward mobility of people in the '80s," said Susan Shilliday. They were people "who found out that even with decent jobs, it was hard to buy a house." Yet no matter how hard they tried, the main characters came across the screen as privileged, narcissistic yuppies.

Marshall found himself overwhelmed by the attention of creating a hit TV show. It also became all-consuming. "It became a calling," he reflected. "It became a way of life." He remembers the experience more for its intensity than its happiness. "Making a television show was very stressful and very difficult. You're juggling the writing of episodes, prepping of episodes, shooting episodes, and then editing them. You're going from one crisis to the next." Every day he felt as if he were trapped in an old silent movie playing Pauline, the damsel in distress tied to a conveyor belt while the buzz saw moved closer. There was always an approaching deadline, always a script that wasn't ready, always a show that needed more editing.

In many ways, the success of *thirtysomething* changed Marshall's life. He was noticed and respected in the industry for the first time. "There was a certain headiness to being recognized in the community," he reflected. He was also something of a minor celebrity. People would come up to him on the street, at the grocery store, and at the movie theater and tell him how much they loved the show. Professionally it gave him the freedom to experiment with ideas and concepts that he had been carrying around in his head for years. Like many of the characters in *thirtysomething*, Marshall had spent his life rebelling against authority. Now younger people were looking up to him as an authority. "It was the first time I was really a boss."

Life at home changed very little. Marshall actually did not make a great deal of money directly from *thirtysomething,* although he used its success to cash in on his next deal. When relatives from the East Coast came to visit, they assumed that Marshall was now living a life of luxury. They were shocked when they discovered that he lived in the same messy house. The only tangible sign of his success was a new Jaguar ("for which I received a suitable amount of torture from everyone who knew me").

On a personal level, Marshall was less anxious and more comfortable with himself. Just as it was becoming fashionable for men to express their feelings, to be soft and emotional, Marshall was moving in the opposite direction. Becoming a man for him meant coming to terms with feelings and behaviors that had been unavailable to him as a child. He allowed himself to be more competitive and confrontational. His fascination with cars during the 1950s turned into a desire to race cars in the 1980s.

Marshall had tapped into the Boomers' fascination with their own psychology, clearing the path for shows like *Seinfeld,* which could boast that nothing was too trivial to inspire a half-hour of comedy. (One episode revolved around the struggle to buy soup from an authoritarian chef.) But the search for reality, the willingness to explore the inner conflict of characters, may have provided an opening to a younger generation with a very different definition of reality. In 1992 MTV launched *The Real World,* which followed the lives of seven attractive youngsters forced to live together for three months in a Manhattan loft. It would take television in a direction that Marshall had never imagined.

PART III
BOOMER NATION:
1992–2004

In the 1990s Boomers assumed power in the United States. "The people who changed the world merely by existing are now in a position to change the world through control of our institutions," observed Martin Ford Puris, an advertising executive who pitched ads to Baby Boomers.

Bill Clinton's election as president in 1992 signified the rise of the Baby Boomers to power. Boomers such as filmmakers Steven Spielberg (1947), Oliver Stone (1946), and Spike Lee (1957), along with superagent Michael Ovitz (1946), were on the Hollywood A list. Raunchy "shock-jock" Howard Stern (1954) and right-wing crusader Rush Limbaugh (1951) dominated the airwaves. Bill Gates (1955) sat on top of the Microsoft empire, which made him the wealthiest man in America. Oprah Winfrey (1954) won the daytime rating wars by focusing on the Boomers' endless fascination with themselves, while David Letterman (1947) became a late-night fixture with his ironic humor and "stupid pet tricks."

Every member of the generation that Abbie Hoffman once advised not to trust anyone over 30 was now well into their third decade. Thanks to the Boomers, America was a middle-aged nation, and society adjusted to their needs even as it started looking toward the generation that would take their place. By the end of World War II the median age reached 30, but it declined over the next few decades with the rising birthrate, hitting bottom in 1970 at 27. As the Baby Boomers aged, America aged with it, the median age increasing from 33.3 in 1990 to 35.3 in 2000. It seemed appropriate that during the 1990s, *Saturday Night Live,* the hip show of the irreverent Boomers, added a new character: Middle-Aged Man, a potbellied superhero who could decipher mortgage rates but not figure out how to program a VCR.

The leading group of Boomers had the highest income of any age group and were the biggest spenders. Boomers born between 1946 and 1955 had an estimated spending power of $1 trillion and a medium family income of $58,889 in 1999. They made up 21.9 million households, and 75 percent were home owners—more than any demographic group. They also had the lowest poverty rate—6.4 percent—of any group. Marketers swarmed over them like locusts, analyzing every detail of their spending habits, no matter how absurd. Boomers were, for example, three times more likely to own a telephone answering machine than their parents, who were twice as likely to purchase a home security system. When Boomers did purchase a home security system, they preferred to pay by check over credit card or cash. Boomers liked paying a fee for joining exclusive travel clubs and getting discounted prices in return. And a higher percentage of Boomers (37.5 percent) felt that restaurant meals had become spicier.

Politicians were not far behind, pushing issues such as health care and Social Security to the top of the nation's agenda. Perhaps the Boomers' greatest impact was on the stock market, which they flooded with savings and retirement money, adding over $4 trillion in value—the largest single accumulation of wealth in history. In the early 1980s the entire mutual fund market totaled $135 billion; by 2000 it topped $7 trillion. Studies revealed that 75 percent of Baby Boomers owned mutual funds, and they accounted for more than one-third of the market increase. Most of the money for mutual funds came from special retirement funds—401(k) accounts—that allowed workers to obtain matching contributions from employers. By 1998 more than 25 million workers had $1 trillion invested in their 401(k) accounts. In 1995, for the first time ever, stocks replaced homes as the primary nest egg for Americans.

Truly, America had become a Boomer Nation. Far from the nightmare of self-indulgence bemoaned by the generation's critics, however, America became a far more civil and safer country. Boomers poured more of their unprecedented wealth into charity than any other age group, doubling the amount of contributions since 1960. The aging of the Boom led to a marked improvement in many of the social indicators used to chart the decline of American civil life. Crime rates plummeted to modern lows. Gun deaths dropped 21 percent between 1993 and 1997. In 1991 there were 2,262 murders in New York City. In 1997 there were 749. The divorce rate held steady. By 1998 there were 208,000 fewer abortions performed than in 1990. At least by comparison to the nadir years of Vietnam and Watergate, America seemed a more optimistic, hopeful place. "Against all predictions," observed the journalist Andrew Sullivan, "the 1990s have turned out to be the most benign decade of the century. Almost every week, to the rising panic of the political and journalistic classes, things seem to be getting better."

ELEVEN

GAINING CONTROL
AT WHAT COST?

Donny with Bill Clinton;   **at the top of his game;**   **Marshall today.**

After locking up the Democratic nomination in the spring of 1992, Bill Clinton sat down with his media advisers to develop a strategy for wresting the presidency away from George Bush, and the Republicans, who had controlled the office since 1981. Casting himself a "new Democrat" who understood the concerns of the struggling middle class, Clinton put his Baby Boom credentials on display throughout the campaign, reminding audiences that he once shook President Kennedy's hand, was nicknamed Elvis, agonized over the draft (and like many of his contemporaries, avoided it), and once memorized Martin Luther King's "I Have a Dream Speech." As a true politician he tried to appeal to all sides; he had tried pot, but assured people that he did not inhale. His wife, Hillary, was a working mother. They named their daughter Chelsea after a Joni Mitchell song. Campaign rallies were smothered in '60s music: the Beatles' "Twist and Shout," "Revolution," and "Here Comes the Sun," along with the Beach Boys' "Good Vibrations."

When Clinton chose another Baby Boomer, Tennessee Senator Al

Gore, as his running mate, pundits announced the 1992 campaign as a generational referendum. "Young Guns: The Generational Gamble," cried *Newsweek*. "The Democrats' New Generation," shouted *Time*. CBS's Bill Plante said Clinton chose Gore "to send a message of generational change." The *San Francisco Examiner* noted that the nominee "has chosen to make the 1992 election a battle of generations." The convention ended with Bill and Hillary, Al and wife, Tipper, boogeying to the beat of Fleetwood Mac's "Don't Stop Thinking About Tomorrow."

Republicans took up the generational challenge, turning the election into a debate over the legacy of the Baby Boom. Marilyn Quayle, wife of Vice President Dan Quayle, tied the Clintons to the radical legacy of the 1960s. "Not everyone demonstrated, dropped out, took drugs, joined in the sexual revolution or dodged the draft," she told the cheering delegates at the Republican Convention. "Dan and I are members of the baby boom generation, too," she said. "And yet our basic understanding of what constitutes good government and a good society is very different from that of the boomers who lead the other party." It was a former White House speechwriter and Bush primary rival, Pat Buchanan, who openly proclaimed that America was in the midst of a culture war, attacking the Democrats for promoting "the amoral idea that gay and lesbian couples should have the same standing in law as married men and women." Clinton, who understood the importance of political symbolism, temporarily neutralized the criticism by offering voters reassuring clips of him leaving a Baptist church with a Bible in hand or speaking movingly about his difficult childhood growing up with an abusive stepfather. He avoided explicit generational appeals and instead tried to win back the middle class by emphasizing the values of hard work and family. Campaigning as a social moderate, he professed his support for capital punishment and promised to "end welfare as we know it," to make the streets safer and the schools better, and to provide "basic health care to all Americans." For traditional Democrats he offered a message of economic populism, promising to soak the rich and fight to preserve popular social programs.

Clinton's message resonated with Democrats in the primaries, but in the fall he needed a media campaign that would sway critical swing voters in key states. John F. Kennedy, a Democrat, may have created the modern media campaign, but it was the Republicans under Ronald Reagan who had turned it into an art form with their "Morning in America" ads in 1984 and the more shrill anti-Dukakis ads in 1988. Clinton, who understood the power of television to shape the agenda, was determined to fight Bush ad for ad on the airways. Borrowing the Republican model, he put together an advertising team that included political professionals and Madison Avenue creatives. Clinton's new team was headed by Mandy Grunwald, a partner in an established Washington political advertising firm, and it included a few other prominent Democratic media firms. They chose Deutsch as the lead Madison Avenue firm and tapped a handful of other commercial executives as part of the team.

A number of Clinton advisers had seen Deutsch's IKEA ads and liked the style, believing that they spoke with a unique voice that could help reach disaffected voters who no longer responded to standard political appeals. "Bringing Deutsch into the inner circle is a signal that they really do want breakthrough advertising, not the cookie-cutter kind of stuff," a campaign staff member said. Grunwald found Donny's ads "in sync with how people think" and with "a great sense of humor." "You could imagine them doing very good antipolitical work in a year when people hate politics," she added. Donny understood why he was chosen: "I think they came to us because they don't want typical political advertising."

Donny's first assignment was to travel to Little Rock after the Democratic Convention to film a series of 30-second spots for the campaign. A political ad campaign is very different from a commercial campaign, as he soon discovered. For the IKEA campaign, for example, Deutsch had developed the strategy, the message, and eventually the ads. In a political campaign, the candidate's advisers decided on the message and wrote the copy. The only thing left for Donny was to shoot the ad. The work itself was mundane, but the highly charged atmosphere of working in a presidential campaign was anything but mundane, and Donny, as always, loved being at the center of the action, even if he was not the focus of attention.

In their first session Clinton's advisers handed the candidate a script for an ad. The governor glanced at it, then exploded. "This is bullshit. This is not what we are supposed to be saying." Before they had a chance to rewrite it, Clinton gestured to Donny to start taping. He would do it off the top of his head. As the camera rolled, Clinton spoke effortlessly, but he ran slightly over by about 4 seconds. Paul Goldman, who was directing the ads with Donny, told Clinton he needed to cut around 4 seconds off his talk. "He closed his eyes. Said 'Okay, let's do it.'" He did it again, editing in his head, finishing in exactly 30 seconds. "You work with the best actor in the world, you give him a 30-second script and he'll never do it in 30 on the first take," Donny remarks.

After the Democratic Convention, Donny traveled with the Clintons and the Gores during a bus trip across the country, collecting dozens of hours of raw footage of Clinton behind the scenes. They were all creatures of television. They knew exactly how to perform in front of the camera. "When the camera was on they would do this snugly thing," observes Paul Goldman. "When the camera was off they would go back to their business."

Clinton's tactics, along with a weak economy and a powerful third-party challenge from Ross Perot, helped the Democrats to unseat Bush and win the election. The new president was 23 years younger than the outgoing president, the greatest age difference since John F. Kennedy replaced Dwight Eisenhower in 1960.

Working on a successful presidential campaign was a heady experience for Donny, and he was not shy about taking credit. He announced to *Adweek* that his firm was "assuming the mantle" of leadership for the new age of advertising. Staffers began calling him "Madonny," drawing parallels between their boss and the glitzy self-promoting star Madonna. He was soon slapped down, however. Controversy was ignited by a *New York* magazine article noting that Donny was claiming a key role in developing ads for the campaign. Clinton's campaign responded by claiming that Deutsch was responsible for two or three spots out of the fifteen to twenty national campaign commercials that made it on the air. "The fact that anyone is getting more credit than the others is kind of sad," said Mandy Grunwald. James Carville, Clinton's campaign chief, was less generous. Deutsch, he said, did 5 percent of the work and claimed 100 percent of the credit.

Nonetheless, Donny's role increased his profile and allowed him to go after bigger clients. "We've always been a sexy agency, but the Clinton campaign put it into another level," he said. "We've gone from a creative hot shop to a serious, national agency."

Donny believed that many larger clients were put off by his style and by his lack of experience. He needed to reassure large accounts by hiring a high-profile executive with a traditional background. Just a few weeks after Clinton's election in November 1992, Donny held a press conference to announce that he had hired Steve Dworin from J. Walter Thompson USA and was changing the name of the firm to Deutsch/Dworin. "Since the day we got together, it has been a true partnership," Donny said. The two partners divided up duties, with Donny focusing on the creative side while Steve developed a strategic vision and management practices. According to *Advertising Age,* Donny "clearly enjoys playing the role of advertising's tortured genius and cowboy-booted bad boy, while Mr. Dworin plays the pinstriped adult trying to keep his rambunctious partner in line." The big question was whether the agency could continue to grow while maintaining its unique style. "Can a big-budget agency keep turning out gritty, low-budget hyper-realistic work?" asked *Advertising Age.* "Or will Deutsch/Dworin gradually lose touch with a particular reality that has been its strength?"

There was an initial wave of good news. Dworin upgraded the staff, bringing in some seasoned veterans from other big firms. In 1993, their first year as partners, the agency secured accounts for Prudential securities ($20 million), Tanqueray ($15 million), Lenscrafter ($35 million), and Hardees ($75 million). But problems emerged almost immediately. Many employees who were used to Donny's personalized and unstructured style resented Dworin's more professional, hierarchical management approach. "I missed the old Deutsch," one worker told *Advertising Age.* "It was raw and crazy. Now the agency is more layered, and account people are getting more involved in the work. People are being brought in from big agencies. There's a different mentality here." Dworin threw temper tantrums and berated workers. "What became very clear after the honeymoon was that he was not a good person, not a nice person," recalled Linda Sawyer. "I felt like people were hiding in their offices."

Employees complained to Donny, but their old boss was surprisingly unresponsive and disinterested. What they did not know was that he was facing an even more painful situation at home: his brief marriage was falling apart. A close friend describes the match as "bad from day one. . . . They were just oil and vinegar." Although he was married, Donny still enjoyed his freedom. In addition to working long hours, he liked going out with his friends, especially on weekends. Jody wanted him to spend more time with her and more time at home. "She wished I had shown her the passion I had for my work," he later told *New York* magazine. They fought almost daily. It created a vicious circle: the more they fought, the more he wanted to stay away, the angrier she became, so the more they fought. His relationship with Jody was failing, but he was developing a close and loving relationship with her daughter, Chelsea. One of the most difficult moments of his life was when he explained to Chelsea that he and her mother were breaking up. Chelsea was only four years old at the time. "We took her to the park and told her and she just started crying." I like having you home daddy, she said over and over again through her tears. "I sat there for hours alone and just wept," Donny recalls. "It was devastating."

At age 35, Donny was facing a crisis point: His personal and professional lives were falling apart. "It was the lowest point of my life." Initially, he turned to drugs and alcohol. "I think I was probably drinking a little too much, maybe doing a little too much coke." His weight ballooned to 225 pounds on a 5-foot 10-inch frame. After months of indecision, he tried a Boomer solution: he went to a therapist. The sessions focused on his insecurities and his childhood, in typical Freudian fashion. Donny had led a sheltered life, managing to extend his adolescence into his mid-30s. He had been cocooned by friendships, personal relationships and more than anything else by his father. Part of the burden he had to bear was that he had inherited his father's business. And while it had been successful under his watch, there were inevitable lingering doubts about his ability. How much of the firm's success was a result of his talent? How much of it was his father's doing? Now that his father was gone, he brought in a partner. The same was true in his personal life. He always had had a girlfriend or, more recently, a wife. "I'd never really been on my own, personally or professionally," he realized. He feared that the breakup of his marriage might condemn him to a perpetual adolescence, and the breakup of his partnership would confirm the professional doubts that everyone had about him.

Donny was careful to keep his bold swagger at the office and in public. Only his close friends knew about his anxiety and his fears, and it was a constant source of conversation. After months of indecision at work and despite the failure of his marriage, Donny decided that he had to act. He had to fire Dworin to prove to himself that he could run an advertising firm and survive outside his father's shadow. He gave Dworin the news and then held a large meeting with all the employees. "It was the first time I ever saw Donny nervous," says Sawyer, who compared Dworin's leaving to the Munchkins in the *Wizard of Oz* after

Dorothy kills the wicked witch. "I saw faces I hadn't seen, and heard laughter that I hadn't heard in a long time."

Donny was not the only one who questioned the future of the agency after Dworin's firing. His departure, wrote the venerable *New York Times* advertising reporter Stuart Elliott, "calls into question the fate of Deutsch/Dworin and whether its impressive growth can continue without him." After the split, some industry watchers established a "Donny watch" to see how long the agency would last.

They are still waiting. Instead of folding, Deutsch expanded, added new accounts, and achieved a new level of creativity. In 1998 the agency won the $250 million national account for Mitsubishi motors. Gaining a major automobile account was a key moment in the transformation of Deutsch from a boutique agency into one of the largest independent full-service agencies in the country. "Once dismissed as an interloper" in most agency boardrooms, remarked *Advertising Age*, "Deutsch now sits near the head of the table." In 1999 Deutsch became the first agency to win *Adweek*'s prize of Agency of the Year in two consecutive years. *Forbes* referred to Deutsch as "one of the fastest-growing and most sought-after shops in America." It had billings of $1.2 billion and offices in Boston, Chicago, Los Angeles, and London. It was credited with a number of edgy campaigns: Mitsubishi credited Deutsch's "Wake Up and Drive" ads for its 25 percent sales growth in the previous year. The agency spent $30 million to transform Baskin-Robbins' recognizable pink spoon into an icon for the small ice cream retailer.

His critics still dismissed Donny as a cocky self-promoter and refused to give him credit for the firm's success. When asked to explain why Deutsch was so successful in the Los Angeles market, one sniffed, "Hollywood is a sound bite town, and Donny gives great sound bites." A New York agency boss sniped: "He's an egomaniac who was obsessed by growth rather than the quality of work that his agency produces." As the *New York Times* put it, "Mr. Deutsch—and by extension, his agency—has had difficulty overcoming an image as a brash parvenu who uses schmooze and mirrors to woo clients and gimmicks and guile to woo customers." In November 1998 *Adweek* featured a display of a group of agency leaders for a full-page portrait in its twentieth-anniversary issue. The caption read in part: "Outspoken? Sure. Successful? Undoubtedly. Popular? Not in all circles. Donny Deutsch has yet to live down his reputation as a braggart who favors publicity stunts."

Friends could track Donny's mood and his sense of himself by observing his fluctuating weight and his taste for clothes. During the '80s he went through the cowboy-banker phase. "He looked like something straight out of a bad Western movie," recalls a friend. In the early '90s, he tried the slicked-back look. "It just looked like someone dropped a can of oil on his head and greased all of his hair back. He looked straight out of a mobster film." During the crisis period when his marriage and partnership were failing, thanks to his weight gain, drugs, and alcohol, "he looked like Joey Buttafuoco," says a friend.

As he approached his 40th birthday, a new, more adult Donny finally emerged. He started working out with a trainer, became religious about eating a low-fat diet, and started dressing in comfortable but toned-down clothes. "You look at him now, and it's like you're looking at the same eyes, the same nose, and the same hands, but everything else is different," observed his administrative assistant, Erin Meyers.

Donny was willing to work up a sweat to get into shape and preserve his youthful appearance. Many Boomers preferred to slow the aging process with a pill, a cream, or an injection. The Pepsi generation was becoming the prune juice generation. Marketers went from selling child-proof caps for medicine to providing easy-to-open caps for seniors. Boomers who once used Retin-A to clear pimples were now using it to erase lines. Sales of home hair coloring products doubled during the 1990s, making it a billion-dollar business. Hot tubs, part of the sexual revolution of the 1960s, were now being used to soothe the aches and pains of middle age. During the 1990s nearly 60 million people used supplements every day, creating a $10 billion market for vitamins, herbs, and minerals. The manufacturer of the sex-enhancing drug Viagra focused its marketing on aging Boomers, becoming the official sponsor of the 2002 concert tour of the '60s rock group Earth Wind & Fire. In the three weeks following its introduction in 1998, the little blue pill accounted for 94 percent of all doctor prescriptions in the United States. Many Boomers also turned to plastic surgery. An estimated 8.5 million cosmetic procedures were performed in 2001—about 50 percent more than the 5.7 million the previous year. Almost half were performed on people aged 35 to 50.

Donny's personality has mellowed with age and success. In 1995

USA Today compared him to the flamboyant television personality Roseanne. "Both are larger-than-life, obnoxious, but lovable, loud-mouths whose working-class acts have made them very wealthy. And both are known best by their first names—Roseanne in Hollywood, Donny on Madison Avenue. The mere mention of their names draws smirks—but infinite interest." A certain cockiness and brashness still defines part of his new adult personality, but he is also capable of being modest and self-effacing. "He's less brassy now," observes a colleague. "He dresses less brassy. He speaks a bit less brassy. He's a little quieter now." He jokes with friends that he does business with blue smoke and mirrors, and he is generous in giving credit to the people around him. His greatest gift, he is fond of saying, is in surrounding himself with people who are smarter than him. "I think it was his personality more than anything else that allowed him to succeed," says friend Perry Shore. "It was not his tremendous business skills. Not his creative skills, or his accountant skills. I think it really was more his charisma and his personality that got him here."

Donny's style reflects the casualness and lack of formality of his generation. The offices, spread out over 90,000 square feet, are a cross between a factory and art gallery. People navigate the expansive space on roller boards. All the offices look exactly the same. There's no hierarchy designated by office size. The glass walls and concrete floors convey an open democratic style. The workplace is very casual. People can wear whatever they want. "If you're being creative," said Meyers, "you can have green hair and wear purple polka dot shorts. He really doesn't care." Growing up in New York, Donny was exposed to a wide variety of people and lifestyles. He grew up after the civil rights revolution, in the midst of feminism, and he watched the gay rights movement unfold. Like many other urban Boomers, he is open and nonjudgmental about people's private lives. His office is in the heart of the gay district in New York's Chelsea area, surrounded by gay bars and restaurants. "Donny is the gayest straight man that I know," said a friend. "There's a lot of gay men in the office who check him out. Donny doesn't care. He loves the attention." He jokes among close friends that he only hires "chicks, Jews, and fags." "The DNA in this place is just off the wall," observes an executive.

For Boomers as a whole, the formula "social liberal, fiscal conservative" would become a mantra used by both Clinton and George W. Bush. Far more than previous generations, Boomers could care less what other people do in their bedrooms or spare time. Surveys reveal a striking correlation between age and social attitudes. Younger people have more liberal views than older people on a variety of issues from gay rights, to interracial dating, to racial equality. Boomers are more socially liberal than their parents, and their Gen X children have only widened the gap.

In Donny's case, ignoring everyone else's private life allows more time to focus on himself. Donny is notoriously vain. He keeps an 8 by 10 picture of himself with a large reflective frame sitting on top of his desk. It is not there because he feels a close connection to the people in the photograph. It sits nearby because he can work at his desk and talk on the telephone while keeping a close eye on his reflection in the frame. "That is the only goddamn reason why that picture is on his desk," observes a former colleague. He is a mirror magnet. "Anytime there is ever a mirror anywhere, he will find it," observes Shore. He's been known to take his shirt off in the office and flex his muscles for Deutsch employees. He often brags that he has the best body of any advertising executive in America. He was known to walk into meetings, plop down on a conference table, and ask: "Tell me something: Is it distracting to have such a good-looking CEO?"

For his 40th birthday, Donny's friends organized a small celebration. Sitting in the festive room, he could not help feeling a little sad. "There's something wrong here." The "something" was that his father was the master of ceremonies for the evening. He thought that by age 40, it should have been his wife and his children who were the most important people in his life. The evening underscored that Donny still had not established a life of his own. He was eager to settle down, get married again, and perhaps start a family.

The opportunity came in 1996 when he was introduced to 25-year-old Stacy Josloff. She grew up in New Jersey and worked selling fashion. They dated for a few years, and Stacy was ready to get married. But Donny liked the freedom that the single life provided, and he did not want to make the same mistake twice. When Stacy presented him with an ultimatum—"If you want to be in my life, you have to make a commitment"—Donny broke things off, and they both started dating other people. After months of indecision, Donny realized that he wanted Stacy back, so he asked her for dinner one night, presented her with a 6-carat diamond, and asked her to marry him.

Once again his friends took a poll on whether he would actually go through with the ceremony. The odds changed weekly. In the end, he went ahead with the wedding. When he walked down the aisle, his friends stood and gave him an ovation. He picked his father to serve as best man. "The happiest I've ever seen him was when his father spoke in his wedding," says friend Stephanie Greenfeld.

In 2000 he also finally put to rest any remaining doubts about his business skills. He sold his company to an international agency, Interpublic Group, for over $270 million—more cash than the entire New York Yankees annual payroll. "The money search is over," he says. Donny remained CEO of the agency, which operated independently under the IPG banner. "The ad industry underestimated me because our agency was small and I went into my father's business—you know, the idiot son syndrome—and I had a big mouth early on and people didn't take me seriously," he told *Forbes* magazine, which listed him among the most underestimated executives in America. "I ended up being the largest independent agency in the world, and sold it last year for $270 million. I had the last laugh."

■

It is not accurate to say that all Boomer men feared commitment or struggled to establish "grown-up" marriages. But as the first generation to live with a 50 percent divorce rate and with so many working women with independent means, Boomer men faced challenges that their parents never experienced. Though very different from each other, Donny and Marshall Herskovitz lived parallel lives in the 1990s in key respects. After years of trying to repair a troubled marriage, Marshall and Susan separated in 1993 and later divorced. Marshall had hoped that intensive counseling and therapy would allow them to bridge their differences, but he was wrong. "We simply grew apart," he remarks. Now in his 40s, Marshall was living alone for the first time in his adult life. He dated occasionally, but he devoted most of his nonwork attention to maintaining a close relationship with his children. More than that, he threw himself into his work, and there was plenty of it.

In 1994, perhaps because of his own preoccupation with preserving his relationship with his children, Marshall tried appealing to the children of Boomers with *My So-Called Life,* a drama about a 15-year-old girl. *Thirtysomething* took the angst of young Baby Boomers seriously; *My So-Called Life* took teenage angst more seriously than it had been treated before. Writing in the *Los Angeles Times,* television critic Howard Rosenberg referred to the show as "a sort of Beverly Hills, 90210, minus the lobotomy." As was often the case with Marshall shows, it received considerable critical acclaim but a limited audience and was canceled after one season. Ironically, an ABC executive complained that only 15-year-old girls were watching. Only two years later WB would target that same audience for hit shows like *Dawson's Creek* and *Buffy the Vampire Slayer.* "We were two years ahead of our time," Zwick said.

In 1998 he started work on a new series, *Once and Again,* which addressed the concerns of Baby Boomers now in their forties. According to Marshall, the drama, which starred Billy Campbell and Sela Ward, focused on "how two grownups with the entire baggage train of their lives behind them will find a way to bring their lives together." He never considered naming the show *fortysomething.* "We knew other people would name the show that, so there was no need for us to." Lily Manning (Sela Ward), the co-owner of a bookstore, with two kids named Grace and Zoe, and Rick Sammler (Billy Campbell), an architect also with two children, named Eli and Jessie, were going through divorces when they met at their children's school. They begin a long, often complicated relationship. They eventually get married and merge their families.

Like the characters in *thirtysomething,* they are constantly forced to choose between conflicting wants and desires. The tension in their thirties, however, was often rooted in the idealism of their youth. By their forties, the Boomers are just trying to survive. Rick and Lily are pulled in so many different directions trying to raise their children and make a living they have trouble making time for each other. "It's older and wiser than *thirtysomething,*" Marshall reflects. "It did not take itself quite as seriously. *Once and Again* was more of a story, while *thirtysomething* was a meditation on life."

Marshall went to great lengths to argue that *Once and Again* was not autobiographical, although he, like the main character in the show, was divorced with two children. The situations the characters faced were unique, but again Marshall reached deep within himself, and his own experience, to uncover insecurities and tensions that animated the show. Taken together, the three shows offer a trilogy of the same Baby Boom family. In *thirtysomething*, Michael and Hope are newlyweds starting a family. In *My So-Called Life*, their children are growing up and experiencing their own turmoil. And in *Once and Again*, the lead couple is divorced, struggling to find love while also sharing the burden of parenthood. They had to contend with problems that the Brady Bunch never faced—drug addiction, the impact of mental illness on the family, anorexia, and a sexual identity crisis. *Once and Again* was steeped in moral ambiguity. The focus was on the complexity of relationships. It evolved around feelings, not action. There were no gruesome murders, dramatic high-speed car chases, or steamy sex scenes. To help explore the thoughts behind the actions, Marshall created black and white interview segments where the characters discussed their feelings with the audience.

Critics hailed it for its realistic portrayal of family dynamics, its great writing, and exceptional acting. As "addictive as a soap opera and as nourishing as a meaty meal," said one near echo of the reaction to *thirtysomething*. "There's no question that *Once and Again* is put together by people with acute powers of observation and an unerring sense of family psychodynamics," observed the *New Yorker*. "They get it. They get the way parents can keep on messing with your head long after you've got gray hairs of your own; they get the way parents have to live with the feeling that whatever they do their children will invariably resent them for it."

Despite the strong critical acclaim, the show failed to attract a large audience. Scheduling problems partly limited its appeal. The show had seven time slots in two and a half years. In its final season, *Once and Again* ranked 103rd among prime-time TV shows, one of the lowest rankings for a network drama series. Whether or not Marshall's formula was dead, there was a clear problem with his demographics. Boomers controlled the country and the industry, but the audience they now needed to attract was much younger. The elusive 18 to 34 age group, not introspective Boomers, was treasured as the holy grail by advertisers.

Marshall believed that the problem was that television viewers did not want to deal with reality. "Most people want TV shows to transport them away from their lives . . . using real life as a reference point is more familiar in the world of movies." The focus on real life problems gave the show a heavy, sometimes depressing tone. "To be honest," said one critic, "it was rarely an uplifting show; even the holiday episodes—the big Thanksgiving meals, the Christmas gatherings—generally ended up with the turkey on the floor, somebody drunk, somebody screaming and somebody bolting out the door." *TV Guide* called *Once and Again* "the best show you're not watching." Robert Bianco, *USA Today's* perceptive critic, said it was "earnest and honest." It forced people to confront "uncomfortable truths: That your children and parents might not be the people you thought they were, or hoped they would be. And that you were required to love them anyway." Bianco pointed out that the show drew about 8 million viewers, which was three times more than MTV's hit *The Osbornes*. "Had *Once* run on cable, it might have run forever."

■

The same generational wave that allowed Boomer-themed shows to dominate television in the 1980s was responsible for drowning them out by the end of the century as advertisers and television executives paddled out to catch the next wave: the 70 million children of the Boomers, born between 1977 and 1995. Boomers, the intense focus of marketing sales pitches since childhood, were now dismissed as "spillovers," as the $36 billion television advertising business catered to the needs of the 18–34 age group. Hollywood, assuming that they were more likely to rush to the theater in the critical opening weekend of a big release, looked to younger audiences to stay afloat. "Baby boom audiences will soon feel the same jolt that perhaps their parents felt when *The Lawrence Welk Show* was jettisoned for *The Monkees*," observed marketing executive John Rash.

Many people questioned the logic of focusing media dollars on Gen X when Boomers still made up a large percentage of the television viewing public and could back up their preferences with purchasing dollars. According to Nielsen, Boomers make up about 40 percent of households watching prime-time television. The average adult between the ages of 25 and 64 spent an average of 248 minutes a day in front of the tube, which amounted to 22 minutes more a day than their children.

Why have advertisers ignored the interests of Boomers who watched more television and possessed more purchasing power? The logic was that older people were more resistant to change, less willing to respond to an advertiser's appeal to change brands. Younger people were more malleable and had not formed strong brand loyalties. In addition, since younger people watch less television, they are harder to reach. The laws of supply and demand dictate that advertisers pay more to reach them. As a result, advertising rates for a show that appeals to those 50 and older are a fraction of the rates that reach people in their 20s. Ironically, advertisers formed many of these assumptions in the 1960s in an effort to tap into the lucrative Boomer market. Over the years, they never challenged the theory, even though the demographics had changed dramatically. Surveys show that Boomers are just as likely to experiment with new brands of soda, beer, and candy as their children. "Madison Avenue people tend to look at aging as if you wake up one day and you're 49 and you can't try new things anymore," complained Madelyn Hochstein, the president of a market research company. Quite possibly, a complicated theory missed a simpler reality: advertisers should reach for the largest audience no matter its age.

The rise of the WB network is a classic example of how the new demographics are changing the way television operates. Just as Brandon Tartikoff transformed NBC in the 1980s by appealing to the cultural tastes of Boomers, the WB has zeroed in on Generation Y. "We saw this swell," said the 35-year-old network president, Jordan Levin. "We paddled on out past the other waves and staked our spot and waited for it to come. We're riding it down, and it's a monster." The network built its base around "power babes" with revealing shirts and sparkling teeth who slay monsters and romance handsome men. Although its prime-time audience is small compared to the major networks—4.4 million in 2002 compared with 12.7 million for CBS—its core audience of viewers between the ages of 12 and 34 attracts top advertising dollars. According to the *New York Times*, advertisers pay $90,000 for a 30-second ad on a typical episode of *60 Minutes*, which is watched by 14 million people with a median age of 60. For a comparable ad on the WB's hot *Smallville*, watched by 7.5 million people with an average age of under 30, advertisers paid $111,000.

Generation X rejoiced that their parents were losing their grip on the nation's popular culture. "Long-awaited baby boomer die-off to begin soon," opined the satirical newspaper the *Onion*. "Before long, tens of millions of members of this irritating generation will achieve what such boomer icons as Jim Morrison, Janis Joplin, Timothy Leary and John

Kennedy already have: death. Before long, we will live in a glorious new world in which no one will ever again have to endure tales of Joan Baez's performance at Woodstock." Boomers, on the other hand, lamented that they were passing the baton to what *Advertising Age* referred to as "that cynical, purple-haired blob watching TV." *Slate* online magazine editor Michael Kinsley half-heartedly complained: "These kids today. They're soft. They don't know how good they have it. Not only did they never have to fight in a war . . . they never even had to dodge one."

In many ways there are important differences in style and manner separating Boomers from Generation X. Not only did Generation X have the misfortune of following a generation twice their size, they grew up in a rapidly changing economy. Between 1979 and 1995 the economy lost 43 million jobs, and outside of Silicon Valley, most of the new jobs offered lower pay and fewer benefits. As a result, Xers have been forced to be more competitive, more materialistic, and more willing to make compromises than their Boomer predecessors at a comparable age. In the 1960s and 1970s idealistic Boomers still believed they could change the world; jaded Xers were more likely to want a new car. "They had the free speech movement; we get political correctness," observed David Greenberg. "They had 'Turn on, tune in, drop out'; we get 'Just say no.' They had communes; we get Melrose Place. They had Apollo; we get the Challenger. They had the pill; we get AIDS." Demographically, Xers are less white, more culturally diverse, and even more socially tolerant. They are twice as likely as their Boomer parents to agree "that there is no single way to live."

Reality television is Gen X's rebellion against the navel gazing of Baby Boomer shows like *thirtysomething*. This generation looks at *thirtysomething* with the same disdain that Boomers once looked at *Father Knows Best*. Since Gen X defined itself in opposition to Boomers, they had a different sense of reality, mutating the quiet introspection of *thirtysomething* and *Once and Again* into the backbiting theatrics of *Survivor*. Marshall's talent was for bringing the viewers into the show by allowing them to empathize with the inner turmoil and confusion of the actor. Reality television is a voyeuristic experience meant to keep the audience distant from the participants. Instead of trying to understand their inner psychology, the viewer is encouraged to judge and mock the contestant. It traces its roots back to the exploitive talk shows that began in the 1980s with Phil Donohue, and in some cases degenerated until they hit rock bottom with Jerry Springer. The shows featured a variety of oddball guests who exposed their innermost demons before a national television audience that took delight in their embarrassment. "It trades on the worst in human nature," Marshall insists. "I detest it."

All of the name calling between generations has obscured the many qualities they share. The Greatest Generation created the prosperity that allowed Boomers to pursue their own agenda. Boomers, in turn, democratized the culture in a way that allowed Xers to develop and nurture their celebration of individualism. In that sense, Xers represent a blossoming of Boomer culture, not a rejection of it. Xers have taken the Boomer ethic of self-fulfillment to new heights, have found new ways of expressing their individualism, and have embellished the antiestablishment streak. They are children of the Boom, and like most children, they tried to break away from their parents. In the end, however, they resemble them more than they would like to admit.

Although Boomers complain about being marginalized by mainstream culture, it is Boomer marketers and television executives who are making the decisions to attract younger audiences. In 1997 Deutsch took over the campaign for the popular soft drink Snapple. Jeffrey Wolf, a Baby Boom executive, decided to focus the campaign on Gen X and Gen Y, who consumed the most soft drinks in the United States. "It is where the business opportunity was," he said. For months, the firm not only conducted focus groups and analyzed market data, it went into the homes of young people to see what posters they had on the walls, what clothes hung in their closets (or lay strewn on the floor), and what CDs they listened to. Using the data, Wolf developed a generational chart (shown here) that highlighted the differences between Gen Y, Gen X, and Boomers. The research revealed both the differences and similarities between Boomers and the younger generation. Gen X defined themselves in opposition to Baby Boomers, while Gen Y, many of them children of the Boomers, were philosophically akin to their parents. Both Boomers and Gen Y grew up during a period of prosperity and shared an overall sense of optimism and idealism, while Gen X were often more jaded and cynical.

Deutsch discovered that younger consumers responded to the same overall style that they had used to reach Boomers during the IKEA campaign. The Boomers had broken the mold, forcing adver-

	BOOMERS	GEN X	GEN Y
The facts	Born between 1946 and 1964	Born between 1965 and 1976	Born between 1977 and 1995
	Currently aged 38–56	Currently aged 26–37	Currently aged 7–25
	78 million	40 million	70 million (36% are 18–24)
	24% are minorities	35% are minorities	37% are minorities
The foundation	Postwar prosperity	Recession	Technology boom/prosperity
	Suburban development	Children of divorce, latchkey kids	Neotraditional family structures
	Rebellion against traditional values	No clearly defined family values	Emphasis on family values
	LSD	Cocaine	Ecstasy
	Rock and roll	Alternative rock	Hip hop/pop, techno
	Vietnam, JFK, Nixon	*Challenger*, AIDS	OJ, Monica, Columbine, and 9/11
	Hippies	Slackers	Entrepreneurs/multitaskers
Core values and attitudes	Self-reliance	Fatalistic	Optimistic/self-enrichment
	Entitlement	Independent	Empowerment
	Experiment	Cope with it	Creative
	Do it my way	Accept and move on	Accept it—do something about it
	Idealism	Pragmatism	Pragmatic idealism
	Internally motivated	Externally motivated	Balanced
Influenced by	Network TV	MTV	Internet
Generational icons	Bill Clinton, John Lennon	Kurt Cobain, JFK Jr., Madonna	Sean Fanning (Napster guy), Tiger Woods
Spirit	Peace, love, happiness	This sucks!	Liv n lrn:)

tisers to deal with a generation that understood the conventions of television. Their children simply took those qualities to the next level. They were more media savvy than their parents, even less willing to buy into a traditional sales pitch. The ads touched on the same individualistic nerve, but in a different place. They also shared a sense of irony. "We are just trying to figure out what is ironic to them," says Wolf. "It is the same themes but a different mind-set based on their life experiences."

The campaign, which launched in spring 2003, used the same rough-cut reality style that the IKEA ads used in the early 1990s. They are designed to make it look as if they could have been produced in someone's basement. There is no strong product message, no sales pitch, or memorable jingle. The central characters are bottles of Snapple dressed in various costumes. One ad features two bottles dressed in tuxedos getting married. Donny gave the campaign his seal of approval in typical style: "Fucking great."

TWELVE

THE NEW BOSSES

Bobby in Cambodia;
© Eberhard Laue, aspect media

Fran with Bill Clinton.

Fran with son David at petition drive;

The Boomers were producing products and selling them to themselves and to everyone else: they were industry and political leaders; they were managing enormous sums of money on Wall Street and in venture capital in Silicon Valley. If some of the most visible parts of American culture were no longer theirs—music, Hollywood, the targets of advertising, and many of the entrepreneurs leading the Internet revolution all coveted a cult of youth—the Boomers were nonetheless the new establishment in almost all walks of life. They had power after rebelling against it for so long.

On October 18, 1993, Fran Visco stood in the East Room of the White House awaiting the arrival of President Clinton and First Lady Hillary Rodham Clinton. Behind her were boxes stacked to the ceiling containing 2.6 million signatures they had collected over the previous months in support of research on breast cancer. Fran traveled from Philadelphia with her mother, her husband, and her 7-year-old son, David. "I'm standing there waiting and it didn't occur to me that I was at the White

House. It didn't really hit me," she recalls. "I mean this man was my age. He was only a couple of years older than me. Then all of a sudden these people come in the door and I saw her, and I saw him, and all of a sudden my stomach started churning. 'Oh my God this is the President of the United States! Fran what are you doing here?'"

The room erupted with applause as the President and First Lady made their way to the stage. "Let's all give a cheer for what we've done," Visco said at the podium. "It's been incredible. Over the past two years, funding has gone from $90 million to $400 million this year. We did that! We're changing the world!" The crowd roared its approval. She read one of the messages that was included in the petition. It was from her son, David. It read: "Mr. President, please stop this disease. I want my mom to live forever."

The key to the organization's approach to politics was its annual convention held every spring at a Washington, D.C., hotel. The conference brought (and still brings) together women from all over the country, from big cities and small rural areas. Some were former activists who campaigned against the Vietnam War and for the ERA. A majority, however, were housewives, teachers, and managers who had never been involved in politics. They represent all age groups, but most were middle-aged Boomers. They shared one thing: They were all either breast cancer survivors or close to someone suffering from the disease. They found comfort in numbers, seeing for the first time hundreds of people like themselves. Their reason for coming to the conference was not to share each other's pain, but to learn how to organize on the local level to apply pressure on Congress to increase funding for breast cancer research. By the 1990s most advocacy groups learned what Bobby Muller had discovered when organizing for Vietnam vets in the 1980s: Real political power rested in the local community, not inside the Beltway. If you wanted to get the attention of a congressman, you apply pressure locally in his or her district. "That's why people take my phone calls and listen to me," says the NBCC's political director. "They know their constituents are behind this organization."

On the first day Fran addressed the group in a packed auditorium, explaining the NBCC's purpose and how they could contribute to eradicating breast cancer. Inevitably, she underscored the sense of urgency by remembering the women who had been at the last conference but were not alive for this one. "Many people look at her as a symbol of something they would love to be," says a participant. "She's smart, tough, outspoken, and fearless." Fran explained that the conference was about power, not therapy. The point was to force the male-dominated medical profession and political establishment to respond to the needs of the breast cancer community. Symbolic gestures were not enough; they needed to exercise power. The members of Congress are public servants. "They are there to serve the people. You elected them." Nonetheless it was therapeutic. "You see people literally sitting taller in their chairs," reflects an observer. "And women in the audience are taking notes and their eyes are getting bigger. You can feel the energy in the room."

The coalition has continued to participate in the medical review process. To give participants some basic background on the scientific process, they created Project Lead, a seminar designed to teach women how to understand and evaluate scientific proposals. Organized by Kay Dickerson, a breast cancer survivor with a Ph.D. in public health, it was a workshop modeled after the antiwar teach-ins of the 1960s. During a four-day intensive program some of the leading scientists in the field taught them about important new developments. They were less interested in generalized studies about basic cell biology or new ways of easing the pain of cancer sufferers. They wanted to see specific proposals that pushed science toward finding a cure for breast cancer. "Yes, you may have a very interesting scientific idea but it doesn't get me any closer to understanding how you treat breast cancer," is how Joanne Howes puts it.

Probably the best example of the success of the NBCC was the passage of the Breast and Cervical Cancer Treatment Act (2000), which provided Medicare benefits to low-income women who were screened and diagnosed in federal screening programs. In 1990 Congress passed legislation providing free mammograms and Pap smears to low-income women without health insurance. It did not, however, include treatment. A woman who was too poor to afford insurance but not poor enough to qualify for Medicaid could be diagnosed but be left without options. "In essence," Visco observes, "it says to women diagnosed with cancer through the screening program: 'Thanks for coming in for a mammogram or cervical exam. You have cancer but there is no guarantee of treatment.'" Visco was fortunate to have a generous private insurance policy that allowed her to get the best treatment possible, and she was convinced that access to quality health care saved her life. Many women were not so fortunate. Many were forced to depend on charity, and often their treatment options were based on what they could afford, not on what they needed. A patient with limited resources, for example, would choose a radical mastectomy instead of the more expensive lumpectomy because she could not afford expensive radiation and chemotherapy treatments.

The coalition built a bipartisan effort in support of legislation sponsored by Rhode Island liberal Republican senator John Chafee to add a treatment component to the Medicare coverage. "Diagnosis without treatment is only half the battle against breast cancer," he said. The first step was to get the support of the chairman of the House Commerce Committee. His chief of staff opposed the idea and refused to raise it with the congressman. "No, there's no way we're ever going to do that," he told Fran, effectively blocking access to the committee. Unable to reach the congressman in Washington, the coalition went into his district and organized constituents. More than a dozen breast cancer survivors attended the meeting and explained why they wanted him to support the bill. When the meeting was over, he said, "By golly we're going to mark this thing up." And he did.

The bill sailed through the House but ran into opposition in the Senate. The coalition decided that it was time to use the media to build support, since it was harder to apply local pressure on the Senate. They organized a press conference featuring a woman from Oklahoma named Tonia Conine. She had breast cancer detected through a CDC screening in March 2000. She had no health insurance but was fortunate to have a doctor who performed the surgery for free. There were, however, follow-up bills for chemotherapy and medication, and her total expenses reached over $9,000. In a tearful press conference she pleaded for Senate passage of the legislation. "The bottom line is at the end of the day when you're an elected official you have to speak to the people that you represent," says Stephanie Katz, the organization's chief lobbyist. "And here is a woman who was screened by a program that the federal government created and then left to a system that really didn't guarantee anything. And it was very, very powerful. Needless to say they got that bill passed pretty quickly after that."

Under the legislation, uninsured patients with incomes up to 250 percent over the federal poverty line, about $35,000 a year for a family of three, would be eligible to have the government pay for all medical expenses in connection with cancer. This would include surgery, radiation, chemotherapy, and follow-up care and medications. The bill passed but quietly. The chief sponsor in the House, Rick Lazio of New York, was running against Hillary Clinton for a Senate seat in New York in 2000. Visco lobbied for a White House signing ceremony, but the administration was unwilling to give Lazio the benefit of a public relations coup in the middle of an election year. On January 4, 2001, just a few days before he left office, however, Clinton held a White House ceremony announcing his efforts to speed up implementation of the policy.

In preparation for the 2000 presidential election, the NBCC developed an aggressive strategy to hold public officials accountable for their position on increased funding for breast cancer treatment. Like many other interest groups, they developed a rating system to grade individual representatives on how they responded to their agenda. Visco complained that too many politicians did little more than wear pink lapel ribbons and support "meaningless resolutions" to show their support for finding a cure. "We're going to be there to say, 'Don't believe that pink ribbon,'" Visco said. "We are going to hold [office-holders] to substantive measures to eradicate breast cancer." If candidates want to court women voters, she warned, they needed to address an issue that affected 2.6 million women every year.

Many traditional scientists have resented the mixing of politics and medicine. The former head of the National Cancer Institute, Samuel Broder, who clashed with Visco in the early 1990s, believed that NBCC politicized the scientific process and rested its claim on the fallacy of direct research. "I call it the iron lung syndrome," he told the *New Yorker*. If scientists' search for a polio cure had been hamstrung by the NBCC's "centrally directed program" instead of an "independent, investigator-driven discovery research," they would have produced "the very best iron lungs in the world—portable iron lungs, transistorized iron lungs." They would not, however, have "developed the vaccine that eradicated polio." Harold Varmus, who moved from the National Institutes of Health to become the president of Memorial Sloan-Kettering, objected to the breast cancer community's distinction between "people who work on a real-life problem and people who work on basic research." All scientific discovery depended on "creative chaos," allowing scientists the flexibility to pursue solutions and not just solve specific diseases.

In 2001 *New Yorker* medical writer Jerome Groopman echoed Varmus's objections, arguing that most major medical breakthroughs were the result of unintended consequences. If there had been a Diabetes Institute in the late 19th century, it would not have funded the research and eventually led to the discovery of insulin. A government institute of polio would not have supported research on the mumps virus, which inadvertently aided in the development of a polio vaccine. "And yet both Congress and the public continue to view open ended scientific investigations as nebulous, self-indulgent, and wasteful of taxpayers' money, and are reluctant to fund them." This new climate forced scientists to talk about imminent cures in order to get the directed research dollars they need. These exaggerated claims were then picked up by the media, which played on the public's false hopes and unrealistic expectations of a cancer cure.

There are other drawbacks. Diseases now look for celebrity spokespersons. Using celebrities is nothing new. Comedian Eddie Cantor raised $1.8 million for polio in the 1930s. Gregory Peck appeared in ads for the American Cancer Society in the 1960s. But the new style of medical politics requires celebrity status to get attention. Every disease now has a face. AIDS has Elizabeth Taylor. Diabetes has Mary Tyler Moore. Christopher Reeve campaigns against spinal cord injuries. Michael J. Fox supports Parkinson's disease research. Michael Milken lobbies for research in prostate cancer. Diseases without celebrities struggle for attention and for resources. "AIDS is the contemporary model for how a group gets a larger share of the pie," says Morton Kondracke, executive editor of *Roll Call.* "Organize your community. Get people to visit members of Congress. And if you can't, find a star who will epitomize the problem."

The bottom line, cried the conservative *American Spectator,* "is that tax dollars are spent disproportionately on a chosen few illnesses, not according to any medical criterion, but in response to the loudest cries of *J'Accuse.*" The result of women Baby Boomers' flexing their muscle was that the health concerns of middle-aged women consumed more federal research dollars than many other diseases that claimed far more lives. Each year lung cancer claimed about 160,400 lives. Breast cancer claimed 44,200. Yet lung cancer received a fraction of the funding. Federal funding for breast cancer research was six times greater than prostate cancer research.

The criticism, however, suggests that science can be an objective process, presided over by dispassionate scientists seeking truth. What Boomer women discovered was that science had always been a political process, pushed in different directions by powerful lobbying groups, including the medical profession and pharmaceutical companies. Breast cancer advocates did not introduce politics to the scientific process; they simply added another pressure group to the equation. The only way to respond to their concerns and satisfy the demands of other constituencies, was to increase the amount of resources the nation devoted to cancer research. "The message we gave to Congress year after year is that the supply has to be bigger," Visco declares. Not surprisingly, a study by the Institute of Medicine, a branch of the National Academy of Sciences, noted that no increase could be "large enough to meet every need or fund every promising lead. Choices must be made and priorities must be set." Boomers, like everyone else, can't have it all, but by growing up to be the most demanding generation in history, they are trying harder than ever to have as much as possible. The results will continue to be impressive.

While NBCC thrived during the 1990s, it was a different story at the VVA, which fell on hard times after Muller's departure in 1987. The VVA suffered for very specific reasons. Initially, when he left to run the separate Vietnam Veterans of America Foundation (VVAF), Bobby took with him the organization's two most important sources of money: the Combined Federal Campaign (CFC) and the receipts from a chain of Vietnam veterans' thrift shops. "He created us and he almost killed us," reflects Ned Foote. Eventually, the thrift shops returned to the VVA, but the bottom line was that there were now two organizations competing for the same limited resources.

Broke and leaderless, the VVA floundered, not recovering a firm footing until the late 1990s. The membership may have resented Bobby's authoritarian style, but he was clearly the driving force in making it a power on Capitol Hill. There was no love lost between Bobby and the new leadership. The hostility was evident in 1993, when Muller attended his first VVA convention since leaving office six years earlier. He traveled to the meeting in Norfolk, Virginia, to support one of his protégés, former army medic Wayne Smith, who was running for president. Smith was supported by many of the original, more radical members of the organization, who complained that it had strayed from its roots. The new leadership, which rallied around the current president, Louisiana attorney James L. Brazee, viewed Smith as a stalking horse for Muller. For many people the election represented another struggle for the soul of the organization. "It's a power struggle with the old guard," said a national board member. "The old guard, who is left of center, sees an organization back on its feet and wants it back now. We say 'no, too many people have worked too hard to hand it over.' " When Bobby wheeled into the convention hall to give a speech, he was booed by the members. They voted to prevent him from speaking, and Bobby was forced to leave.

Since it was not a membership organization, the VVAF allowed Bobby to pursue his own agenda without interference from below. He used the new organization to build support for two major initiatives: diplomatic recognition of Vietnam and an international ban on land mines.

Bobby believed that veterans needed to take the lead in the drive to recognize Vietnam. In addition to orchestrating visits to Vietnam, Bobby lobbied the business community to put pressure on the administration. "It was the principal focus of our organization's work for a number of years," he reflects. His organization published a newsletter every week on developments in Indochina. He convinced the Vietnamese to allow Americans to visit the country. The visits, he said, would allow American officials to experience "the grace of the Vietnamese people." Since he had developed close contacts with a number of Vietnamese officials, they would often check with him before granting a visa. There was only one person whom Bobby recommended against receiving a visa: Arizona Congressman, and later Senator, John McCain, a navy pilot who spent more than five years in a Vietnamese prison camp. Initially Bobby felt that McCain was so full of hatred for the Vietnamese that nothing could turn him around.

In 1985 McCain, who got a visa anyway, traveled back to Vietnam for the first time with Walter Cronkite for a television show marking the tenth anniversary of the fall of Saigon. Over the next few years he returned more than a half-dozen times. The experience helped turn

McCain around. By the early 1990s he was leading a bipartisan group of Vietnam veterans in Congress for reconciliation. In 1991 he supported the Bush administration's decision to establish a "road map" leading to diplomatic relations. According to the agreement, the Vietnamese promised to cooperate in the search for American MIAs and agreed to pull their troops out of neighboring Cambodia. For its part the United States promised to lift the trade embargo against Vietnam and eventually establish full diplomatic relations. The American Legion, the nation's largest veterans' group, opposed the initiative, as did groups dealing with MIA-POW questions.

That was the situation that former antiwar protester Bill Clinton inherited in January 1993. Although politically Bobby had a lot in common with Bill Clinton, initially he had little respect for the man. Bobby admired people, even his opponents, who had "guts." You had to prove your mettle to Bobby by enduring adversity, overcoming pain, and, most of all, standing up for what you believe in. "Courage for me means swimming against the tide," said the former lieutenant who enjoyed the thrill of charging up the hill. "To be willing to expose yourself to failure and ridicule." Clinton may have been a talented politician, but he had no backbone. "He was a man without principle," Muller said. Clinton lied about his actions during Vietnam. "He weaseled out of the draft, but he refused to oppose the war. He managed to avoid the draft and avoid service." Oddly enough Clinton would earn Bobby's respect later by his toughness in standing up to the media scrutiny during the Monica Lewinsky affair. "How you can get up every morning and face the media when you know the whole world knows that you have a little pee-pee that hangs to the left I will never know," he says. "The fact that this guy can take the types of hits he's taking and stand up every day and keep going is inspirational."

Just as it took an anti-Communist Republican to go to China, Bobby feared that it would probably take a hawkish veteran to break the ice with Vietnam. But Clinton surprised him. He sought political cover from three well-known Vietnam veterans: Republican John McCain and Democrats Robert Kerrey (D, Nebraska) and John Kerry (D, Massachusetts). Clinton, Bobby observes, was a reluctant convert who "got dragged along" by outspoken vets. "Because he didn't serve, because he was intimidated by the military he was slow to pick up the cause." The Vietnamese honored their commitment to the United States, helping

Pentagon teams exhume graves and track down parts of old parachutes. In February 1994 Clinton lifted the trade embargo the United States had imposed thirty years earlier, at the beginning of the war.

In July 1995 President Clinton, saying it was "time to heal" the divisions caused by a war two decades ago, announced the establishment of formal diplomatic relations with Vietnam. "We can now move on to common ground. Whatever divided us before, let us consign to the past." The ceremony in the White House was a portrait of the Baby Boom generation's response to the war. A president who protested against the war and avoided military service was flanked by two veterans who fought and suffered: John McCain and Bob Kerrey. Sitting in the front row, just a few feet away from the president, was Bobby Muller, veteran turned antiwar activist. Referring to them, Clinton said, "They served their country bravely. They are of different parties. A generation ago, they had different judgments about the war which divided us so deeply. But today, they are of a single mind. They agree that the time has come for America to move forward on Vietnam."

Although Clinton was willing to put closure on one issue left over from the war, he was reluctant to move on another. In 1984 Bobby had returned to the killing fields of Cambodia, a country that "not only experienced war, it experienced genocide." Outside Phnom Penh he went to a torture center that had been transformed into a museum. "I emotionally felt the horror and the terror of what had gone on and I got this chill through the deepest part of me." It tapped into another side of Bobby's personality—a profound pessimism. Part of what drives and gets him up every day, gives him some of his kinetic energy, is an impending sense of doom. He worked so hard because the stakes were so high. "We're fucked," he thought to himself after viewing the torture chamber. "We ain't going to make it. Once you understand what human beings are capable of doing, once you get that, you realize that genetically we're built to do this because we do it generation after generation after generation. There's something about our genetic makeup that allows us to go down that path of darkness and get to the point that we do what is absolutely unimaginable to each other. There are no limits. There are no constraints. If we don't fundamentally change this dynamic at some point, somehow, somebody's going to take this the distance and we're going to light it up."

He needed a new cause into which he could channel that manic energy. He was struck by the numbers of war survivors who were missing legs. Most had stepped on land mines left over from the Vietnam War, and most of the mines were put there by the United States. Bobby had personal experience with land mines, having stepped on one during an early combat mission in Vietnam. He walked away unscathed, but many other soldiers were not so lucky. Mines were the chief cause of American casualties in the Vietnam War, by some estimates killing or wounding nearly 65,000 U.S. soldiers. "When I was on the hospital ship, the guys that cried the loudest were either burn victims or victims of land mines who suffered a traumatic amputation of a limb. And when they changed the dressing on that limb those guys would cry— literally, I swear, would cry—for their mothers."

The problem was worldwide. There were more than 60 million mines buried in sixty-eight countries. Estimates are unreliable, but most experts claim that mines continue to claim over 20,000 lives a year. "That's right: $3 antipersonnel landmines had killed more people than all the Cold War weapons of mass destruction combined," Bobby notes. Most land mines were designed to wound, not kill. For every solder wounded, at least two others were removed from combat to provide assistance. The problem was that after the battle, the mines remained to prey on civilians. And they were indiscriminate. "Every other weapon got put away after the war," Bobby says. "But land mines were still causing horribly debilitating and painful injuries" to innocent civilians who don't have the luxury of being able to leave a war-torn country. "It was the poorest of the poor, the most vulnerable within the society, who were invariably winding up the victims of land mines," he reflects. "It was the kids, either playing or bringing animals out to graze, that were getting blown up. In Cambodia, one of every 236 individuals was an amputee. Even when they never explode, the mines, which often weigh only a few ounces, can cripple economic development in poverty-strapped nations.

The VVAF established a prosthetic clinic on the outskirts of Phnom Penh, which emerged within a few years as the national rehabilitation center for the country. Every month it produced more than 140 prostheses and 30 wheelchairs. In addition to helping the victims of land mines, Bobby wanted to organize an international campaign to ban their use. In September 1992 he teamed up with Thomas Gebauer, head of Medico International in Frankfurt, Germany. A few weeks later Bobby hired Jody Williams, who as deputy director of Medical Aid in El Salvador had been responsible for running its project for wounded children in El Salvador. The *Washington Post* referred to Muller and Williams as "classic baby boomer lefties who've made a difference." Both were shaped by antiwar crusades. Vietnam was the defining experience of Bobby's life. For Williams it was the Reagan administration's intervention in the tiny Central American nation of El Salvador during the 1980s. Both possessed a strong sense of moral outrage, a keen understanding of the media, and a handy ability with sound bites.

The aim of the campaign was not only to ban the manufacture and use of land mines, but to equate antipersonnel mines with poison gas and chemical weapons. In 1992, Bobby approached Vermont senator and antimine crusader Patrick Leahy. "I'll help you. But, Bob, you gotta understand something," Leahy told Muller, "it's going to take years." "That's okay," Bobby responded. "We're going to stay with you." The same year Leahy quietly pushed into law a moratorium on the export of antipersonnel mines. In 1993 he got it extended for three years by a vote of 100 to 0. "Bobby was my inspiration, my conscience on this issue," Leahy said. The one-year ban offered a clear signal to the international community that the United States was serious about the land mine issue. The campaign picked up momentum when, in a 1994 speech to the United Nations, President Clinton called for "ridding the world" of antipersonnel land mines. The following year the International Committee of the Red Cross abandoned its policy of neutrality on political issues and joined the campaign.

Clinton, however, under pressure from the Pentagon, began backtracking. In part he was responding to political pressures at home. When Republicans gained control of the Congress in 1994, the beleaguered president was convinced that he had to move closer to the center, co-opting the conservative agenda at home while appearing strong on foreign policy issues. He was also influenced by growing military tension with North Korea. In the event that the 1.3-million-strong North Korean army tried rushing across the DMZ, the United States would use its million-plus mines to slow the approach. "My primary responsibility is to protect the young people that I or one of my successors will have to send into battle," Clinton said. "I don't want them hamstrung by some decision I make today."

Although Clinton explained his reluctance as a matter of principle, Bobby was convinced it was all about fortitude. "The Pentagon's job is to acquire weapons, not to go to a president asking to be stripped of them," Bobby told *Maclean's* in 1997. "Because Clinton didn't serve, because of his deference to the military, he's a coward when it comes to standing up to the Pentagon." Bobby attended a meeting with Clinton in the White House to discuss the issue. "Mr. President, what more can we do" to help you on this issue? he asked. "You can get the Joint Chiefs off my ass," Clinton responded. "I can't afford a breach with the Joint Chiefs." He did, however, promise he would get rid of these weapons in a time frame they could live with.

While Bobby was running into opposition within the United States, Jody Williams was having great success rallying other nations to the cause. She bypassed the glacial United Nations and patched together an international coalition of private and public groups, orchestrating a successful media strategy to sway public opinion and force reluctant nations to join. Diana, the late Princess of Wales, lent her star quality to the land mine issue with visits to victims in Bosnia and Angola. Williams made good use of emotional images of children without legs, but nothing grabbed headlines more than the pictures of Diana tip-toeing through a mine field in Angola and comforting victims in Bosnia. "We don't have the same kind of emotional images to convey our position," said U.S. Army Colonel Thadd Buzan, a military–political affairs strategist in Korea.

The question emerged: How important was U.S. participation in the campaign? Muller and Williams split on the answer. Bobby believed that without U.S. participation, a treaty would be toothless, and he wanted to work with the administration to develop a treaty that it could sign. Bobby worked hard to build public support to make it politically feasible for Clinton to go along with it. "The Pentagon didn't give a shit about land mines," he says. They feared that a successful campaign to ban land mines would create a precedent that could endanger munitions they really cared about. What would be next? Cluster bombs? Bobby's plan was to provide the administration with political cover by recruiting high-profile military officials to publicly support the ban and he corralled more than a dozen generals, including Persian Gulf War hero Norman Schwarzkopf. The president "has a real problem, and we've got to help him solve it," he said. A master of public relations, Bobby tried to mold public opinion by using pop stars to get his message out. The way to connect with people was not through high-sounding speeches, he believed, but through music and entertainment. Most of all, he hoped to neutralize Pentagon worry by assuring them that his efforts were not part of a master plan by antiwar pacifists to neuter the American military.

Williams, riding the fast-moving international wave, refused any hint of compromise to appease the United States, believing that international opinion would eventually embarrass Clinton into signing. "She [Williams] was running around the world being little Miss Land Mine Queen," Bobby recalls, criticizing the United States and undermining his efforts to build bridges with the administration and the Pentagon. Instead of working through established channels, she painstakingly assembled a coalition of more than 1,000 non-governmental organizations in more than sixty nations. These groups lobbied, pressured, and cajoled their governments to support the ban. After listening to Williams talk with reporters, Bobby said he hoped the Pentagon "won't get the idea that we are a bunch of backwoods, leftover Woodstock activists."

The differences between Muller and Williams exposed another crack in the Baby Boom. The 1960s may have produced a new style of activism and an impatience for change, but it did not produce agreement on tactics and strategy. Williams was the unreformed radical who resisted working within the system. Like many of Bobby's former antiwar friends, she remained deeply distrustful of "the establishment" and reluctant to compromise principle for short-term gain. In many ways, her philosophy was similar to Bobby's during his early years in the antiwar movement. During the 1980s, however, Bobby made the move to the center. Realizing that change was often slow and incremental, he chose to work from the inside.

In December 1997 the campaign succeeded in getting 120 nations to sign a comprehensive ban on the global production and use of land mines. The United States, Russia, and China were among only a small number of global powers that refused to sign. "For the first time the majority of nations of the world will agree to ban a weapon which has been in military use by almost every country in the world," said Jean Chrétien, Canada's prime minister. The press hailed the treaty as a major breakthrough in the campaign to ban land mines and praised

Williams for her herculean efforts. That year the International Campaign to Ban Land mines received the Nobel Peace Prize. Williams rushed from Washington back to her house in Vermont; dressed in tank top and worker overalls, she stood barefoot on her front lawn to address reporters after the announcement of the award. She called President Clinton a "weenie" who was not "on the side of humanity" for failing to endorse the ban. She accepted the prize as a personal reward, downplaying the role played by the International Campaign. "I don't think she has a clue that this was a stupid thing to do, to put herself out in front," a VVAF staff member told the *Washington Post*. "She could have gotten the prize and very magnanimously said, 'I owe this to Leahy and Bobby Muller.' She could have afforded to be gracious and magnanimous. But that's not her nature."

Many people believed that Bobby Muller, not Jody Williams, should have received the Nobel Prize since he was the architect of the campaign and Williams was his employee. But Bobby had ambivalent feelings about the campaign. The ban represented a pyrrhic victory without American participation. "You can have every nation in the world agree to something, but if the United States doesn't support it, the agreement is hollow, it doesn't work." It went back to the lesson Bobby learned when he first came to Washington on behalf of Vietnam veterans: You can't have a treaty that is based on morality. True success in politics required both morality and power, and without the United States, the treaty lacked any sanction.

There was no ambivalence in his views of Jody Williams, especially her behavior after receiving the Nobel Prize. "I had to applaud this bitch at the end of the day," he recalls of the Nobel ceremony when she accepted the prize. "But I really wanted to drive a stake through her heart." He fired her from her $60,000 job at the foundation, claiming she was an "out-of-control" employee who had stolen credit for a grassroots campaign that he had organized and hundreds of others helped make successful. The antiwar protester who once shouted down the president of the United States complained that she had ruined a perfect photo op. "This could have been done in the [National] Press Club. We could have had Senator Leahy standing next to her. Boom. We could have added a controlled press statement that would have stepped up to what a laureate would be expected to say. . . . She could have gotten dressed, for God's sakes!"

The campaign to ban land mines cost millions of dollars, but money was no longer a problem for Bobby since he had remarried into one of the wealthiest families in America. His first wife, Virginia, never fully recovered from the harassment campaign in 1987. Over the next few years she suffered from a series of major illnesses, including kidney failure. She grew frail and weak, suffered from frequent infections, and was no longer able to work. "I said goodbye to Virginia at least six times," Bobby says. Each time she bounced back. A heavy smoker, she was diagnosed with lung cancer in January 1995 and died on July 4, 1996. Later that year Bobby married Solange MacArthur, a physician and granddaughter of insurance magnate John D. MacArthur, one of the three wealthiest men in America at the time of his death in 1978. During the 1990s Solange poured millions of dollars into Bobby's political activities, essentially bankrolling the campaign to ban land mines. He moved into Solange's expansive townhouse in Washington, along with Virginia's granddaughter, Kayla, whom Bobby continued to raise as his own daughter. That comfortable arrangement came to an end in March 2003 when Solange filed for divorce.

Medical advances also improved the quality of his life in the 1990s. Bobby's injuries had robbed him of any sexual function for nearly twenty-five years. It did not, however, prevent him from experiencing sexual pleasure or from giving it to his partners. "People should understand that you can have a very satisfying sexual relationship without having an erection for the purpose of sexual intercourse," he observes. "In fact, when a guy is not distracted because of his own sensations [he] can better pay attention to [his] partner's needs. It ends up being extremely gratifying and rewarding for a woman." Since 1997 drugs such as Viagra have allowed Bobby to have erections. In addition, medical procedures using electrical stimulation have allowed him to experience orgasms. Bobby had the procedure for the first time in the mid-1990s. He went to a local hospital where a doctor implanted an electrical device into his rectum to stimulate the prostate and produce an orgasm. "Just when we got to showtime there was a class of nursing students" walking past his room. The doctor invited them in to watch. "So I am getting it off for the first time in over 20 years in front of a dozen nursing students," he says proudly. Now he uses a specially calibrated vibrator that can produce an orgasm simply by touching the penis.

Bobby has been spared the typical health problems that often plague people confined to wheelchairs: bedsores, urinary tract infections, circulatory problems, excessive weight gain. According to his neurologist, despite being confined to a wheelchair for more than thirty years, physically Bobby is in the "top one percent of all paraplegics." He remains active, exercises daily, and watches his diet. He has not lost his sense of adventure. He has jumped from airplanes, securely hooked to an experienced skydiver. He has taken up scuba diving. "The water neutralizes his disability," reflects brother Roger. "It is the one place where he can be like everybody else." Bobby has benefited from the Boomer expansion of individual rights to include the disabled. Since passage of the Americans with Disabilities Act (ADA) in 1990, a federal law prohibiting discrimination against people with disabilities, Bobby can eat at almost any restaurant, travel on trains and airplanes, attend concerts and sporting events. "The biggest pain-in-the-ass for me is transferring in and out of the car, or from the sofa into the wheelchair and getting your clothes realigned." For him, being a paraplegic is "an inconvenience, not a problem."

■

No generation agrees on everything. Yet beneath petty tactical disputes, what defined the rise of Baby Boomers in politics was their style. Boomers were the first generation to grow up with television and the first to appreciate and reward politicians of all ages who make use of its powerful images to shape debate. They understand the power of television to convey messages that bypass traditional power brokers and appeal directly to people in their homes. They are antibureaucratic, less willing to work within existing institutions, and more willing to create their own. The ethic of self-fulfillment infused their approach to politics. Politics is always about vying for power, but Boomers have added a new tone of impatience. For breast cancer survivors the central question was not what new scientific breakthrough will lead to more effective chemotherapy, but what science can do today to help them. The generation that grew up having its every need catered to by marketers and its expectations whetted by prosperity, the generation that commanded attention because of its sheer size, was bound to change the nature of politics in America.

Boomers understand how mass media have changed the way the public understands and responds to issues. "To make stuff happen, values trump data," Bobby says. The Boomer generation that came of age with television and with highly charged emotional debates over Vietnam, civil rights, and gender roles instinctively thinks about politics as a clash of cultures, not a debate over complicated public policy choices. Television appeals to emotions, not to intellect. Conservatives learned this lesson during the 1980s, and progressives played catchup during the 1990s. Today Boomer political discourse is about values and emotions, not intellect and reason.

The most significant contribution Boomers have made to American politics has been in their genius in developing sophisticated well-organized interest groups like the NBCC and VVA. The Boomer generation was less loyal to either ideology or to party than their parents. For their parents, political parties faced each other like opposing armies on the battlefield, fighting over clearly marked ideological terrain. Boomers prefer guerrilla tactics to conventional warfare, roaming across the political battlefield, choosing an opportune time to strike. Whether liberal or conservative, they inherited from the 1960s a sense of self-righteousness, a gift for public theater, a disdain for compromise, and a lust for battle. They have created a new decentralized political universe perfectly suited to a generation that was skeptical of authority and bureaucracy and disloyal to either party or candidates.

Muller described his approach to politics with the acronym KISS: "Keep it Simple, Stupid." The key to success in politics, he learned, was to find a cause that has a strong emotional appeal that can be explained in a thirty-second sound bite. His friend, former Senate Majority Leader and fellow Boomer Tom Daschle, told Bobby in 1997 that he had finally "learned how to play the game." The key to success in Washington is to "take a very small piece of the action" and "stay focused on it for years." The land mine campaign, he says, was "Politics 101." You get a powerful senator to support your cause, you hire the best lobbyists and public relations team in Washington, you raise and spend millions of dollars, and you gradually build your political base. Bobby, who came to Washington in 1978 full of moral indignation, believed that he would change policy almost overnight through self-righteous appeals to the socially conscious. Two decades later, he had learned to fight as the consummate insider.

Conservatives learned the same lessons and brought a similar style to politics. "I question authority, which is why I want to dismantle the state," declares a conservative Boomer. During the 1980s the Heritage Foundation, a conservative think tank, held weekly meetings for young activists who called themselves the "third generation." The first generation had rallied around William F. Buckley's *National Review* in the 1950s, and the second helped elect Ronald Reagan in 1980. The third generation formed a host of new lobbying groups and think tanks to push their agenda. As the journalist Nina Easton observed, their leaders—Bill Kristol, an adviser to Dan Quayle and founder of the *Weekly Standard,* antitax crusader Grover Norquist, and affirmative action critic Clint Bolick—were the flip side of their liberal counterparts. They created a myriad of interrelated public interest groups around Washington that combined shrewd politics with ideological fervor. They were part, Easton says, of the "question authority generation" and they fought with "all of the hubris and irreverence and impatience for change that characterized the 1960s Leftists who came before them."

Boomers were not the first generation to develop powerful interest groups, but they perfected the art of interest group government. They turned JFK's famous dictum on its head: "Ask not what you can do for your country. Ask what your country can do for you." Many scholars looking for political power in modern America still focus on voters, the political parties, and powerful elected leaders. In the Boomer nation, real power lies in the web of new interest groups, often based in Washington, but with local offices and chapters in key congressional districts across the country. The most enduring legacy of the '60s and '70s was the hundreds of local and national organizations created by women's groups and environmentalists to further their agenda inside the Beltway and in the election booth, long after it had lost support at the polls: The National Organization for Women, Consumer Federation of America, Environmental Defense Fund, National Women's Political Caucus, National Association for the Repeal of Abortion Laws, Friends of the Earth. Initially, conservatives were slow to organize, but by the late '70s and '80s, they had adopted the style and organization of the left and created their own counterestablishment: the Christian Coalition, National Right to Life Committee, Federalist Society, Institute for Justice, and Free Congress Foundation.

Interest groups are nothing new in Washington, but they have proliferated at an astonishing rate since the 1960s. In 1956 Gale Research's *Encyclopedia of Associations* listed fewer than 5,000 special interest groups; by 1994 that number had swelled to over 20,000. A 1990 survey found that 70 percent of Americans belonged to at least one interest group, and nearly 25 percent claimed membership in four or more. The "old era of lobbying by special interests—by a well-connected, pluto-cratic few—is as dead now as slavery and Prohibition," observes jour-nalist Jonathan Rauch. "We Americans have achieved the full democra-tization of lobbying: influence-peddling for the masses."

The contrast between Bobby Muller and Fran Visco reveals key dif-ferences in Boomer style. Both are strong, independent-minded leaders with a clear sense of right and wrong and supreme confidence in their own ability. But they created very different organizations. The problem with building an organization that appeals to Boomers is their skepti-cism. In creating the VVA, Bobby thought vets would give him their support, knowing he had their best interest in mind. But this generation distrusted elites and wanted to have a voice in the process. His goal of creating a powerful top-down advocacy group that would respond to his agenda ran against the spirit of the times and the desire of the very people he wanted to represent. Visco maintained tight control over her organization's agenda, but NBCC was from the beginning created as a grassroots organization where the local chapters had the opportunity to speak their minds and influence policy. Muller wanted to speak for his generation without always listening to their voices. When they did finally speak, he realized that many of them spoke a different language. The experiences of the Vietnam generation were so varied that it was impossible for one man, or one organization, to represent them.

Visco built NBCC on the foundation of feminism; Muller tried to build VVA on the fractured base of the Vietnam War. Realizing that women were divided on most other major issues of the day, from gay rights to abortion, NBCC made the decision to focus exclusively on the one issue on which all could agree: increased funding for breast cancer. Bobby went in the other direction, insisting that the organization address a wide range of highly charged political issues that went beyond the hard-core issues that could unite a majority of Vietnam vets—Agent Orange, improved GI benefits. By broadening the agenda, he left him-self open to criticism from both left and right. Vietnam-generation vets had different needs from older veterans, and many of the traditional organizations were unresponsive to their needs. But they remained too fractured to agree on a broad agenda of reform.

THIRTEEN

NEW CHALLENGES; LOST OPPORTUNITIES

Alberta getting her Ph.D.;

Liz and Andres in Paris.

Choice is a good thing in life, and the more of it we have, the happier we are. Authority is inherently suspect," the journalist Alan Ehrenhalt observed, summing up the attitude of the Boomer generation. In the 1990s, however, now moving well into middle age, many Boomers including Ehrenhalt were questioning their generation's blind celebration of individualism and opportunity. "The world of choice has brought us a world of restless dissatisfaction," he wrote, while the "suspicion of authority has meant the erosion of standards of conduct and civility." Ehrenhalt was nostalgic for the world of his parents and the neighborhood in Chicago where he grew up. It was a world, he wrote, of "limited choices" but "lasting relationships" where community meant "not subjecting every action in life to the burden of choice, but rather accepting the familiar and reaping the psychological benefits of having one less calculation to make during the course of the day."

Is it possible to have an individualistic utopia, a country in which even the army's advertising slogan became "An Army of One," and still feel the spirit of community? By the end of the century, the Home Shopping Network, a televised flea market, had 23,000 incoming phone lines that could handle 20,000 calls a minute. The average supermarket stocked as many as 24,000 different items—three times the magnitude in 1990 and twenty-times more than in the 1950s. The days of the mom-and-pop store are mostly dead. A Barnes and Noble 30,000-square-foot superstore showcases over 175,000 different book titles and more than 30,000 CDs and cassettes. They sold one of every eight books purchased in the United States. Sophisticated software allows direct marketers to identify specific groups for their sales pitch. The makers of swimming pool floats, for example, can target pool owners living in upscale zip codes, in warm weather states, who purchased items from expensive gift magazines with their American Express card. On the Lands' End web site, customers enter their body proportions, and the computer creates a figure of their body to model clothes.

Technology has expanded the range of choices for Boomers, and none has been more influential than the creation of the PC, the explosion in software, and the development of the World Wide Web. While a handful of Boomers—Microsoft's Bill Gates and Paul Allen, Apple's Steve Jobs—played key roles in the explosive growth of the PC, Boomers did not pioneer the invention of the Internet. They did, however, embrace it and help spread its influence. A 2001 Nielsen Home Technology Report showed that 57 percent of Boomers had access to the Internet compared with 45 percent of all adults. Nearly a quarter of all Boomers logged onto the Internet at least once a day, and they spent more time online than any other age group. "The popular media image of Xers surrounded by high-tech computer products and ensconced in digital lifestyles is inaccurate," reported the authors of the Yankelovich report on generational marketing. "It's the information-hungry Boomers who spend the most money on computers, faxes, cell phones, and related high-tech gear."

The Internet empowered individuals by putting vast amounts of unfiltered information at their fingertips. In medicine, patients used the Internet to find out about new treatments, breaking the monopoly that physicians once had on medical information. In business the sharing of electronic documents flattened hierarchies and gave lower-level employees access to huge amounts of information previously the purview of managers. Investors could bypass stockbrokers and plan retirement benefits on-line. By allowing people to communicate effortlessly across thousands of miles, the Internet gave rise to the "virtual corporation," in which employees and managers were located in different places. Politicians used the Internet to bypass the traditional media and communicate their message directly to voters.

All of these web-using browsers discovered that it was one way to create communities of connection. If Ehrenhalt's old neighborhood culture was forever gone, lots of small communities across geographic lines were now possible. America Online (AOL), the largest Internet provider in the United States, claimed 30 million members by 2001. More than three-quarters of its subscribers used anonymous chat rooms to meet people who share similar interests. People from all over the globe joined together in virtual town halls to discuss issues of mutual interest. Teenagers in San Diego could discuss music with peers in Boston and Washington; a senior citizen in Texas mourning the death of a loved one could find solace with someone in Florida; an AIDS patient in San Francisco could share treatment ideas with doctors in New York. The technology reconfigured the consumer society, providing buyers with new options and increased power. "The Internet is nothing less than a revolution in commerce," pronounced *Business Week*.

There was more diversity than ever before on the shelves of America's real and virtual stores. There was also more diversity among the shoppers—more, in fact, than anyone had intended. In 1965, while the front pages of newspapers focused on the Voting Rights Act as the second landmark civil rights legislation in two years, another bill passed that would change the complexion of American schools, cities, and towns even more than would integration. In July, standing in the shadow of the Statue of Liberty, Johnson signed the Immigration Act of 1965. "The bill that we sign today is not a revolutionary bill," he said, but it did "repair a very deep and powerful flaw in the fabric of American justice." The new legislation replaced the old national origins system, which restricted percentages based on outdated 19th-century quotas, with a family preference system that gave priority to close relatives of existing citizens.

In a classic case of unintended consequences, the legislation produced a chain of migration that would confound efforts to control immigration. According to the Census Bureau, by the early 1990s, over 1 million new legal immigrants were arriving in the United States every year, accounting for almost half of U.S. population growth. Most of these immigrants settled in large cities in a handful of states—New York, Illinois, and New Jersey, as well as Florida, Texas, and California. By 1990 the population of Los Angeles, the nation's second-largest city, was one-third foreign born. Los Angeles was also home to the second-largest Spanish-speaking population (after Mexico City) of any city on the North American continent. New York's foreign-born population, like Los Angeles's, also approached 35 percent of its total populace in 1990, a level the city last reached in 1910. In 1960 Miami was about 75 percent Anglo. By 1987 it was 15 percent Anglo, with Cubans making up the largest immigrant group, along with African Americans, Haitians, Salvadorans, Jamaicans, Puerto Ricans, and Nicaraguans. Three-quarters of the residents spoke a language other than English at home.

Many Americans worried about the cohesiveness of American culture in such a multicultural era and questioned its ability to absorb and assimilate so many different cultural influences. "Is it really wise to allow the immigration of people who find it so difficult and painful to assimilate into the American majority?" asked conservative journalist Peter Brimelow. Liberal historian and former Kennedy adviser Arthur Schlesinger, Jr., gave powerful expression to the cultural fears in his influential book *The Disuniting of America,* which lamented the "cult of ethnicity" that had arisen "to protect, promote, and perpetuate separate ethnic and racial communities." Like many other social commentators, Schlesinger worried that the melting pot was losing its ability to forge a national identity that transcended ethnic and racial appeal. "One wonders," he wrote, "will the center hold? Or will the melting pot give way to the Tower of Babel?"

For Boomers, fears of cultural anarchy produced a wave of nostalgia. "The generation that proclaimed the Age of Aquarius," observed a journalist, "is now busy buying and selling the Age of Nostalgia." In 1974, 54 percent of Americans said that the present was better than the "good old days." Only 37 percent disagreed. Asked the same question during the booming 1990s, however, and the numbers flipped: 56 percent preferred the past, 32 percent the present. Politicians tapped into that longing. In 1996, 73-year-old Republican senator Robert Dole, a survivor of World War II and certified member of the Greatest Generation, tried turning his campaign into a referendum on the Baby Boom. In his acceptance speech in San Diego, he told his audience "I remember" a time when things in America were better, a time of "tranquility, faith, and confidence in action." He accused the president's generation of being "an elite who never grew up, never did anything real, never sacrificed, never suffered, and never learned." On the same night Bill Clinton was in fashionable Jackson Hole, Wyoming, celebrating his 50th birthday by singing Beatles songs.

The most dramatic examples came from popular culture. Sixties rock stars from the Eagles to the Beach Boys to the Rolling Stones packed concert stadiums. TV shows from the 1960s, like *The Addams Family, The Brady Bunch, The Flintstones,* and *Mission Impossible,* found their way to the big screen. In *Crooklyn* filmmaker Spike Lee revealed what it was like growing up in 1970s Brooklyn, complete with eating Trix cereal and watching *The Partridge Family.* Advertisers jumped on the bandwagon, using Rolling Stones music to sell Pepsi and James Brown's hit "I Feel Good" to sell laxatives. Charlie the Tuna reappeared on store shelves. Sales of Coke soared after it re-created its older contour bottle in 1994. Baltimore's Camden Yards and Cleveland's Jacobs Field helped Boomer baseball fans remember the ballparks of their youth. Even the 1960s icon, the Volkswagen Beetle, made a comeback by appealing to the generation's lost idealism. "If you sold your soul in the '80s," the ad declares, "here's your chance to buy it back." The Nickelodeon cable channel became the most popular cable channel among Boomers by recycling sitcoms from the 1960s in its *Nick at Night.* The median age of its viewers was 43.7.

The Boomer ambivalence toward change infused the new urbanism movement spearheaded by Elizabeth Platter-Zyberk and Andres Duaney. Community, they argued, depends on creating a social space where people can gather, discuss issues, and form friendships. Traditional towns constructed private residences around parks and squares to encourage social interaction. It is the lack of a geographically defined public space that has contributed to the decline of community life and produced a host of social problems. Since suburbs are spread out, people are forced to spend an inordinate amount of time in their cars. Instead of spending quality time with families and friends, harried suburbanites are either sitting in traffic commuting to work or ferrying children to school and play.

They had a point. Between 1982 and 2000 the U.S. population grew by 20 percent, but the amount of time Americans spent in traffic increased by a staggering 236 percent. Atlanta led the nation in the average distance its commuters travel each day to work—36.5 miles round-trip. Seattle residents spent an average of 59 hours stuck in traffic a year, sixth highest in the nation. "We moved to the suburbs to get lawns and a country setting," complained an environmentalist. "Now we find we are sitting in traffic going to work and going to get a quart of milk."

Like an earlier generation of suburban critics, Liz and Andres worry about the impact of the suburbs on children. Social critics in the 1950s feared that Boomers growing up in the suburbs would turn into a generation of conformists. Advocates of the new urbanism worry that the suburbs will now turn the children of Boomers into a generation of bored, isolated social misfits. "A child growing up in such a homogeneous environment is less likely to develop a sense of empathy for people from other walks of life and is ill prepared to live in a diverse society," they argue in their book, *Suburban Nation*. A rash of teen school shootings seemed to confirm their fears. The most deadly attack took place in April 1999 at Columbine High School in Littleton, Colorado. During the final week of classes, two disgruntled and heavily armed students killed twelve classmates and a popular teacher and planted thirty pipe bombs and other explosives before taking their own lives.

Children aside, the real target for new urbanist ideas were aging Baby Boomers. Boomers without children at home were the fastest-growing family type by the end of the decade. By 2010, 36 million households, almost one-third, will be empty nesters. The "sandwich generation" finds themselves caregivers to groups on opposite ends of the age spectrum—parents and children—and urbanism makes it easier for them to care for both without having to travel great distances. A 2002 survey by Del Webb, the largest developer of retirement communities, showed that Boomers hoped to retire in communities that provided reasonable services within a short walking distance. They wanted more amenities—more parks, a greater variety of shopping, more natural beauty, and less traffic.

In 1991 a small group of new urbanists gathered in Yosemite National Park and drew up a document called the Ahwahnee Principles. They agreed that planning "should be in the form of complete and integrated communities containing housing, shops, workplaces, schools, parks, and civic facilities." Reflecting their belief in the pedestrian village, they argued that these activities should be "within easy walking distance of each other" and "of transit stops." It called for creating a community of diverse housing types "to enable citizens from a wide range of economic levels and age groups to live within its borders." It should place public interest over private interest and "contain an ample supply of specialized open space in the form of squares, greens, and parks."

In 1993 the principles became the founding document for the Congress of the New Urbanism, which was chaired by Elizabeth and run by Peter Katz. Herbert Muschamp, architecture critic for the *New York Times,* referred to the congress as "the most important phenomenon to emerge in American architecture in the post–Cold War era." The congress, which he called "the only organized nationwide movement of consequence initiated by baby boom architects," challenged "the conventional wisdom that members of this individualistic generation are incapable of collective action."

During the early to mid 1990s Liz and Andres, whom *Architectural Record* dubbed "the king and queen of New Urbanism," spent as much time traveling and lecturing as they did designing. Liz's understated style and scholarly manner was more appropriate for academic audiences, so she spent most of her time on college campuses. Andres has become the provocateur for the movement. Part prophet, part showman, and part promoter, he traveled almost every week, appearing at building conventions and civic meetings. Tapes of his lectures circulated around the architectural community. The audiences loved him, but many of his peers dismissed him as glib, sentimental, and arrogant.

The movement received a boost in 1996 when the new urbanism became the inspiration for Disney's new town of Celebration, near Orlando, Florida. Liz and Andres participated in the draft stage of the town, although another architect was chosen to build it. "We were the ones who introduced the idea of a town and not a golf club community," Liz reflects. Disney's decision to build the town based on the concept of traditional neighborhood development showed that ideas considered radical just ten years earlier had gone main-

stream. Celebration covered nearly 5,000 acres, took nine years and
$2.5 billion to build, and was home to 5,000 residents in 2000. Like
Seaside, Celebration was designed to provoke a sense of nostalgia for
small-town life with its front porches, picket fences, and tidy gar-
dens.

The movement's success trickled down to building fads everywhere. Across the country, developments promised buyers mixed-
use areas, pedestrian friendliness, front porches, and Victorian street
lamps. Many cities knocked down high-rise buildings and replaced
them with townhouses with front porches and picket fences. By the
end of the 1990s nearly every major metropolitan area in the United
States had a suburban Main Street project underway. The town of
Valencia, California, 30 miles north of Los Angeles, built a half-mile-
long Main Street called the Town Center Drive, featuring a pedestrian bridge that linked new apartments to a regional mall. Haile
Plantation near Gainesville, Florida started work on a 1,700-acre
planned community, which included a one-third-mile-long Main
Street. In Rockville, Maryland, town officials replaced their boarded-
up downtown mall with a $300 million mixed-use development that
included a four-block Main Street. The Department of Housing and
Urban Development devoted billions of dollars to a project to use
new urbanist principles to redesign the nation's public housing
stock. According to the *New Yorker,* by 2000 there were 200 traditional neighborhood developments in the United States.

In 2001 the *New York Times* claimed that "traditional-neighbor-
hood developments" were "considered by many real estate theorists
to be the leading edge." Seaside, once considered a "novel experiment," had become "a source of admiration and emulation." It is not
hard to understand why developers wanted to emulate Seaside's success. In the early 1980s its lots had sold for as little as $15,000. By
2000 a cemetery plot cost more. Beachfront lots sold for between
$1.6 million and $2.3 million. Away from the beach, lots start at
$300,000. Houses that sold for less than $100,000 in the early 1980s
were selling for more than $500,000 by 2000.

Liz, however, feared that developers were co-opting some of the
language and icons of new urbanism without buying into its social
philosophy. The new urbanists denounced it as "neo-porchism."
"The middle ground," she told a conference of new urbanists in

1997, "will reinforce the worst characteristics of each type." Big developers were "jumping on the Main Street bandwagon without appreciating the intricacies that can make or break a public realm." The new urbanism was not about picket fences and front porches, she insisted. At its heart it was about creating a new sense of community, fighting against the trend toward mass consumerism that defined postwar American life. "At its core, new urbanism isn't an architectural movement, even if most of its founders are architects," observed Alan Ehrenhalt. "It is part of the broader reaction to the past three decades of individualist excess, and the desire for an end-of-century social reconnection in American life." Instead of lots of Seasides, however, America was filling its suburbs with McMansions—front porches and Victorian details notwithstanding.

There is little evidence that Americans are willing to abandon their spacious homes in the suburbs or abandon their cars as the new urbanists wish. Between 1992 and 1997 Americans developed about 3.2 million acres of open land every year, nearly double the rate during the 1980s. In 1920 there were about ten people living on every acre of land in America's cities and suburbs; by 1990 there were only four. The result was a suburban landscape made up of strip malls and cookie-cutter residential areas. Sprawl eroded about 50 acres of valuable farmland every hour. "Where Old Macdonald had a farm, a hamburger joint now stands," noted the *Economist.*

Politics also stands in the way of the new urbanists. Critics on the left claim they spend too much time refashioning new suburban developments and not enough time dealing with deteriorating cities or questioning America's dependence on the automobile. "Trying to design one's way out of a profound social crisis is like trying to cure obesity with a tight fitting corset," complained a critic. "One may wind up with a thinner waistline, but elsewhere the fat will bunch up and spill over in a way that is more unsightly than ever." But on the other hand they were criticized for imposing too many rules and regulations and for ignoring what the conservative columnist Fred Barnes called "an irrefutable fact of American life." "For all the scorn that's heaped on the suburbs—and especially on subdivisions of nearly identical houses on the fringe of metropolitan areas—people like living there."

Polls revealed that the vast majority of Americans still associated the suburbs with better schools, low crime, and convenient shopping.

Ironically, while most people said they wanted to live in the suburbs, they preferred that most development take place in the city. "Their ideal arrangement," wrote the authors of a study on suburban sprawl, "is to get into the castle and pull up the drawbridge the minute they cross the moat." "What's the difference between an environmentalist and a developer?" asked a popular joke. "The environmentalist already has his house in the mountains." Americans seem to like the new urbanism more in theory than in practice. "I hate being forced to choose between hideous sprawl and preapproved nostalgia," said architecture critic Ada Louise Huxtable. She described it as a choice between "the real awful and the awful unreal."

The emphasis on small town life also ran counter to another dominant trend of the decade: the growth of mass consumer stores. Consumers in our fast-paced individualized society may like browsing the small boutique stores that line Main Street, but they spend their money at convenient discount stores promising low prices and standardized service. As children, Baby Boomers craved McDonald's burgers and fries; as middle-aged adults, they prefer double espresso with low-fat milk at Starbucks. The result is the same: large chain stores like Borders Books, Banana Republic, The Gap, and Hollywood Video have replaced many of the mom-and-pop bookstores and funky coffee shops associated with small town life. By 2003 retail giant Wal-Mart was the largest private employer in the country. With $243 billion in sales, it was the nation's biggest retailer of jewelry, socks, underwear, toys, and food. On any given day, its sales were larger than the gross domestic product of more than thirty-six nations.

The lament about the decline of civic life and the desire to restore a sense of community is the result of Boomer self-flagellation about not living up to the standards of their parents' generation, which was widely celebrated throughout the decade. Boomers have found their own ways to build very different kinds of community. "For every bridge club or Masonic temple that has folded, there are countless AIDS advocacy groups or Usenet discussion groups to take their place," observed Francis Fukuyama. The experiences of Fran Visco and Bobby Muller suggest that Boomers are not less involved; rather, they are choosing to get involved in different ways. The kinds of civic organizations that Liz and Andres hope to re-create were ideal for a generation that shared a consensus about social goals and how to pursue them. Boomers, on the other hand, grew up in a diverse culture that celebrated individual expression. With Washington filling many of the roles once played by private groups, Boomers created grassroots interest groups instead of local civic organizations.

By the end of the 1990s, "The paradox of being fresh by being traditional has played itself out," Paul Goldberger remarked. "Young architects don't like things that look old." Many in the profession dismissed the new urbanists as "merchants of nostalgia," pointing out that the movement is based on the false assumption that a carefully designed small town will encourage civilized behavior. "But that assumes that architecture and design have a lot more power over people's lives than they do," observed Goldberger. "The lovely main street of Stockbridge doesn't guarantee that a healthy community will exist in Massachusetts any more than the harsh red brick high-rise towers of Stuyvesant Town rule out a sense of community in Manhattan."

Liz and Andres have been stung by criticism from the academy. Architecture places a premium on being creative and coming up with new concepts. The idea of integrating tradition is anathema to the profession. Liz draws back from Andres's often exaggerated claims about the possibility of new urbanism to change behavior. Her expectations are more modest. She believes people look to the physical environment for a sense of continuity and stability. In a world where technology is changing things constantly, our social world is in constant flux, and the economy is unpredictable, she simply wants stability.

Ironically, while Liz and Andres have devoted their professional lives to re-creating the small town community with its emphasis on family and togetherness, they have created a very modern family life. In addition to running their own design firm, DPZ, Liz serves as dean of the architecture school at the University of Miami. She spends her days moving back and forth between the academic and business worlds, essentially juggling two full-time positions. Liz and Andres established a clear division of labor at home and the office. They do not work on the same projects, and when they do, one or the other is the boss. At home Liz is careful to avoid falling into the domestic trap. "Every day she is very careful not to be typecast," says Andres. They share responsibilities around the house. Andres's grandmother, who lives with them in the Miami home, makes dinner. "I set the table, Liz heats it up. My grandmother does the dishes."

Their life revolves around their work. They stopped taking vacations because they found it difficult to relax. At home in the evening they read. Andres estimates that they go to Blockbuster once a year to rent a movie. His musical tastes are classical; she likes rock and roll. Elizabeth's religious faith never wavered. She grew up in a Catholic family and has practiced her faith in a quiet manner her whole life.

Liz has some reservations about not having children, but raising a family was harder for older Boomers than for younger ones. "For women to be an architect was so different and seemed to be such a hurdle, that it didn't seem possible to do both," she says. Older Boomers were the first to enter the professions in large numbers. She wanted to make her mark in the world, and that meant competing with men. "There's a small window of years that I'm a part of where you will find that many women who did advance in the profession made the choice to not have kids," she reflects. Attitudes toward women in the workplace changed slowly. "I'm part of that group that thought we had to wait to have children. We all thought we had to wait and make our mark in business or in our profession first. And then when it came around to making the decision, it was too late."

Alberta Wilson, by contrast, was ready for a world in which one size fits all. After graduation from Tabernacle in 1996, she contacted Charles Ruffin, her seventh-grade teacher in Philadelphia, looking for a teaching job. It was perfect timing. He and a small group at the Beulah Baptist Church were trying to set up a new Christian school. Ruffin had spent thirty-one years as a teacher in the Philadelphia public school system and was convinced that it was failing. It certainly was doing nothing to instill Christian values. "He got the church to see that as part of our missionary effort we need to educate our children," recalls Deacon Jenkins. "He started from the ground up."

Since becoming pastor at Beulah in 1978, Ruffin had been moving the church to the right, instilling it with fundamentalist values and his burden to spread the word through teaching. He preached a tough fundamentalist message, telling his parishioners they had to do more than just listen to the gospel; they had to live it. "Most members of the church confessed Christ but they did not live as Christians," says Jenkins. If you accept Jesus Christ, you cannot live in sin: you cannot have sex outside of marriage, buy lottery tickets, smoke, drink, or do drugs. In 1991 Ruffin saw the realization of his plan to expand the church with the opening of a small day care center. Soon afterward, the church began organizing two-week summer camps to expose youth to both God and nature.

It was a natural next step to establish a Christian day school. The Philadelphia school system, the eighth largest in the United States, was a disaster by any standard. As the middle class fled to the suburbs or opted for private urban schools, the city system was left with the poorest and least-motivated students. By the 1990s more than half of its students failed standardized math and reading tests; nearly 70 percent lived at or below the poverty line. The dropout rate was around 50 percent. On any given day, one in four students was absent. Ruffin formed a fellowship of church members who taught in the public school system. Most of the members were Baby Boom teachers who were frustrated by the bureaucracy and lack of discipline in the public schools and saw the fellowship as a way to offer guidance and support to one another. By 1996 they started planning for a day school. Most members of the fellowship became founding members of the board of directors.

Although he did not realize it at the time, Ruffin was riding a generational wave of devotion. There was a strong correlation between raising families and finding religion, and evangelical schools positioned themselves to attract Boomers returning to religion. In 1983 only 12.9 million of Boomers had children under 18, according to the Census Bureau. By 1993 the number of Boomer parents had risen to 21 million.

Ruffin told Alberta about his plans and invited her to come to Philadelphia to meet the board and interview for the position as principal. After a preliminary interview, they offered Alberta the job at a salary of $35,000. She immediately accepted. Woody quit his job, they packed their bags, and they moved into a modest two-story duplex in northeastern Philadelphia. What Alberta did not know was that a power struggle was taking place behind the scenes. Some members of the board were deeply suspicious of her, especially of her belief that women should be subservient to men. They wanted a religious school, but not one centered on strict fundamentalist teachings. In between the time Alberta accepted the job and the first day of school in September, the board demoted her from principal to school administrator. While her precise duties were never spelled out, the change was designed to allow the board to retain the power to make decisions about educational philosophy while limiting Alberta's role to carrying out their wishes.

When school opened after Labor Day, Alberta realized she had a far more pressing problem than bureaucratic politics: only five students had enrolled. Pastor Ruffin had optimistically expected that the day care center would serve as a feeder for the school. He had hoped to open the school with kindergarten through third-grade classes. Instead, they had one very small kindergarten class. Most parents simply could not afford the $65 weekly expense, especially since they could send their children to local public school for free. Not only was the class small, but problems developed almost immediately between Alberta and the school's lone teacher, who resented Alberta's fundamentalist views and "drill instructor" style. Alberta insisted that the teacher wear a dress every day. She was not permitted to talk on the phone while school was in session. The biggest problem was that Alberta required her to be in her office every morning at 8:00 A.M., thirty minutes before school started, for "devotional," which consisted of Alberta's lecturing her about what the Bible told her to teach each day.

In October, after two months of school, the crisis came to a head. Pastor Ruffin, who shared Alberta's views, came to her rescue. Although slowed by an aggressive cancer, he summoned the physical and political strength to disband the board, encourage the teacher to leave, and make Alberta principal with broad powers. Beulah was going to be a fundamentalist school. The shakeup ended the political dispute, but it did not stop the rumblings about Alberta's rigid style. The first two years witnessed a complete turnover in staff. "We represent Christ and we are models for the children," she told teachers and staff while continuing to insist on the early-morning devotional. "It was a struggle for most of us to be here on time," recalls a teacher. "We had to be here at 8:00 A.M., not 8:01, but 8:00 A.M." Alberta would not allow teachers to play contemporary music in the classroom or permit students to go on field trips to amusement parks. She banned copies of the popular *Harry Potter* books, complaining that they preached witchcraft. The conflicts did not prevent the school from growing. In 1997 they ended the year with fourteen students in kindergarten. In 1998 there were fifty-four kids up to third grade. The next year there were seventy-four students and four grades. In 2000, they had ninety-two students up to the sixth grade.

Like many other fundamentalist schools, Beulah's used the "A Beka" education system from the largest publisher of Christian education books in the country. Its world history text dates the origins of human history with Adam and Eve, "the smartest, most perfect man and woman ever to live on this earth." It claims that the Bible's account of the serpent in the Garden and the Flood are true, and it makes a special point of challenging evolution—"the false idea that man began as an animal and slowly changed (evolved) into man." Some Christian schools teach evolution as a theory along with creationism, but A Beka makes no compromises with secularism. "There is no evidence at all that the first men were hairy 'ape men' and that after many centuries they gradually lost their hair and started to wear clothes."

It was not just what they taught but the way they taught it that made Beulah and other Christian schools like it so different. Many parents who enrolled their children did not have strong feelings about the curriculum; they were looking for the discipline and structure that had been missing from their own childhoods. Only a small number of the children's parents are members of the church; more than half are from broken homes. Beulah insists that at least one parent of each child must "be saved," which reinforced discipline at home. The school enforced a strict regime on its premises. Uniforms are required. Boys wear yellow shirts and green plaid ties; the girls wear yellow blouses and green plaid jumpers. Teachers did not paddle the children, but parents were invited to perform the ritual. "Some parents come and bring a belt and spank their children now," Alberta observes.

Alberta's deep Christian faith and Boomer values inspired her involvement in the school choice movement. The movement's roots were planted in two unlikely sources. One was free market economists like Milton Friedman, who in the 1950s argued that competition would not only produce quality private schools, it would force public school to improve. The other was 1960s liberal reformers who saw choice as a way of empowering the poor by offering them vouchers to attend better schools. Lyndon Johnson briefly considered including a voucher program as part of his war on poverty, and liberal foundations like the Ford Foundation funded experiments with local schools. The issue died down until the 1990s, however, thanks to the intransigence of the teachers' unions and the impracticality of choice anywhere but in cities. In the '90s, it reemerged as a key part of the conservative agenda. In recent years conservatives have merged the economic and equity arguments, claiming that school choice would force failing schools to improve at the same time that it empowered poor people.

Like the new urbanism, the school choice movement has blurred ideological lines and forged new coalitions. The school choice movement has been unique in its ability to forge a coalition between African Americans, who make up the vast majority of public school students, and conservative whites. The movement has also built bridges between the faithful and the unchurched at a time when the nation is deeply divided over religious issues. A 1999 survey by the Joint Center for Political and Economic Studies found that 60 percent of blacks favored vouchers, including two-thirds of Baby Boomers, compared with 53 percent of the overall population. Many of the African Americans who support choice, whether Boomers or not, were parents of school-age children who had lost faith in the public school system. Cleveland's school choice program was forged by Fanny Lewis, a born-again mother of a school-aged child, and Clint Bolick. In Wisconsin African American lawmaker Polly Williams, a single mother who represented a predominantly black district in Milwaukee, wrote the state's voucher law.

Alberta realized that vouchers were the only way that many poor families would be able to send their children to private Christian schools. In 2000 she resigned from Beulah to run for mayor of Philadelphia on a pro-voucher educational reform platform. Most people were surprised that this political novice, who had never before expressed interest in government and knew little about Philadelphia politics, wanted to run. She had worked in local elections while at Tabernacle, but Philadelphia was not Virginia Beach. She was unfazed by the criticism. "I sent for the paperwork to be placed on the ballot," she recalls, "began to prepare myself by taking government and political classes at a local college, as well as read up on issues in politics." A few months later, however, she learned that Pennsylvania had enacted legislation, the Educational Improvement Tax Credit, which gave tax credits to businesses that donate to scholarship or educational improvement organizations. Those organizations could then use the donations to help families pay for nonpublic school tuition. Maybe she did not have to run for mayor, after all, but instead she could create a private foundation to help funnel money to private schools.

Vouchers were a tough sell in Pennsylvania, where the state constitution specifically outlawed using public money for private schools. "No money raised for the support of the public schools of the commonwealth shall be appropriated to or used for the support of any sectarian school," it declared in language that reflected earlier Protestant panic over Catholic separatism. In searching for assistance, she discovered a wide range of organizations devoted to helping promote the school choice movement. One of the largest, Children First America, based in Texas, coordinated grassroots efforts to establish and fund choice programs. Parents, the group argued, have "the fundamental right to choose their children's schools," and their mission is to educate parents about their options and to raise private scholarship money to support choice programs. "When I met Alberta, she was searching for what to do next," recalls Children First's Ron Harris. "We helped crystallize her thought process and walk her through, hand in hand, on building her scholarship program." She had only a vague idea about wanting to help parents, but through her conversations with Children First, Alberta defined three goals for her new organization: to put money in the hands of parents so that children could attend Christian schools, educate parents so they could become active in the lives of their children, and assist local Christian schools to renovate buildings and attract students. "There is no other scholarship program in the country that has that mission," observes Harris. Before filling out the paperwork to establish a foundation, she needed to come up with a name. "I did not know what to name the corporation," she recalls, "but knew that I believed God had 'called' me, so I named it Faith First Educational Assistance."

Alberta hailed the landmark Supreme Court decision in June 2002 that let stand the Cleveland school voucher program, calling it a "remarkable milestone in education." In that decision the Court declared that the Cleveland voucher plan was constitutional, despite the fact that some public money ended up in religious coffers, because parents could use their money—a maximum of $2,250—for either religious or nonreligious schools. The program did not specifically promote religion and violate the separation between church and state. "The Ohio program is entirely neutral with respect to religion," said Chief Justice William Rehnquist. Clarence Thomas, the only African American on the Court, added that vouchers were needed to save children from "inner city public schools that deny emancipation to urban minority students."

Like the new urbanism, supporters of school choice draw from both deeply conservative and profoundly modern traditions. Sometimes Alberta sounds like Jerry Falwell; at other times she sounds like Huey Newton, her former idol from her Black Panther days. She sees choice as a religious issue because parents are commanded by the Bible to "train up a child in the way he should go: and when he is old, he will not depart from it" (Proverbs 22:6). Her arguments, however, are often based on appeals to equity and entitlement: poor children are entitled to receive the best education possible. Alberta described school choice as an educational freedom movement and the next step in the struggle for civil rights. The existing public school establishment discriminates against poor children, especially poor African American children, by relying on geography in a world where the poorest neighborhoods almost always have the worst schools. "In a lot of urban areas we have traded race-based segregation for means-based segregation," observes Donna Wilson of Children First. "The people with the money have left the public school system. The people left behind are the ones with no choices."

The arguments in favor of school choice are shaped by Boomer culture and by the most sacred of all Boomer principles: the right of each individual to make choices about his or her future. "You have the right to choose just about everything in America except the school your kids go to," observes Wilson. The school choice movement views education as another consumer product, not a public trust that needs to be preserved. It seemed inevitable that a generation nurtured on variety cereal packs would demand the same power of choice on an issue as important as their child's education.

The choice movement also reflects the Boomer antipathy toward bureaucracy, dismissing public schools as "the last great monopoly left in America." Like many of their fellow Boomers, advocates of school choice had lost faith in public institutions. In the past, education had been considered too important to be left up to private groups. In its place they offer a conservative version of "power to the people"—taking power from public school bureaucracies and placing it in the hands of individual families. "It is about empowerment," declares Ron Harris of Children First America. Howard Fuller, the head of the Milwaukee-based Black Alliance for Educational Options and former veteran of the black power movement, saw no contradiction between his former radicalism and his support for a conservative initiative. "Our argument back then was power to the people," he said. "You tell me how you empower people in America if you don't ever give them control over the money."

The old model of integration viewed schools as a valuable tool in mixing races and backgrounds. The new model places more emphasis on efficiency than on integration. In fact, many supporters of school choice dismiss the goal of racial mixing altogether. The public position of movement leaders is to emphasize equal resources, stressing that it is more important to provide minority students with equal resources than it is to mix them with white students. But from the beginning the driving force behind the movement has been Christian conservatives like Alberta who view choice as a way of promoting religious education. In essence, they are practicing their own version of identity politics when they argue that mixing black students and white students is less important than instilling a strong religious identity.

There are numerous obstacles in her path. While Alberta and other school choice advocates blame "liberal teachers' unions" for blocking their efforts at reform, her problems are closer to home. The white conservatives who have spearheaded the movement have worked hard to keep the religious dimension of school choice in the background, emphasizing instead the secular benefits of choice. They realize that most Americans do not want to tear down the wall separating church and state. Alberta also supports a sweeping voucher program that would allow parents to send their children to any school of their choice, including private schools in the suburbs. "I believe the ideal would be to have universal vouchers whereby children would benefit regardless of their family's income level," she observes. "And yes, these children should be allowed to receive vouchers to attend schools in the suburbs." However, white suburban voters, the backbone of the Republican Party, have shown little enthusiasm for school choice programs that would mix urban and suburban children.

Alberta had always been more interested in promoting grassroots cultural changes than she was in politics. By the late 1990s many religious conservatives were returning to their original mission of saving souls, not winning elections. "After spending millions of conservative Christian dollars, after a White House dominated for 12 years by Ronald Reagan and George Bush and a Congress run by Republicans since 1995, are we better off today than we were 20 years ago?" asked Cal Thomas and Reverend Edward Dobson. "A fair-minded person would have to answer no," they concluded. Social conservatives raised money, recruited foot soldiers, and staffed the phone banks for Republican candidates who ignored them after the election. Despite all their efforts they had few tangible victories to their credit: public attitudes on many social issues had become more liberal, abortion was still legal, the gay rights movement continued to gain momentum. Paul Weyrich, a founder of modern social conservatism, announced that "politics has failed" and conservatives had "lost the culture war." "I no longer believe that there is a moral majority," he confessed. At its peak in the mid-1990s, the Christian Coalition had local chapters in forty-eight states. By 2000 the organization had lost its chief organizer, Ralph Reed, maintained a local presence in only seven states, and was hobbled with a $2.5 million deficit.

Perhaps what dispirited social conservatives most of all was the public's lackluster response to the impeachment of Bill Clinton. The year-long drama that led up to the trial and consumed much of the nation's attention centered on an affair between Clinton and former White House intern Monica Lewinsky. When charges surfaced, a defiant president denied having had sexual relations with "that woman." After he made the same denials in a civil case and to a grand jury, Kenneth Starr, the owl-faced special prosecutor in the case, recommended that the president be impeached and removed from office for "high crimes and misdemeanors." To support his conclusion, he delivered a steamy 445-page report to the House detailing the affair and offering eleven potential grounds for impeachment.

Kenneth Starr was born twenty-eight days before Clinton in the neighboring state of Texas. Both men grew up in humble circumstances, went east to college and law school, and stayed home during the Vietnam War (Starr had a medical deferment for psoriasis). Starr met President Kennedy the day before he died, but, unlike Clinton, did not shake his hand. His idol was Richard Nixon. Clinton and Starr emerged from the 1960s on opposite sides of the cultural divide. Clinton identified with the decade's youthful experimentation; Starr clung more tenaciously to his fundamentalist faith and strict values. While Clinton worked his way up the ranks of the Democratic Party, Starr established his credentials as a conservative jurist, serving as solicitor general under President George Bush before accepting appointment as special prosecutor investigating allegations of Clinton wrongdoing in the earlier Whitewater affair.

The conflict between these two Boomers, and the debate over impeachment itself, transformed into a larger cultural war between liberals and conservatives over the legacy of the 1960s. For all of the carefully choreographed images of Clinton walking out of church with his wife in one hand and the Bible in the other, the president remained for millions of conservatives the poster child of a generation of self-indulgent Boomers: a pot-smoking, draft-dodging, truth-parsing womanizer. Impeaching the president, declared a prominent conservative, would "kill off the lax morality of the sixties." *The Wall Street Journal* editorialized that Starr was "not just prosecuting Bill Clinton; he was prosecuting the entire culture that gave birth to what Bill Clinton represents." Republican House leader Tom DeLay (R, Texas), called the contest over impeachment "a debate about relativism vs. absolute truth." For liberals, however, the struggle was about preserving individual freedom and defending the legacy of the '60s from the moralizing right wing. Harvard Law professor Alan Dershowitz wrote a book entitled *Sexual McCarthyism,* which compared Starr's pursuit of Clinton to Joseph McCarthy's witch hunts of the 1950s. Many on the left viewed impeachment as the revenge of the old power brokers who resent the gains made by women and minorities since the 1960s. "Bill Clinton is guilty of not being owned by the good ol' southern boys, or the good ol' eastern Establishment," thundered African American congresswoman Maxine Waters.

It seemed only fitting that the nation's first Baby Boom president would produce a scandal over his private behavior. His defenders drew a distinction between private sins and public crimes. Richard Nixon had engaged in a systematic abuse of the government to frustrate his opponents and maintain his hold on power. Clinton simply wanted to have a little fun in the Oval Office. His behavior was wrong, and he should be punished, but he should not lose his job. Most conservatives rejected the distinction, insisting that the integrity of the office was at stake.

Inevitably, the struggle over impeachment transformed into a clash of values. Their parents' generation dealt with substantive issues of war and peace, the haves versus the have-nots, black against white. Boomers never had to contend with such momentous issues. Deterrence tamed and eventually won the Cold War. All citizens enjoyed basic rights. A thriving economy and modest welfare state provided a minimum standard of living. Boomers had the luxury to devote much of their time and energy to self-exploration, expanding the range of individual expression and freedom. The new lines of conflict in the Boomer nation were over culture and values. The nation was evenly divided between those who felt the president should provide a moral example and those who agreed with the statement: "As long as he does a good job running the country, a president's personal life is not important."

Much to the chagrin of social conservatives, the more evidence they produced of Clinton's wrongdoings, the higher his ratings soared. He left office with the highest approval rating of any postwar president. After the Democrats bucked the tide and won seats in the 1998 congressional elections, conservatives raised the white flag. Virtues king Bill Bennett admitted that he was "not in sync" with public opinion and lamented the death of outrage.

Just two years later, however, the 2000 election served as the real public referendum on both Clinton and the Boomer legacy. For all their differences in style and personality, George Bush and Al Gore had a great deal in common: both were Baby Boomers who came of age during the 1960s, sons of privilege and power who cast themselves as outsiders. The 2000 election was the first time since 1928 that a presidential election took place during a time of peace and prosperity without an incumbent seeking reelection. Without an overwhelming problem to galvanize voters, the candidates targeted issues of primary concern to Boomers and older Americans: pre-scription drugs, managed care, education, Social Security and Medicare reform.

The specifics of the policy debate were lost in the larger discussion over the cultural legacy of the 1960s. Just as the Depression and World War II had framed political debate for the previous generation, the challenge to authority during the 1960s provided the frame of reference for Boomers. In the 2000 election the cultural clash moved from the streets to the election booth. The Republicans turned Bill Clinton into a symbol of '60s excess, vowing to return honor and dignity to the White House. George W. Bush learned from the Dole debacle in 1996 and the public backlash against the Republican impeachment process that Boomers resented self-righteous moralizing of conservatives just as much as they were appalled by Clinton's indiscretions. The Republican nominee took a different tack, praising his generation's success in promoting the rights of women and minorities and preserving the environment while ruefully admitting that "at times, we lost our way." "Our current President embodied the potential of a generation," he told Republican delegates meeting in Philadelphia. "So many talents. So much charm. Such great skill. But, in the end, to what end?"

Bush, whose adolescence was a haze of partying and drinking, appealed to the nation as a reformed Boomer who had seen the light later in life. Gore was the principled, if somewhat stiff, veteran who captured his generation's idealism while remaining faithful to traditional values. The transition from Clinton to Gore represented "a new phase in the life of his own baby boom generation," observed the political analyst William Schneider. "They've moved on from sex, drugs, and rock 'n' roll to family, work, and responsibility." The vice president had to perform an awkward "Tennessee two-step"—embracing Clinton-era prosperity while distancing himself from the president's misdeeds. His first step was to pick as his running mate Connecticut senator Joseph Lieberman, who supported Clinton's agenda but harshly criticized his personal behavior.

Judging from the popular vote, Gore won the debate—barely. According to the electoral college, however, Bush won the election even more narrowly. The results revealed a deeply divided nation. Republicans scored best among white, religious, married, and suburban voters;

Democrats did best with single, nonreligious, and urban voters. Like the rest of the nation, Boomers divided their votes evenly: 49 percent for Bush, 48 percent for Gore. Nearly 80 percent of Bush supporters believed the Clinton scandals were "very important"; only 18 percent of Gore voters agreed. On the issue that mattered most to Alberta, 76 percent of Bush voters supported school vouchers. Observed the journalist Andrew Sullivan, "America is currently two nations, as culturally and politically alien as they are geographically distinct."

■

The British journalist Godfrey Hodgson once remarked that "Americans love change but they hate to be changed." We change our hairstyles and clothing fashions, but we rarely alter our underlying ideals and values. He had a point, and it helps to explain why Christian fundamentalists and the new urbanists encountered so many obstacles during the 1990s. Many aging Boomers longed for the simplicity of their childhoods—the closely knit neighborhoods overflowing with other children, the strong bonds of community, the clearly defined rules of conduct. The memories were often imaginary—life always seems less complicated in the past—but no less vivid. Alberta Wilson embraced fundamentalism for the opposite reasons: to escape the chaos and confusion of her childhood and to create a moral universe with inalterable standards of good and evil.

For most Boomers, however, the appeal of nostalgia and traditional values competed with their embrace of the consumer culture. Boomers wanted all of the benefits of an individualistic, consumer-driven society: the big house in the suburbs, wide-screen television with access to hundreds of channels, and a local Wal-Mart or Sam's store for convenient one-stop shopping. But they also wanted less suburban sprawl, fewer cars on the road, and a greater sense of community spirit. Boomers lamented the decline of traditional values, but they did not want anyone telling them how they should live their lives. They enjoyed the benefits of immigration—even small suburban communities contained Thai and Middle Eastern restaurants in addition to the now common Chinese and Mexican eateries—but fretted about the fragmentation of American culture. In many ways, the intense social divisions of the 1990s were a product of these Boomer internal conflicts.

WE ARE ALL BOOMERS NOW

During the same week that Congress voted to impeach Bill Clinton, Tom Brokaw's sentimental homage to his father's generation climbed to the top of the *New York Times* best-seller list. Earlier that summer, Americans flocked to theaters to watch Steven Spielberg's *Saving Private Ryan*. Inevitably the comparison was made between the self-indulgent Boomers, represented by Bill Clinton, and the courageous representatives of the "Greatest Generation" who stormed Omaha Beach, risking their lives to save democracy. "What strikes me," observed the columnist Ellen Goodman, "is how serious, how important their struggle was. A matter of life and death. By comparison, the impeachment conflict that threatens to define our wasteful generation is frivolous, foolhardy. A matter of sex and lies."

Boomer bashing, much of it by Boomers, became a popular sport by the late 1990s. "Baby Boomers are the most obnoxious people in the history of the human race," wrote the journalist Joe Queenan. "They're stupefyingly self-centered, unbelievably rude, obnoxious beyond belief, and they're everywhere." David Brooks accused Boomers of being hypocritical sellouts who wanted to make a ton of money without being a part of the hated establishment. Even Clinton adviser Paul Begala got into the act. "I hate the Baby boomers," he wrote. "They're the most self-centered, self-seeking, self-interested, self-absorbed, self-indulgent, self-aggrandizing generation in American history."

The Boomer self-criticism ignores a fundamental fact: by almost any statistical standard, America is better off now than it was in 1945. "The paradox of our time is that we are feeling bad about doing well," noted the economist Robert Samuelson. Life expectancy increased from 65.9 years in 1945 to 75.7 years in 1995. Per capita income more than doubled, from $6,367 to $14,696. The number of high school graduates more than tripled (25 percent to 81 percent), and the percentage of adults completing college increased from 5 to 22. In 1949 the poverty rate stood at 39.7 percent. In 1994, 14.5 percent of Americans fell below the poverty line. Although the gap between rich and poor has grown wider, by an absolute standard the poor are better off today. According to one study, more than 40 percent of Americans living below the poverty line own their homes, 72 percent have washing machines, 92 percent have air conditioners, and 72 percent own cars.

The Boomer emphasis on self-fulfillment has been blamed for nearly every social ill, from the breakup of traditional families to the rise in teen drug use. There is another side to the story, however. During the 1950s many unhappy couples stayed together because of the social stigma associated with divorce. Today, polls show that an overwhelmingly majority of Americans (four of five) are happy with their lives. Of course there are good reasons to decry high divorce rates, especially when children are involved, but the fact is, we are as happy now as we have ever been. Only Icelanders are more content.

Why, if our quality of life has improved so dramatically, do Boomers seem to complain so much? It's an old paradox of expectations and reality. Just as the Progressive era a century ago witnessed an explosion of utopian expectations and political activism, only to collapse during World War I because utopia had not yet arrived, so has the Boom created a backlash of perception that is divorced from the reality. Boomers were raised in a world of seemingly unlimited possibilities, when economists promised an end to the boom-and-bust cycle that had confounded previous generations, when American military might allowed a cold peace to replace the threat of permanent war, and when rising standards of living promised equal opportunity and an end to social discord. "We didn't merely expect things to get better," Samuelson observed about the post–World War II world. "We expected all social problems to be solved."

The gap between expectation and reality has produced a tidal wave of skepticism and cynicism. "Disillusionment is always linked to optimism," observed the sociologist Christopher Jencks. "If you never thought things were going to be good, you're not as disillusioned." If Boomers are dissatisfied, it is not because they have not achieved great things. Instead, it is because they judge their achievements by an unrealistic standard of success. Growing up in an age of television, Boomers have learned to look almost instinctively to Washington, and in particular to the White House, to provide a solution or a new program to address every social ill. At the same time they are deeply skeptical of government and its leaders. A 1996 survey found that 72 percent of Baby Boomers agreed that "the government is completely out of touch with what Americans like me face every day." Baby Boomers want less government, but they also want Washington to find jobs for everyone who wants to work. They want government to do more for the poor, but not expand welfare. They want it all: new social programs, lower taxes, and a balanced budget. The gap between what they expect of government and how much they are willing to pay for it mirrors what they expect of themselves compared to what they achieve.

The Boomer preoccupation with self-examination took on a more serious tone after the terrorist attacks on September 11, 2001. Every generation experiences some searing national tragedy that shifts public debate and shapes perceptions for years to come. The collapse of the twin towers of the World Trade Center, a symbol of American global economic power, and of the burning gash in the Pentagon, the symbol of American military might, will be remembered along with other days of infamy: the attack on Fort Sumter, the 1929 stock market collapse, Pearl Harbor, the Kennedy assassination. At Pearl Harbor, 2,403 people were killed and 1,178 wounded; of the dead, only 68 were civilians. On the first day of the Normandy invasion on June 6, 1944, 1,465 died. Before nightfall on September 11, 2,813 civilians were dead, making it the bloodiest day since September 17, 1862, when 6,300 Union and Confederate soldiers were killed or mortally wounded in the Civil War battle of Antietam. "It is clear now, as it was on December 7, 1941, that the United States is at war," said former CIA director R. James Woolsey. "The question is: with whom?"

That question was quickly answered, when the U.S. invaded Afghanistan, and later, Iraq, but another remained in doubt: Are the Boomers up to the challenge? "For years, we Americans enjoyed a carefree, self-indulgent disconnect from the rest of the world," observed the political analyst Gloria Borger. "Then we were attacked at home, suddenly unified by an external enemy—even a nameless, stateless one. Overnight, once untethered baby boomers, who envied the resolve and spirit of World War II's 'greatest generation,' were facing an unprecedented test of their own." "We came of age declaring the age of Aquarius and the dawn of an era of perfection," observed the former editor in chief of *American Demographics* magazine. "The times may now be finally putting to bed the idea that life is easy." "The life-altering events of September 11, 2001, will test our mettle at a time of national crisis," observed Joe Hallett of the *Columbus Dispatch*. "Our fathers knew how to respond. Our grandfathers knew how to respond. Will we? For baby boomers, this is our defining moment. Can we subjugate self-preservation to national sacrifice, self-indulgence to the cause of humanity? Can we lead? This is our time. The legacy of a generation hangs in the balance."

During the 1930s many people expressed similar concerns about the generation that would later be hailed as America's "greatest." "Their adolescence was divided between the crass materialism of the jazz 1920s and the shock of the economic collapse," observed Maxine Davis after traveling the country talking to teens in the mid-1930s. "Can we depend upon them now to live and work and carry on in our beliefs of democracy, individual liberty, and freedom?" she asked. The answer was not reassuring. She found the generation to be apathetic, overwhelmed by the complexity of "modern" society, lacking in faith and conviction. They were the most dispirited in American history, she argued, to the point that if past generations had demonstrated similar qualities "there would be no Lexington and Concord, no Vicksburg or Bull Run." Reflecting the pervasive isolationism of the age, more than 80 percent of young Americans in the 1930s told *Literary Digest* they would not fight unless an enemy attacked American soil. "They are utterly lacking in any sense of responsibility toward the conduct of this nation," she observed. It was "a decadent, vitiated generation, a cancer in the vitals of our people."

That generation would prove the pessimists wrong in places like Iwo Jima, Normandy, and Bastogne. The difference today is that Boomers are the ones holding power and making the decisions about how to respond to terrorism, rather than wearing fatigues and carrying arms. They will be making their contribution not on the battlefield but in the strategy sessions and the boardrooms. Immediately after the attacks, President Bush told his advisers that the terrorist threat would give new meaning and purpose to the Boomer generation, providing them with the opportunity to prove their mettle and demonstrate the same courage and commitment that their fathers had shown in World War II. On September 20 the president issued a generational call to arms before a joint session of Congress and an anxious nation. "In our grief and anger, we have found our mission and our moment," he declared. "Our nation—this generation—will lift a dark threat of violence from our people and our future," he pledged. "We will not tire, we will not falter, and we will not fail."

Each generation learns the lessons of the past and tries to apply them—often incorrectly—in their own time. The grandparents of Boomers passed on to their children the lessons of Versailles following World War I—that the United States needed to avoid military alliances with European nations. Those lessons produced a powerful isolationist movement that prevented the U.S. from responding in the 1930s to the rise of Adolf Hitler. The parents of Boomers learned "the lessons of Munich" that appeasement led only to greater sacrifice and more bloodshed down the road, which helped unite the country against Communism in the late 1940s and 1950s. Boomers, however, learned conflicting lessons about one key offshoot of that conflict: Vietnam. Even after September 11, the use of American power provoked sharp disagreement. The president and his supporters bypassed Vietnam and invoked the Pearl Harbor analogy, comparing Osama bin Laden and Saddam Hussein to Adolf Hitler. His critics pointed out the dangers of getting sucked into a conflict thousands of miles away with an elusive enemy on unfamiliar soil.

Bush may have seen the war on terrorism as a way to purge the nation of its self-centered ways, but he fought it with a minimum of disruption at home. "Has there ever before been a leader who combined so much martial rhetoric with so few calls for sacrifice?" asked New York Times columnist Paul Krugman. The president planned to wage war against the Taliban in Afghanistan and later against Saddam Hussein in Iraq without altering his prewar agenda. Despite the escalating costs of the war and a disappearing surplus, the president pushed the Jobs and Growth Tax Relief Reconciliation Act of 2003 through Congress, slashing taxes by $330 billion. His Democratic opponents, mute on the theme of sacrifice, hoped to stimulate a sag-

ging economy by spending the money on programs that benefit
their most loyal supporters.

On the day of the 9/11 attack, Bobby Muller pulled together his
team at the Vietnam Veterans of America Foundation. "Our world
has totally changed," he told them. He hoped that the attacks would
convince Americans to look at the world in a different way. "It was
an extraordinary opportunity to pull the nation together to sacrifice
for the common good," to ask Americans to cut back on foreign oil
and develop alternative fuels. "Instead, we drop bombs on the poorest nation on earth. It's fucking completely nuts." His concerns were
shared by Marshall Herskovitz—"Instead of mobilizing to act on its
best impulses, [the nation] was mobilized to act unilaterally and
self-righteously"—and by Fran Visco, who went searching for her
old peace buttons from the Vietnam era. Most of the nation, by
contrast, including a majority of Boomers, shared Alberta Wilson's
view. "I support my president," she declared. "I believe that he is
God's man."

Debate about Iraq notwithstanding, the war on terror has shown
that the Boomers and their children are no less patriotic than previous generations. Support for the armed forces remains strong, and
the forces themselves—commanded by Boomer generals—have
been extraordinarily effective. The Army's advertising slogan—"An
Army of One"—was initially ridiculed when it was rolled out prior
to 9/11 as a way to attract recruits to a centralized, disciplined calling
in an age of decentralized individualism. Yet thanks to Boomer-
driven technology, the Army is in fact more decentralized than ever
before—and correspondingly effective.

■

At each stage in the life cycle, Boomers have shaped American culture. How will they change the nation as they move into their retirement years? Their purchasing patterns will continue to change as
they age, which will mean not only longer lines at the Early Bird Special but a significant reshaping of the economy. The 45 to 64 age
group makes up 36.5 percent of restaurant spending and 38 percent
of the home furnishings market; they also require more prescription
drugs and other health care products. It is a good bet that those
industries will benefit from the aging of the Boom, while others—

toy manufacturers, for example—will experience rough sailing. Many businesses are already gearing up for the Boomers' onslaught. The Marriott hotel chain planned to open hundreds of new retirement communities, many specially designed for residents with cognitive disorders. The Mayo Clinic requires medical students to wear goggles, earplugs, and gloves to familiarize themselves with the diminished sensory capacity of an aging population.

Economists fret about the ability of the Social Security system to meet the demands of new retirees. In 2000 there were 3.4 workers contributing to Social Security for every person over age 65. In 2030 there will be only 2.0 workers for every senior. Modern medicine, which has extended life spans, allows Boomers to live longer—and require benefits longer—than their parents' generation. The AARP, one of the most powerful lobbying groups on Capitol Hill, will ensure their voices are heard. Pessimists predict labor shortages along with soaring taxes and deficits as the nation struggles to balance the gap between wage earners and dependents. The age gap threatens to change the lines of cleavage in American politics, replacing today's ideological battles between left and right with a war between the young and the old.

It is unlikely that the nation will ever again experience such an influential generational bulge. The Boom was the product of unique historical forces coming together to create the perfect generational wave. World War II served as a dramatic backdrop, marking a clear break with the generation raised in the 1930s. Since it was bracketed on either side by birth troughs, the Boom's edges appeared sharper and its influence greater. Their parents grew up in a world consumed with depression and war; Boomers were raised amid promises of prosperity and peace interrupted by limited war. The Boom coincided with the emergence of television, the maturation of mass media, and the skillful advertisers who used it to forge a sense of shared generational identity—an identity reinforced on the playground and in the classrooms of their overcrowded schools. Boomers grew up in a unique moment in the nation's history—a time of unprecedented economic growth and unparalleled expectations about the future. But the same forces that made the Boomers unique now work to blur future generational distinctions. Television and movies helped mold a truly national identity that blended the many local and regional cultures into a broader—and largely idealized—notion of what it means to be an American. Since that national culture was initially directed at Boomers as young consumers and then controlled by them, it includes their unique generational imprint. Today, American culture is Boomer culture. For better or worse, that is unlikely to change. America is a Boomer Nation.

NOTES

Except as otherwise indicated here or in the text, all quotes are from interviews with the author.

Introduction   The Long Boom
Page

1   *"It seems to me,"*   "Sixty-Six Million More Americans," *Fortune*, January 1954, 95.

    And the babies kept coming   Daniel Seligman and Lawrence A. Mayer, "The Future Population 'Mix,'" *Fortune*, February 1959, 94 and 222.

2   *"Just imagine how much"*   Sylvia F. Porter, "Babies Equal Boom," *Reader's Digest*, August 1951, 6.

    In 1958 Life *magazine*   Landon Jones, *Great Expectations: America and the Baby Boom Generation* (New York: Coward, McCann and Geoghegan, 1980), 41.

    Yet as the decade progressed   Landon Jones, *Great Expectations*, 24.

3   *In the 1930s the social scientist*   Karl Mannheim, *Ideology and Utopia* (New York: Harcourt, Brace, 1936); "The Sociological Problem of Generations," in *Essays on the Sociology of Knowledge* (New York: Oxford University Press, 1952); William Strauss and Neil Howe, *Generations: The History of America's Future, 1584–2069* (New York: William Morrow, 1991), 8; and *The Fourth Turning: An American Prophecy* (New York: Broadway Books, 1997).

4   *Demographers themselves do not always*   Susan Mitchell, *American Generations*, 2nd edition (Ithaca: New Strategist Publications, 1998), 22.

5   *"By pitching so many things"*   Susan J. Douglas, *Where the Girls Are: Growing Up Female with the Mass Media* (New York: Times Books, 1994), 24–25.

    In 1958, 64 toy manufacturers   "Mattel Credits TV, 52-Week Ad Push for Success in Volatile Toy Market," *Advertising Age*, November 25, 1958, 84–85; "Mattel Built Toy Market Share via Year-Round TV, Still Hikes Spending," *Advertising Age*, October 19, 1960.

By some estimates Howard Smead, *Don't Trust Anyone Over Thirty: The First Four Decades of the Baby Boom* (New York: The Writers Club Press, 2000), 64.

Eugene Gilbert, who referred Dwight Macdonald, "Profiles: Eugene Gilbert," *New Yorker,* November 22, 1958; Eugene Gilbert, "Why Today's Teenagers Seem So Different," *Harper's Magazine,* November 1959, 76–79; "A New, $10 Billion Power: The U.S. Teenage Consumer," *Life,* August 31, 1959, 83; Thomas Hine, *The Rise and Fall of the American Teenager* (New York: HarperCollins, 2000), 237–38.

6 *In the 1950s Boomer parents* Raymond Serafin, "The Auto 'Boom,'" *Advertising Age* (April 1, 1996), S1.

Boomers were raised in a period James T. Patterson, *Grand Expectations: The United States, 1945–1974* (New York: Oxford University Press), 61–65.

"Never had so many" Steven M. Gillon, *The American Paradox: A History of the United States Since 1945* (Boston: Houghton Mifflin, 2003), 81.

Many states passed mandatory James Bryant Conant, *The American High School Today: A First Report to Interested Citizens* (New York: McGraw-Hill, 1959); "Students: On the Fringe of a Golden Era," *Time,* January 29, 1965, 57; Thomas Hine, *The Rise and Fall of the American Teenager,* 242–43 and 252–55.

8 *The institution that solidified* David Farber, *The Age of Great Dreams: America In the 1960s* (New York: Hill and Wang, 1994), 49–57.

Television separated the Boomers Paul C. Light, "The First TV Generation," in Stuart Kallen, *The Baby Boom* (San Diego: Greenhaven Press, 2002), 41; James L. Baughman, *The Republic of Mass Culture* (Baltimore: Johns Hopkins University, 1992), 41–47.

9 *Studies showed that the average* David Farber, *The Age of Great Dreams,* 56; Gillon, *The American Paradox,* 88–92.

As young children *Washington Post,* April 21, 1985; Daniel C. Hallin, *The Uncensored War: The Media and Vietnam* (New York: Oxford University Press, 1986), 211–16.

If television ads bombarded For the best discussion of Freud's impact on American thought see: E. Fuller Torrey, *Freudian Fraud: The Malignant Effect of Freud's Theory on American Thought and Culture* (Bethesda, Maryland: Lucas Books, 1992). Also useful are: Yiannis Gabriel, *Freud and Society* (Boston: Routledge, 1983); and Nathan G. Hale, Jr., *The Rise and Crisis of Psychoanalysis in the United States* (New York: Oxford University Press, 1995).

10 *"Benjamin Spock probably did more"* E. Fuller Torrey, *Freudian Fraud,*
132.

Spock, whose The Common Sense Thomas Maier, *Dr. Spock: An American Life* (New York: Harcourt, 1998), 204–11; Landon Jones, *Great Expectations,* 54–65.

11 *Later, when many Spock babies* E. Fuller Torrey, *Freudian Fraud,* 247; Alfred Kazin, "The Freudian Revolution Analyzed," *New York Times Magazine,* May 6, 1956, 218.

As Kenneth Keniston wrote Kenneth Keniston, *Young Radicals: Notes on Committed Youth* (New York: Harcourt, Brace & World, 1968), 235.

According to the pollster Daniel Yankelovich, *New Rules: Searching for Self-Fulfillment in a World Turned Upside Down* (New York: Random House, 1981), 2.

Not surprisingly, the word lifestyle Peter Clecak, *America's Quest for the Ideal Self: Dissent and Fulfillment in the 60s and 70s* (New York: Oxford University Press, 1983), 9–34; David Farber, *The Age of Great Dreams,* 55.

12 *In 1940 only 11 percent of women* Cheryl Russell, *The Master Trend: How the Baby Boom Generation is Remaking America* (New York: Plenum Press, 1993), 33.

13 *In 2000, surveys by* USA Today, January 13, 2000.

14 *According to the economist* Paul Light, *Baby Boomers* (New York: Norton, 1988), 78.

There is also evidence to suggest Paul Light, *Baby Boomers,* 80–82

15 *Generations, like individuals, change* Kenneth L. Woodward and Paul Brinkley-Rogers, "All of Life's Stage," *Newsweek,* June 6, 1977, 83.

As life expectancy expanded See the pioneering work of Daniel J. Levinson, *The Seasons of a Man's Life* (New York: Ballantine Books, 1978); and *The Seasons of a Woman's Life* (New York: Ballantine Books, 1997).

Part I   The Cult of Youth
Page

19 *"The twentieth century"* Daniel Seligman and Lawrence A. Mayer, "The Future Population 'Mix,'" *Fortune,* February 1959, 222–23.

In 1965, 41 percent of all David Burner, *Making Peace with the 60s* (Princeton; Princeton University Press, 1996), 136–38; Terry H. Anderson, *The Movement and the Sixties: Protest in America from Greensboro to Wounded Knee* (New York: Oxford University Press, 1995), 95–96.

20 *With so many young people*   Terry H. Anderson, *The Movement and the Sixties*, 61–64.

Boomers were not the driving force   Steven M. Gillon, *The American Paradox: A History of the United States Since 1945* (Boston: Houghton Mifflin, 2003), 278.

The story of the first   Robert J. Ringer, *Looking Out for #1* (New York: Fawcett Crest, 1977); Peter Clecak, *America's Quest for the Ideal Self: Dissent and Fulfillment in the 60s and 70s* (New York: Oxford University Press, 1983), 247–62; Gillon, *The American Paradox*, 279.

21 "*The high-school set*"   "Pleasures of Possession," *Newsweek*, March 21, 1966, 71–72; Mary Wells Lawrence, "The 60s: Baby Boom, Creative Boom," *Advertising Age*, June 18, 1990, 66.

As Boomers graduated from college   Melinda Beck, "The Baby Boomers Come of Age," *Newsweek*, March 30, 1981, 34.

Chapter 1   The Boomer Generation
Page
24 *The number of marriage licenses*   Joseph S. Clark, Jr., and Dennis J. Clark, "Rally and Relapse, 1946–1968," in Russell F. Weigley, ed., *Philadelphia: A 300-Year History* (New York: W.W. Norton, 1982), 668–70.

Boosters claimed that television   "Television," *Evening Bulletin*, May 1, 1949, Urban Archives, Temple University, Philadelphia.

25 *In 1939 Thayer, Inc.*   Joseph Nolan, "Boom in Baby Buggies," *New York Times Magazine*, February 21, 1954.

Sales of baby food   "Babies Mean Business," *Advertising Age*, August 9, 1948, 22–23.

Elementary school enrollment   "More Than Two-Million New Consumers a Year," *Business Week*, August 29, 1953.

In 1947 more than sixty-four   *New York Times*, June 9, 1947.

27 "*The nation is getting*"   *New York Times*, January 26, 1961.

31 *That mixed message*   J. Ronald Oakley, *God's Country: America in the Fifties* (New York: Dembner Books, 1986), 294–99.

Many Hollywood films   Nancy Woloch, *Women and the American Experience*, 2nd edition (New York: McGraw Hill, 1994), 478–92; Rosalind Rosenberg, *Divided Lives: American Women in the Twentieth Century* (New York: Hill and Wang, 1992) 138–79; Steven M. Gillon, *The American Paradox: A History of the United States Since 1945* (Boston: Houghton Mifflin, 2003), 135.

32   *In 1942, Alfred Kinsey*   James H. Jones, *Alfred C. Kinsey: A Biography* (New York: W.W. Norton, 1997).

"What was unique to us"   Ruth Rosen, "The Female Generation Gap: Daughters of the Fifties and the Origins of Contemporary American Feminism," in Linda Kerber, ed., *U.S. History as Women's History: New Feminist Essays* (Chapel Hill: University of North Carolina Press, 1995), 318.

According to a 1993 Congressional   *Chicago Sun-Times*, September 19, 1993.

34   *In August 1957* Bandstand   Steven D. Stark, *Glued to the Set: The 60 Television shows and Events That Made Us Who We Are Today* (New York: Free Press, 1997), 68–72.

35   *In 1940 less than*   Lynn Rosellini, "When a Generation Turns 40," *U.S. News and World Report*, March 10, 1986, 60.

36   *Between 1940 and 1950*   "Philadelphia's Negro Population: Facts on Housing," Philadelphia Housing Association, October 1953, Urban Archives, Temple University, Philadelphia.

40   *Before the fad was over*   "U.S. Again is Subdued by Davy," *Life*, April 25, 1955, 27.

With the exception of   Oakley, *God's Country*, 362–63.

42   *In the waning days*   "The Explosive Generation," *Look*, January 3, 1961, 17.

When President Kennedy   Walter Cronkite, *A Reporter's Life* (New York: Alfred A. Knopf, 1996), 305; Paul Light, *Baby Boomers* (New York: Norton, 1988), 166–67; Steven D. Stark, *Glued to the Set*, 111–14.

Chapter 2   The Vietnam Division
Page

47   *The term, and the worry*   For a good discussion on contemporary fears of juvenile delinquency, see the five-part series in *Saturday Evening Post*, "The Shame of America," January 1955.

49   *Lyndon Johnson dreaded*   Steven M. Gillon, *The American Paradox: A History of the United States Since 1945* (Boston: Houghton Mifflin, 2003), 202–203.

While confidently predicting victory   Michael Beschloss, "I Don't See Any Way of Winning," *Newsweek*, November 12, 2001, 58.

50   *When Johnson suddenly escalated*   Christian G. Appy, *Working-Class War: American Combat Soldiers and Vietnam* (Chapel Hill: University of North Carolina Press, 1993), 17–19; Lawrence M. Baskir and William A. Strauss, *Chance and Circumstance: The Draft, the War, and the Vietnam Generation* (New York: Knopf, 1978), 5.

52 *By the time he took a commercial* Gillon, *The American Paradox,* 237–38.

54 *A standard tour of duty* Kim Willenson, *The Bad War: An Oral History of the Vietnam War* (New York: New American Library, 1987), 76.

58 *Ron Kovic, who lived* Ron Kovic, *Born on the Fourth of July* (New York: McGraw-Hill, 1976), 39.

60 *Bobby got his revenge* "Assignment to Neglect: From Vietnam to a VA Hospital," *Life,* May 22, 1970, 24–32.

64 *Richard Nixon, however* Godfrey Hodgson, *America In Our Time* (Garden City, New York: Doubleday, 1976), 384–96; "Man and Woman of the Year: The Middle Americans," *Newsweek,* January 5, 1970, 15.

67 *After young people rallied* Frederick G. Dutton, *Changing Sources of Power: American Politics in the 1970s* (New York: McGraw-Hill, 1971), 27–56; Jerry Hagstrom, "Baby Boom Generation May Have to Wait a While to Show Its Political Clout," *National Journal,* April 28, 1984.

It never worked that way The figures are based on voters 18–24 according to CBS News exit polls. See: Jerry Hagstrom, "Baby Boom Generation May Have to Wait a While to Show Its Political Clout," 804; *Los Angeles Times,* April 27, 1986.

71 *In 1971, the pollster* Jonathan Rauch, "Vietnam Veterans Are Wondering Whether They Have a Friend in the VA," *National Journal,* July 18, 1981, 1291.

Chapter 3   Growing Pains
Page

73 *The nation was in the midst* "Students: On the Fringe of a Golden Era," *Time,* January 29, 1965, 57; "Man of the Year," *Time,* January 6, 1967, 18–23.

74 *The women of her generation* David Allyn, *Make Love, Not War* (Boston: Little Brown, 2000), 33–34; Steven M. Gillon, *The American Paradox: A History of the United States Since 1945* (Boston: Houghton Mifflin, 2003), 218.

76 *"In the 1950s as in"* Yankelovich, *New Rules: Searching for Self-Fulfillment in a World Turned Upside Down* (New York, Random House, 1981), 96.

Just as important, Boomer couples Paul Light, *Baby Boomers* (New York: Norton, 1988), 115.

Rising divorce rates were just Daniel Yankelovich, *New Rules,* 98; Lynn Rosellini, "When a Generation Turns 40," *U.S. News & World Report,* March 10, 1986, 60.

77 *"Our findings"* "How's Your Sex Life," *Newsweek,* September 1, 1975, 57.

79   *By the 1980s, 25 percent*   Nancy Woloch, *Women and the American Experience*, 2nd edition (New York: McGraw Hill, 1994), 558–63; Peter Clecak, *America's Quest for the Ideal Self: Dissent and Fulfillment in the 60s and 70s* (New York: Oxford University Press, 1983), 182–85.

80   *The most dramatic change*   Gillon, *The American Paradox*, 292–94.

81   *All of these changes in law*   Ruth Rosen, *The World Split Open: How the Modern Women's Movement Changed America* (New York: Viking, 2000), 320–27; Winifred D. Wandersee, *On the Move: American Women in the 1970s* (Boston: Twayne Publishers, 1988), 170; Gillon, *The American Paradox*, 295–96.

83   *Music emerged during the 1960s*   Maurice Isserman and Michael Kazin, *America Divided: The Civil War of the 1960s* (New York: Oxford University Press, 2000), 161; Terry H. Anderson, *The Movement and the 60s: Protest in America from Greensboro to Wounded Knee* (New York: Oxford University Press, 1995), 92–95.

The most popular group   George Lipsitz, "Who'll Stop the Rain?," in David Farber, *The Sixties: From Memory to History* (Chapel Hill, University of North Carolina Press 1994), 206–34; "Hear That Big Sound," *Life*, May 21, 1965, 83.

According to Life *magazine*   Gillon, *The American Paradox*, 217.

87   *In 1968, for example*   Lawrence M. Baskir and William A. Strauss, *Chance and Circumstance: The Draft, the War, and the Vietnam Generation* (New York: Knopf, 1978), 32–33.

90   *The generation's size worked*   John E. Schwarz, *America's Hidden Success: A Reassessment of Twenty Years of Public Policy* (New York: Norton, 1983), 124–29; John W. Hawks, "The Next Boom in Real Estate," *American Demographics*, May 1991, 48.

Included in those numbers   Melinda Beck, "The Baby Boomers Come of Age," *Newsweek*, March 30, 1981, 34.

92   *During the '50s and '60s*   Kirse Granat May, *Golden State, Golden Youth: The California Image in Popular Culture, 1955–1966* (Chapel Hill: University of North Carolina Press, 2002).

93   *California may have fallen*   Peter Biskind, *Easy Riders, Raging Bulls* (New York: Simon & Schuster, 1998), 14–15.

Beginning in the late '60s   David A. Cook, "Lost Illusions: American Cinema in the Shadow of Watergate and Vietnam, 1970–1979," in *History of the American Cinema* (New York: Scribner, 2000), 1–24; Robert Sklar, *Movie-Made America* (New York: Random House, 1975), 286–304; Diane

Jacobs, *Hollywood Renaissance* (New York: Dell Publishing, 1977), 1–22; Robert Phillip Kolker, *A Cinema of Loneliness* (New York: Oxford University Press, 1980), 1–15.

Hollywood's decision to pursue   Aniko Bodroghkozy, *Groove Tube: Sixties Television and the Youth Rebellion* (Durham: Duke University Press, 2001), 199–216; Steven D. Stark, *Glued to the Set: The 60 Television Shows and Events That Made Us Who We Are Today* (New York: Free Press, 1997), 142.

96   *Los Angeles housed*   "One Pace Back, Two Paces Forward," *The Economist*, April 3, 1982, 77.

Chapter Four   Finding God
Page

98   *The Philadelphia explosion*   *Report of the National Advisory Commission on Civil Disorders* (New York: E.P. Dutton, 1968), 128–35.

The rate of serious crime   "The Crime Wave," *Time*, June 30, 1975, 10–17.

99   *"The Negro masses"*   Steven M. Gillon, *The American Paradox: A History of the United States Since 1945* (Boston: Houghton Mifflin, 2003), 229.

100 *The experiment was a miserable*   The local newspapers were filled with reports of violence. See: *Evening Bulletin*, "South Philadelphia High School and Crime," Urban Archives, Temple University, Philadelphia. Especially useful are: 10 January 1968, 19 January 1968, 20 January 1968, 17 March 1968, 11 May 1968, 13 May 1968.

101 *Many other African American women*   Lee Rainwater and William L. Yancey, *The Moynihan Report and the Politics of Controversy* (Cambridge: Harvard University Press, 1967) includes the report along with critical commentary.

102 *Like many of the other social*   Gilbert Steiner, *Social Insecurity: The Politics of Welfare* (Chicago: Rand McNally, 1966), 33; James T. Patterson, *America's Struggle against Poverty 1900–1994* (Cambridge: Harvard University Press, 1994), 171.

105 *The Nation of Islam*   *Washington Post*, May 9, 1993.

107 *For many African American leaders*   Allen J. Matusow, *The Unraveling of America* (New York: Harper and Row, 1984), 345–75.

110 *Alberta's experience with*   Kenneth L. Woodward, "Born Again!" *Newsweek*, October 25, 1976, 68.

Perhaps the most well-known   TRB, "Leap of Faith," *New Republic*, May 8, 1976, 8; Kenneth Woodward, "Born Again!," 68.

Many Boomers who had turned Wade Clark Roof, *A Generation of Seekers: The Spiritual Journeys of the Baby Boom Generation* (New York: HarperCollins, 1993).

111 *Unlike their parents* Barbara Kantrowitz, "In Search of the Sacred," *Newsweek,* November 29, 1994; Richard Cimino and Don Lattin, "Choosing My Religion," *American Demographics,* April 1999, 62; Wade Clark Roof, *Spiritual Marketplace: Baby Boomers and the Remaking of American Religion* (Princeton; Princeton University Press, 1999), 3–15.

In many ways Richard Higgins, "Sold on Spirituality," *Boston Globe,* December 3, 2000, 19; Peter Clecak, *America's Quest for the Ideal Self: Dissent and Fulfillment in the 60s and 70s* (New York: Oxford University Press, 1983), 115–56.

112 *"Choice so much"* Jeffrey L. Sheler, "Spiritual America," *U.S. News and World Report,* April 4, 1994, 48.

"People are looking" *Boston Globe,* December 3, 2000.

By some estimates Marc Spiegler, "Scouting for Souls," *American Demographics,* March 1996, 42; *New York Times,* April 16 and 18, 1995.

Millions of other Americans "Getting Your Head Together," *Newsweek,* November 6, 1976, 56–62; Gillon, *The American Paradox,* 279–80.

Part II   The Great Shift
Page
117 *By the mid-1980s, they* Michael Shay, "Baby-boomer rock 'n' roll," *Advertising Age,* September 2, 1985, 16; Robert J. Samuelson, "The Binge is Over," *Newsweek,* July 10, 1989, 35; Melinda Beck, "The Baby Boomers Come of Age," *Newsweek,* March 30, 1981, 34.

118 *Evidence of a new culture* Bill Barol, "The Eighties Are Over," *Newsweek,* January 4, 1988, 40; Nicolaus Mills, "The Culture of Triumph and the Spirit of the Times," in Nicolaus Mills, *Culture in an Age of Money: The Legacy of the 1980s in America* (New York: Ivan Dee, 1990), 11–28; Steven M. Gillon, *The American Paradox: A History of the United States Since 1945* (Boston: Houghton Mifflin, 2003), 391.

Many observers dismissed *Newsweek,* December 31,1984; Beth Brophy, "Middle-Class Squeeze," *U.S. News & World Report,* August 18, 1986, 36; Hendrik Hertzberg, "The Short Happy Life of the American Yuppie," in Nicolaus Mills, *Culture in an Age of Money,* 66–82; John L. Hammond, "Yuppies," *Public Opinion Quarterly,* Winter, 1986, 487–98.

119 *At the same time, Boomer* *New York Times,* November 30, 1995.

"The parenting motto" *Tampa Tribune,* September 15, 1996.

Advertisers jumped on *Newsday,* October 5, 1988.

120 *Prosperity, advances in medical* Lynn Rosellini, "When a Generation Turns 40," *U.S. News & World Report,* March 10, 1986.

Perhaps the single biggest *Washington Post,* August 18, 1996.

Chapter 5 *The Prolonged Adolescence of Donny Deutsch*
Page

124 *His generation also had* "Students: On the Fringe of a Golden Era," *Time,* January 29, 1965, 56.

125 *A 1971 survey* Timothy Miller, "Dropping Out of Society," in Stuart A. Kallen, ed., *The Baby Boom* (San Diego: Greenhaven Press, 2002), 95; Steven M. Gillon, *The American Paradox: A History of the United States Since 1945* (Boston: Houghton Mifflin, 2003), 279.

Despite all the scorn "Get Up and Boogie," *Newsweek,* November 8, 1976, 94–100.

126 *In 1970 a presidential* David Allyn, *Make Love, Not War: The Sexual Revolution, an Unfettered History* (Boston: Little, Brown, 2000), 186.

You did not have to sneak David Allyn, *Make Love, Not War,* 228–45; Gillon, *The American Paradox,* 280–81.

127 *The liberalization of all things* Martin Duberman, *Stonewall* (New York: Dutton, 1993); David Allyn, *Make Love, Not War,* 145–165; "Stonewall," *Newsweek,* July 3, 1989, 56–7; Gillon, *The American Paradox,* 290–91.

128 *After graduation Donny* Deutsch (unpublished autobiography), 180.

Donny returned to New York Deutsch (unpublished autobiography), 181.

129 *Donny bounced around* Deutsch (unpublished autobiography), 181–82.

David Deutsch & Associates was a small Deutsch (unpublished autobiography), 182.

In 1984 Donny put together *Advertising Age,* March 13, 1986.

An ad for Japanese *Crain's New York Business,* August 24, 1987.

130 *In July 1989 the agency used* *New York Times,* July 7, 1989.

131 *Deutsch's main task* Judith Graham, "IKEA furnishing Its U.S. Identity," *Advertising Age,* September 17, 1989.

It was a challenge IKEA Campaign, no date, Linda Sawyer Papers.

132 *These categories, driven by* Cynthia Rigg, "IKEA Ad Campaign Makes Virtue Out Of N.J. Turnpike," *Crain's New York Business,* May 21, 1990, 14;

Alison Fahey, "IKEA Building a Loyal Following with Style, Price," *Advertising Age*, January 28, 1991, 23.

Boomer lifestyle, according Leah Rickard, "Friendship and Choice Now Thicker than Blood," *Advertising Age*, November 7, 1994, 17.

Perhaps the most provocative Kate Fitzgerald, "IKEA Dares to Reveal Gays Buy Tables, Too," *Advertising Age*, March 28, 1994, 3; *The Washington Post*, May 19, 1994.

134 *At that time, 1989* New York Times, March 29, 1994, 20; *Plain Dealer* (Cleveland), April 5, 1994.

Left unsaid was that Times (London), April 6, 1994.

These risky ads made Los Angeles Times, June 5, 1994.

The ads also revealed Rosser Reeves, *Reality in Advertising* (New York: Knopf, 1961), 34; *New York Times*, March 31, 1991.

135 *That style no longer* New York Times, March 31, 1991; *Washington Post*, May 29, 1986.

136 *All of Deutsch's ads* Warren Berger, "Vox Populi," *Advertising Age*, January 1, 1994.

One of Donny's favorite Melanie Wells, "Bad Boy Makes Good," *Forbes*, November 29, 1999.

There were times when Donny Leslie Savan, *The Sponsored Life: Ads, TV, and American Culture* (Philadelphia: Temple University Press, 1994), 263–64; Deutsch (unpublished autobiography), 171.

137 *The office atmosphere* New York Times, February 16, 1992.

Newsweek *commented that* Annetta Miller and Seema Nayyar, "Captain Outrageous," *Newsweek*, October 31, 1994.

Chapter 6   The Way We Wish We Lived Now
Page

140 *Young couples looking for* Kenneth T. Jackson, *Crabgrass Frontier: The Suburbanization of the United States* (New York: Oxford University Press, 1985), 231–45; Larry Van Dyne, "The Making of Washington," *Washingtonian*, February, 2000.

141 *At the time, social critics* Steven M. Gillon, *The American Paradox: A History of the United States Since 1945* (Boston: Houghton Mifflin, 2003), 102–03.

145 *"There was something lonely"* Jane Leifer, "The Trials of the Coed 100," *Princeton Alumni Weekly*, May, 1973.

147 *Liz had never been politically* Diane Ghirardo, *Architecture After Mod-*

ernism (London: Thames and Hudson, 1996), 7–17; Vincent Scully, *American Architecture and Urbanism,* 1st ed. (New York: Praeger, 1969), 7.

148 *Although Scully was an intimidating*   *New York Times,* January 27, 1991.

154 *The desire to create*   Ron E. Roberts, *The New Communes: Coming Together in America* (Englewood Cliffs, New Jersey: Prentice-Hall, 1971), 47–62; Timothy Miller, *The 60s Communes: Hippies and Beyond* (Syracuse, New York: Syracuse University Press, 1999), xx; "Year of the Commune," *Newsweek,* August 18, 1969, 89–90.

"Everyone swam nude"   Steven M. Gillon, *The American Paradox: A History of the United States Since 1945* (Boston: Houghton Mifflin, 2003), 215–16.

158 *There were a few basic*   Andres Duaney and Elizabeth Platter-Zyberk, "The Neighborhood, the District, and the Corridor," in Peter Katz, ed., *The New Urbanism: Toward an Architecture of Community* (New York: McGraw-Hill, 1994), xvii–xx.

159 *Building in Seaside started*   Jerry Adler, "Suburbs; the new burb is a village," *Newsweek,* December 26, 1994.

Andres and Liz were hailed   Kurt Anderson, "Is Seaside Too Good to be True?" in David Mohney and Keller Easterling eds., *Seaside: Making a Town in America,* (New York: Princeton Architectural Press, 1991), 43.

Seaside was "Bobo" paradise   Anderson, *Seaside,* 44–46; David Brooks, *Bobos in Paradise: The New Upper Class and How They Got There* (New York: Simon & Schuster, 2001).

160 *Ironically, Seaside's commercial*   Philip Langdon, "A Good Place to Live," *Atlantic,* March 1988.

Since there was little   Greg Bush, in interview with Elizabeth Platter-Zyberk, July 28, 1997.

Andres aspired to be   Philip Langdon, "A Good Place to Live."

Andres volunteered his services   James Howard Kunstler, *Home From Nowhere* (New York: Simon & Schuster, 1996), 213.

161 *Their calls for a new*   "Neighborhood Reborn," *Consumer Reports* 61, no. 5 (May, 1996): 24.

Banks and insurance companies   "Bye-Bye, Suburban Dream; Paved Paradise," *Newsweek,* May 15, 1995.

162 *By the end of the 1980s*   Philip Langdon, "A Good Place to Live."

Nevertheless, the Boomers   *Milwaukee Journal Sentinel,* April 21, 1996; *Austin American-Statesman,* October 26, 2002.

Although they expressed frustration   *Washington Post,* November 7, 1999.

163 *"If today's suburbs"* *The Denver Post,* November 12, 1995.

"A large part of" *USA Today,* April 23, 2003.

Chapter 7 The New Power Politics
Page

164 *By 1978 there were a number* James S. Olson and Randy Roberts, *Where the Domino Fell: America and Vietnam, 1945–1990* (New York: St. Martin's Press, 1991), 268–69.

165 *Arriving in Washington in January* "Speaking Out for the Vietnam Vet," *National Journal,* September 2, 1978, 1400.

166 *The advice came just as* Bobby Muller, Subcommittee on Administrative Law and Governmental Relations, Committee on the Judiciary, House, 98th Cong., 2nd sess., March 21, 1984. U.S. Government Printing Office, 1984.

Ironically, the organized veterans' Timothy B. Clark, "Veterans' Groups Are Battling the 'Anti-Vet' President," *National Journal,* September 2, 1978.

167 *The older organizations pointed* Kirk Victor, "A Different Drummer," *National Journal,* March 12, 1988, 669.

168 *While there was no open policy* Paul Light, *Baby Boomers* (New York: Norton, 1988), 103–04.

There were clear generational Wilbur J. Scott, *The Politics of Readjustment: Vietnam Veterans Since the War* (New York: Aldine De Gruyter, 1993), 8.

Although they often dismissed Wilbur J. Scott, *The Politics of Readjustment,* 84.

169 *Bobby argued that Vietnam vets* Jonathan Rauch, "Vietnam Veterans Are Wondering Whether They Have a Friend in the VA," *National Journal,* July 18, 1981, 1291.

170 *One of the biggest issues* Gerald Nicosia, *Home to War: A History of the Vietnam Veterans' Movement* (New York: Crown Publishers, 2001), 434–505, 587–96.

The CVV adopted its philosophy Jonathan Rauch, "Vietnam Veterans Are Wondering Whether They Have a Friend in the VA," 1291.

This position put them Scott, *The Politics of Readjustment,* 39.

Veterans were faced with David E. Bonior, "The Vietnam Veteran: a History of Neglect" (lecture, Wayne State University, Detroit, Mich., October 28, 1985).

171 *In November 1978 the older* "50 Percent Increase in Some Veterans' Pensions Approved," *Congressional Quarterly,* October 28, 1978: 3165–66.

Bobby viewed the legislation "Muller Demands: Take Welfare Out of VA," *Stars and Stripes,* November 2, 1978.

Initially Bobby had high hopes *Washington Post,* April 28, 1979.

The CVV was also disappointed "Bert Carp and Ellen Goldstein to Pat Bario and Mike Chanin," November 14, 1978, Carter Presidential Library, Name File—Muller.

172 *The dismissive comment about* Jonathan Rauch, "Vietnam Veterans Are Wondering Whether They Have a Friend in the VA."

"No steps we take" *Washington Post,* May 29, 1979.

174 *In January, on the same day* The Associated Press, January 31, 1981.

176 *During his 1980 presidential campaign* George C. Herring, "The 'Vietnam Syndrome' and American Foreign Policy," *Virginia Quarterly Review,* LVII (Fall 1981): 594–612.

During the 1970s Hollywood Olson and Roberts, *Where the Domino Fell,* 273–74.

The Rambo movies perpetuated H. Bruce Franklin, "The POW/MIA Myth," *Atlantic,* December 1991; Gerald Nicosia, *Home to War,* 302–09.

178 *That put them at odds* *Washington Post,* June 5, 1980.

He had hoped that Vietnam "Vietnam veterans; On the Ho Chi Minh Trail," *Economist,* November 12, 1983.

Bobby reflected many of the doubts Steven M. Gillon, *The American Paradox: A History of the United States Since 1945* (Boston: Houghton Mifflin, 2003), 353–54.

181 *Bobby thought the* Scott, *The Politics of Readjustment,* 146.

182 *Bobby was typically* *Washington Post,* December 29, 1981.

While playing up its concern Gerald Nicosia, *Home to War,* 395–401.

183 *More than 150,000 people* Tom Morgenthau, "Honoring Vietnam Veterans— at Last," *Newsweek,* November 22, 1982.

The convention elected *Washington Post,* November 26, 1983.

Prophetically, he warned *Washington Post,* November 11, 1983.

184 *For the next few years* Jonathan Alter and Kim Willenson, "Vietnam: The Unknown Soldier," *Newsweek,* June 4, 1984.

188 *The failure in Vietnam* Joseph Nye, "In Government We Don't Trust,"

Foreign Policy 108 (September 22, 1977): 99; *Washington Post,* January 31, 1980; Gillon, *The American Paradox,* 311–12.

189 *Changes in the structure* Bernadette A Budde, "Business Political Action Committees," in Michael Malbin, ed., *Parties, Interest Groups, and Campaign Finance Laws* (Washington, D.C.: American Enterprise Institute of Public Policy Research, 1979), 9–15; David Adamany, "The New Faces of American Politics," *Annals* 486 (July 1986): 18–21.

Chapter 8 The "Second Stage" and Other Struggles for Women
Page
191 *In August 1980 the* New York Times Ruth Rosen, *The World Split Open: How the Modern Women's Movement Changed America* (New York: Viking, 2000), 338.

The struggle for a constitutional Jane J. Mansbridge, *Why We Lost the ERA* (Chicago: University of Chicago Press, 1986), 8–19; Ruth Rosen, *The World Split Open,* 332–33.

192 *The women's movement split* Betty Friedan, *The Second Stage* (Cambridge: Harvard University Press, 1998), 3–5; *Christian Science Monitor,* October 28, 1981; Bella Abzug, "Forming a Real Women's Bloc," *The Nation,* November 28, 1981, 576; Ruth Rosen, *The World Split Open,* 335.

195 *She came to realize what millions* Sandra G. Mannix, "Attorney Declares War On Breast Cancer," *The Legal Intelligencer,* April 29, 1992, 4.

196 *Boomers became adults* James T. Patterson, *The Dread Disease: Cancer and Modern American Culture* (Cambridge: Harvard University Press, 1987), 303.

197 *Just as women demanded* Barron H. Lerner, *The Breast Cancer Wars* (New York: Oxford University Press, 2001), 178.

198 *Kushner was often forced* Marilyn Werber Serafini, "Biomedical Warfare," *National Journal,* February 1, 1997.

Boomer expectations of medicine Cheryl Clark, "A Generation in Control," *San Diego Union-Tribune,* October 7, 2001.

In addition to its roots Chris Bull, "Grim Reality," *The Advocate,* July 27, 1993, 24–26.

199 *Their tactics, though controversial* New York Times, June 5, 2001; Steven M. Gillon, *The American Paradox: A History of the United States Since 1945* (Boston: Houghton Mifflin, 2003), 374–75.

200 *If the women's movement*   *New York Times,* February 28, 1993.

201 *As Love went on her book*   *Los Angeles Times,* December 5, 1993.

     During one televised debate   *Boston Globe,* June 27, 1990.

     She became annoyed   *Los Angeles Times,* December 5, 1993.

202 *Fran took the Amtrak*   *Newsday,* October 4, 1993.

     It was "like this epiphany"   Robert Bazell, *Her-2: The Making of Herceptin, a Revolutionary Treatment for Breast Cancer* (New York: Random House, 1998), 124.

203 *The growing political ferment*   *Washington Post,* April 19, 1994.

205 *The leadership shared a common*   *Los Angeles Times,* May 24, 1992.

     The disagreements reflect larger   *Washington Post,* April 19, 1994.

207 The Washington Post *took note*   *Washington Post,* April 19, 1994.

208 *Most Democrats supported*   *New York Times,* June 29, 1994.

209 *The coalition set up*   *Los Angeles Times,* February 18, 2002.

Chapter 9   *The New Fundamentalism*
Page

212 *Not surprisingly, memories*   Tom Morganthau, "Decade Shock," *Newsweek,* September 5, 1988, 14.

     Both perspectives oversimplify   Todd Gitlin, "Straight from the Sixties: What Conservatives Owe the Decade They Hate," *American Prospect,* May–June, 1996, 54.

217 *Not only was Tabernacle*   Joel A. Carpenter, *Revive Us Again: The Reawakening of American Fundamentalism* (New York: Oxford University Press, 1997), 57–75.

218 *No one embraced that*   Dudley Clendinen, "The Righteous Stuff," *Lear's* magazine May 1993, 59.

     In 1967 Bell moved   Dudley Clendinen, "The Righteous Stuff," 83.

     Practicing the biblical teachings   Rod Bell, Sr., *The Mantle of the Mountain Man* (Greenville, South Carolina: Bob Jones University Press, 1999), 129.

219 *Bell reserved most of his ire*   Rod Bell, Sr., *The Mantle of the Mountain Man,* 128–31.

     Bell's growing political activism   William C. Berman, *America's Right Turn: From Nixon to Bush* (Baltimore, Maryland: Johns Hopkins University Press, 1994), 60–63; "Thunder From the Right," *New York Times Magazine,* February 8, 1981, 23.

Despite their doctrinal   Burt Solomon, "Christian Soldiers," *National Journal* (February 24, 1996), 410; *Houston Chronicle,* June 19, 1993.

220 *Religious fundamentalists found*   Peter Clecak, *America's Quest for the Ideal Self: Dissent and Fulfillment in the 60s and 70s* (New York: Oxford University Press, 1983); William Berman, *America's Right Turn,* 64–72 and 76–91. Glazer later published the essay in a book with the same title. See: Nathan Glazer, *The Limits of Social Policy* (Cambridge: Harvard University Press, 1990), 117; Steven M. Gillon, *The American Paradox: A History of the United States Since 1945* (Boston: Houghton Mifflin, 2003), 299.

In addition to New Right   Peter Schrag, "The Silver Anniversary of Proposition 13," *California Journal,* June 1, 2003, 22; Gillon, *The American Paradox,* 299–300.

221 *Losing faith in government*   A James Reichley, *Faith in Politics* (Washington, D.C.: Brookings Institution Press, 2002), 298; Dinesh D'Souza, "Jerry Falwell's Renaissance," *Policy Review* (Winter, 1984): 34; Walter Shapiro, "Politics and the Pulpit," *Newsweek,* September 17, 1984, 24.

223 *While pleading for a return*   "Praise the Lord and Pass the Loot," *The Economist,* May 16, 1987, 23; Gillon, *The American Paradox,* 391.

224 *Religious conservatives created*   Nina J. Easton, *Gang of Five: Leaders at the Center of the Conservative Crusade* (New York: Simon & Schuster, 2000), 216.

As Reed's observation   Wade Clark Roof, "The Baby Boom's Search for God," *American Demographics,* December 1992, 50.

225 *By the 1980s the gap*   Walter Shapiro, "Politics and the Pulpit," *Newsweek,* September 17, 1984, 24.

Reagan's appeals worked   A James Reichley, *Religion in American Public Life* (Washington, D.C.: Brookings Institution, 1985), 319–31; "Praise the Lord and Pass the Loot," *Economist,* May 16, 1987, 23.

Reagan's successor   *New York Times,* September 27 and October 16, 1988.

228 *She continued teaching*   Alberta C. Wilson, "The Biblical Teaching Concerning Women," Ph.D. diss., Tabernacle Baptist Theological Seminary, May 5, 1996.

229 *As she thought about life*   Alberta C. Wilson, *From the Ghetto by Grace to Glory* (Columbus, Georgia: Brentwood Christian Press, 1996).

Chapter 10   Boomer Culture
Page
230 *In Hollywood in the 1970s*   New York Times, October 30, 1988.

Newsweek *went so far*   Richard Turner, "The Kid Who Saved Television," *Newsweek,* January 5, 1998, 82; *Los Angeles Times,* July 2, 1989, May 2, 1991, and October 30, 1992.

Movies were no different   Los Angeles Times, April 9, 1998.

231 *A number of shows*   New York Times, October 30, 1988; Brian D. Johnson, "Prime-Time Decline," *Maclean's,* October 31, 1988, 60.

Nostalgic Boomers could tune   San Diego Union-Tribune, December 6, 1988.

In 1989 VH1 tried   New York Times, August 7, 1989.

233 *The movie aired on*   New York Times, March 21, 1983.

Despite the complaints   New York Times, March 22, 1983.

TV Guide *called*   TV Guide, March 19, 1983, a–6.

The movie received   New York Times, July 8, 1983.

236 *It was their nightmare*   Terrance Sweeney, "Fortysomething," *Written By,* May 2000.

238 *Over the next few seasons*   New York Times, September 22, 1996.

239 *The show tackled another*   Thirtysomething Stories (New York: Pocket Books, 1991).

240 *Most critics praised*   Harry F. Waters, "The Over 30 Crowd," *Newsweek,* December 21, 1987.

"Watching thirtysomething *every week"*   Dan Wakefield, "Celebrating 'The Small Moments of Personal Discovery,'" *TV Guide,* June 11, 1988, 35.

The New York Times *said the show*   New York Times, February 24, 1988.

Another critic referred to   New York Times, December 20, 1988.

Dissenters argued that   San Francisco Chronicle, May 28, 1991.

241 *Another critic dismissed the show*   Los Angeles Times, April 19, 1988.

The show was a unique generational   Eva S. Moskowitz, *In Therapy We Trust: America's Obsession with Self-Fulfillment* (Baltimore: Johns Hopkins University Press), 6; Steven M. Gillon, *The American Paradox: A History of the United States Since 1945* (Boston: Houghton Mifflin, 2003), 280.

242 Thirtysomething *broke with*   Patricia Hersch, "Thirtysomethingtherapy,"

Psychology Today, October 1988, 62–63; *The New York Times,* September 22, 1996.

243 *The show also reinforced* New York Times, September 22, 1996.

Part III Boomer Nation
Page
245 *In the 1990s Boomers assumed* Martin Ford Puris, "Lessons for Baby-Boom Futurists," *Advertising Age,* June 26, 1989.

246 *The leading group of Boomers* "A Profile of American Baby Boomers," MetLife Mature Market Institute; George P. Moschis, *The Maturing Marketplace: Buying Habits of Baby Boomers and their Parents* (Quorum Books: Westport, Connecticut, 2000).

Politicians were not far Boston Globe, April 23, 1999.

247 *Truly, America had become* New York Times, October 17, 1990; "The Gospel of Wealth," *Economist,* May 30, 1998, 19; David Gergen, "A Sense of Belonging," *U.S. News & World Report,* December 6, 1999, 108.

At least by comparison Sunday Times, July 5, 1998.

Chapter 11 Gaining Control: At What Cost?
Page
248 *When Clinton chose another* Howard Fineman, "Sixties Coming of Age," *Newsweek* July 20, 1992, 32.

249 *Republicans took up the generational* USA Today, August 20, 1992.

250 *A number of Clinton advisers* "Coming Soon: Great Spots and Friction," *National Journal,* August 1, 1992, 1790.

Grunwald found Donny's ads Barbara Lippert, "How They'll Play in Adland," *Adweek,* July 13, 1992; *New York Times,* July 4, 1992; *Washington Post,* July 4, 1992.

251 *Working on a successful presidential* Noreen O'Leary, "The Donnybrook," *Adweek,* January 18, 1993.

He was soon slapped Noreen O'Leary, "The Donnybrook."

Nonetheless, Donny's role Melanie Wells, "Deutsch Shares Bright Spotlight," *Advertising Age,* November 16, 1992.

Donny believed that many Melanie Wells, "Deutsch Shares Bright Spotlight."

252 *The big question was* Warren Berger, "Vox Populi," *Advertising Age,* January 1, 1994.

There was an initial   Warren Berger, "Vox Populi."

Employees complained to   Steve Fishman, "Donnie Deutsch: From Ad Man to Mayor?" *New York,* May 5, 2003.

254 *Donny was not the only*   *New York Times,* February 17, 1994.

Instead of folding   Laura Petrecca, "The Best Agencies: Deutsch Raises the Bar to Earn Agency of the Year Honor," *Advertising Age,* January 25, 1999.

In 1999 Deutsch became   Melanie Wells, "Bad Boy Makes Good," *Forbes,* November 29, 1999.

It was credited with   Melanie Wells, "Bad Boy Makes Good."

The agency spent $30 million   Warren Berger, "Vox Populi."

His critics still dismissed   Laura Petrecca, "The Best Agencies: Deutsch Raises the Bar to Earn Agency of the Year Honor."

A New York agency boss   Francesca Newland, "Newsmaker: Donny Deutsch," *Campaign,* August 20, 1999.

As the New York Times *put*   *New York Times,* December 4, 1998.

255 *Donny was willing to work*   *Los Angeles Times,* November 28, 1999; Paula Span, "Dye Hard," *Washington Post Magazine,* May 3, 1998, 18.

During the 1990s nearly 60   *Washington Post,* February 6, 1999.

The manufacturer of the sex-enhancing   Michael J. Weiss, "Chasing Youth," *American Demographics,* October 2002, 9.

Many Boomers also turned   *Columbus Dispatch,* June 23, 2002.

Donny's personality has mellowed   *USA Today,* April 26, 1995.

257 *In Donny's case*   Steve Fishman, "Donnie Deutsch: From Ad Man to Mayor?"

258 *In 2000 he also finally*   Katarzyna Moreno, "On Your Mind," *Forbes,* May 14, 2001, 34.

In 1994, perhaps because   *Los Angeles Times,* August 24, 1994.

259 *As was often the case*   *Indianapolis Star,* August 5, 1999.

260 *Critics hailed it for its realistic*   *The San Diego Union-Tribune,* January 4, 2001.

"There's no question that"   Nancy Franklin, "Again and Again: Fortysomethings In Love," *New Yorker,* January 24, 2000.

Marshall believed that the problem   *St. Petersburg Times,* April 15, 2002.

The focus on real life   *USA Today,* April 15, 2002.

261 *The same generational wave*   *St. Petersburg Times,* March 25, 2002.

Many people questioned Pamela Paul, "Targeting Boomers," *American Demographics,* March 2003, 2.

262 *"Madison Avenue people"* *New York Times,* January 6, 2003.

The rise of the WB network *New York Times,* January 6, 2003.

Generation X rejoiced Daniel Okrent, "Twilight of the Boomers," *Time,* June 12, 2000, 72.

263 *Boomers, on the other hand* Jeff Giles, "Generalizations X," *Newsweek,* June 6, 1994, 62.

In many ways there are Heather R. McLeod, "The Sale of a Generation," *American Prospect* Spring 1995, 93.

"They had the free speech" Heather R. McLeod, "The Sale of a Generation."

Demographically, Xers are Margot Hornblower, "Great Xpectations," *Time,* June 9, 1997, 58–69.

264 *Although Boomers complain* Jeffrey Wolf, "Snapple Campaign," Account Planning, Deutsch, Inc.

Chapter 12   The New Bosses
Page
268 *The room erupted with* *Washington Times,* October 20, 1993; Karen Stabiner, *To Dance With the Devil: The New War on Breast Cancer* (New York: Delacorte, 1997), 14.

270 *The coalition built a bipartisan* *New York Times,* October 24, 2000; *The Plain Dealer* (Cleveland, Ohio), August 28, 1999.

271 *In preparation for the 2000 presidential* *The Hill,* November 10, 1999.

Many traditional scientists have resented *Los Angeles Times,* November 5, 1995.

272 *In 2001 New Yorker medical* Jerome Groopman, "The Thirty Years' War," *New Yorker,* June 4, 2001.

There are other drawbacks Claudia Kalb, "Stars, Money, and Medical Crusades," *Newsweek,* May 22, 2000.

The bottom line Michael Fumento, "The Squeaky Wheel Syndrome," *American Spectator,* December 1998.

273 *Not surprisingly, a study* Michael Fumento, "The Squeaky Wheel Syndrome."

Broke and leaderless *Chicago Sun-Times,* August 5, 1993.

276 *"They served their country"* *Washington Post,* July 12, 1995.

He needed a new cause   Bobby Muller (transcript of Nobel Peace Laureate Conference, University of Virginia, Charlottesville, VA, 1998).

277 *The problem was worldwide*   *The Charleston Gazette,* August 22, 1997; Bobby Muller (transcript of Nobel Peace Laureate Conference, University of Virginia, Charlottesville, VA, 1998); David C Morrison, "A Weapon That Keeps on Killing," *National Journal,* July 17, 1993, 1843.

278 *The* Washington Post *referred*   *Washington Post,* March 22, 1998.

279 *Although Clinton explained*   Bruce Wallace, "The Battle to Ban Land Mines," *Maclean's,* July 1, 1997, 34; Bobby Muller (transcript of Nobel Peace Laureate Conference, University of Virginia, Charlottesville, VA, 1998).

While Bobby was running   *Seattle Times,* December 14, 1997.

280 *Williams, riding the fast-moving*   *St. Louis Post-Dispatch,* October 19, 1997.

In December 1997 the campaign   *Christian Science Monitor,* February 3, 2000; *Washington Post,* January 21, 1997; *New York Times,* September 20, 1997.

281 *"I don't think she has"*   *Washington Post,* March 22, 1998.

284 *Muller described his approach*   Bobby Muller, transcript of Nobel Peace Laureate Conference, University of Virginia, Charlottesville, VA, 1998.

Conservatives learned the same   Nina J. Easton, *Gang of Five: Leaders at the Center of the Conservative Crusade* (New York: Simon & Schuster, 2000), 18; Benjamin Hart, "Abbie Hoffman's Nightmare," *Policy Review* (Fall, 1987): 72.

285 *Interest groups are nothing*   Jonathan Rauch, "The Hyperpluralism Trap," *New Republic,* June 6, 1994, 22.

Chapter 13   New Challenges; Lost Opportunities
Page

287 *"Choice is a good thing"*   Alan Ehrenhalt, *The Lost City: The Forgotten Virtues of Community in America* (New York: Basic Books, 1995), 1–32.

Is it possible to have   *Boston Globe,* December 26, 1999; Cheryl Russell, The Master Trend," *American Demographics,* October 1993, 28.

288 *Technology has expanded*   Pamela Paul, "Targeting Boomers," *American Demographics,* March 2003, 2.

"The popular media image"   J. Walker Smith and Ann Clurman, *Rocking the Ages: the Yankelovich Report on Generational Marketing* (New York: HarperBusiness, 1997), 127.

289 *In a classic case of unintended* David M. Reimers, "An Unintended Reform: The 1965 Immigration Act and Third World Immigration to the United States," *Journal of American Ethnic History* 2 (Fall 1983): 9–28; *New York Times,* July 19, 1987; James P. Smith and Barry Edmonston, eds., *The New Americans: Economic, Demographic, and Fiscal Effects of Immigration* (Washington, D.C.: National Academy Press, 1997), 3.

290 *Many Americans worried about* Peter Brimelow, *Alien Nation* (New York: Random House, 1995); Richard Lamm and Gary Imhoff, *The Immigration Time-Bomb: The Fragmenting of America* (New York: Dutton, 1985); Arthur M. Schlesinger, Jr., *The Disuniting of America: Reflections on a Multicultural Society* (New York: Norton, 1992), 15–18.

For Boomers, fears of *Washington Post,* August 18, 1996; Joe Klein, "Saxophone vs. Sacrifice," *Newsweek,* March 18, 1996.

291 *The most dramatic examples* Brian D. Johnson, "Yabba dabba déja vu,"*Maclean's,* May 30, 1994; Rebecca Piirto Heath, "What Tickles Our Funny Bones," *American Demographics,* November 1996.

292 *"We moved to the suburbs"* Jerry Adler, "Bye-Bye Suburban Dream," *Newsweek,* May 15, 1995, 40.

Like an earlier generation Andres Duaney, Elizabeth Platter-Zyberk, and Jeff Speck, *Suburban Nation: The Rise of Sprawl and the Decline of the American Dream* (New York: North Point Press, 2000), 118–22.

Children aside, the real Pulte Homes, Press Release, "Boomers Eyeing Retirement Prefer Comfort, Energy Efficiency Over High Style"; *Atlanta Journal-Constitution,* November 8, 1998; Rochelle Stanfield, "The Aging of America," *National Journal,* July 20, 1996.

In 1991 a small group *New York Times,* June 2, 1996.

293 *In 1993 the principles* *New York Times,* June 2, 1996.

During the early to mid 1990s Clifford A. Pearson and John E. Czarnecki, "Urbanism of the New and Everyday Varieties Inspires a Trio of Books," *Architectural Record,* September, 2000.

294 *The movement's success trickled* Paul Goldberger, "It Takes a Village," *New Yorker,* March 27, 2000.

In 2001 the New York Times *claimed* *New York Times,* December 9, 2001.

Liz, however, feared Alan Ehrenhalt, "The Dilemma of the New Urbanists," *Governing Magazine,* July 1997; Charles Lockwood, "Main Street Goes Suburban," *Architectural Record,* March 1998.

295 *The new urbanism was not* Alan Ehrenhalt, "The Dilemma of the New Urbanists."

"Where old Macdonald" "Not Quite the Monster They Call It," *Economist*, August 21, 1999.

Politics also stands Daniel Lazare, "Mouseketopia," *These Times*, March 17, 1997.

But on the other hand Fred Barnes, "Suburban Beauty; Why Sprawl Works," *Weekly Standard*, May 22, 2000.

Polls revealed that Larry Van Dyne, "As Far as the Eye Can See," *Washingtonian*, February 2000; *Houston Chronicle*, March 19, 2000.

296 *The emphasis on small town* Charles Lockwood, "Main Street Goes Suburban."

The lament about the decline *Washington Post*, May 28, 2000.

297 *By the end of the 1990s* Paul Goldberger, "It Takes a Village."

299 *Although he did not realize* *Plain Dealer* (Cleveland), December 25, 1994.

301 *Like many other fundamentalist* *Washington Post*, September 17, 1999.

302 *Like the new urbanism* *New York Times*, October 9, 2000; *Washington Times*, October 23, 2000.

Many of the African Americans *New York Times*, June 29, 2002; *Plain Dealer*, June 30, 2002.

303 *Alberta hailed the landmark* *Washington Post*, June 28, 2002.

305 *Howard Fuller, the head* *New York Times*, October 9, 2000.

306 *Alberta had always been* Cal Thomas, "'Not of this World,'" *Newsweek*, March 29, 1999, 60; *Washington Post*, March 18, 1999; *St. Louis Post-Dispatch*, March 19, 1999.

307 *Impeaching the president* Steven M. Gillon, *The American Paradox: A History of the United States Since 1945* (Boston: Houghton Mifflin, 2003), 445–46; *Washington Post*, December 27, 1998; Alan Dershowitz, *Sexual McCarthyism: Clinton, Starr, and the Emerging Constitutional Crisis* (New York: Basic Books, 1998).

308 *Inevitably, the struggle over* *Washington Post*, December 27, 1998.

309 *Bush, whose adolescence* William Schneider, "It's About to Become Gore's Convention," *National Journal*, August 15, 2000.

Judging from the popular vote Voter News Service via CNN.com.

Epilogue   We Are All Boomers Now
Page
311 *During the same week*   *Boston Globe*, December 31, 1998.

   Boomer bashing, much   Joe Queenan, *Balsamic Dreams: A Short but Self-Important History of the Baby Boomer Generation* (New York: Henry Holt, 2001), 9 and 15.

   David Brooks accused   Paul Begala, "The Worst Generation," *Esquire*, April, 2000.

   The Boomer self-criticism   Robert J. Samuelson, "Great Expectations," *Newsweek*, January 8, 1996, 24.

   Life expectancy increased   *Times* (London), December 26, 1999.

312 *Why, if our quality*   Robert Samuelson, "How Our American Dream Unraveled," *Newsweek*, March 2, 1992, 32.

   The gap between expectation   *Times* (London) December 26, 1999.

   If Boomers are dissatisfied   *Washington Post*, August 18, 1996.

313 *The Boomer preoccupation*   *Washington Post*, September 12, 2001.

   That question was quickly   Gloria Borger, "The day evil came home," *U.S. News & World Report*, September 24, 2001, 34.

314 *"We came of age"*   *Washington Post*, June 10, 2003.

   "The life-altering events"   *Columbus Dispatch*, September 16, 2001.

   During the 1930s many   Maxine Davis, *The Lost Generation: A Portrait of American Youth Today* (New York: Macmillan, 1936), 3–9 and 365–72.

315 *Bush may have seen*   *New York Times*, February 11, 2003.

INDEX

ABOUT THE AUTHOR

STEVE GILLON has taught at Yale University and Oxford University and is currently a professor of history at the University of Oklahoma. He is also the resident historian of the History Channel, where he hosts a Sunday morning show, *HistoryCenter,* and has appeared in numerous specials, including "History vs. Hollywood." He is the author of many books and articles about modern American history.

ork lifts whizzed and assembly lines ran and people scurried and machines whirred and whistles blew and people scampered and wheels turned and cranks cranked and people scuttled and it was all a nonstop kaleidoscopic blur of energy and action and noise and controlled frenzy throughout the manufacturing department.

Signs were everywhere, pointing to the Manufacturing Manager's pursuit of higher Quality.

Quality: The Key to Productivity read one.

Higher Quality Means Higher Productivity read another variation on the same theme.

Better Means Faster and Faster Means Better read a third, slightly more oblique exhortation hanging in the assembly area.

Which is where The Boss, the right-hand man, the left-hand man, and the Manufacturing Manager were now in their tour of the manufacturing department.

"We've been making a lot of Quality progress here," said the Manufacturing Manager, gesturing toward a group of workers diligently affixing the little hooks to the bodies of commas.

"Poor Quality here, the hooks fall off. Hooks fall off, commas get rejected. Commas get rejected, one of two things happen: Either they get scrapped, or they get reworked. Either way, productivity goes to pot—and you can't have that in a manufacturing operation!"

"No, no," said the left-hand man.

"Of course you can't," said the right-hand man.

"Well, the problem's gone! We fixed it!" stated the Manufacturing Manager, decisively.

But although his tone was most decisive, the Manufacturing Manager's eyes betrayed just the barest hint of doubt. And although the Manufacturing Manager was oblivious to that slight twinge, The Boss was not.

Just as I thought, thought The Boss.

"That's great news," said The Boss. "Just how did you do it? What are the workers doing now that's caused Quality to go up?"

"Why don't you ask one of them?" said the Manufacturing Manager. "Pick anyone you like. Just don't slow them down."

The Boss approached a worker on the line. "Good morning," he said.